The Reading Commitment
SECOND EDITION

The Reading Commitment

SECOND EDITION

Michael E. Adelstein
UNIVERSITY OF KENTUCKY

Jean G. Pival
UNIVERSITY OF KENTUCKY

HARCOURT BRACE JOVANOVICH, INC.

NEW YORK   SAN DIEGO   CHICAGO   SAN FRANCISCO   ATLANTA
LONDON   SYDNEY   TORONTO

Requests for permission to make copies of any part of the work should
be mailed to: Permissions, Harcourt Brace Jovanovich, Publishers, 757 Third
Avenue, New York, N.Y. 10017.

ISBN: 0-15-575572-2

Library of Congress Catalog Card Number: 81–84322

Printed in the United States of America

PREFACE

This collection of essays is primarily designed to provide composition students with well-written, interesting, and stimulating prose models. In addition, it furnishes pedagogical aids to instructors concerned with improving student reading skills. Often, because of the emphasis on writing in composition courses, this subsidiary instruction in reading has been haphazard and incidental—more by chance than by design. *The Reading Commitment* attempts to rectify this situation by alerting students to the specific relationships that exists between perceptive, critical reading and effective writing. Thus the selections in *The Reading Commitment* were chosen for their readability and appeal to students with varying reading skills, and for their potential usefulness in teaching the critical reading techniques that contribute to better analysis and better writing.

The Introduction sets up a three-step reading approach: Pre-Reading, Analytical Reading, and Reflecting. The questions that precede and follow each selection are based on this method. Each of the three steps emphasizes reading skills that can be applied to the development of good writing habits. The "Pre-Reading" device of finding the subject of a piece and the author's approach to it can help students see the importance of planning their papers in the pre-writing phase. The "Analytical Reading" step emphasizes a close analysis of structure and content. The suggested steps in the "Reflecting" process—Point, Organization, Support, Synthesis, and Evaluation—all stress the rhetorical considerations common to both reading and writing. The "From Reading to Writing" assignments are designed to relate the reading techniques to suggested student themes.

Because an awareness of overall structure is essential to both reading and writing, nearly all the essays appear in their original, uncut form. Some, like Sally Carrighar's narrative and the description by Annie Dillard, though they are excerpted from longer works, stand as independent essays. A few, such as Robert Lipsyte's definition of "SportsWorld," are entire chapters of books. All are well unified, however, and are appropriate for discussion in a single class period; occasionally, two related short pieces could be assigned. A wide variety of models is provided—more than seventy in all—so that instructors will have the opportunity to choose those most interesting and most suitable for their students.

We have deliberately limited ourselves to selections that are contemporary in character. They are written in the style and language that students will be expected to emulate; thus, they serve as more practical models than "classic" essays from eighteenth- and nineteenth-century writers. In addition, we agree with the advocates of experiential writing that students write best about contemporary subjects that are pertinent to their experience (for example, personal development, values, education, conservation, sports), that are of enduring interest, and about which students have some prior knowledge. Because we also believe that novice writers can profit from an acquaintance with the rhetorical strategies of professional writers, the book includes many selections by nationally acclaimed authors who are masters of contemporary idiom: writers such as Maya Angelou, Isaac Asimov, Saul Bellow, Wendell Berry, Joan Didion, John Ciardi, E. B. White, and Tom Wolfe.

The Instructor's Manual that is available to users of this textbook suggests answers to the questions accompanying each selection and offers advice on discussion techniques and on motivating students to write. The manual also includes syllabuses correlating *The Reading Commitment,* Second Edition, with *The Writing Commitment,* Second Edition, and with the *Harbrace College Handbook,* Ninth Edition, for instructors who want to use this book with a composition text. Finally, there is an alternative table of contents arranged according to the rhetorical strategies used in the selections and a bibliography of works dealing with the teaching of reading and writing.

In the Second Edition, we have deleted several outdated selections and have substituted essays by Ellen Goodman, Gail Godwin, Neil Postman, James Fallows, and other well-respected contemporary writers. We have also placed more stress on expository writing by increasing the number of essays in that section and by reorganizing it into clearer subdivisions. In addition, the writing assignments have been updated and revised to provide an audience for student writing.

In making these changes, we are grateful for the advice and suggestions of many instructors using the First Edition. Of particular help in this respect were many members of the freshman English staff at the University of Kentucky, particularly David Godfrey, Martha Gehringer, Chris Cetrulo, and Elvin Holt. Among other colleagues we are especially indebted to are Dallas High, Alfred L. Crabb, Jr., and Kenneth Davis. We have also profited greatly from the assistance of many people at Harcourt Brace Jovanovich. For his encouragement, kindness, and guidance, we are most grateful to Eben W. Ludlow, Executive Editor and our sponsoring editor there. And we are also highly appreciative of the work of Paula Lewis, our manuscript editor, and of the sincere dedication and painstaking care of Carolyn Viola-John, who edited the book in the final crucial months. But the greatest debt of gratitude we owe to our patient and long-suffering spouses, Carol and Joe, for their understanding during years of bookish neglect.

MICHAEL E. ADELSTEIN
JEAN G. PIVAL

CONTENTS

vii

Proposition Argument: Formal 312

Problem-Solution Argument: Informal 351

Problem-Solution Argument: Formal 363

THEMATIC TABLE OF CONTENTS

Values

Women

Writers and Writing

Youth

The Reading Commitment

SECOND EDITION

Introduction

WHY READ?

In 96 percent of American households at least one television set is turned on for an average of more than six hours a day. So it is not surprising that with so much competition for people's time, they read little. But why should people want to read?

People read not only to satisfy their curiosity about others—TV stars, film and sports celebrities, political figures—but also to improve themselves. Many articles and books offer advice about varied subjects: ways to earn more money and manage it prudently; ways to select a career, a mate, or a used car; ways to win everything from new friends to a better job.

In addition, people turn to the printed word for facts and figures both to satisfy their own craving for specific detail (note the popularity of the *Guinness Book of World Records*) and to impress others with their knowledge. Why else do sports fans study batting averages, total yards gained rushing, and endless other data?

And so the printed word—in newspapers, magazines, and books—provides information about sports and politics and hobbies and consumer tips and vacation ideas and personal health. Reading provides information that interests people and that makes people interesting.

Besides serving a practical purpose, reading provides sheer pleasure. It's fun to read for fun. Even though television offers a similar escape, reading for enjoyment persists. Readers turn to all kinds of stories—tales of love, adventure, romance, war, and science fiction—for the pleasure of mentally leaving their everyday lives and participating in the thrilling experiences depicted on the printed page. Reading has not only survived the Age of Television, but with the advent of the relatively inexpensive and nearly always available paperback, it has boomed among adults. Why?

One answer is that reading offers more choices than television does. As a reader, you can choose from an almost infinite variety of printed stories. You can decide when you want to read instead of being confined to a network schedule. You can read anywhere—in a tent, a bus, a subway, a plane, in a beach chair, or in bed.

Another answer is that reading provides the pleasures of the imagination. John Keats, the English poet, referred to this form of enjoyment when he wrote that "heard melodies are sweet, but unheard ones are sweeter." Television provides the "heard" melodies, showing in close-ups and with fine fidelity how everyone and everything looks and sounds. Reading furnishes the sweeter "unheard" melodies, allowing readers to imagine for themselves the world described on the printed page. This difference may account for television's usual inability to do justice to a novel or a short story.

In addition to offering information and enjoyment, reading can enrich our lives. Television appeals mainly to the eyes and ears, reading to the mind. Occasionally television presents meaningful dramas and documentaries, but most of the time it offers a bland diet of fast-food hamburgers, Coke, and french fries—little to stick with you and nourish you from one day to the next. Reading supplies the necessary vitamins and proteins that strengthen the mind, providing wisdom: an understanding of self and others, of human relationships, and of the nature of the world we inhabit. The printed page usually offers us a unique opportunity to meet a more experienced and intelligent person—alive or dead—who provides a special insight into life or a different vision of the world. It enables us to enrich our minds with the best that has been thought and said since the dawn of civilization.

To extend your mind and to broaden your understanding is to acquire a new way of seeing and knowing that will increase your awareness of yourself, of others, and of life itself. Naturally, reading is not the only means to this end; you can learn a lot from experience. But you cannot experience everything yourself, and you can be bruised and scarred in the process. Experience is a slow and painful teacher; the printed page offers more wisdom at less cost. There the finest minds have preserved the benefit of their experience. All their learning, joys, sorrows, and hopes await you if you read—and comprehend what you read.

The last point—to comprehend what you read—requires that you read actively, intelligently, and critically. That is one objective of this book: to help you read better and enjoy it more. We'd like to turn you onto reading because the information, enjoyment, and enrichment you will derive from it can make your life richer and more stimulating.

Another objective of this book is to help you improve your writing. Truly, people who read well usually write well. "A writer," according to Saul Bellow, "is a reader moved to emulation." Just as you can improve your playing of tennis or basketball or the violin by watching professionals, so you can improve your writing by analyzing how professional writers present their ideas clearly, interestingly, and convincingly. There will be more about this subject—how reading helps writing—later in this book.

Now that we have had our say about reading, let us conclude with the words of a famous author, Virginia Woolf, from her essay, "How Should One Read a Book?" To fellow readers she wrote of her fantasy about Judgment Day when the avid readers of the world appear with "the great conquerors and lawyers and statesmen" to receive their reward. She prophesied that

the Almighty will turn to Peter and will say, not without a certain envy when He sees us [the readers] coming with our books under our arms, "Look, these need no reward. We have nothing to give them here. They have loved reading."

We hope this book will help you to love reading, too.

HOW TO READ BETTER

Obviously, you can read. But like most college students, you'd probably like to improve your reading: you'd like to be able to concentrate better, to read faster, to remember more of what you've read, and to analyze and evaluate it more effectively. You may have already found that college professors expect you to read, understand, remember, and draw inferences from assignments of fifty to one hundred pages for each of their class meetings. How can you cope with this heavy reading load?

To begin, you should be aware that there are at least three levels of reading. The first, which might be termed basic reading, you learned in elementary school. There you became acquainted with the alphabet, mastered some system of word or phonetic perception, and gradually acquired a basic vocabulary.

Another level of reading, which might be termed analytical, involves understanding the full meaning and implications of a written sentence or passage. This level requires not merely a passive act of word recognition, but an active attempt to determine the total message and experience being conveyed. Analytical reading consists of perceiving the central idea, relating subordinate ideas to it, understanding the key words, realizing the logical assumptions, and discerning the reasons supporting the ideas.

The third level, evaluative reading, consists of formulating a critical judgment about the written work. Evaluative reading requires a questioning attitude, one that constantly challenges the logic of the written statement, searches for the writer's prejudices, weighs the significance of the points, attacks the evidence, considers the stylistic effectiveness of the writing, and then relates the ideas and feelings to other views about the subject.

As a college student, you should have few problems with basic reading. But you may feel that your analytical reading skills need to be improved. You can test yourself on this memorable sentence from the Declaration of Independence:

We hold these truths to be self-evident, that all men are created equal, that they are endowed by their Creator with certain unalienable rights, that among these are life, liberty, and the pursuit of happiness.

You should be familiar with the vocabulary here except for *unalienable,* the archaic form of our modern word *inalienable,* used here with *rights* in the sense of "rights not to be taken away from anyone." With that explanation, you should fully understand the sentence.

But do you? For example, exactly what are the self-evident truths and what do they mean? Are you aware that the sentence has a cause-and-effect structure: all men are created equal because all men are endowed by their Creator with certain unalienable rights. Looking at the effect ("all men are created equal"), did you wonder about the word *men?* Did you assume that it referred only to adult males? Or does it include females, young people, non-Americans? And when you read the word *created,* did you wonder whether men or people could be created equal but then could lose their equality? Is there anything to indicate that people, having been born equal, should continue to be equal throughout their lives? Which brings us to the word *equal.* In what sense are people equal? We know that human beings by virtue of their genetic makeup are not equal physically or mentally, and we realize that not all babies have the same opportunities, either socially, culturally, or materially. Exactly what, then, does the word *equal* mean in this context?

Turning next to the cause—the self-evident truth about unalienable rights—we discover that three are specified: life, liberty, and the pursuit of happiness. The right of *life* seems simple to understand: it means that no one can take away another's life. But what about the death penalty? Does a murderer also have an "unalienable" right to life? Does an unborn fetus? Does an incurably ill patient maintained on life-supporting machines? And exactly what does *liberty* mean? Freedom from taxes, from service in the armed forces, from driving restrictions, from a fine for smoking marijuana? But perhaps even more complicated is *pursuit of happiness.* Let us assume that *happiness* requires personal definition, people deciding to what extent it involves wealth or peace of mind or something else. What about *pursuit?* What is specifically implied in the right to *pursue,* or *seek,* happiness?

Our purpose in wrestling with this sentence is to illustrate the questioning attitudes involved in analytical reading. As you may realize, the sentence is not a simple one, but mature readers should be able to analyze its structure and realize its implications. Acquiring this skill is difficult, requiring patience and concentration, and it may be a lifelong venture, as Henry David Thoreau stated in *Walden:*

To read well, that is, to read true books in a true spirit, is a noble exercise, and one that will task the reader more than any exercise which the customs of the day esteem. It requires a training such as athletes underwent, the steady intent almost of the whole life to this object.

Indeed, just as athletes improve their ability in golf, tennis, basketball, and other sports through detailed instruction, grueling practice, and personal evaluation, you may similarly improve your reading skills.

In this Introduction and in the introduction to each part of the book, you will find some instruction to improve your reading; in the sections you will discover well-written, contemporary, interesting selections for reading practice; and with each one you will find questions that will allow you and your instructor to evaluate your comprehension and to help you relate the reading skills to your writing.

We have tried to choose challenging and stimulating prose pieces written for mature readers. Hard-cover books are generally designed for such readers, as are most popular magazines, such as *Time, Newsweek, Redbook,* and *Sports Illustrated.* Reading the selections in this book should not only interest you but also benefit you—by enlarging your mind, increasing your awareness, expanding your understanding, stimulating ideas for writing, and showing you how to proceed in your own papers.

STEPS IN THE READING PROCESS

PRE-READING

The reading process should begin not with the first words on the first page but with a prior survey called pre-reading. Its purpose is to prepare you for reading: to let you know what you're about to find so that you can adjust yourself accordingly. It's like getting ready for a trip by going over the route and learning about some of the key places, or planning for a football game by studying the past records of the teams and familiarizing yourself with their players, formations, game strategies. You can get more out of a book or article by preparing for reading it. But how?

With a book or textbook, the title and subtitle should provide some inkling of its contents, as should the publisher's statements, which may appear on the front or back of the jacket, inside the jacket-flaps, or on the front or back cover of a paperback book. The table of contents provides a handy outline, while the index offers a listing of the particulars covered. Equally important is the preface or foreword, which many readers unfortunately ignore, but which writers use for stating their purpose and the background of the book. Also, you might flip through the opening and closing chapters: the first usually announces the author's purpose and the problem or issue the book will deal with; the last will often provide a summary. Finally, any printed biographical information about the author may prove helpful.

Pre-reading the selections in this book is somewhat similar. The titles, subtitles, and the brief biographical sketches usually provide clues. Then division and subdivision headings, if there are any, can help. Opening and closing paragraphs are especially valuable because they usually contain key ideas. Skimming the first few sentences of other paragraphs can also be rewarding, often disclosing important points or revealing a summary, both occasionally introduced by a number. For instance, note the clue furnished by the word *two* in the first sentence of the following paragraph:

So there are two rival explanations for the falling turnout at the Presidential polls. Maybe it is because of the way the news comes across through TV and the other media. Maybe it is because of the discouraging state of today's world.

—Ithiel de Sola Pool, "Why Don't People Vote?"
TV Guide, 23 October 1976, p. 6.

This short paragraph in the middle of the article summarizes the ideas and helps you to remember the "two rival explanations."

Another pre-reading clue may take the form of a question that the writer poses and then answers in several following paragraphs; for example:

What can these courses in ethics accomplish? One objective is to help students become more alert in discovering the moral issues that arise in their own lives. . . .

Another major objective is to teach students to reason carefully about ethical issues. . . .

A final objective of these courses is to help students clarify their moral aspirations. . . .

—Derek C. Bok, "Can Ethics Be Taught?"
Change, October 1976, p. 28

Note how the opening question, the numbered sentence, and the opening sentences of the subsequent paragraphs present the main ideas. Pre-reading may not always reveal important information in such an accessible form, but it can often provide direction and purpose to your reading.

ANALYTICAL READING

The second step in the reading process is similar to effective listening, requiring many of the same skills. Think of the written page as a person speaking. Constantly react by mentally asking the writer: What's the point here? Does it make sense? Is it important? How is each point related to the main one and to the previous one? What are some of the key words? Also, anticipate what the writer may say—just as you often do in a conversation— and compare the statements with your own ideas.

Obviously, to question and to compare ideas requires that you concentrate on the printed page instead of thinking about the big game, the weekend date, or the month's bills. The best way of forcing yourself to concentrate and of avoiding the need to reread paragraphs or pages is to have a pencil or high-light marker in hand. With either of these, you will actively look for key words or important sentences to note. We prefer a pencil because in addition to underlining, you can more easily write comments or make marks in the margin, and bracket or circle words or allusions whose meaning you cannot understand from context and need to look up. In addition, you can signal reasons or causes and emphasize key points by writing appropriate numbers in the margins or by drawing arrows or similar markers. By actively involving yourself in analytical reading, you will concentrate better and comprehend more.

REFLECTING

So much for pre-reading and analytical reading. Now for the third step: reflecting. This process involves not only thinking about what you have read but also evaluating it. To help you achieve these objectives, you might want to follow our five-question approach, easily remembered by the acronym POSSE. Yes, in reading you're actually hunting—not for desperadoes, obviously, but for ideas and implications in the reading material. POSSE provides you with a systematic process to follow in the form of a series of questions:

1. What is the **P**oint of the selection? In other words, what is the theme, thesis, or controlling idea?
2. How are the ideas **O**rganized? Do they follow a chronological, spatial, cause-effect, or other pattern?
3. How are the ideas **S**upported? Are examples, illustrations, facts, reasons, testimony, or other evidence offered?
4. How can these ideas be **S**ynthesized, or compared or contrasted with my own or other people's experiences and ideas about the subject?
5. How should I **E**valuate the ideas? How clearly, concisely, convincingly, and effectively are the ideas stated? How important are they?

The first three questions focus on reviewing what you've learned from pre-reading and analytical reading. You should be able to state the author's main idea in your own words, describe the organizational pattern, and point out the supporting evidence used. One way to think about this review is to conceive of it as a reply to a friend who has asked you what you read, what it was about, what the main ideas were, and how they were substantiated. If you cannot respond to these questions fully, then you need to reread the work, searching for the answers. Only after you have grasped fully the point, organization, and support should you proceed to the final two questions.

The first of these questions, relating to synthesis, asks you to compare and contrast the written ideas with your own experiences and ideas or with those of other people to gain a broader understanding of the subject and the importance of the author's contribution. You may, of course, know so little about some subjects that you are unable to relate to the ideas. If so, then you cannot synthesize. But if you have had any personal experience with the subject, either directly or indirectly, you can compare and contrast. If you have just finished reading a review about a film you have seen or have read other reviews about, then you can synthesize. Or if you have read an article about high school vandalism, experienced it in your school, or discussed it with your friends, then you can relate these views to the author's. But, on the one hand, you should realize that your experience may not be typical; on the other hand, you need not feel awed by a work just because it is printed. Recognize your limitations, yet be prepared to disagree when you can find solid reasons and evidence for doing so.

Then you are ready for the most complex of all the reading tasks—evaluation. Of course, you probably do this naturally. When you finish a book or article, you usually have some reaction. You know the extent to which you found it enjoyable, interesting, significant, or useful. In talking to friends, you may recommend it or not. A good evaluation is based on your reaction, but it also requires that you have sound reasons for your opinion.

What is initially difficult is determining what standards to apply: obviously, an article about planting tomatoes cannot be evaluated by the same criteria as an argument against the death penalty. Another problem is that standards are not quantitative (based on, say, the number of words or paragraphs) but qualitative, depending on the reader's taste and experience both with the subject itself and with writing in general. For example, judging a review of a new rock album requires some knowledge about rock music standards and some acquaintance with other such reviews.

Moreover, an evaluation is not only a personal reaction but a critical one. As a person, you have certain private and emotional responses conditioned by your past life. As a critic, you should strive to be fair, informed, impartial, objective. Consequently, it would be perfectly understandable for you to cry or be moved emotionally at a movie but to criticize it afterward for being too sentimental. As an example, you may be stirred by the death of a boy's dog in the film, but as a critic, you may realize after reflecting that this scene was cheap, trite, and unnecessary. The same "split personality" approach—personal and critical—applies to reading a personal narrative, a descriptive essay, or an argument. You may dislike it or disagree with it for personal reasons, but then praise it because you realize its value and effectiveness.

Evaluation should be attempted only after you try to understand the work completely, having analyzed it carefully and reflected on it fully. We stress this point because in our experience, students often tend to dismiss a written work because it requires effort. We hope you will realize that many complex ideas cannot be stated simply. Therefore, you should make a reasonable attempt to understand what authors have written before faulting their work. Be certain that you have made the commitment that mature reading demands.

In evaluating, you are on safe ground when you point out in what ways the written material is based on misinformation, incomplete information, or faulty logic. Or you may question whether the generalizations are sound, the evidence sufficient, or the solution practical. By evaluating the written work on these and similar terms, you are basing your judgment on more objective and widely accepted reasons than if you relied solely on your personal taste and response. As as result, you will be reading and reacting with more insight, intelligence, and sophistication.

It is easier to discuss these three steps in the reading process—pre-reading, analytical reading, and reflecting—than to tell you exactly how to proceed. The best learning is in the doing. In the following pages, we provide you with examples of personal, descriptive, expository, and argumentative writing to acquaint you with the characteristics of these rhetorical forms, to provide you with models for your own writing, and to present you with reading samples that should interest, stimulate, and challenge you. In the introduction to each part of the book, we make suggestions for developing the pertinent pre-reading, analytical reading, and reflecting techniques. In addition, we offer questions at the beginning and at the end of each selection to help you improve your reading skills. But it is up to you to apply our suggestions—to make the reading commitment.

FROM READING TO WRITING

You might well ask at this point, "How does all this work on reading help in writing?" Contrary to folklore, good writing rarely results from spontaneous, original inspiration. The truth is that good writers don't reinvent the wheel, don't devise a whole new technique of writing every time they produce a new work. True, they learn from their own past experiences, but they also profit from writers whose works they admire. They become voracious readers, learning consciously and unconsciously from everything in print. They learn to read not only with an eye to form, to language, and to style, but to the use of other writers' techniques in their own writing. They know that writing is a problem-solving endeavor—often a slow and painful one because each problem must be solved anew. Thus, because they reveal how others have solved some of the problems you face in your own writing, critical reading skills and habits can be valuable to you as a writing tool.

As you read good writing, try to develop a sensitivity to strategies that you can adapt and imitate in your own writing. Also, as you learn to analyze other writing, to note its merits and discern its weaknesses, you will become more critical and concerned about your own writing. As you watch good tennis players or guitarists play, you learn from them. And as you read and analyze good writing, you learn from it. In this way, your reading can help to improve your writing.

1 PERSONAL WRITING

Personal writing is the most intimate and informal of all writing. Addressed to one's self or a few close friends or a limited group of sympathetic readers, it is like the free and easy conversation between two close friends, the warm exchange among guests at a small dinner party, or the chatty after-dinner speech delivered to an informal, congenial gathering of people. The primary aim is to entertain, to strike responsive emotional chords, rather than to inform or persuade. Consequently, the form is usually narrative, the writer telling a story or relating an incident. Because there is little need for the precise word choice and the objective clarity required in informative writing, the writer chooses language for its interest, color, and spontaneity. And because personal writing appeals primarily to the reader's emotions, relating observations and events that are common to human experience, writers find that dialogue and sensory description are techniques especially helpful to their purpose.

Consequently, it is not surprising that the voice projected in this kind of writing is closer to informal spoken language than we find in any other form. The authors of personal writing try to sound like themselves—honestly and authentically using their own voices, free of the formality often used in speaking to strangers. When this honest and natural quality is achieved, the writers themselves are revealed: we learn something about them as private people—age, sex, aspirations, secret longings, insecurities, values, responses to other people. Perhaps the closest, most intimate introduction to the writer is achieved in reading diaries and journals, where writers usually note their own thoughts for their own personal satisfaction and enjoyment. Less revealing, perhaps, is the self-portrait painted for the reader in letters and autobiographical narrative or anecdote, where the writer may engage in some role-playing. Least intimate of all the forms of personal writing is the personal essay, which often has the purpose of informing as well as entertaining.

KINDS OF PERSONAL WRITING

DIARIES, JOURNALS, AND LETTERS

Because diaries, journals, and letters are written close to the time of the event, they may more nearly capture the essence of the diarist. This characteristic is most vividly noticeable in the letter from Anne Morrow Lindbergh: written in her first year at college, it reveals the voice of an eager, bubbly young woman.

The Lindbergh piece and the other selections from journals demonstrate another characteristic of personal writing: vivid, concrete details that recreate the experience for us. We feel overwhelmed with Anne Morrow Lindbergh as she writes about her schoolwork. We share the intimate reading of poetry with Sylvia Plath and her friend; we find Alan H. Olmstead's collie pup as appealing as he does; and we can sense Michael Parfit's cold misery as the rain falls on his sleeping bag.

Although a journal entry should achieve this richness of detail and individual voice, it need follow no prescribed form. We can try our hand at any kind of writing that suits our fancy—narrative, essay, or even poetry. The key word is *experiment*.

AUTOBIOGRAPHICAL NARRATIVE

Autobiographical narrative is not quite so free as diary writing. Because it is written to a broader audience, it needs to be tighter in organization. Like fiction, autobiographical narrative has a unifying action or situation limited by a span of time. The action can consist of a single episode, as in the selections from *I Know Why the Caged Bird Sings* and *All God's Dangers.* The latter piece tells of the risks run by a courageous black man during a brief shopping trip to a racially bigoted small town. The action can also span a longer time, the writer recounting in sequence a number of related experiences, as in Sally Carrighar's account of her summer in the Canadian woods. Finally, two related incidents that happen far apart in time can be narrated, as in the story of how the young son of Ernest Hemingway lied in order to impress his famous father and how, long afterward, his father still felt pain and disappointment.

But whether the action is limited to one single episode or to a series of related ones, it does serve as a unifying device for autobiographical narrative. And although time may be handled in other ways, the simple chronological treatment, moving from an earlier time to a later one, is perhaps the most common and effective organizational scheme.

PERSONAL ESSAY

Most formal of all types of personal writing is the personal essay. Generally, personal essays are strongly thematic; that is, their unity is achieved through a main idea or thread of recurring experiences. Ralph Schoenstein's essay, for instance, comments on the many times that first his grandfather and then he himself worried over things beyond their control; Studs Terkel's newsboy weaves together the incidents that have made distasteful his job of delivering papers.

The main purpose of a personal essay, however, is not merely to tell a story, but to comment or to give one's personal reactions to recurring events or situations. The chronological order that can effectively organize a single happening can become cumbersome in discussing numerous situations and the relationships between them. Therefore, writers of personal essays provide a unifying or focusing statement to guide the reader—a statement that introduces the subject and reflects the writer's attitude toward that subject. Sometimes this sentence opens the essay, as in Schoenstein's "My grandfather's hobby was worrying, and although hobbies are not usually thought of as being inheritable, I am a talented worrier, too." Other writers may place the focusing statement at the end of an introductory paragraph or two. But it almost always appears early in the essay guiding the readers on their way through the subject, and at the same time, establishing the writer's tone.

The personal essay, unlike expository or argumentative writing, frequently reflects a voice that is casual, amused, ironic, sometimes carrying a tone of mock seriousness. Even when the tone is serious, the subject matter of the personal essay—a situation that is irritating or disconcerting, perhaps, but certainly not earthshaking—keeps the essay from being weighty and ponderous.

TACTICS FOR READING PERSONAL WRITING

PRE-READING

In the Introduction to this book, we recommended that you follow certain pre-reading procedures, such as thinking about the title, then skimming the opening and closing paragraphs. Obviously, these procedures are a little difficult to follow when reading short personal writing. Often, as in diary entries and letters, there is no title, and you certainly don't want to diminish the pleasure of reading a narrative by learning the outcome before you actually read the selection. But there are some things you can do to prepare yourself to read a piece of personal writing intelligently.

Remembering that there is a thematic relationship between the title and the content of what follows it, and if there is a title, you might examine it with these questions in mind:

1. Are there words in the title I don't know the meaning of? Look up words you are unsure of in a dictionary. Often, titles have a thematic significance, so it is important to understand the words before reading.
2. If names appear in the title, do you know anything about the people or places referred to? Again, the dictionary may give sufficient information. But you may need to refer to an encyclopedia to get the knowledge you need for a better understanding of the work.

Once you have scrutinized the title, look for information about the essay. As we suggested in the Introduction, background information is sometimes provided between the title and the opening paragraph in editorial statements or captions, or sometimes in a footnote. This material can give you an idea about what kind of person the writer is, maybe even about the situation described in the article. If you are reading a book, follow our earlier suggestion to skim the dust jacket or the flyleaf.

You may be wondering whether these preliminary steps are necessary. Remember, this procedure is intended to add to your appreciation of the work. It is like tasting a new food dish: you often want to know what the ingredients are before you will even taste it. Similarly, you will probably enjoy your reading more if you taste the content first, preparing your mind to get maximum satisfaction and nourishment from the work. And this brings us to the final step in the pre-reading process—skimming the opening paragraph. If the work is well written, you should glean some idea of the situation, the mood the writer wants to project, the time context, and perhaps an introduction to some of the characters. Now you are ready to read!

ANALYTICAL READING

Many proficient readers prefer to go through a narrative twice: first for the enjoyment and suspense of the plot, then to make themselves aware of more subtle aspects of the work. Other readers would rather absorb everything in one sitting. Whichever method they prefer, critical readers train themselves to get more out of narrative writing than just the story. Certainly, they are aware of the sequence of events, but they are also sensitive to the tone projected by the narrator, to the relationships between characters and between events, and to the influence of the events on individual characters. In addition, critical readers look for developments that signal shifts in the action or that foreshadow the outcome. Sorting these out as they read can lead to their complete satisfaction at the end of the story; they do not feel confused or cheated by the outcome of the story because they had failed to respond to some signal from the writer.

So far we have talked about how to read narrative writing in general. Because personal writing relies so heavily on narrative—because accounts of events appear so often in letters, diary and journal entries, autobiographical narratives, and even personal essays—it is similar in many respects to fictional narrative. Thus we can apply many of the same reading tactics to personal writing that we do to fiction. Essentially, all narrative involves these questions: WHO? WHAT? WHERE? WHEN? HOW? So, as you read, keep these questions in mind and underline key passages to aid you in your analysis:

WHO?   Who is the writer/narrator? Who are the other characters? What kind of people are they?

WHAT?   What are the relationships of the characters to each other and to the events of the story? How do the events and the characters' reaction to them reveal something about the kind of people the characters are?

WHERE?   Where does the action take place? What does the setting
         contribute to the story?
WHEN?   When does the action take place? Is there any significance
         to its occurring at this time?
HOW?   How does the writer organize the narrative and reveal the
         tone? How does the writer influence the reader's feelings
         about characters and events?

REFLECTING

When you have read through the work, you are ready to enter the third
stage of the reading process—reflecting on what you have read. As we indicated in the Introduction, this is the time to summarize the content in order
to make sure you have assimilated or digested the material; to determine
how the writer organized the work and how he or she supported the points
made; to synthesize and evaluate. Let's see how our POSSE approach can
help you to search out a critical method for evaluating personal writing.

*What is the **P**oint of the selection?* With the possible exception of the
personal essay, instruction is not usually the main purpose of personal writing. Even so, the reader often leaves a work of personal narrative with new
knowledge, fresh insight, or a broadened understanding of human nature.
The reader can share vicariously any lesson learned by the narrator—the
shame felt by a son who seeks approval from his father by dishonest means
or the conclusions about living things reached by a young girl after she kills
a porcupine for no reason. If there is an insight implicit in the story, then
you should be able to summarize the work, stating that point.

*How is the material **O**rganized?* Most narrative, as we have said, is
organized by chronological sequence. If you found that the story moves
easily from one event to the next, you can be sure that the writer has provided clues to the time sequence for you, as on page 65, paragraph 18 of the
selection by Maya Angelou: "*Before* the girls got to the porch . . . ," "They
came *finally* . . . ," "*At first* . . . ," "*Then* one . . . ," "*Another* said. . . ." Skim
each selection after reading, making yourself aware of such signals. Eventually, the use of these devices will become second nature to you and will be
useful in both your reading and your writing.

*How are the ideas **S**upported?* Support in other forms of writing is
achieved by using examples, citing authority, and the like. But personal
writing, particularly narrative, does not lend itself to these techniques. True,
the personal essay often contains them, but autobiographical narrative uses
other devices to support the writer's views or attitudes. An important contribution to this support is made by the tone or voice projected in the work. A
look at the language chosen by the writer at critical points in the narrative
can reveal personal attitudes toward the subject. Note, for example, Anne
Morrow Lindbergh's vivid language when she refers to her schoolwork
(pages 19-20, paragraphs 2, 6): "coils are tightening," "it hounds me doggedly." Her word choice convinces you that she finds the work demanding.

In "The Road Less Traveled," note how Michael Parfit's analogy between backpacking and the excitement and sadness of leaving home sets up the ambivalent attitude toward backpacking that is apparent throughout his essay. And observe how Alan Olmstead's language in describing his puppy reveals his affection for her: "A lovely, gentle little lady."

Another question to ask yourself about the writer is this: Do I find the voice relaxed, honest, natural, and informal? Word choice is not the only factor in creating voice—sentence structure and length can also contribute. Fairly simple sentences, numerous sentence fragments, and dialogue sentences help create a familiar voice, while longer, more complex sentences project an air of formality and distance. Thus, the voice the author assumes in writing can lend the same kind of aid that the voice of the speaker does in a talk to an audience.

How can this work be Synthesized with my own or other people's ideas on the same subject? A good way to synthesize personal narrative is to use the technique we often practice in conversation. When we are in a group of people telling stories and anecdotes, one story usually leads to another. Think of how often you have heard such phrases as "That reminds me of the time . . ." and "Speaking of baseball, remember the game. . . ." When that happens, we are synthesizing the elements of the conversation, relating them thematically to similar episodes in our own experience or the experience of others. Likewise, something in a piece of personal writing—the subject, the tone, one of the characters—may remind us of a similar element in another piece. Comparison of the two leads to a synthesis that deepens our understanding of each.

How do I Evaluate the selection? This step should be the simplest of all. All of us can readily define our emotional reaction to a work. If you've followed the other steps outlined here, you should have little trouble giving specific reasons why you liked, disliked, or were unmoved by the selection.

FROM READING TO WRITING

Moving from reading to writing in any particular medium is somewhat like changing from spectator to participant. A basketball game or a piano concert looks easy when someone else is making all the necessary moves and coping with the techniques of the process. So too in reading personal writing. It is easy to become so caught up in a gripping narrative or an entertaining personal essay that you are not conscious of the "moves" of the writer. But when you yourself start to write, you wish that you had been more observant in your reading. Developing the kind of reading habits that we have suggested can help you make the transition from watcher to doer—from reader to writer. As you become aware of the tactics that writers of good narrative use, you can transfer these to your own writing problems. If you make yourself conscious of how the writers in this book have handled problems of organization, sentence strategies, word choice, dialogue, and establishment of tone, then you should begin to see ways to employ these in your writing—not in blind imitation, but in intelligent adaptation.

Diaries, Journals, and Letters

A LETTER ABOUT COLLEGE WORK
Anne Morrow Lindbergh

BIOGRAPHICAL SKETCH

Anne Morrow Lindbergh was born in Englewood, New Jersey, in 1906. She graduated from Smith College in 1927, and married Charles A. Lindbergh in 1929. Following the kidnapping and murder of their young son in 1932 and the notoriety surrounding that tragedy, the Lindberghs moved to England. Their return to the United States, at the outbreak of World War II, was marked by renewed notoriety surrounding Lindbergh's opposition to U.S. involvement in the war. Besides her letters and diaries, Mrs. Lindbergh's published works include Listen: The Wind, A Gift from the Sea, *and a novel,* Dearly Beloved.

PRE-READING

1. On the basis of the biographical sketch, what benefits do you think Mrs. Lindbergh gained from preserving a diary and collection of letters written when she was young?

2. Check the dates of the selection. Approximately how old was the writer?

3. Read the first two paragraphs of the letter. What is the mood of the writer?

[Northampton, April 22, 1925]

Mother darling—

¹ I am terribly sorry not to have written for so long but it has been so frantically crowded and I have been very discouraged and I couldn't bear to write "from the depths"!

² It is a little better now. The work seems to be piling up frightfully and the coils are tightening. Finals are pushing from the other side and it gives you a permanent hounded feeling.

³ And I'm *not* doing any outside things. Not a thing! Really. I don't see anyone that isn't in my classes or in my house and all the time that's not spent at classes is spent studying. Perhaps I get stale.

FROM Anne Morrow Lindbergh, *Bring Me a Unicorn: Diaries and Letters of Anne Morrow Lindbergh, 1922–28* (New York: Harcourt Brace Jovanovich, 1971, 1972), pp. 20–21. Copyright © 1971, 1972 by Anne Morrow Lindbergh. Reprinted by permission of Harcourt Brace Jovanovich, Inc.

19

⁴ Writing for Miss Kirstein takes *hours*, too. And it needs consecutive hours. I haven't any consecutive hours except at night and on Sunday. Sunday is always one long stretch of work from morning until quite late, without even the break of going to classes.

⁵ I do wish I had some alibi for such inefficiency—something like having appendicitis or being in love, or brain fever—but I haven't *any* excuse—I am a healthy contented sane creature but I seem to work like molasses.

⁶ I think a great deal of it is because I can't seem able ever to drop it from my mind and get away from it and come back refreshed. That is awfully silly of me, but wherever I go I take it all with me—all the paraphernalia of work—mental paraphernalia. I look at a birch tree through a mist of gym shoes, course cards, alarm clocks, papers due, writtens, laundry boxes, choir practices, bills, long themes, and *exams*—etc. It hounds me doggedly and I think much too much about it and it makes me discouraged, and when I'm discouraged I can't do *anything*. This sounds so much worse than it is. I really shouldn't get discouraged. It is just because I can't see anything outside of college. It is so absorbing that it has loomed all out of proportion and I feel cut off from everything else.

⁷ But, Mother, in spite of this torrent of complaints, I love it—I really do—and I wouldn't stop for anything in the world. I've never had anything like it before. It is thrilling and absorbing and wonderful.

⁸ *I'm not taking any writing course* [next year]. Do you think that's awful? Of course there will be a good deal of writing in Eng. 19, and reports to make and write in the History. The reason I'm not taking it is that I won't have time to do them all as fully as I want to, if I do. Besides, I've learned from Miss Kirstein's course that (thrilling as she and it are) I really need more to think about and less to write about. Nothing I write has any backbone to it and it won't have until I absorb more. Do you think it's very silly?

ANALYTICAL READING

1. What do you suppose Lindbergh means by "from the depths" in the first paragraph? What change enables her to write the letter?

2. What does Lindbergh blame for the "permanent hounded feeling" she experiences (paragraph 2)? Are the teachers too demanding? Is she incapable of meeting the standards of Smith College? Or does she perceive some other failing in herself?

3. Evidently Lindbergh knew her mother would be disappointed about her not taking a writing course in the following year. How does Lindbergh attempt to justify her decision?

REFLECTING

Point: What does Lindbergh hope to make her mother realize? Try to summarize the central idéa or theme in one sentence. Which of Lindbergh's sentences best states this idea?

Organization: Does Lindbergh ramble on and on in the letter, or is there some general organizational plan? How is paragraph 6 organized and developed? What is the effect of ending with a question? Does Lindbergh introduce a new and separate subject in the last paragraph about next year, or is the subject related to the preceding paragraph or some other idea in the letter?

Support: Refer to specific words, sentences, and fragments that establish the natural, informal voice of the writer. Is Lindbergh convincing about her real attitude toward college? Why and how? In this text, several of the words are italicized. How did they appear in her handwritten letter? Explain the use of brackets in the first sentence of paragraph 8.

Synthesis: Do you or your friends share any of Lindbergh's feelings about the first year at college? Do you need consecutive hours for writing? Discuss the implications of the sentence in paragraph 8: "I really need more to think about and less to write about."

Evaluation: Is Lindbergh's letter interesting, sincere, and natural? Is there a conversational effect to it? Does she make her main point convincingly?

FROM READING TO WRITING

1. Write a letter home or to a friend explaining in detail some problem of adjusting to college, a job, life in a dorm or away from home, or some other new experience. Try to capture Lindbergh's friendly, conversational tone.

2. Write a letter to your parents about some decision that you know will not please them. Try to make them understand your reasons.

3. Write a letter to a favorite high school teacher or coach about your initial reaction to college. Imagine as you write that you are having a face-to-face conversation.

4. Write a letter to your parents about how difficult it is to study because there are so many exciting things going on outside of class, such as getting to know new and interesting people, attending meetings, and the like.

THE BEGINNING OF A CAREER
Sylvia Plath

BIOGRAPHICAL SKETCH

Sylvia Plath (1932–1963) was born in Boston, Massachusetts, educated at Smith, and attended Cambridge University in England on a Fulbright scholarship. There she married the English poet Ted Hughes. She is best known for her autobiographical

FROM Sylvia Plath, *Letters Home: Correspondence 1960–63*, ed. Aurelia Schober Plath (New York: Harper & Row, 1975), pp. 86–90. Copyright © 1975 by Aurelia Schober Plath. Reprinted by permission of Harper & Row, Publishers, Inc.

novel, The Bell Jar, *which dealt with her depression and was published after her suicide. Her highly regarded poetry appeared in three volumes:* The Colossus *(1960) and the posthumous* Ariel *(1965) and* Uncollected Poems *(1965). Because of her impressive poetry, her concern about women's oppression, and her tragic death, she has gained a wide following. In these letters she writes to her mother, Aurelia Plath, who encouraged her to become a writer.*

PRE-READING

1. Read the biographical sketch. To whom are the letters addressed?

2. Check the dates on the letters. How many days are involved? How old was Plath at the time?

3. Read the first paragraph below. Where is Plath at the time of the writing? What is the situation?

The Belmont Hotel, Cape Cod
June 11, 1952

[1] Your amazing telegram [*telegram announcing $500* Mademoiselle *prize for "Sunday at the Mintons," which I forwarded**] came just as I was scrubbing tables in the shady interior of The Belmont dining room. I was so excited that I screamed and actually threw my arms around the head waitress who no doubt thinks I am rather insane! Anyhow, psychologically, the moment couldn't have been better. I felt tired—first night's sleep in new places never *are* peaceful— and I didn't get much! To top it off, I was the only girl waitress here, and had been scrubbing furniture, washing dishes and silver, lifting tables, etc. since 8 a.m. Also, I just learned since I am completely inexperienced, I am not going to be working in the main dining room, but in the "side hall" where the managers and top hotel brass eat. So, tips will no doubt net much less during the summer and the company be less interesting. So I was beginning to worry about money when your telegram came. God! To think "Sunday at the Mintons' " is *one* of *two* prize stories to be put in a big national slick!!! Frankly, I can't believe it!

[2] The first thing I thought of was: Mother can keep her intersession money and buy some pretty clothes and a special trip or something! At least I get a winter coat and extra special suit out of the Mintons. I *think* the prize is $500!!!!!!!!!

[3] ME! Of all people! . . .

[4] So it's really looking up around here, now that I don't have to be scared stiff about money . . . Oh, I say, even if my feet kill me after this first week, and I drop 20 trays, I will have the beach, boys to bring me beer, sun, and young gay companions. What a life.

[5] Love, your crazy old daughter. (Or as Eddie said: "One hell of a sexy dame"!)

x x x Sivvy

* Aurelia Plath's note.

June 12, 1952

⁶ No doubt after I catch up on sleep, and learn to balance trays high on my left hand, I'll feel much happier. As it is now, I feel stuck in the midst of a lot of loud, brassy Irish Catholics, and the only way I can jolly myself is to say, "Oh, well, it's only for a summer, and I can maybe write about them all." At least I've got a new name for my next protagonist—Marley, a gabby girl who knows her way around but good. The ratio of boys to girls has gotten less and less, so I'll be lucky if I get tagged by the youngest kid here. Lots of the girls are really wise, drinking flirts. As for me, being the conservative, quiet, gracious type, I don't stand much chance of dating some of the cutest ones . . . If I can only get "in" as a pal with these girls, and never for a minute let them know I'm the gentle intellectual type, it'll be O.K.

⁷ As for the *Mlle* news, I don't think it's really sunk in yet. I felt sure they made a mistake, or that you'd made it up to cheer me. The big advantage will be that I won't have to worry about earning barely $300 this summer. I would really have been sick otherwise. I can't wait till August when I can go casually down to the drug store and pick up a slick copy of *Mlle,* flip to the index, and see ME, one of two college girls in the U.S.!

⁸ Really, when I think of how I started it over spring vacation, polished it at school, and sat up till midnight in the Haven House kitchen typing it amidst noise and chatter, I can't get over how the story soared to where it did. One thing about *Mlle* college fiction—although that great one last year by the Radcliffe girl was tremendous and realistic—I remembered the first issue I read where there were two queer part-fantasies, one about the hotel the woman kept for queer people, and the other about an elderly married couple. So I guess the swing of the pendulum dictated something like good old Henry and Elizabeth Minton. Elizabeth has been floating around in my head in her lavender dress, giggling very happily about her burst into the world of print. She always wanted to show Henry she could be famous if she ever worked at it!

⁹ One thing I am partly scared and partly curious about is Dick's reaction when he reads the story in print. I'm glad Dick hasn't read it yet, but Henry started out by being him and Elizabeth me (and they grew old and related in the process). But nevertheless I wonder if Dick will recognize his dismembered self! It's funny how one always, somewhere, has the germ of reality in a story, no matter how fantastic . . .

¹⁰ I get great pleasure out of sharing it [*her feeling about the story*] with *you,* who really understand how terribly much it means as a tangible testimony that I *have* got a germ of writing ability even if *Seventeen* has forgotten about it. The only thing, I probably won't have a chance to win *Mlle* again, so I'll try for a guest editorship maybe next year or my senior year, and set my sights for the *Atlantic.* God, I'm glad I can talk about it with you—probably you're the only outlet that I'll have that won't get tired of my talking about writing . . .

¹¹ Speaking again of Henry and Liz, it was a step for me to a story where the protagonist isn't always ME, and proved that I am beginning to use imagi-

nation to transform the actual incident. I was scared that would never happen, but I think it's an indication that my perspective is broadening.

[12] Sometimes I think—heck, I don't know why I didn't stay home all summer, writing, doing physical science, and having a small part-time job. I could "afford" to now, but it doesn't do much good to yearn about that, I guess. Although it would have been nice. Oh well, I'll cheer up. I love you.

Your own Sivvy

June 15, 1952

Dear Mother,

[13] . . . Do write me letters, Mommy, because I am in a very dangerous state of feeling sorry for myself . . . Just at present, life is awful. *Mademoiselle* seems quite unreal, and I am exhausted, scared, incompetent, unenergetic and generally low in spirits . . . Working in side hall puts me apart, and I feel completely uprooted and clumsy. The more I see the main hall girls expertly getting special dishes, fixing shaved ice and fruit, etc., the more I get an inferiority complex and feel that each day in side hall leaves me further behind . . . But as tempted as I am to be a coward and escape by crawling back home, I have resolved to give it a good month's trial—till July 10 . . . Don't worry about me, but do send me little pellets of advice now and then.

June 24, 1952

[14] . . . Last night I went on a "gang" birthday party at the "Sand Bar" where we sang and talked for a few hours. There were about forty of us kids from the hotel. I managed by some magic to get myself seated next to a fellow in his first year at Harvard Law—and he was just a dear . . . The best part was when we came back. It was a beautiful clear starry night, and Clark went in to get me two of his sweaters to wear because it was cold, and brought out a book of T. S. Eliot's poems. So we sat on a bench where I could just barely read the print, and he put his head in my lap and I read aloud to him for a while. Most nice. The only thing is I am so inclined to get fond of someone who will do things with me like that—always inclined to be too metaphysical and serious conversationally—that's my main trouble . . . So glad to hear the check from *Mlle* is real. I hardly could believe it. Just now I am mentally so disorganized that I can't retain knowledge or think at all. The work is still new enough to be tiring, what with three changes a day into uniforms, and I am so preoccupied by mechanics of living and people that I can't yet organize and assimilate all the chaos of experience pouring in on me. In spite of everything, I still have my good old sense of humor and manage to laugh a good deal of the time . . . I'll make the best of whatever comes my way.

ANALYTICAL READING

1. Is the tone of these letters reminiscent of that in Anne Morrow Lindbergh's letter? Are there similarities in the writing techniques?

2. Would you classify the language as formal or informal? Natural or affected? Cite examples from the work to support your choice.

3. What is the relationship between "Sivvy" and her mother? How is this revealed?

REFLECTING

Point: Is there one subject or theme that runs through all four letters? Are there other ideas common to all the letters? Discuss.

Organization: In the first letter, how does Plath organize the material? What devices does she use to move the discussion from one paragraph to the next?

Support: What methods does Plath use to support her points? How does she achieve a conversational style?

Synthesis: The letters dwell on Plath's adjustment to her new situation. Relate this to the Lindbergh selections.

Evaluation: Did you find the letters interesting? Why or why not? Do you find any clue in the letters to Plath's suicide eleven years later? Did you find relationships between the Plath and the Lindbergh letters? What?

FROM READING TO WRITING

1. Write a letter about a current problem to someone you feel is completely sympathetic to you.

2. Write a letter to someone close to you concerning a recent triumph you've had, such as an A grade, a job advancement, or a part in a play. Try to write as if you were telling the person about it face to face.

AN OLD MAN'S JOYS AND FEARS
Alan H. Olmstead

BIOGRAPHICAL SKETCH

Alan H. Olmstead (1910–1980) became editor of the Manchester Evening Herald *in 1941 and also wrote a triweekly column for other Connecticut papers, including* The Connecticut Yankee. *In addition, he was the author of* In Praise of Seasons *(1977) and several unsigned essays for* The New Yorker's *"Talk of the Town" section. During the first six months of his retirement, he kept a diary—published under the title* Threshold—*to record "some of the disappointments, pleasures, and reflections of a new traveler into that state of joblessness sometimes known as the Golden Age."*

FROM Alan H. Olmstead, *Threshold: The First Days of Retirement* (New York: Harper & Row, 1975), pp. 57–63, 113–114. Copyright © 1975 by Alan H. Olmstead. Reprinted by permission of Harper & Row, Publishers, Inc.

PRE-READING

1. From the biographical sketch, what do you find out about Olmstead's situation as he starts the journal? Why do you think the name of the book is *Threshold?*

2. From the titles of the individual entries, what can you guess about the nature of their content? Are you sure you know the meanings of *euphoria* and *via?*

Old Man's Puppy

Thursday, Oct. 26

[1] After some noonday carpentry, which gave a rough finish to the dog house, and an afternoon of search which ranged from the Connecticut Humane Society's kennels to a final pet shop in Hartford, we came home with a puppy—a dark-faced, relatively unmarked shepherd-collie. She is, we hope, essentially the same dog we have always had on the place. Within five seconds of being put down on her new home ground, she had the heart of whichever one of us she ran to with tail wagging in a beginning of all the games she and we were going to play together. Still, this was not the usual kind of puppy homecoming. Hitherto, much of the tenderness of bringing a new puppy home was rooted in the fact that the puppy was being brought home to a child. The child and the puppy would grow up together, in mutual happy innocence, until they came to that tragic parting of the ways resulting from the difference in their life spans. The death of the dog who had once been their puppy—that was often, for the children, their first introduction to the ineffably sweet sadness of death, an emotional experience which at once awed and absorbed them by its compulsive, convulsive powers. This time, although SJ is home for vacation and was reenacting her own previous bringing home of her first puppy, this was not another child's puppy. It was an old man's puppy which came home today. The games she gets to play will be old man's games. He is to be her chief companion, and she will have to listen as he whispers to her some of his old man's problems. There is a different strain of sentiment in this kind of relationship, because now the life span of the puppy and the life span of the human being paired with the puppy have just about an equal number of years to run, if both are lucky. She is a lovely, gentle little lady, and we hope to find her a happy kind of name, one fit for a companionship to the end of a journey.

Euphoria, Via Yo-Yo

Friday, Oct. 27

[2] There is no better therapy than that of building a dog house, and no better healer of the spirit than a puppy. Between the two, those doldrums—

that spell of depression in which, feeling myself lashed by the world and its circumstance into a series of petty defeats, I also began lashing myself—have disappeared. The human spirit can stand only so much of one kind of feeling and then turns and twists, by whatever process it may take, by whatever degree of irrationality may be required, to something different. The dog house stands there, in front of the garage, a momentarily successful enterprise created by saw and hammer and nails. The puppy, still uneasy about unknown worlds, still flatteringly in love with the person it knows best in place of its mother, plays safely in the yard, away from the damage it might do gardens, away from the lifelong danger waiting for it out in the street. If a recovery of the spirit is inevitable and is going to happen anyway, these are at least substantive ingredients for the change. But the truth is that if it hadn't been a dog house and a puppy it would have been something else which produced this turn from depression to euphoria. Strip it down to its essential movements, and the human mood is as complicated as a yo-yo.

Afraid of Halloween

Tuesday, Oct. 31

[3] The fear of the unknown is most powerful among the very young and the very old. With the very young the great curative, curiosity, usually comes to the rescue. With old people there is almost no curiosity as to which particular young neighborhood identity may be hiding beneath the Halloween mask at the door. With old people there is a dread, in this era of violence, of the possible appearance of tricksters a little older and meaner than children. With old people there are magnified memories, from past Halloweens, of such things as the soft vegetables splattered against the door, or the homemade bomb exploded in the mail box, or of the night long ago when adult friends, in playful mood, played their roles so well we didn't realize who they were until they had been hulking large and strange inside our home for too many strained minutes. But the real trouble with old people on Halloween is that there are no young people inside the house to go to the door, to play the guessing game with the tots, to muster the spirit to answer and mingle in the challenges of Halloween. So there comes the time when, instead of having jack-o'-lanterns burning in the window, the people in the house sit huddled into their deepest chairs, down below window-sill level, with as few lights as possible showing anywhere and no outside light at all, and try to let a television program distract their minds from the possible imminence of a knock on some door. Tonight the shameful, craven story was this: sitting in such fear, neither of us moved immediately when the one knock of the evening—a timid, two-thump-only knock—did come, and by the time one of us got to the door and turned on the outside light, what must have been a very small goblin had gone. We felt sorry for the small goblin, but more sorry for ourselves.

To You Coming After

Saturday, Dec. 16

⁴ Entry after entry, day after day, reveals this diarist totally wrapped up in the narrowing perceptions of his own particular station in life. Has he nothing to offer except this gossipy exchange of pensioner experience with other "Golden Agers"? Is this the most that life is about—to get this far, and then play the last few innings of the game from a contemplative wheel chair? What if there stumble into this diary some younger people not looking for pensioner experience, but drawn by love or curiosity to see what it may be like, between these covers? Has the old man nothing to say to or for them? Yes, indeed, all you who are coming after, and here is a slice of it. One of the sweet sadnesses very high in the feeling of all us older ones is that of a worried affection for all the younger people who are still strung out in the struggle along the path, who do not know their ending, or how they are going to make it. Every birth that comes after one is at once a miracle and a cruelty; one rejoices in the new life; one anticipates the sorrow the innocence thus born must inevitably encounter. One has to feel guilty, some of the time, for ever having helped bring anybody into this sadistic world. So I, the diarist, am sad for all you young people, the ones I know and love and those I merely observe, and I have this wish for all of you, that life may be as kind to you as it can, and that you all, for your part, may be as kind to one another as you can. I wish mercy upon you all, and joy that is seasoned with proportion and sense so it won't decay on you, and I beg of you not to expect too much happiness from any source. At the same time I fiercely enjoin you not to be too cautious in guarding yourself against those moments of beauty and tenderness, or those instincts for perceiving potential nobility and dignity in the human behavior, which keep lingering on from your childhood. You have to learn to take all things together, layering and reflecting one upon another, compensating, marrying, conserving, spending, juggling, borrowing—and never take any final verdict from either evidence or experience but keep playing the possibility that some day, if you are lucky, you may end up loving and wishing well to the humanity in everybody. You may then discover that however you audit the human experience, it somehow manages to come out a plus, too, like people. Run along, now, to your young busyness, to your terrible maturity, to your first blank awarenesses of the end, but with your options of the spirit always open, to whichever of the ages of man is next for you.

ANALYTICAL READING

1. What is the general tone of the selections? Do you feel that the writer of this journal is addressing a specific or general audience? Why?

2. What is the writer's attitude toward his dog? Toward children? Toward young people? Toward retirement? How does he communicate this?

3. What kind of person do you think the writer is? Support your answer by citing specific passages that illuminate his personality.

REFLECTING

Point: Is there a message or philosophy contained in the selections? If so, is it one from which all readers can benefit, or just retired people?

Organization: How does the writer organize the individual entries? Does each contain its own unity of idea? Discuss. What theme holds them all together? Describe the effect of the last sentence in each.

Support: Does Olmstead use contrast and comparison in supporting his theme? If so, where and how?

Synthesis: Do these selections also deal with adjustment? Compare them with the Lindbergh and Plath selections. Does Olmstead make you more aware of your relationship to your pet and your Halloween experiences? Does Olmstead regret old age? Or does he accept it and if so, how?

Evaluation: What do you think of the advice given to young people? Which selection did you like the best? The least? Why? Do you find Olmstead's writing to be mature, interesting, perceptive, and sincere? Justify your opinion by citing examples.

FROM READING TO WRITING

1. Write a journal entry about an experience that represented a transition in your life. Try to write it so that it not only helps you to better understand your feelings but also might help someone else to make a similar adjustment.

2. Write a journal entry about your acquisition of a new pet. If possible, write several sequential entries, tying them together with a common theme.

3. Try to analyze for your classmates why Halloween was exciting to you as a child. Was it only the candy you received that appealed to you?

THE ROAD LESS TRAVELED

Michael Parfit

BIOGRAPHICAL SKETCH

Michael Parfit (1947–   ) was born in London and grew up in England, the United States, and Brazil. In 1971 he graduated from the University of Southern California with a degree in journalism. Parfit began free-lance writing in 1971 and since then has written a book, Last Stand at Rosebud Creek *(1980) and since then has published in* The New York Times, *the* Christian Science Monitor, *and the* Wall Street Journal. *He is also a regular contributor to* New Times.

FROM Michael Parfit, "The Road Less Traveled," *The New York Times Magazine,* July 25, 1976, pp. 12, 16–17, 19, 22. Copyright © 1976. Reprinted by permission of the Sterling Lord Agency, Inc.

PRE-READING

1. What does the title mean to you? As you read, see how close your meaning is to Parfit's.

2. Skim the first paragraph. Does it give you an idea of what the subject is? How does it relate to the title?

3. What in the biographical sketch hints that Parfit might prefer independence and solitude?

[1] Discovering backpacking is a bit like leaving home for the first time. There's a mixture of pain and new freedom, and your family is not sure it approves. The comparison is imperfect, of course; the pain of the hike is only physical, and from backpacking you always return. But there's a root similarity. In wilderness, as in that first apartment, you find independence that you didn't know was there.

[2] Consider the core experience, shared even by Colin Fletcher, whose book "The Complete Walker" is still the best how-to in the backpacking field. You have come to the end of a dirt road in mountainous country. Beyond the fringe of the road's end is an understory of laced willows, thorned wild roses and gooseberry, out of which rise trees hung with moss. This, you realize, is the extent of man's reach; beyond here is the territory of the weasel, the rat, the bear, the rattlesnake and—who knows?—the wolf. Beyond here you dare not travel.

[3] Then, just as you secure these boundaries in your mind and turn away, the brush parts, and there appears a human being of normal stature who calmly states that he or, just as likely, she has been back in there for a week. It's like an unexpected door opening in stone. It happened to me in the California Sierras in 1968, and though the person was a vegetarian who looked and talked like an oboe and appeared somewhat off his feed, the jolting of vision that he produced opened a new concept of spaciousness and freedom in me which, after a few hundred miles of subsequent back-country travel, I retain.

[4] So today, Monday, I am preparing a pack for a trip into a minor wilderness about 100 miles north of Los Angeles. The place I am going is not a mecca like California's John Muir Trail or the Eastern states' Appalachian Trail, so I won't call unnecessary attention to it by name as if its qualities were rare. It's just an empty place of mountain, desert and river valley, preserved largely because a century of settlers found it inhospitable, and I'll be spending four days there—not much time, but enough to slake my restlessness.

[5] As if to assert its domain, the urban life I am temporarily quitting rushes around me as I pack: film to buy, letters to write, errands to attend to in advance, people to call. I calm this storm of preparation by chanting a kind of rosary, a list supplied, thoughtfully, by a backpacking store that sells all the items the list requires. In beads, it would dangle to the floor. "Pocketknife, snakebite kit, adhesive tape, aspirin, insect repellent, compass, matches, needles, fishhooks, string, rope, pliers, mirrors, sleeping bag, ground cloth, foam

mattress, short pants, long pants, poncho, toilet paper, hat, rope, cooking pots, primus stove, food, tent. . . ."

⁶ Civilization, which has contributed the aluminum-frame belted backpack to ease wilderness travel, has now gone the other way by providing useless weight in the form of guidebooks that detail wilderness routes. The books are complete with graphs of trail ups and downs which resemble fever charts and have a vaguely similar function, expressing degrees of sweat. Fine for office daydreams, but destructive of mood and mystery in the manner of fluorescent tubes hung in catacombs. This way, ladies; please mind the abyss.

⁷ I will take, instead, the ultimate symbol, a topographic map. And I will flout the list and leave my six-pound, two-person tent behind. This is my tribute to the wilderness prophet John Muir, founder of the Sierra Club, who carried only dried bread and tea in a burlap sack. Besides, in this wilderness, in this season, it absolutely never rains.

⁸ Tuesday morning. A beginning. Like a kid crying "Salvation!" I expect a miracle from the first steps, a sudden relief of worldly burdens the first time I turn a corner and cut away from the road. It never happens. I have put on the pack, 35 pounds, tied on Vibram-soled boots, crossed a small river called the Manzana, walked for an hour and a half and so far feel only continued restlessness, the urge to push faster than my new weight will let me, and, from a fold of sock, the start of a little pain. Perhaps it's like meditation, or tennis, the inner game: Ask too much of it and you lose it all, double-faulting into the wind. There's more release than grasp in the sport, and it all comes slowly, like the accumulating miles.

⁹ The trail winds along the Manzana, named after apple trees but lined with oaks. It is summer, the dry season in this part of the country, and the river is low and warm, making its way languidly from pool to pool, thick with algae the color of straw. There are small, hungry trout in these pools, and when I stop for a drink they gather around my immersed fingers and nibble at my nails and my ring. The sensation is strange, like being kissed by tiny people, and it creates a false but delightful feeling of communication.

¹⁰ I flip a white pebble in the pool and watch them fight over it, then share some crumbs of my "gorp," a mixture of nuts, raisins, granola and M&M's, which they devour like piranhas. Most of them, of course, will die as the river shrivels in the summer's heat, so there's no point in becoming too attached. Still, when the sun finally persuades me to remove my boots and swim in the pool, the little trout kiss my feet.

¹¹ Later, drying on a rock, I study the "topo" map, a maze of contour lines speckled with interesting names: Cold Spring, Manzana Narrows, Big Cone Spruce Camp, White Ledge, Hurricane Deck, Sulphur Spring, Sweetwater Canyon, the Sisquoc River. The last holds more promise than just the ring of its Chumash Indian name: It is the heart of this wilderness, and so becomes my goal.

¹² You begin a backpack determined to subvert normal, goal-oriented existence to the point of walking onward with nowhere to go, and then you find

that goals are necessary to keep you going. Without them, you'd sit down on a rock after a mile, pant, and eat all your gorp. So I find my devotion to reaching the Sisquoc grows as my body tires.

¹³ I am climbing, weaving back and forth up a slope covered with manzanita, the red-skinned savage bush, and dry grass, on which occasional scarlet buglers, small elongated wildflowers, blare silent messages to invisible bees. I had forgotten, as I always do, that the most intense experience of a backpack is its labor. I am not spending my day examining the sublime filigree of nature; I'm spending it in toil, sweat running down my back and in my eyes, watching only the dust of the trail a yard ahead, not for the detail of its diatomaceous soil, but for loose obstacles.

¹⁴ But here is an interesting paradox. The longer I trudge, committing myself to the achievement of the Sisquoc, and the more important the goal becomes to the maintenance of the hike, the less it really matters, except as a device, like a shoehorn to pry me out of laziness and get me moving. If I rest a minute, the desire to get there fidgets at my ankles, but once I'm up and hurting, it disappears in the intensity of the moment.

¹⁵ In the end there is a summit—White Ledge—and I remove the pack and lie back on hot white sandstone. As I luxuriate upon it—who would have thought stone could be so comfortable?—here, too, is a kind of communication. I do not condone talking to plants (except in whispers), much less to rock, but for a short time up here I feel a kind of physical unity with the earth which, I suspect, could be described as mystical and thus robbed of meaning. I am an Aquarius on stone made by a sea, smoothed by rain. Rock and water, uplifted, tearing down, rebuilding, one grain at a time. For a moment here as I lie in hot darkness under my hat, the relationship seems alive beneath me, and my role somehow a participant, but the feeling escapes me. Perhaps it is just a delusion of fatigue; as my body recovers, the Sisquoc, now visible down the canyon, beckons again.

¹⁶ I skid down inclines in matted chaparral of greasewood, more pleasantly known as chemise, and manzanita, through a transition zone of grass, dry and white in the late-afternoon light, into the belly of the canyon. Here, although the creek that slithers over bedrock has already gone south for the year, is a green confusion. The naturalist in me, an amateur of near incompetence, delights and rebels in the same acre. . . .

·   ·   ·

¹⁷ On Wednesday I reach the Sisquoc, hiking down White Ledge canyon in avenues of chaparral to a camp 13 miles from the nearest road, and, temporarily out of goals, I enter the best and least time-conscious period of backpacking. Now I can relieve myself of the pack's burden and settle in, attending to numerous small and agreeable tasks. I gather firewood—bits of dry manzanita and Digger-pine cones sticky with resin which burn with a hot red flame and a smell of oil. I reorganize my pack, taking out my nesting cooking pots and a box of rice for this evening's meal.

¹⁸ A backpacking menu is a study in lightness. An incredible selection of freeze-dried foods is available in the multitude of backpacking stores now sprouting up everywhere like mushrooms in damp soil. You can even get freeze-dried strawberry ice cream, if you must. But I usually stick to one-pot meals that stick to me. I don't go as far as some backpackers in my obsession with ounces, cutting the margins off maps and the handle off my toothbrush, but simplicity is part of the joy.

¹⁹ After unrolling my three-pound Dacron sleeping bag and my foam pad—much warmer and only slightly less comfortable than an air mattress—I prospect for a sleeping spot, a pleasant job which involves several periods of prone contemplation. Having thoroughly tested a level bit of ground near an oak, I spend the rest of the day hiking packless down the river, fishing for trout with small, gray flies and considerable success. The river is low, small enough to cross on dry stones, but it pools up under sandstone and shale cliffs, and here the 10-inch trout gather in clear green water to feed. It's like fishing in an aquarium and requires no effort.

²⁰ In fact, in comparison with yesterday's sweat, this whole day seems to be an orgy of ease, of heavy-lidded laziness in the sun. I have no responsibility but the maintenance of my own life, so this is deeper than ordinary relaxation, which I usually take fitfully against a background of impending decisions. I sit on stones, listen to water, walk, wade, catch fish, and dawdle, while the day slips away. And when I return to camp at dusk with half a dozen trout on a willow-branch stringer, I am happily weary and ready for sleep. "When my days are over," an anonymous backpacker has written the wilderness register near my camp, "bury me here." I can imagine no purer rest.

²¹ As the sun drops like a comet into a bank of clouds over White Ledge, I eat rice and trout so fresh they curl in the pan, and I savor the solitude. . . .

.   .   .

²² I go to sleep content, with only the company of mice rustling in oak leaves and frogs on the river singing in rhyme, but late that night I am awakened by a sound I have heard too often: the soft patter—as meaningful as an adder's hiss—of rain.

²³ My inner clock immediately rusts into immobility, and I prepare for a long, slow dawn. How many times have I done this—gone out into dry country with only faith in the forecast as my shelter? And how many times has it rained? . . .

²⁴ Few of the minor regrets of life are as poignant as wishing you had brought a tent. In gentle rain like this, dampness accumulates slowly with an inexorable lack of mercy, giving you enough time for anticipation and remorse before engulfing you in simple misery.

²⁵ Tonight, though, I go through all the preliminaries without the catharsis: Before enough rain has fallen to penetrate the sleeping bag, the storm pauses and I go back to sleep, humid but fundamentally dry. And when I awake to an

earthenware sky, I have enough time to find a small cave before the rain returns.

²⁶ In and out of sunshine, the rest of the trip drifts toward its end. But on the last day, Friday, I am caught by a new compulsion: to get out, back to the city. Ease has aged, and suddenly I am wondering, What's been going on out there in the human turmoil, what's the news? Without a radio, which would be sacrilege, I'm as remote as a star, and anything can happen. Some friends went backpacking for two weeks in early August 1974; you know what they missed. When they came out and the papers were talking about President *Ford,* they felt like Rip van Winkle. In this sense, backpacking amplifies the pace of life by showing you how much goes on while you're away. Often, instead of returning from the back country filled with a new serenity, I come out scrabbling to catch up. In the wilderness, as well as outside, change commands, and this valley is full of the evidence of fire and flood, but compared to the land the human metabolism flashes like gunpowder in the flint-shadowed pan.

²⁷ So I hustle away over White Ledge and back down the Manzana, knowing, in the end, that backpacking is little more than a partial escape—a retreat into the simplicity of hard work and physical pleasure which allows you to cheat on those taxes levied against you by civilization that you pay in pace and pressure. If you want to retain your hold on what we pompously call reality, you have to come back, hang the pack in the shed like a husk of skin and again confront the 20th century. So if you think of backpacking as salvation, it'll disappoint you. All it does is offer a small door in stone, marked Visitors Only, into another world.

ANALYTICAL READING

1. As you read, did you make yourself aware of the events in each day? Can you outline them?

2. Can you describe the place that Parfit chose for the trip?

3. Is Parfit's account written only for himself or to a larger audience? What part does his tone and word choice play in revealing his concept of audience?

4. Does he make use of figurative language such as analogy, simile, or metaphor? Cite some examples.

5. Were you aware of the variety of sentence structure? If not, examine paragraph 8 and discuss the sentences in it.

6. Did you learn anything about backpacking? Equipment? Cooking techniques? What does information such as this contribute to this article?

7. Can you give the meaning of the following words: *topographic, catacombs, abyss, chaparral, filigree, paradox, orgy?* Why is the word *orgy* particularly appropriate?

8. Explain the paradox the author mentions in paragraph 13.

REFLECTING

Point: Summarize in one sentence what you think the message of the article is. How does Parfit reveal his attitude about backpacking?

Organization: Obviously, the author uses chronological organization. But does he find other ways to organize some of the material? Demonstrate.

Support: Can you find specific sentences that act as support to the main point Parfit makes about backpacking? How does he support the attitude set up in the opening paragraph? What details suggest that he is writing to an audience that has little experience with backpacking?

Synthesis: Does Parfit's trip remind you of a backpacking or camping trip you have taken yourself or heard about? How?

Evaluation: What was your reaction to the work? Did you find it interesting, dull, informative? Can you support your emotional reaction by citing specific evidence? How effective is the last paragraph? What is your attitude toward the writer?

FROM READING TO WRITING

1. Write a journal entry about an event you plan for next weekend. Try to emulate Parfit's inclusion of instructional materials without making it into a "how-to" paper. Experiment with fresh, figurative language.

2. Reconstruct an interesting experience from a recent trip and write about it to a general audience.

3. Write about your first trip away from home: your preparations, your apprehensions, your feelings of strangeness, your disappointments, your pleasant experiences, your realizations. You might, for example, write about a trip with the Scouts or the Sierra Club, a trip to the beach, a high school class trip.

Autobiographical Narrative

MADELINE

Loren Eiseley

BIOGRAPHICAL SKETCH

Loren Eiseley (1907–1977) was born in Lincoln, Nebraska, and received a Ph.D. in anthropology from the University of Pennsylvania, where he served as head of the Anthropology Department, dean, and curator of the University's museum. The recipient of many national and international honors and awards, a frequent lecturer, and a member of numerous scholarly organizations, government task forces, and boards of directors, he wrote innumerable articles for scientific journals and national magazines. His verse and prose have appeared in many literary anthologies. Among his most highly respected books are The Immense Journey *(1957),* Darwin's Century *(1958), and* Francis Bacon and the Modern Dilemma *(1963).*

PRE-READING

1. From the biographical sketch, do you imagine Eiseley to be serious, playful, matter-of-fact, or what?

2. From skimming the first paragraph, can you guess what the narrative will be about? What kind of cat is a "prima donna"? Do you imagine the story about her will be light and entertaining or somewhat serious? Why?

¹ Maddy was what we called her familiarly. Madeline was her real name and she was a prima donna and a cat—in that order. Maddy was a cat that bowed, the only one I have ever encountered. She is part of my story, what one might call the elocution or stage part. We patronized each other. Maddy performed her act, and I assumed the role of her most ardent admirer. In discharging this duty I learned a great deal from Maddy, my patroness, whom I here acknowledge.

² I have known a good many cats in my time—some that scratched, some that bit, some who purred, and even one who, by my standards at least, talked. I liked Maddy, I suppose, because we had so much in common. Maddy was an isolate. Maddy lived with three other more aggressive and talented animals who took the major attention of my host. Maddy, by contrast, was not so much

FROM Loren Eiseley, *All the Strange Hours: The Excavation of a Life* (New York: Charles Scribner's Sons, 1975), pp. 133–37. Copyright © 1975 by Loren Eiseley. Excerpt from "Madeline" is reprinted by permission of Charles Scribner's Sons.

antisocial as shy, when you came to know her. She wandered a little forlornly in back rooms and concealed herself under furniture, or in a recess above the fireplace.

[3] Maddy, in short, wanted a small place in the sun which the world refused to grant her. She was at heart simply a good-natured ginger cat in a world so full of cats with purrs less hoarse that Maddy, like many of us, had learned to slink obscurely along the wall and hope that she might occasionally receive a condescending pat. Nothing was ever going to go quite right for Maddy. In this we reckoned without poor Maddy's desperation. She discovered a talent, and I, at least, among her human friends, was appalled at how easily this talent might have gone unguessed, except for a chance episode and an equally uncanny tenacity on Maddy's part. Maddy learned to bow.

[4] Perhaps you may think, as a human being, that this is a very small accomplishment indeed. Let me assure you that it is not. On four feet it is a hard thing to do and, in addition, the cat mind is rarely reconciled to such postures. No one among us in that house, I think now, realized the depths of Maddy's need or her perception.

[5] It happened, as most things happen, by accident, but the accident was destined to entrap both Maddy and ourselves. She was ensconced in her favorite recess upon the mantle of the fireplace, watching us, as usual, but being unwatched because of the clever gyrations of one of her kindred down on the floor. At this point, Mr. Fleet, our host, happened to stoop over to adjust a burning log in the fireplace.

[6] Easing his back a moment later, he stood up by the mantle and poked a friendly finger at Maddy, who came out to peer down at the sparks. She also received an unexpected pat from Mr. Fleet. Whether by design or not, the combination of sparks and the hand impinging upon her head at the same time caused Maddy to execute a curious little head movement like a bow. It resembled, I can only say, a curtsey, an Old World gesture out of another time at the Sun King's court.

[7] Maddy both hunched her forefeet and dropped her head. All she needed to complete the bow was a bonnet or a ribbon. Everyone who saw applauded in astonishment and for a few moments Maddy, for once, was the center of attention. In due course that would have been the end of the matter, but a severe snowstorm descended over our part of the state. We were thus all housebound and bored for several days. This is where Maddy's persistence and physical memory paid off; on the next night upon the mantle she came out of her own volition, and bowed once more with precisely similar steps. Again everyone applauded. Never had Madeline received such a burst of affectionate encouragement. If there were any catcalls they could only have come from her kin beneath the davenport. Her audience was with her. Maddy seized her opportunity. She bowed three times to uproarious applause. She had become the leading character in the house. The event had become memorable. Maddy, no more than a dancer, would forget the steps and the graceful little nod of the head. It became an evening routine.

[8] I have said that in the end both Maddy and her audience were entrapped. It happened in this way: finally the snow went away and we, all except Maddy, tried to resume our usual nocturnal habits—the corner bar, the club, the book. But the bow had become Maddy's life. She lived for it; one could not let her down, humiliate her, relegate her unfeelingly to her former existence. Maddy's fame, her ego, had to be sustained at any cost, even if, at times, her audience was reduced to one. That one carried, at such times, the honor of the house. Maddy's bow must be applauded. Maddy would be stricken if her act began to pall.

[9] To me the act never did pall. More than once I gave up other things to serve as a substitute audience. For, you see, I had come to realize even then that Maddy and myself were precisely alike; we had learned to bow in order to be loved for our graceless selves. The only difference was that as a human being living in a more complex world it had taken me longer to develop the steps and the routine. I talked for a living. But to talk for a living, one must, like Maddy, receive more applause than opprobrium. One must learn certain steps.

[10] I was born and grew up with no burning desire to teach. Sea captain, explorer, jungle adventurer—all these, in my childhood books, had been extolled to me. Unfortunately my reading had not included the great educators. Thus upon completing my doctorate I had no real hope in those still depressed times of 1937 of finding a university post. While I was casting about for a job among newspaper folk of my acquaintance, word came that I had been proffered a position at the University of Kansas.

[11] Most of the midwestern universities of that period had joint departments of sociology and anthropology, or at best one tame anthropologist who was expected to teach in both fields. When I appeared that fall before my first class in introductory sociology I realized two things as I walked through the door. I did not dare sit down. I did not dare use my notes for anything but a security blanket to toss confidently on the table like a true professor. The class was very large. A sizable portion of the football squad was scattered in the back row. I was, I repeat, an isolate like Maddy. If I ever lost that audience there would be chaos. The class met every day in the week.

[12] Each night I studied beyond midnight and wrote outlines that I rarely followed. I paced restlessly before the class, in which even the campus dogs were welcome so long as they nodded their heads sagely in approval. In a few weeks I began to feel like the proverbial Russian fleeing in a sleigh across the steppes before a wolf pack. I am sure that Carroll Clark, my good-natured chairman, realized that a highly unorthodox brand of sociology was being dispensed in his domain, but he held his peace. By then everything from anecdotes of fossil hunting to observations upon Victorian Darwinism were being hurled headlong from the rear of the sleigh. The last object to go would be myself. Fortunately for me, the end of the semester came just in time.

[13] At the close of the first year I had acquired, like Madeline the ginger cat, some followers. I had learned figuratively to bow and I was destined to keep

right on bowing through the next thirty years. There was no escape. Maddy had taught me how necessary it was that one's psyche be sustained. An actor, and this means no reflection upon teaching, has to have at least a few adoring followers. Otherwise he will begin to doubt himself and shrink inward, or take to muttering over outworn notes. This is particularly true in the case of a cat who has literally come out of nowhere to bow under everyone's gaze on a fireplace. Similarly I had emerged as a rather shy, introverted lad, to exhort others from a platform. Dear Maddy, I know all you suffered and I wish I could think you are still bowing to applause. You triumphed over your past in one great appreciative flash. For me it has been a lifelong battle with anxiety. . . .

ANALYTICAL READING

1. What is the relationship between the cat and the narrator? Is Maddy merely a pet?

2. Is the story really about Maddy, or is it about the narrator?

3. How does the author use analogy, or unusual comparison?

4. Is there any evidence that the writer has a sense of humor?

5. What kind of self-image does the writer project as a teacher and as a person?

REFLECTING

Point: Does Eiseley draw a conclusion only about his own life, or does the message extend to all of us? Summarize the message in the narrative.

Organization: This selection is in two parts. Indicate where the division occurs. What device does Eiseley use to make the transition? How does he sustain focus throughout? How does he link the two parts?

Support: How does the comparison between Maddy's learning to bow and Eiseley's learning to teach support the main point of the article? What specific details help?

Synthesis: It is sometimes said that pets take on the characteristics of their owners. Do you think this happens here? Has it happened to you?

Evaluation: Did you find that the selection effectively revealed Eiseley's character? Does the character in the narrative fit the conception of him that you derived from the biographical sketch? What devices help the reader to "know" the narrator? What makes this famous man appear so human?

FROM READING TO WRITING

1. For your classmates, write an autobiographical narrative about your relationship with a pet. As Eiseley did, try to choose one episode or ritual that illustrates the relationship.

2. For your classmates, write an autobiographical narrative about your playing a role, perhaps modeling your behavior after an older sibling or adult.

TO MAKE PAPA PROUD
Gregory H. Hemingway, M.D.

BIOGRAPHICAL SKETCH

Gregory H. Hemingway (1931–   ), the youngest son of Ernest Hemingway, lives and practices medicine in New York. He is not a professional writer, but his book Papa: A Personal Memoir *won high praise from Norman Mailer, in the preface to the book, for its "remarkable achievement" in portraying the real Ernest Hemingway. Other critics have hailed his ability for recapturing the bittersweet father-son relationship.*

PRE-READING

1. From the title of the book and the biographical sketch, what kind of relationship would you expect to find between Gregory and his famous father?

2. Skim the first two paragraphs. What task has the father set for the son? How would you react to such instruction from your father?

3. What is the setting? How old do you think the son is at the time of the story?

¹ That summer in Havana I read papa's favorites, from *Huckleberry Finn* to *Portrait of the Artist as a Young Man:* like him, I sometimes had two or three books going at the same time. Then papa steered me to the short story masters, Maupassant and Chekhov. "Don't try to analyze—just relax and enjoy them."

² "Now," papa said one morning. "Try writing a short story yourself. And don't expect it to be any good."

³ I sat down at a table with one of papa's fine-pointed pencils and thought and thought. I looked out the window, and listened to the birds, to a cat crying to join them; and to the scratch of my pencil, doodling. I let the cat out. Another wanted in.

⁴ I went to papa's typewriter. He'd finished with it for the day. Slowly I typed out a story and then took it to him.

⁵ Papa put his glasses on, poured himself another drink, and read, as I waited. He finished it and looked up at me. "It's excellent, Gig. Much better than anything I could do at your age. Only change I'd make is here," and he pointed to the line about a bird falling from its nest and finding, miraculously, that if it flapped its wings, it wouldn't crash on the rocks below.

⁶ "You've written . . . 'All of a sudden he realized he could fly.' Change 'all of a sudden' to 'suddenly.' Never use more words than you have to—it detracts from the flow of action." Papa smiled. I hadn't seen him smile at me

like that for a long time. "But you've won the lottery, pal. Writing takes study, discipline, and imagination. You've shown me with this that you have the imagination. And if you can do it once, you can do it a thousand times. Imagination doesn't leave you for a long time, maybe never. Dostoyevsky was fifty-seven when he wrote *Crime and Punishment.*

[7] "God, I used to get sad in Key West when people sent me their work and I could tell after reading one page that they didn't have it and never would. I answered every goddamn letter, usually saying that writing well was mainly a matter of luck, that to be given a great talent was like winning a million-to-one lottery; and if you weren't blessed, all the study and self-discipline in the world wouldn't mean a thing. If their letter had something like 'Everybody says I'd make a great engineer but what I really want to do is write,' I'd answer, 'Maybe everybody isn't wrong and you'll probably make an excellent engineer and then forget all about writing and be delighted you never went into it.'

[8] "I wrote hundreds of letters like that and I was getting a dollar a word in those days.

[9] "Later, when there were even more letters, I shortened my answers to 'Writing is a tough trade. Don't get mixed up in it if you can help it.' They probably thought, 'That conceited son of a bitch probably hasn't even read my stuff. But because he can write, he makes a big exclusive thing of it.'

[10] "The important thing is, Gig, that now I can teach *you* because you have the tools. And, in all immodesty, I know a lot about the trade.

[11] "I've wanted to cut down for a long time. The writing doesn't come so easily for me anymore. But I'll be just as happy helping you as doing it myself. Let's have a drink to celebrate."

[12] Only once before can I remember papa being as pleased with me—when I tied for the pigeon-shooting championship. And he was confident that there was another winner in the family when I entered the short story for a school competition and won first prize.

[13] Turgenev should have won the prize. He wrote the story. I merely copied it, changing the setting and the names, from a book I assumed papa hadn't read because some of the pages were still stuck together.

[14] I didn't feel like a winner and wondered how long it would be before papa found out that the only creative contribution I had made to the story was to alter "suddenly" to "all of a sudden."

[15] Fortunately I wasn't around when papa discovered my plagiarism. It got back to me that someone asked him if his son Gregory wrote. "Yes," he replied, with gusto and sparkle, flashing that "say cheese" smile he sometimes affected. "Gregory writes an occasional bad check." And, of course, everyone laughed.

[16] Someone in that crowd might have thought, "What a brutal bastard to make such a callous wisecrack about his son. I guess all those stories I've heard about him being a hard-shell bully are true."

[17] Hard-shelled, yes, but I helped make that shell.

ANALYTICAL READING

1. When in the story do you first suspect the plagiarism?

2. As you read, did you feel vicarious guilt? How does the dialogue between father and son help the reader to feel the son's guilt? Is the writer's use of dialogue more effective than simply telling the reader that he felt guilty?

3. In what other ways do we learn of the son's feelings of guilt? Why?

4. What do you learn of the relationship between the writer and his father?

5. Is the language used in the dialogue realistic? Discuss, citing examples. Is there any significance in the father's reference to the son as "Gig" early and "Gregory" later?

REFLECTING

Point: Do you think this selection is only an interesting personal narrative about a son and his famous father, or does it also serve as a moral lesson?

Organization: Where in the narrative does the point of the story become clear? Can you construct a sentence outline that reveals the organizational structure? Does the fact that the plagiarism is not admitted until late in the selection add to or detract from the narrative? Is the one-sentence conclusion effective? Why?

Support: Hemingway uses two incidents to indicate or dramatize the damage done by his plagiarism. What are they? How do "Papa" Hemingway's remarks about writing submitted to him and about his own writing contribute to the narrative?

Synthesis: Can you recall a time when one of your actions made you ashamed afterwards? Does young Hemingway's shame arise from public exposure or because of his love for his father? Is the son reevaluating his father's reputation?

Evaluation: Do you think the ending is effective? Can you suggest another way of handling it? What would be the effect of omitting the last two paragraphs? Can you understand why the son might be motivated to plagiarize? Can you understand and perhaps excuse him?

FROM READING TO WRITING

1. Think of a time when you were humiliated or embarrassed by one of your actions or decisions. For a general audience, write about it in narrative form, relying heavily on dialogue and events to provide an example from which others might learn.

2. For your classmates, write about an incident in which you did something that you hoped would win approval from someone. Be sure to reveal the relationship involved, but avoid telling your audience how you felt in so many words. Before you write, work out a skeletal organizational scheme similar to the one you found in the Hemingway narrative.

GOD'S DANGERS IN TOWN

Theodore Rosengarten

BIOGRAPHICAL SKETCH

All God's Dangers is a remarkable book, an oral history in the words of Nate Shaw, a cotton farmer from Alabama. While a Ph.D. candidate at Harvard University, Theodore Rosengarten won an Ethnic Studies grant from the Ford Foundation which enabled him to interview on tape the eighty-five-year-old Shaw. In the 1930s Shaw joined a sharecroppers union and later, in a shootout with people trying to break up the union, he shot at a sheriff. For that offense, he spent twelve years in prison under often brutal conditions, but managed to retain his independent spirit. The quality of that spirit comes through in this selection from the book.

PRE-READING

1. From the title of the book, what do you expect from the narrative?

2. After reading the biographical sketch, what might you expect the language in the selection to be—casual and conversational, formal and stiff, or what?

3. The first few paragraphs set up the situation. What is it? Does the narrator imply trouble?

¹ One day I told my wife, "Darlin, I'm goin to Apafalya to get me a load of cotton seed hulls for my cows and some meal."

² She said, "Darlin, you goin to town, I want you to get Rachel and Calvin some shoes"—they was the two oldest.

³ Told her, "All right. I'll do that."

⁴ She didn't know what number they wore but here's what she done: she went and took the measure of their foots and told me to get em shoes just a little longer than the measure from the heel to the toe. Well, I was fully determined to do it—and that was some of my first trouble.

⁵ I drove into Apafalya, hitched my mules, and walked into Mr. Sadler's store to get some shoes for the children first thing; then I was goin to drive on down to the carbox at the depot and load me a load of hulls and meal. Had my cotton bodies on my wagon—

⁶ I went on into Mr. Sadler's store and there was a big crowd in there. The store was full of white people and two or three colored people to my knowin. And there was a crippled fellow in there by the name of Henry Chase—Mr. Sadler had him hired for a clerk, and several more, maybe three or four more clerks was in there and some was women clerks. I walked in the store and a white lady come up to me and asked me, "Can I wait on you?"

FROM Theodore Rosengarten, *All God's Dangers: The Life of Nate Shaw* (New York: Alfred A. Knopf, 1974), pp. 162–70. Copyright © 1974 by Theodore Rosengarten. Reprinted by permission of Alfred A. Knopf, Inc.

[7] I told her, "Yes, ma'am, I wants a couple of pair of shoes for my children."

[8] And she took the measures and went on to the west side of the store and I went on around there behind her. She got a ladder, set it up, and she clumb that ladder and me standin off below her. There was a openin between the counters—and I was standin down there, just out of the way of the little swing-door and she was searchin from the front of that store nearly down to where I was.

[9] And this Chase fellow, he was kind of a rough fellow and it was known—a heap of his people there in town didn't like him. So she was busy huntin my shoes and she'd climb that ladder and take down shoes, measurin em, and she'd set em back up if they wouldn't do, didn't come up to that straw measure. And she was just rattlin around there, up the ladder and down it, and this here Chase fellow was standin off watchin. After a while he come around there, showin his hatred, showin what he was made of, that's all it was. And there was a old broke down—it had been cut in two at the bottom—a old, tough brogan shoe sittin there on the counter, a sample, you know. And he walked through there by me to get behind that counter where she was. I was standin on the outside waitin on her patiently, weren't sayin nothin. And he didn't like that white lady waitin on me, that just set him afire—I knowed it was that; I'd never had no dealins with him, no trouble with him noway—and he remarked, "You been in here the longest—" right in my face.

[10] I said, "No sir, I haven't been in here but just a little while."

[11] The white lady spoke up too; said, "No, he hasn't been here very long. I'm tryin to find him some shoes."

[12] He said, "You been in here the longest, you too hard to suit."

[13] I said, "No sir, all I'm tryin to do is buy me some shoes to match the measure for my children's foots."

[14] She said, "No, he hasn't been here but a short while."

[15] Good God, when she said that he grabbed that old shoe up—he didn't like her to speak up for me—grabbed that shoe up and hit at my head with it. I blocked his lick off. Well, when I blocked his lick off—he'd a hit me side the head with that old shoe, or on the face; no doubt he woulda cut me up—he throwed that shoe down. He seed he couldn't hit me with it, I was goin to block him off. He dropped that shoe back down on the counter and out from between there he come and run down to the low end of the store. And Mr. Sadler kept shovels, hoes, plow tools, and every kind of thing down there, on the low end, back end of the store. Chase runned down there and picked him up one of these long-handled shovels and he whirled around and come back—he just showed that he was given to split me down with that shovel. He come back—he begin to get close to me and I sort of turned myself to him one-sided.

[16] I said, "Don't you hit me with that shovel"—told him to his head, didn't bite my tongue—"don't you hit me with that shovel."

[17] He wouldn't say nothin. Just stood there and looked at me, wouldn't move up on me. Kept that shovel drawed, lookin at me, lookin at me, lookin at

me. I just dared him to hit me with that shovel—I never told him what I'd do and what I wouldn't. Well, he stood there and let into cussin. He disregarded that white lady, just stood there with that shovel on him, cussin me, lookin like all he wanted was a chance. I'd a turned my head and he'd a hit me, looked like from the way he acted.

¹⁸ All right. We got up a loud talk and all the people in the store noticed it. After a while, a fellow by the name of Howard Crabtree—old Dr. Crabtree was a horse doctor and this was his son—runned up there and started his big mouth. And this cripple man Chase tellin me all the time, "Get out of here, you black bastard. Get out of here." Tryin to run me out the store and I hadn't done a thing to him.

¹⁹ And this Crabtree, he runned up, "Naw, he aint goin to hit you, but goddamnit, get out of here like he tells you."

²⁰ I said, "Both of you make me get out. Both of you make me get out."

²¹ Couldn't move me. The white lady had done disbanded and got away from there. I stood my ground when this here Howard Crabtree runned up and taken Chase's part. I said, "I ain't gettin nowhere. Both of you make me get out."

²² Chase runned back and put the shovel where he got it from and down the aisle on the far side of the store he went. And there was a ring of guns there, breech-loaders. I kept my eyes on him, watchin him. I weren't goin nowhere. The white lady went on back to huntin my shoes after Chase left from there—he come out from the back of the store and went on down to where that ring of guns was, sittin right in the front as you go in the door. And he grabbed up one of them single barrel breech-loaders—that's when a white man befriended me and several more done so until I left town. There was a white gentleman clerkin in there, Mr. Tom Sherman—I seed this here Henry Chase grab that gun and break it down, run his hand in his pocket and take out a shell and put it in there. Totin shells in his pocket so if anything happened that he needed to shoot somebody—picked up a gun and broke it down and unbreeched it and run his hand in his pocket, pulled out a shell and stuck it in there, then breeched it back up and commenced a lookin for a clear openin to shoot at me. I just considered it for a bluff—he weren't goin to shoot me there in that man's store, surely. And I watched him close, he jumpin around lookin, first one way then the other, holdin that gun in his hands, lookin. And Mr. Tom Sherman just quit his business when he seed Chase drop a shell in that gun, walked right on up to him and snatched the gun away. Chase didn't resist Mr. Sherman—that was a heavy-built man. Mr. Sherman took that gun out of his hands, unbreeched it, took that shell out of it, set the gun back in the ring and stood there by that ring of guns. Out the store Chase went.

²³ Well, by that time, the white lady done got my shoes. I turned around and paid her for em. She wrapped em nice and I took the shoes and went on out the back door—it was handy; I come in the back door and I went back out it. I didn't go down the front. Chase'd gone out of there and I didn't want no trouble with him.

²⁴ So, out the back door I went and I turned to the left and walked on out in the middle of the street, goin to my wagon. And when I got out to where I could see clear, Aunt Betsey Culver, Uncle Jim Culver's second wife, was sittin in the street on a buggy. Uncle Jim was over there by Sadler's store, he seed all that happened there. I walked up to the buggy and howdyed with my auntie—didn't talk about that trouble neither. I just set my shoes in the foot of the buggy and was standin there talkin with her. And after a while I happened to look down the street and here come that cripple Chase fellow—he was a young fellow too, and he walked in kind of a hoppin way, one leg drawed back—and the police was with him, old man Bob Leech, settle-aged white man. They was lookin for me and they come up to me quick. Chase pointed at me and said, "That's him, standin right yonder; that's him, standin there at that buggy."

²⁵ Old man Leech walked up to me, looked at me, looked me over. And by me standin kind of sideways at Chase in the store, he done went and told the police that I acted just like I had a pistol in my pocket. Well, he never did see my hand. I had on a big heavy overcoat that day, just what the weather called for. So, he pointed me out to the police; police walked on up to me but wouldn't come right up to me, not very close.

²⁶ He said, "Consider yourself under arrest."

²⁷ I looked at him, said, "Consider myself under arrest for what?"

²⁸ "Uh, consider yourself under arrest."

²⁹ I asked him again, "Consider myself under arrest for what?"

³⁰ "That's all right; that's all right."

³¹ Come up to me and patted me, feelin for a gun. I said, "You want to search me"—I just grabbed that big overcoat and throwed it back—"search me, search me, just as much as you please. Search me."

³² He got up close enough to run his hands around me, feelin my hip pockets. He didn't find no gun. I had no gun, I didn't tote no gun around thataway. He said—he talked kind of through his nose, funny. And I called him in question about every word he spoke to me. He said, "Well, c'mon go with me."

³³ I said, "Go with you where?"

³⁴ "Gowanup-t-th-maya-uvtawn."

³⁵ I couldn't understand him.

³⁶ "Gowanup-t-th-maya-uvtawn."

³⁷ I said, "To the mayor of town?"

³⁸ He talkin thataway and I couldn't hardly understand him, talkin through his nostrils, looked like. I understood him but I just kept him cross-talked. Well, I started not to go—my mind told me, 'Go ahead with him, don't buck him.'

³⁹ He carried me on down the street and hit the left hand side of town goin in—left my shoes in my uncle's buggy. And I went on. Got down there and went up the stairs—the stairsteps come down to the walkway. The mayor of town was upstairs. And by golly, when I got up there, who was the mayor of

town? Doctor Collins! Dr. Collins knowed me well, been knowin me a long time. Walked on into his office and old man Leech, the police, spoke to him. And before he could say anything, Dr. Collins seed who was with him. He said, "Why, hello. What you doin with Shaw up here?"

⁴⁰ "Well, him and Henry Chase got into it down there in Sadler's store."

⁴¹ Dr. Collins said, "Um-hmm." Dr. Collins was a pretty heavy-built man himself. He said, "Well, Mr. Leech, where is Chase?"

⁴² "He down there in town somewhere, in the streets."

⁴³ "Um-hmm."

⁴⁴ "And they got into it in Sadler's store."

⁴⁵ "Mr. Leech, go down there and get Chase and bring him up here."

⁴⁶ The old police went down and got Chase, brought him up there. He come up hip-hoppin, hip-hoppin—that's the way he walked, doin just that-away every step he took. Chase said, when he got up there, "Hi, Doc."

⁴⁷ Dr. Collins said, "Howdy, Henry."

⁴⁸ I was standin there listenin. He said, "Henry, did you and this darky—" he wouldn't say nigger neither; that was a white man, and there was some more of em in this country wouldn't call you nigger. Dr. Collins said, "Henry, did you and this darky get into it down there in Sadler's store?"

⁴⁹ He said, "Yeah." But wouldn't tell nary a thing he done, uncalled for. "He was down there in Sadler's store—" wouldn't tell what I was waitin on or nothin, just told what he wanted Dr. Collins to know— "was down there in Sadler's store and we got into it"—wouldn't tell him what we got into it about—"and I told him to get out of there and he gived me a whole lot of impudent jaw."

⁵⁰ Dr. Collins said, "Um-hmm. Who seed that beside you, Henry?"

⁵¹ "Well, Howard Crabtree seed it."

⁵² And the whole store seed it but none of em weren't busyin theirselves with it. Mr. Tom Sherman seed it and he went and took that gun away from him. Dr. Collins said, "Um-hmm. Well, go down, Mr. Leech, and get Howard Crabtree and bring him up here."

⁵³ Chase said, "And he kept his hand behind him like he had a gun in his hip pocket."

⁵⁴ Crabtree walked up with his big-talkin self. Dr. Collins said, "Crabtree, did you see this darky and Henry Chase get into it down there in Sadler's store?"

⁵⁵ "I did. I did. I seed it every bit."

⁵⁶ "Well, Crabtree, would you—"

⁵⁷ "He had his hand behind him—" told the same lie Chase told—"had his hand behind him and he kept a tellin Chase not to hit him, better not hit him, and givin up a lot of other impudent jaw."

⁵⁸ Dr. Collins said, "Um-hmm. Crabtree, would you swear that he had his hand in his hip pocket?"

⁵⁹ "No, no"—he jumped back then—"no, I wouldn't swear he had his

hand in his hip pocket, but he looked like he had it in there. I don't know where his hand was, he had on that big overcoat."

60 "Um-hmm," Dr. Collins said, "Um-hmm."

61 Dr. Collins knowed me well. Never gived nobody no trouble, tended to my business, let other folks alone, I didn't meddle in things. And at that time I had a good name, right there in Apafalya, I'd been there since I was a little boy up till I was grown and after.

62 Dr. Collins said, "Well, the little old case don't amount to nothin. I'm just goin to throw it out."

63 After Crabtree told him he wouldn't swear I had my hand in my hip pocket, Dr. Collins asked me, "Shaw, did you have a pistol?"

64 I said, "No, Doctor, I aint seed a pistol in I don't know when. I had no pistol."

65 Chase allowed to him, "He went out the back way; he coulda carried it out there and stashed it."

66 Well, good devil, just as sure as my Savior's at his restin place today, I didn't have no pistol, never thought about no pistol.

67 All right. They whirled and left from up there when Dr. Collins said he was just goin to throw the little case out. And when they started out, I started out right behind em. Dr. Collins throwed his finger at me—"Shaw, this way; Shaw, Shaw."

68 I was lookin back at him and I stopped. He said, "Just be yourself and stay up here a few minutes; that'll give em time to get away from down there, clear em out, then you can go."

69 I just made myself at home, stood there. After a while, Dr. Collins said, "Well, you can go ahead now. Mess don't amount to nothin nohow, that's the reason I throwed it out."

70 When I got down the stairsteps onto the walkway, there was Mr. Harry Black, man I had done my guano dealin with, and there was a fellow went around there in Apafalya, heap of folks called him Tersh Hog—that was Mr. Bob Soule, went for a cousin to Cliff Soule. He lived out about a mile from Apafalya and he didn't take no backwater off nobody. If a thing weren't right, he were goin to fix it right. Some of em didn't like him because they had to pass around him, white folks. And I seed him walk the streets right there in Apafalya with his pistol in his—just like a law, only he'd carry his pistol in his coat pocket, and that handle was hangin out over the pocket. Didn't nobody give Mr. Bob Soule no trouble in Apafalya and nowheres else he went. So, Mr. Bob Soule was standin there at them steps when I come down, and Mr. Harry Black and Mr. Ed Hardy—I knowed them definitely and there was a couple more of em, bout five altogether standin there when I come down. They said, "Hello, Nate. Hello, Nate."

71 I stopped and spoke to em polite and they was polite to me. Well, Uncle Jim Culver had done stood there too at the bottom of the steps while his trial business was goin on and he heard them white men speak this: "If that nigger

comes down from up there with any charges against him, we goin to paint this damn place red."

[72] I didn't know—I didn't hear em say it. Uncle Jim told me, "They was standin there for a purpose. I done stood here and listened at em. Said, 'If that nigger comes down from up there with any charges against him, we goin to paint this damn place red.' "

[73] All of em knowed me well: I'd traded with Mr. Harry Black and Mr. Ed Hardy and they had passed confidence with me. And Mr. Bob Soule, he loved justice. When I walked down amongst em, all of em, I knowed em, looked in their faces, standin huddled there where the stairway hit the walkway. They was satisfied. They left there when I left.

[74] Uncle Jim added his advice: "Things are hot here, son. Now you go on up the street and get your mules and wagon and turn around and go on back home."

[75] I said to myself, 'The devil will happen before I do that.'

[76] And he said, "Don't come back, don't come back through town. Go on home. Take your mules and go on home now."

[77] I went on up there and pulled my mules back and hitched the traces and untied em from the post they was hitched to—both of em hitched to the same post and them inside traces dropped—set up on my wagon and went just as straight, just as dead straight right back down through Apafalya as I could go. Uncle Jim was standin there and he told some fellow, "There that boy goin right back through town and I told him to get his mules and wagon and go on back home."

[78] But I was game as a peacock. I just went straight to his buggy and got my shoes out and carried em to my wagon, hitched my mules back, crawled up in the wagon over them high bodies, right down dead through town I went. And when I got down close to where the railroad runned under that bridge there in Apafalya I turned to my left and went on down to the depot. Loaded my hulls and meal—and when I left, I had a straight way right out from there up the back streets of town toward home.

[79] One day after that, Uncle Jim got at me bout goin back down through town. I told him, "I aint no rabbit, Uncle Jim. When a man's mistreated that-away and he got friends and they proves it, he don't need to be scared. Of course, it's a dangerous situation and if I'd a been guilty of anything, I'd a took low."

[80] There was a old colored fellow down at the door at Sadler's store the whole time this ruckus was goin on inside. Mighta been inside himself at the start but he runned out if he was; he acted like he runned out. And he stood where he could see me. And do you know he just stood there and beckoned to me that whole time, he beckoned to me to run out. That just roused the whole store up. The old man tickled me. He was a pretty heavy-built old man and he weren't as high—his head, he could have walked under a tall horse and never touched it. Heavy-built old colored man. And he had on one of these old

frock-tail coats and it hit him just below the knee and it was cut back like a bug's wings. And he just stood there and bowed and beckoned for me to run out there. And every time he'd bow, that old coat would fly up behind him and when he straightened up it would hit him right back there below the bend in his legs. Tickled me, it tickled me. I thought it was the funniest thing I ever saw. He was scared for me and wanted me to run out of there. I didn't run nowhere. I stood just like I'm standin today—when I know I'm right and I aint harmin nobody and nothin else, I'll give you trouble if you try to move me.

ANALYTICAL READING

1. Does the narrator's language contribute to or detract from the authenticity of the account? Cite examples.

2. As you read, were you aware of the relationships of the characters to one another? How are these revealed in the narrative?

3. Is it more accurate to describe the narrator as aggressive and militant or as respectful and courageous?

4. Where does the incident take place? Is the setting important?

5. What do you think is the turning point of the story?

REFLECTING

Point: Is the purpose of the narrative simply to dramatize the brutality of some whites toward blacks? Is there more than one main point? How does the narrator communicate his message to the reader?

Organization: What is the organizational pattern? Do you think it is characteristic of narrative writing? Is it violated by the last paragraph? If so, why?

Support: What events and human relationships help to support the narrator's points in the story? What particular words and phrases help to make the story realistic?

Synthesis: How does this story compare with others like it, such as *Roots* or the selection by Maya Angelou (pages 63–66)? Would you say that this story makes a comment about the human spirit? How do you account for Shaw's courage?

Evaluation: How did you react emotionally to the story? Do you think the narrator demonstrates self-pity in telling about the incident? Illustrate. How does the narrator show that some white people treated him fairly?

FROM READING TO WRITING

1. Using as much dialogue as possible, write a narrative for a college audience about an incident in your own life when you were placed in some kind of danger.

2. For your classmates, write a personal narrative about a time when you had unexpected difficulty in making a purchase, returning something, or complaining about some defect.

UNUSUAL WRITING LESSONS
Robert M. Pirsig

BIOGRAPHICAL SKETCH

Robert M. Pirsig (1928–   ) was born in Minneapolis, received a B.A. and M.A. from the University of Minnesota, where he later served as an instructor in English composition before taking a similar position at the University of Chicago. He has also worked as a technical writer for several companies and served as an official of the Zen Meditation Center in Minneapolis. In 1974, he was awarded a Guggenheim fellowship. Since the publication in 1974 of Zen and the Art of Motorcycle Mainte-nance, *for which he later received an award from the American Academy of Arts and Letters, he has written articles for several periodicals. The book is an autobiograph-ical narrative of his motorcycle journey across the United States with his young son. But it is also a journey back to sanity and to a recognition of values. In this selection and throughout the book, Pirsig uses the name Phaedrus for the old personality he is trying to leave behind.*

PRE-READING

1. From the title of Pirsig's book and the biographical sketch, do you expect the book to be unconventional? Why? What does the incongruous pairing of an Oriental religion and motorcycles tell you about Pirsig's mind?

2. Skim the first two paragraphs. Pirsig talks of Quality in the first paragraph and begins the narrative in the second. Can you assume from this that his personal experience will somehow relate to Quality? What catches the reader's interest in the opening paragraphs and suggests the main idea of the selection?

[1] Today now I want to take up the first phase of his [Phaedrus'] journey into Quality, the nonmetaphysical phase, and this will be pleasant. It's nice to start journeys pleasantly, even when you know they won't end that way. Using his class notes as reference material I want to reconstruct the way in which Quality became a working concept for him in the teaching of rhetoric. His second phase, the metaphysical one, was tenuous and speculative, but this first phase, in which he simply taught rhetoric, was by all accounts solid and prag-matic and probably deserves to be judged on its own merits, independently of the second phase.

[2] He'd been innovating extensively. He'd been having trouble with stu-dents who had nothing to say. At first he thought it was laziness but later it became apparent that it wasn't. They just couldn't think of anything to say.

[3] One of them, a girl with strong-lensed glasses, wanted to write a five-hundred-word essay about the United States. He was used to the sinking feel-ing that comes from statements like this, and suggested without disparagement that she narrow it down to just Bozeman [Montana].

FROM Robert M. Pirsig, *Zen and the Art of Motorcycle Maintenance* (New York: William Morrow & Co., 1974), pp. 190–94, 270–72. Copyright © 1974 by Robert M. Pirsig. Reprinted by permission of William Morrow & Company, Inc.

[4] When the paper came due she didn't have it and was quite upset. She had tried and tried but she just couldn't think of anything to say.

[5] He had already discussed her with her previous instructors and they'd confirmed his impressions of her. She was very serious, disciplined and hard-working, but extremely dull. Not a spark of creativity in her anywhere. Her eyes, behind the thick-lensed glasses, were the eyes of a drudge. She wasn't bluffing him, she really couldn't think of anything to say, and was upset by her inability to do as she was told.

[6] It just stumped him. Now *he* couldn't think of anything to say. A silence occurred, and then a peculiar answer: "Narrow it down to the *main street* of Bozeman." It was a stroke of insight.

[7] She nodded dutifully and went out. But just before her next class she came back in *real* distress, tears this time, distress that had obviously been there for a long time. She still couldn't think of anything to say, and couldn't understand why, if she couldn't think of anything about *all* of Bozeman, she should be able to think of something about just one street.

[8] He was furious. "You're not *looking!*" he said. A memory came back of his own dismissal from the University for having *too much* to say. For every fact there is an *infinity* of hypotheses. The more you *look* the more you *see*. She really wasn't looking and yet somehow didn't understand this.

[9] He told her angrily, "Narrow it down to the *front* of *one* building on the main street of Bozeman. The Opera House. Start with the upper left-hand brick."

[10] Her eyes, behind the thick-lensed glasses, opened wide.

[11] She came in the next class with a puzzled look and handed him a five-thousand-word essay on the front of the Opera House on the main street of Bozeman, Montana. "I sat in the hamburger stand across the street," she said, "and started writing about the first brick, and the second brick, and then by the third brick it all started to come and I couldn't stop. They thought I was crazy, and they kept kidding me, but here it all is. I don't understand it."

[12] Neither did he, but on long walks through the streets of town he thought about it and concluded she was evidently stopped with the same kind of blockage that had paralyzed him on his first day of teaching. She was blocked because she was trying to repeat, in her writing, things she had already heard, just as on the first day he had tried to repeat things he had already decided to say. She couldn't think of anything to write about Bozeman because she couldn't recall anything she had heard worth repeating. She was strangely unaware that she could look and see freshly for herself, as she wrote, without primary regard for what had been said before. The narrowing down to one brick destroyed the blockage because it was so obvious she *had* to do some original and direct seeing.

[13] He experimented further. In one class he had everyone write all hour about the back of his thumb. Everyone gave him funny looks at the beginning of the hour, but everyone did it, and there wasn't a single complaint about "nothing to say."

[14] In another class he changed the subject from the thumb to a coin, and got a full hour's writing from every student. In other classes it was the same. Some asked, "Do you have to write about both sides?" Once they got into the idea of seeing directly for themselves they also saw there was no limit to the amount they could say. It was a confidence-building assignment too, because what they wrote, even though seemingly trivial, was nevertheless their own thing, not a mimicking of someone else's. Classes where he used that coin exercise were always less balky and more interested.

[15] As a result of his experiments he concluded that imitation was a real evil that had to be broken before real rhetoric teaching could begin. This imitation seemed to be an external compulsion. Little children didn't have it. It seemed to come later on, possibly as a result of school itself.

[16] That sounded right, and the more he thought about it the more right it sounded. Schools teach you to imitate. If you don't imitate what the teacher wants you get a bad grade. Here, in college, it was more sophisticated, of course; you were supposed to imitate the teacher in such a way as to convince the teacher you were not imitating, but taking the essence of the instruction and going ahead with it on your own. That got you A's. Originality on the other hand could get you anything—from A to F. The whole grading system cautioned against it.

[17] He discussed this with a professor of psychology who lived next door to him, an extremely imaginative teacher, who said, "Right. Eliminate the whole degree-and-grading system and then you'll get real education."

[18] Phaedrus thought about this, and when weeks later a very bright student couldn't think of a subject for a term paper, it was still on his mind, so he gave it to her as a topic. She didn't like the topic at first, but agreed to take it anyway.

[19] Within a week she was talking about it to everyone, and within two weeks had worked up a superb paper. The class she delivered it to didn't have the advantage of two weeks to think about the subject, however, and was quite hostile to the whole idea of eliminating grades and degrees. This didn't slow her down at all. Her tone took on an old-time religious fervor. She begged the other students to *listen*, to understand this was really *right*. "I'm not saying this for *him*," she said and glanced at Phaedrus. "It's for *you*."

[20] Her pleading tone, her religious fervor, greatly impressed him, along with the fact that her college entrance examinations had placed her in the upper one percent of the class. During the next quarter, when teaching "persuasive writing," he chose this topic as a "demonstrator," a piece of persuasive writing he worked up by himself, day by day, in front of and with the help of the class.

[21] He used the demonstrator to avoid talking in terms of principles of composition, all of which he had deep doubts about. He felt that by exposing classes to his own sentences as he made them, with all the misgivings and hang-ups and erasures, he would give a more honest picture of what writing was like than by spending class time picking nits in completed student work or

holding up the completed work of masters for emulation. This time he developed the argument that the whole grading system and degree should be eliminated, and to make it something that truly involved the students in what they were hearing, he withheld all grades during the quarter.

. . .

[22] This road keeps on winding down through this canyon. Early morning patches of sun are around us everywhere. The cycle hums through the cold air and mountain pines and we pass a small sign that says a breakfast place is a mile ahead.

[23] "Are you hungry?" I shout.

[24] "Yes!" Chris [Pirsig's eleven-year-old son] shouts back.

[25] Soon a second sign saying CABINS with an arrow under it points off to the left. We slow down, turn and follow a dirt road until it reaches some varnished log cabins under some trees. We pull the cycle under a tree, shut off the ignition and gas and walk inside the main lodge. The wooden floors have a nice clomp under the cycle boots. We sit down at a tableclothed table and order eggs, hot cakes, maple syrup, milk, sausages and orange juice. That cold wind has worked up an appetite.

[26] "I want to write a letter to Mom," Chris says.

[27] That sounds good to me. I go to the desk and get some of the lodge stationery. I bring it to Chris and give him my pen. That brisk morning air has given him some energy too. He puts the paper in front of him, grabs the pen in a heavy grip and then concentrates on the blank paper for a while.

[28] He looks up. "What day is it?"

[29] I tell him. He nods and writes it down.

[30] Then I see him write, "Dear Mom:"

[31] Then he stares at the paper for a while.

[32] Then he looks up. "What should I say?"

[33] I start to grin. I should have him write for an hour about one side of a coin. I've sometimes thought of him as a student but not as a rhetoric student.

[34] We're interrupted by the hot cakes and I tell him to put the letter to one side and I'll help him afterward.

[35] When we are done I sit smoking with a leaden feeling from the hot cakes and the eggs and everything and notice through the window that under the pines outside the ground is in patches of shadow and sunlight.

[36] Chris brings out the paper again. "Now help me," he says.

[37] "Okay," I say. I tell him getting stuck is the commonest trouble of all. Usually, I say, your mind gets stuck when you're trying to do too many things at once. What you have to do is try not to force words to come. That just gets you more stuck. What you have to do now is separate out the things and do them one at a time. You're trying to think of what to *say* and what to say *first* at the same time and that's too hard. So separate them out. Just make a list of all the things you want to say in any old order. Then later we'll figure out the right order.

[38] "Like what things?" he asks.

[39] "Well, what do you want to tell her?"

[40] "About the trip."

[41] "What things about the trip?"

[42] He thinks for a while. "About the mountain we climbed."

[43] "Okay, write that down," I say.

[44] He does.

[45] Then I see him write down another item, then another, while I finish my cigarette and coffee. He goes through three sheets of paper, listing things he wants to say.

[46] "Save those," I tell him, "and we'll work on them later."

[47] "I'll never get all this into one letter," he says.

[48] He sees me laugh and frowns.

[49] I say, "Just pick out the best things." Then we head outside and onto the motorcycle again.

[50] On the road down the canyon now we feel the steady drop of altitude by a popping of ears. It's becoming warmer and the air is thicker too. It's good-bye to the high country, which we've been more or less in since Miles City.

ANALYTICAL READING

1. What is Pirsig's tone? How do you think he feels toward his students? Toward his son? Support your opinion by citing examples.

2. What seems to be Pirsig's main concern about his students' writing? What devices does he use to deal with their problems? With his son's problem?

3. The incidents in the narrative parallel a development of ideas in the writer's mind. Show the relationship between the incidents and the new ideas.

4. Compare the language of the opening paragraph with that of the rest of the narrative. Which is more concrete? What do you think is the effect of less abstract language? How do you feel about the author's referring to himself as *he* instead of *I*?

REFLECTING

Point: Does Pirsig make more than one point in the narrative? What? Do you think he makes a point about Quality? If so, what is it?

Organization: The excerpt has almost a double organizational scheme: one is the chronological order of the narrative, the other is a progression of points made about freshman English and the grading system. Outline the two and express their relationship to each other.

Support: Does the narrative sufficiently support the points made by Pirsig? Do you feel that he makes a strong case for Quality as "a working concept"? Discuss. Is ample evidence offered to show that schools teach students to imitate? Does it seem natural that a class would be hostile to the idea of eliminating grades?

Synthesis: How do the instructions that Pirsig gives to his student and his son relate to your own experiences in composition classes? How do you react to his recommendations about the grading system? What did you learn about teaching and teachers as your read the selection?

Evaluation: Compare the effectiveness of this narrative with that of the Hemingway and Eiseley selections. Specifically, compare whether the ending of each resolves the problem raised in each.

FROM READING TO WRITING

1. Write a short narrative for a general audience about a personal experience that illustrates the statement, "The more you *look* the more you *see*."

2. For your classmates, write an account of a brief activity that you engage in almost daily, but never look at closely. Provide as much detail as possible. Suggestions: walking a path that you take every day to class; standing in line for a meal at the dorm; the routine you follow in getting ready for studying or for a date.

3. Write a narrative for a teachers' magazine showing how students do or do not cater to the whims of college or high school teachers.

A WILDERNESS EXPERIENCE
Sally Carrighar

BIOGRAPHICAL SKETCH

Sally Carrighar was born in Cleveland, Ohio. She won immediate fame with her first book, One Day on Beetle Rock, *published in 1944. Her works, most of them dealing with nature and man's relationship to it, have earned her a reputation as a naturalist and conservationist. Other books include* One Day at Teton Marsh, Icebound Summer, Wild Heritage, *and* Home to the Wilderness, *from which this selection comes.*

PRE-READING

1. From the title of Carrighar's book, what would you expect her attitude toward the wilderness to be?

2. After skimming the first paragraph, what do you know of the situation? Note Sally Carrighar's age at the time of the narrative. Was this a new experience for her?

[1] As amazing as miracles was a morning in June the year that I was fifteen and woke up in a tent on an island in Canada. We had arrived by lake steamer

FROM Sally Carrighar, *Home to the Wilderness* (Boston: Houghton Mifflin, 1973), pp. 89–97. Copyright 1944 by Sally Carrighar. Copyright © 1973 by I.C.E. Limited. Reprinted by permission of Houghton Mifflin Company.

the previous night and, tired after the long trip from Kansas City, had gone straight to bed. Now it was daylight. I got up quickly, quietly and slipped out to see this new world.

² The tent was a short way back from the shore with a path leading down to a little dock. I walked to the end of it. Ripples were gently rearranging the pebbles along the beach but the lake was smooth. Its wide and beautiful surface, delicate silver-blue, streamed with a mist that disappeared as I watched, for the light of the early sun, splintering on the tops of the mainland evergreen trees, was starting to fall on the mist and dissolve it. Curiously the lake's level surface seemed to be moving in alternate glassy streams, right and left, an effect that sometimes occurs on quiet water, I don't know why.

³ The bay in front of the dock was framed by the shores of the mainland, which curved together from both sides to meet in a point. At that vertex another island, rocky and tall, rose from the water. It looked uninhabited; and although a few cabins were scattered along the mainland, between and behind them was unbroken forest. It was my first sight of a natural wilderness. Behind our tent too, and several other tents here and a house in their midst, was the forest. Over everything, as pervasive as sunshine, was the fragrance of balsam firs. It was aromatic and sweet and I closed my eyes and breathed deeply to draw in more of it.

⁴ Voices from some of the tents meant that others were stirring. At the house wood smoke rose from the chimney, another redolent fragrance mingling soon with the smell of bacon frying. It is a combination familiar to everyone who has known woodland mornings. There would be talk at breakfast, the meeting with strangers—a loss. The sunrise across the wild northern lake seemed a kind of holiness that human chatter was bound to destroy a little. The water, so still and lucent, beyond it the dark mystery of the forest, and the firs' fragrance: for this sacred experience, enjoyed alone, I would get up at dawn every day during that summer.

⁵ We would be here for three months with my father joining us for July. Neither of my parents had been here before but friends, the Wymans from Painesville, had written to say that they knew of this island in the Muskoka Lakes and suggested our spending some weeks there together. After three summers in Kansas City, where the temperature day and night can stay above ninety, we were going to get away somewhere, and since my father had not been back to his native Canada for some time, the Wymans' idea appealed to my parents.

⁶ On the island were five or six visiting families. Some had children of whom only one was a girl near my age. She would turn out to be very lively, never happy unless she was engaged in some boisterous game. I thought of her as an enemy. The family who owned this tiny resort were named White. They had several grown sons and a daughter. One of the sons, Dalton, nineteen, was just back from Montreal where he had won the junior world championship in canoeing. He was dark-haired and tall, with a puckish smile, to me that year probably the most glamorous youth in the world. One could never, of course, hope to be friends with him.

[7] At the back of the house were a large vegetable garden, two or three sheds and an old boat with grass growing up through its timbers. Past them one reached a thicket. I pushed through it that first afternoon, into the woods beyond.

[8] The brush was thinner here but the trees grew densely. I wandered on, memorizing some landmarks: this boulder, this berry bush, this fallen log. I looked back. All had disappeared! It was a different grove when one turned around.

[9] The house was no longer in sight and my heart beat faster. I was lost! But one couldn't get lost on an island, although this one was large, three and a half miles long. It was only necessary to find the shore, mostly rocky and wild, and follow it back. But I still felt lost and curiously afraid.

[10] The trees, vaguely and strangely, were menacing. Not in any park, cemetery or pasture had I ever been so entirely enclosed by trees. These were massive, like giants. One surrounded by them felt helpless. They spread above, forming together a cavelike dark. They were presences. *Which way had I come*—where was the shore!

[11] Fear of trees is an old reaction, still a familiar emotion on primitive levels. Eskimos camping among trees, found along Northern rivers, dare not settle down beneath one for the night until they have stood off and thrown a knife into its trunk. Many other tribes have been awed by trees. If a branch has been broken off, if its bark has been damaged, or in the case of having to fell it, an apology would be made to a tree. The blood of a slaughtered animal was brushed onto it, or it was given a drink of water. In the Punjab, a former province of India, human sacrifices were made to a certain tree every year. Trees and groves in many parts of the world have been considered sacred.

·   ·   ·

[12] In the Canadian woods I didn't believe consciously that a tree might be hostile. I was just strangely uneasy there in the eerie atmosphere of the grove. One can name this dread and call it claustrophobia, which probably is an ancient fear. A prehistoric man might have felt trapped in dense woods, and recently Sir Frank Fraser Darling, the eloquent conservationist, has said that many modern people are afraid of a wilderness, which is why they are so willing to see it destroyed. Anyway I was slightly alarmed by that island forest, and although I was rather eager to know what was there I couldn't force myself to continue farther.

[13] My going and coming were noted, for I met Dalton on the way back and he said, "You didn't stay in the woods very long."

[14] "I was getting lost." He smiled with amusement.

[15] There were always three or four canoes pulled up on the beach. One day I got one of them out on the water and was floundering around in it when Dalton came down to the dock. He called, "Try to bring it back to the beach and I'll show you how to paddle." I sat in the bow facing him as with his strong, quick stroke he shot us out onto the lake. There he gave me the first

lesson, demonstrating the right way to hold the paddle, how to turn it so smoothly in pulling it back that a canoe doesn't vary its course by an inch. "Line up the prow with some tree on the shore," he said, "and don't let it swing either side off the trunk." In shallow water again we changed places and awkwardly I tried to put into practice what he had demonstrated. A skill, a start in learning a new skill—inspiring prospect—from this young man who himself was dedicated to perfecting a skill: was it possible that we might have something in common?

¹⁶ The Whites had a piano. It was in the sitting room of the house and I could no more stay away from it than I could have gone without food. My frequent playing must have been a trial to some of the other guests, especially a violinist who practiced several hours a day in his tent (a situation I didn't remind him of when I met him years later in San Francisco where he was teaching the young Yehudi Menuhin). But Dalton enjoyed my music. He used to come and stand at one end of the piano with his elbow on top, listening and watching.

¹⁷ He gave me more paddling lessons and after a while I too could hold a canoe's prow on the trunk of a shoreline tree. In the afternoons I went out with him in his racing canoe, as ballast he said, while he kept up his training. His canoe was a little sliver of a thing with graphite all over the outside to make it slip through the water faster. In Montreal he had paddled a mile in four minutes and seven seconds, a record which probably has been beaten many times, but when he dipped in his paddle, his canoe leapt away like a dolphin.

¹⁸ He landed us on the mainland one day and said, "Let's take a little walk." With a companion one could enjoy a forest. Besides, the trees here were of varying heights, they didn't form caves. It was an intricate scene, everything was prolifically growing—and dying. The ground was a litter of brown leaves and fir needles and sticks. It was unkempt compared with a park but fascinating.

¹⁹ All around us was limber movement. The grasses and wildflowers bent quivering in the flow of the breeze and the trees above were a green ruffling commotion. Their leaves, as they tossed and swung, seemed to be cutting the sky into bits, to be scattered as scraps of sunlight along the ground.

²⁰ Birds were lacing the air, in and out of the trees and bushes. One on the ground was jumping forward and scratching back through dead leaves and one, also searching for insects, was spiralling upon a tree trunk, pressing its stiff, short tail on the bark as a prop. At that time, in June, most of the birds would be feeding young, Dalton said, and they had to work all day catching insects for them. Besides this bright movement of wings, then, there must be thousands of tinier creatures doing whatever insects do on a summer afternoon: a world everywhere *alive*.

²¹ Dalton seemed to have realized that I knew almost nothing about what was here and was showing me things: a porcupine's tracks, a bee tree, a fox's burrow. He knocked on a tree and a flying squirrel poked its little head out of a hole. It was all wonderful, even exciting, but strange.

[22] We came out on a small elevation. Below was a meadow brimful of yellow-green sunlight. Perhaps this was the pleasantest way to enjoy a forest: with trees and brush at your back but a wide escape if anything should approach from behind. Unmentionable were wolves, bears. (They may have been there in fact. That forest is now built up but resorts not far away advertise that guests can hear wolves baying.) Dalton had brought his rifle. Was he just thinking of shooting something for fun, or was the gun for protection?

[23] The thought of escape was still there. Compare a park: only a few, spaced-out trees were allowed to grow, their dead branches were pruned away, the flowers were all in neat beds, the grass was kept mowed, never allowed to become weeds or "grasses." All controlled, therefore safe.

[24] Here the plants grew their own way and the animals went their own way—one might appear anywhere, any time. No one knew what might happen—did happen, for there were dead broken trees among the live ones. Everything was wild—naturally. That was the meaning of forests of course, that they were wild. Therefore unpredictable.

[25] Yet the wilderness was a beautiful, even enchanting place with its graceful movement and active life. Even underfoot if one scratched away the brown leaves as the bird had done, one might come upon small, secret lives. But might there be things that would bite? I had heard of tarantulas. With a feeling of cowardice, shrinking back, I wanted to leave, to return to the wide placid lake. And then I did something which made it seem that, on nature's terms, I had no right to be here at all.

[26] Dalton said, "Look!" Pointing: "There's a porcupine in the crotch of that tree over there." One of the wild inhabitants of this forest, only medium sized for an animal, sat on the branch, his back a high curve, with his quills raised and bristling. He might be lying like that to let the sunshine come into his fur, warm down to his skin. He looked sleepy. Dalton handed the rifle to me and said, "Let's see if you can hit it."

[27] He showed the way the gun should be held, braced against my shoulder, how to sight the target along the barrel. "Now pull the trigger back with your right hand—slowly, just squeeze it." I pulled the trigger and with astonishment saw the porcupine fall to the ground.

[28] Dalton was full of praise. "Very good! I didn't think you could do it." We went down along the side of the meadow. Beneath the tree lay the porcupine, limp and still. Even his fur and quills were that, lifeless now. Looking smaller, this was the little creature who, a few moments earlier, had been up on the bough wrapped in sunshine, enjoying life. I burst into tears.

[29] Dalton went over alone the next day and drew out the quills and brought them to me to decorate the basket of scented sweet-grass that I, like all the women, was making. I gave them away. . . .

[30] I never returned to the mainland forest alone, but by midsummer I'd made my own a small peninsula on the island. Paddling along its shore one morning I had tied the canoe to a tree overhanging the lake and sat in its shade doing embroidery. The point—it was the southern tip of the island—was nar-

row, not more than fifty yards wide. Through its trees I could see across to the bay on the other side and the center was open, with a thin cover of grass and wildflowers among sun-warmed rocks. It looked perfectly safe and I went ashore to investigate.

[31] There was no trail leading away from here, the point seemed private, peculiarly mine, and it pleased me very much. I came back the next day and then other days. Sometimes I walked about but more often sat under one of the trees, which were firs and quivering aspens, listening to the songs of the birds and watching them and a squirrel who was always there. I had a wonderful feeling—I had had it too with the chipmunk—that I was acceptable here, that I was liked, for they made little overtures even before I started feeding them bits of bread. Perhaps it helped that I talked to them.

[32] Gradually, a few moments one day, more moments the next, being there in that small safe woodland began to seem almost the same experience as making music, as the way, when I played the piano, I *was* the music, my physical body feeling as if it dissolved in the sounds. I could say my dimensions then were those of the melodies and the harmony that spread out from the piano in all directions. I had no consciousness of my individual self.

[33] Tenuously, imperfectly that Canadian summer, the same thing happened when I would walk around the peninsula, unafraid. It was not a wide going out and out, as with music, but again by losing myself—this time by becoming identified with whatever I was especially aware of. It happened first with a flower. I held a blue flower in my hand, probably a wild aster, wondering what its name was, and then thought that human names for natural things are superfluous. Nature herself does not name them. The important thing is to *know* this flower, look at its color until the blueness becomes as real as a keynote of music. Look at the exquisite yellow flowerettes in the center, become very small with them. *Be* the flower, be the trees, the blowing grasses. Fly with the birds, jump with the squirrel!

[34] Finally I spent every morning there. No one knew where I had gone.

ANALYTICAL READING

1. In this narrative, Sally Carrighar moves from being a stranger to becoming a part of the wilderness. Trace the steps in this progress.

2. In her descriptions of the Canadian island, to what senses does Carrighar appeal? Illustrate.

3. How does Carrighar use comparison in the selection? How do these comparisons help to explain the killing of the porcupine?

4. What kind of person was Dalton? Do you think he and the writer were similar?

5. What is Carrighar's relationship to Dalton? Does that relationship help to explain the killing of the porcupine? Why does she say that she "never, of course, hoped to be friends with him"?

6. Can you give the meaning of these words: *lucent, redolent, claustrophobia, graphite?*

7.   Reread the eight paragraphs (18–25) preceding the encounter with the porcu-
     pine. How do they heighten the horror of killing the porcupine? Why does she
     shoot it?

REFLECTING

Point: What point does Carrighar make about the relationship of humans with the
     wilderness? How does it relate to the attitudes toward trees that she mentions?

Organization: Does Carrighar rely mainly on chronological organization? Support
     your answer. Divide the narrative into several main sections, showing their
     functional relationships. For example, what purpose does the paragraph about
     the piano serve?

Support: Discuss Carrighar's use of the following to support her message: (1) de-
     scription, (2) her experiences with animals, (3) her feelings about trees and
     flowers.

Synthesis: Compare the message in paragraph 33 with Pirsig's recommendation to
     his student. Relate Carrighar's experiences with Parfit's.

Evaluation: Do you find Carrighar's language effective? Does she create images? List
     some sentences that strike you as especially effective. Be able to justify your
     choices. Does she convince you of her changed attitude toward being alone in
     the woods? Do you grow to share her reverence toward nature?

FROM READING TO WRITING

1.   Write a narrative for your classmates about a time in your own life when hurting
     or killing an animal gave you a new awareness of life and your relationship to
     other creatures.

2.   Describe for your classmates your own first awareness of the beauty of nature or
     your first feelings of oneness with it. Avoid flowery generalities; try to be as
     specific in your statements as Carrighar is.

GRANDMOTHER'S ENCOUNTER
Maya Angelou

BIOGRAPHICAL SKETCH

*Maya Angelou (1928–   ) was born in St. Louis. She started her career as a
dancer, touring Europe and Africa in* Porgy and Bess. *Her acting roles include* Cabaret for Freedom, *Genêt's* The Blacks, *and the TV version of* Roots. *A civil rights
activist, she worked with Martin Luther King, Jr., and the Southern Christian Leadership Conference. Her book,* Gather Together in My Name, *is a continuation of the*

book from which this selection is taken, I Know Why the Caged Bird Sings. *Her most recent book is* And I Still Rise.

PRE-READING

1. What relationship do you see between the title of the book the selection comes from and the information in the biographical sketch?

2. From skimming the first paragraph, what do you expect the selection to be about? Who is the main character?

¹ "Thou shall not be dirty" and "Thou shall not be impudent" were the two commandments of Grandmother Henderson upon which hung our total salvation.

² Each night in the bitterest winter we were forced to wash faces, arms, necks, legs and feet before going to bed. She used to add, with a smirk that unprofane people can't control when venturing into profanity, "and wash as far as possible, then wash possible."

³ We would go to the well and wash in the ice-cold, clear water, grease our legs with the equally cold stiff Vaseline, then tiptoe into the house. We wiped the dust from our toes and settled down for schoolwork, cornbread, clabbered milk, prayers and bed, always in that order. Momma was famous for pulling the quilts off after we had fallen asleep to examine our feet. If they weren't clean enough for her, she took the switch (she kept one behind the bedroom door for emergencies) and woke up the offender with a few aptly placed burning reminders.

⁴ The area around the well at night was dark and slick, and boys told about how snakes love water, so that anyone who had to draw water at night and then stand there alone and wash knew that moccasins and rattlers, puff adders and boa constrictors were winding their way to the well and would arrive just as the person washing got soap in her eyes. But Momma convinced us that not only was cleanliness next to Godliness, dirtiness was the inventor of misery.

⁵ The impudent child was detested by God and a shame to its parents and could bring destruction to its house and line. All adults had to be addressed as Mister, Missus, Miss, Auntie, Cousin, Unk, Uncle, Buhbah, Sister, Brother and a thousand other appellations indicating familial relationship and the lowliness of the addressor.

⁶ Everyone I knew respected these customary laws, except for the powhitetrash children.

⁷ Some families of powhitetrash lived on Momma's farm land behind the school. Sometimes a gaggle of them came to the Store, filling the whole room, chasing out the air and even changing the well-known scents. The children crawled over the shelves and into the potato and onion bins, twanging all the time in their sharp voices like cigarbox guitars. They took liberties in my Store that I would never dare. Since Momma told us that the less you say to white-

folks (or even powhitetrash) the better, Bailey and I would stand, solemn, quiet, in the displaced air. But if one of the playful apparitions got close to us, I pinched it. Partly out of angry frustration and partly because I didn't believe in its flesh reality.

⁸ They called my uncle by his first name and ordered him around the Store. He, to my crying shame, obeyed them in his limping dip-straight-dip fashion.

⁹ My grandmother, too, followed their orders, except that she didn't seem to be servile because she anticipated their needs.

¹⁰ "Here's sugar, Miz Potter, and here's baking powder. You didn't buy soda last month, you'll probably be needing some."

¹¹ Momma always directed her statements to the adults, but sometimes, Oh painful sometimes, the grimy, snotty-nosed girls would answer her.

¹² "Naw, Annie . . ."—to Momma? Who owned the land they lived on? Who forgot more than they would ever learn? If there was any justice in the world, God should strike them dumb at once!—"Just give us some extra sody crackers, and some more mackerel."

¹³ At least they never looked in her face, or I never caught them doing so. Nobody with a smidgen of training, not even the worst roustabout, would look right in a grown person's face. It meant the person was trying to take the words out before they were formed. The dirty little children didn't do that, but they threw their orders around the Store like lashes from a cat-o'-nine-tails.

¹⁴ When I was around ten years old, those scruffy children caused me the most painful and confusing experience I had ever had with my grandmother.

¹⁵ One summer morning, after I had swept the dirt yard of leaves, spearmint-gum wrappers and Vienna-sausage labels, I raked the yellow-red dirt, and made half-moons carefully, so that the design stood out clearly and masklike. I put the rake behind the Store and came through the back of the house to find Grandmother on the front porch in her big, wide white apron. The apron was so stiff by virtue of the starch that it could have stood alone. Momma was admiring the yard, so I joined her. It truly looked like a flat redhead that had been raked with a big-toothed comb. Momma didn't say anything but I knew she liked it. She looked over toward the school principal's house and to the right at Mr. McElroy's. She was hoping one of those community pillars would see the design before the day's business wiped it out. Then she looked upward to the school. My head had swung with hers, so at just about the same time we saw a troop of the powhitetrash kids marching over the hill and down by the side of the school.

¹⁶ I looked to Momma for direction. She did an excellent job of sagging from her waist down, but from the waist up she seemed to be pulling for the top of the oak tree across the road. Then she began to moan a hymn. Maybe not to moan, but the tune was so slow and the meter so strange that she could have been moaning. She didn't look at me again. When the children reached halfway down the hill, halfway to the Store, she said without turning, "Sister, go on inside."

[17] I wanted to beg her, "Momma, don't wait for them. Come on inside with me. If they come in the Store, you go to the bedroom and let me wait on them. They only frighten me if you're around. Alone I know how to handle them." But of course I couldn't say anything, so I went in and stood behind the screen door.

[18] Before the girls got to the porch I heard their laughter crackling and popping like pine logs in a cooking stove. I suppose my lifelong paranoia was born in those cold, molasses-slow minutes. They came finally to stand on the ground in front of Momma. At first they pretended seriousness. Then one of them wrapped her right arm in the crook of her left, pushed out her mouth and started to hum. I realized that she was aping my grandmother. Another said, "Naw, Helen, you ain't standing like her. This here's it." Then she lifted her chest, folded her arms and mocked that strange carriage that was Annie Henderson. Another laughed, "Naw, you can't do it. Your mouth ain't pooched out enough. It's like this."

[19] I thought about the rifle behind the door, but I knew I'd never be able to hold it straight, and the .410, our sawed-off shotgun, which stayed loaded and was fired every New Year's night, was locked in the trunk and Uncle Willie had the key on his chain. Through the fly-specked screen-door, I could see that the arms of Momma's apron jiggled from the vibrations of her humming. But her knees seemed to have locked as if they would never bend again.

[20] She sang on. No louder than before, but no softer either. No slower or faster.

[21] The dirt of the girls' cotton dresses continued on their legs, feet, arms and faces to make them all of a piece. Their greasy uncolored hair hung down, uncombed, with a grim finality. I knelt to see them better, to remember them for all time. The tears that had slipped down my dress left unsurprising dark spots, and made the front yard blurry and even more unreal. The world had taken a deep breath and was having doubts about continuing to revolve.

[22] The girls had tired of mocking Momma and turned to other means of agitation. One crossed her eyes, stuck her thumbs in both sides of her mouth and said, "Look here, Annie." Grandmother hummed on and the apron strings trembled. I wanted to throw a handful of black pepper in their faces, to throw lye on them, to scream that they were dirty, scummy peckerwoods, but I knew I was as clearly imprisoned behind the scene as the actors outside were confined to their roles.

[23] One of the smaller girls did a kind of puppet dance while her fellow clowns laughed at her. But the tall one, who was almost a woman, said something very quietly, which I couldn't hear. They all moved backward from the porch, still watching Momma. For an awful second I thought they were going to throw a rock at Momma, who seemed (except for the apron strings) to have turned into stone herself. But the big girl turned her back, bent down and put her hands flat on the ground—she didn't pick up anything. She simply shifted her weight and did a hand stand.

[24] Her dirty bare feet and long legs went straight for the sky. Her dress fell

down around her shoulders, and she had on no drawers. The slick pubic hair made a brown triangle where her legs came together. She hung in the vacuum of that lifeless morning for only a few seconds, then wavered and tumbled. The other girls clapped her on the back and slapped their hands.

[25] Momma changed her song to "Bread of Heaven, bread of Heaven, feed me till I want no more."

[26] I found that I was praying too. How long could Momma hold out? What new indignity would they think of to subject her to? Would I be able to stay out of it? What would Momma really like me to do?

[27] Then they were moving out of the yard, on their way to town. They bobbed their heads and shook their slack behinds and turned, one at a time:

[28] " 'Bye, Annie."

[29] " 'Bye, Annie."

[30] " 'Bye, Annie."

[31] Momma never turned her head or unfolded her arms, but she stopped singing and said, " 'Bye, Miz Helen, 'bye, Miz Ruth, 'bye, Miz Eloise."

[32] I burst. A firecracker July-the-Fourth burst. How could Momma call them Miz? The mean nasty things. Why couldn't she have come inside the sweet, cool store when we saw them breasting the hill? What did she prove? And then if they were dirty, mean and impudent, why did Momma have to call them Miz?

[33] She stood another whole song through and then opened the screen door to look down on me crying in rage. She looked until I looked up. Her face was a brown moon that shone on me. She was beautiful. Something had happened out there, which I couldn't completely understand, but I could see that she was happy. Then she bent down and touched me as mothers of the church "lay hands on the sick and afflicted" and I quieted.

[34] "Go wash your face, Sister." And she went behind the candy counter and hummed, "Glory, glory, hallelujah, when I lay my burden down."

[35] I threw the well water on my face and used the weekday handkerchief to blow my nose. Whatever the contest had been out front, I knew Momma had won.

[36] I took the rake back to the front yard. The smudged footprints were easy to erase. I worked for a long time on my new design and laid the rake behind the wash pot. When I came back in the Store, I took Momma's hand and we both walked outside to look at the pattern.

[37] It was a large heart with lots of hearts growing smaller inside, and piercing from the outside rim to the smallest heart was an arrow. Momma said, "Sister, that's right pretty." Then she turned back to the Store and resumed, "Glory, glory, hallelujah, when I lay my burden down."

ANALYTICAL READING

1. How old is the narrator? What kind of relationship does she have with her grandmother?

2. Were you aware of the language used? How does Maya Angelou indicate regionalisms and dialect variations in the story? Do these characteristics add authenticity to the narrator's voice? Refer to specific expressions: why, for example, is *powhitetrash* one word?

3. What do the first four or five paragraphs contribute to the narrative?

4. What is the tone in the story? Does it shift? When? If so, does this contribute to our knowledge of the narrator's feelings? Does the foreshadowing in paragraph 15 add to or detract from the account?

5. What do you find out about the physical environment and the way the characters lived? How is this information revealed?

6. What do you think the narrator learned from the episode? Why did she draw the heart in the dust? Has the incident affected her attitude toward the children?

REFLECTING

Point: What do you think the message is? Does the reader gain some understanding as the narrator does? Do you think the reader might learn things that the narrator is unaware of?

Organization: Does Maya Angelou use only a chronological organization? What do the opening paragraphs do for the overall organization of the story?

Support: How does Maya Angelou use action, emotional response of the narrator, language, and images to support the message of her story?

Synthesis: In what ways is this story related to the Nate Shaw selection? To other stories you may have read or know about (*Roots,* for example)? Contrast the reactions of the young and old black women. How do you account for the differences?

Evaluation: Did you find the situation believable? Why? Does the ending come close to excessive sentimentality? If you planned to present this narrative as a play, how would you have it end? Does the incident suggest realistically the threat that the blacks felt from the whites? Is it effectively depicted here?

FROM READING TO WRITING

1. Write a short narrative for a general audience about a situation that somehow threatened you or a person close to you. Without making direct moralistic statements, try to write the story so that the reader can infer a moral lesson about human relationships.

2. For your classmates, describe an experience you have had involving a bully or an intimidating person. Use dialogue and perhaps try to explain the cause or causes of your characters' actions.

JAMES DICKEY'S GLORY

James Dickey

BIOGRAPHICAL SKETCH

James Dickey (1923–   ) was born in Atlanta, graduated from Vanderbilt University (where he played football) with B.A. and M.A. degrees, and flew more than a hundred combat missions in World War II. Now a professor of English at the University of South Carolina, he has worked in advertising, has been poet in residence at several schools, and served as a consultant in poetry to the Library of Congress for two terms. He is the author of numerous books of poetry, including Buckdancer's Choice, *which won the National Book Award in 1966. Among his many prose works are several books of literary criticism and critical articles, and the novel* Deliverance, *which was a Literary Guild selection and was made into a popular movie.*

PRE-READING

1. From the biographical sketch, what would you expect Dickey's "glory" to be?

2. From the title and the first paragraph, how would you identify the "glory"?

¹ In 1940 I was a senior in high school. My main sport was football, but my preference was really track. I was a big strong animal who could run fast, and I gloried in this fact. My conference, though I lived in Atlanta, was not the conference in which the big Atlanta high schools competed. I ran in the North Georgia Interscholastic Conference, or N.G.I.C., as it was popularly known. The high-hurdles event, which was my specialty, was often held on grass, up the middle of a football field. This was the case at the 1940 N.G.I.C. meet. We qualified in the afternoon, all of us trying hard but not so hard as to tire ourselves out for the night's final. In the trials I lost to a fine hurdler from Canton, Georgia, and then went out with him, soaked with shower water, and got a cheeseburger. I felt that I had not run well, that my start had been bad, that I had not been able to get a good grip on the turf with my spikes, that I had been too high over the hurdles, that my finish had been poor. But my conqueror had set a new N.G.I.C. record, and he should have.

² When I suited up for the finals, though, I was ready. I felt that I had come to run. It was a cool night, and there were several hundred people in the stands, and, when they called the hurdles final, a great many people were clustered about the finish line, where the tape glimmered with ghostly promise for the winner. I ran in the next lane from the boy from Canton. We shook hands: a new friendship, a fierce rivalry, for I knew he would give no quarter, and I knew damn well that I wasn't planning to give any. We got down on the blocks. Before us was a green sea of grass with faint line stripes from spring

FROM *Esquire*, October 1976, p. 81. © 1976 by Esquire, Inc. Reprinted by permission of Esquire Magazine.

practice across it. I concentrated on getting as much pressure on my legs as I could. I would try to get off well, though I was too big to hope for a really fast start. The gun cracked, and we were gone. I paid no attention to where anyone else was but concentrated on form and on picking up speed between hurdles. But I could dimly sense the Canton boy. At the fifth hurdle I could tell that we were dead even.

³ The finish-line crowd was coming at us like a hurricane. I concentrated on staying low over the hurdles and made really good moves on the next three. I began to edge him by inches, and by the next two hurdles I thought that if I didn't hit the next two I'd make it. I also said to myself, as I remember, *don't play it safe. Go low over the last stick, and then give it everything you've got up the final straight.*

⁴ But I did hit the last hurdle. I hit it with the inner ankle of my left foot, tearing the flesh to the bone, as I found out later, and the injury left a scar which I bear to this day. However, my frenzied momentum was such that I won by a yard, careening wildly into the crowd after the tape broke around my neck. I smashed into the spectators and bowled over a little boy, hitting straight into his nose with my knee. He lay on the smoky grass crying, his nose bleeding, and I came back, blowing like a wounded stallion, everybody congratulating me on a new N.G.I.C. record. But I went to the boy, raised him up in my arms, wiped the blood from his nose, tried to comfort him, and kissed him. That raising-up of an injured, unknown child was the greatest thing that I have ever gleaned from sports.

ANALYTICAL READING

1. What does Dickey mean by "glory"? How does it compare to your preconceived notions?

2. How old do you think Dickey was at the time of the incident? Where did it take place?

3. Is there an ironic twist at the ending of the story? How does Dickey prepare the reader for it?

4. How does Dickey use description to heighten the sense of total concentration?

5. As you read, were you aware of how Dickey uses sentence structure to emphasize the speed and urgency of the race? Review the second paragraph describing the race, listing the length and kinds of sentences you find there.

REFLECTING

Point: Does the story make a statement about human priorities? Discuss.

Organization: Except for the first paragraph, the story is arranged chronologically. What purpose does the first paragraph serve?

Support: In questions 4 and 5 above, you looked at the description and sentence techniques. Do these also serve as support? How? What specific details make the selection vivid? How effective are such images as "The finish-line crowd was coming at us like a hurricane" and "I came back, blowing like a wounded stallion"?

Synthesis: Compare Dickey's experience with Sally Carrighar's. What do they have in common? How are they different?

Evaluation: Did the story hold your suspense and interest? Why? Would the story have been more or less successful if Dickey had explained why the raising up of the child was so important to him? How does the ending flatter the reader?

FROM READING TO WRITING

1. For your classmates, write a short narrative about a time when you participated in a competitive event and things turned out differently than you had expected.

2. Write a narrative for your classmates titled "_____'s Glory," putting your name in the blank.

3. Write a narrative about how sports contributed to the development of your character. Establish a particular audience before you begin: for example, readers of your college newspaper's sports page.

THE PERFECT PICTURE
James Alexander Thom

BIOGRAPHICAL SKETCH

James Alexander Thom, a native of Indiana and a graduate of Butler University (Indianapolis), has been a police reporter, feature writer, a financial editor for the Indianapolis Star, *and an editor of the revived* Saturday Evening Post. *Now a free-lance writer, he has been a contributor to* Reader's Digest, National Geographic, *and* The Country Gentleman. *His novels include* Spectator Sport *(1978). He is currently working on a novel based on the Revolutionary War. At present he is a lecturer in the school of journalism at Indiana University.*

PRE-READING

1. From the title, what profession would you expect the narrator to be in?

2. After skimming the first paragraph, what do you know of the narrator and the plot?

3. Describe the tone the writer establishes in the opening paragraph.

¹ It was early in the spring about 15 years ago—a day of pale sunlight and trees just beginning to bud. I was a young police reporter, driving to a scene I didn't want to see. A man, the police-dispatcher's broadcast said, had acciden-

FROM *Reader's Digest*, August 1976, pp. 113–14. Copyright © 1976 by The Reader's Digest Association, Inc. Reprinted with permission.

tally backed his pickup truck over his baby granddaughter in the driveway of the family home. It was a fatality.

² As I parked among police cars and TV-news cruisers, I saw a stocky, white-haired man in cotton work clothes standing near a pickup. Cameras were trained on him, and reporters were sticking microphones in his face. Looking totally bewildered, he was trying to answer their questions. Mostly he was only moving his lips, blinking and choking up.

³ After a while the reporters gave up on him and followed the police into the small white house. I can still see in my mind's eye that devastated old man looking down at the place in the driveway where the child had been. Beside the house was a freshly spaded flower bed, and nearby a pile of dark, rich earth.

⁴ "I was just backing up there to spread that good dirt," he said to me, though I had not asked him anything. "I didn't even know she was outdoors." He stretched his hand toward the flower bed, then let it flop to his side. He lapsed back into his thoughts, and I, like a good reporter, went into the house to find someone who could provide a recent photo of the toddler.

⁵ A few minutes later, with all the details in my notebook and a three-by-five studio portrait of the cherubic child tucked in my jacket pocket, I went toward the kitchen where the police had said the body was.

⁶ I had brought a camera in with me—the big, bulky Speed Graphic which used to be the newspaper reporter's trademark. Everybody had drifted back out of the house together—family, police, reporters and photographers. Entering the kitchen, I came upon this scene:

⁷ On a Formica-topped table, backlighted by a frilly curtained window, lay the tiny body, wrapped in a clean white sheet. Somehow the grandfather had managed to stay away from the crowd. He was sitting on a chair beside the table, in profile to me and unaware of my presence, looking uncomprehendingly at the swaddled corpse.

⁸ The house was very quiet. A clock ticked. As I watched, the grandfather slowly leaned forward, curved his arms like parentheses around the head and feet of the little form, then pressed his face to the shroud and remained motionless.

⁹ In that hushed moment I recognized the makings of a prize-winning news photograph. I appraised the light, adjusted the lens setting and distance, locked a bulb in the flashgun, raised the camera and composed the scene in the viewfinder.

¹⁰ Every element of the picture was perfect: the grandfather in his plain work clothes, his white hair backlighted by sunshine, the child's form wrapped in the sheet, the atmosphere of the simple home suggested by black iron trivets and World's Fair souvenir plates on the walls flanking the window. Outside, the police could be seen inspecting the fatal rear wheel of the pickup while the child's mother and father leaned in each other's arms.

¹¹ I don't know how many seconds I stood there, unable to snap that shutter. I was keenly aware of the powerful story-telling value that photo would have, and my professional conscience told me to take it. Yet I couldn't make my hand fire that flashbulb and intrude on the poor man's island of grief.

[12] At length I lowered the camera and crept away, shaken with doubt about my suitability for the journalistic profession. Of course I never told the city editor or any fellow reporters about that missed opportunity for a perfect news picture.

[13] Every day, on the newscasts and in the papers, we see pictures of people in extreme conditions of grief and despair. Human suffering has become a spectator sport. And sometimes, as I'm watching news film, I remember that day.

[14] I still feel right about what I did.

ANALYTICAL READING

1. What do we learn of the narrator's feelings about the assignment? About the old man? What words indicate the writer's sympathy and emotional involvement?

2. As you read, were you aware of the devices the writer used to indicate the time sequence? Check back to find examples.

3. Unlike the writers of many of the other narrative selections, Thom uses very little dialogue. What advantage can you see in this?

4. The descriptions in the story are often photographic. Choose one that you think has strong pictorial characteristics and analyze how that effect is achieved.

REFLECTING

Point: The writer makes a rather obvious point. Summarize it in one sentence. Where in the article is it presented? How is the reader prepared for it?

Organization: How is the story organized? Jot down a simple outline of the time elements in the story. Has the author eliminated unnecessary details to focus on the scene with the child and grandfather?

Support: How do the detailed descriptions help to support the message of the story? Discuss the effectiveness of the phrase "island of grief" (paragraph 11)?

Synthesis: How do you feel about this conflict between professional and personal ethics? Does Dickey's narrative relate to this conflict?

Evaluation: This story could easily have been handled as a sentimental tear-jerker or as an obvious moral sermon. Does the writer avoid these traps? Justify your opinion. Did the writer do right? Did he have a responsibility to newspaper readers? How do television cameramen treat comparable episodes?

FROM READING TO WRITING

1. Write about an episode in your life that involved a moral decision. Indicate how you feel today about the decision you made.

2. Write about a time when the demands of a job, sport, or other activity conflicted with your personal ethics.

3. Write for your classmates either about how you decided not to do something enjoyable or advantageous because you knew it was wrong, or about something unpleasant or disadvantageous you did because you knew it was right.

Personal Essay

LOOK FOR THE RUSTY LINING
Ralph Schoenstein

BIOGRAPHICAL SKETCH

Ralph Schoenstein (1933–   ) was born in New York and earned a B.A. from Columbia University. He has been active as a television writer-producer and journalist. His nonfiction sports story "A Giant Fan's Lament" won him the Grantland Rice Memorial Award in 1962. He has written many books, the most recent of which are Citizen Paul *(1978) and* Yes My Darling Daughters *(1976). His humorous essays have appeared in numerous magazines and anthologies.*

PRE-READING

1. Of what popular saying is the title a rephrasing? What do you expect the title to contribute to the tone of this personal essay?

2. After skimming the first paragraph, indicate the sentence that you think is the focusing statement—the one that introduces the subject to the reader?

3. From skimming the first paragraph, do you expect this to be a serious essay? What sets the tone?

[1] My grandfather's hobby was worrying, and although hobbies are not usually thought of as being inheritable, I am a talented worrier, too. My grandfather's glum genes, which skipped my merry father, have reflowered in me as a major, all-purpose anxiety. A few weeks ago, for example, I learned that collapsing stars called black holes may soon suck up all the matter in the universe. Because I read this in *Vogue,* I hoped at first that the black holes were some kind of fad—a celestial pop event like Kohoutek or UFOs—but then I saw that the author of the article had been twice a visting Member at the Institute for Advanced Study, in Princeton, and I knew that another crisis was at hand. Ominously, the Institute is just down the street from where I do *my* worrying.

[2] The end of the universe should have been a splendid challenge for a gifted worrier like me, but mostly it upset me in a new and worrisome way, because it made me realize that I was spread too thin. When I found the black-

FROM *The New Yorker*, February 3, 1975, p. 31. Reprinted by permission of the author.

hole story, I hadn't nearly come to the end of an earlier wonderful worry of mine about the polar ice cap melting and raising the level of the Atlantic Ocean enough to submerge the entire East Coast. I had been thinking of moving my family to Saskatchewan, but now that I was falling behind in my worrying, I had to worry if Saskatchewan might be tastier for a black hole than Princeton. On the other hand, Princeton was closer to those African killer bees that have been inexorably moving north from Brazil—the ones that made me decide not to visit Central America last winter. The bees are getting very close to Central America, and Panama may be the only place where there is a chance to turn them back. Of course, even if it had only butterflies, Panama would still be a worrisome vacation spot for me, because it is said to be riddled with as much anti-American feeling as Boston.

³ In these terrible days, I often think of my grandfather, who was a nervous wreck in a simpler and happier time. His worries were transient and nicely manageable: When would Mel Ott start hitting again? When would Eleanor Roosevelt collapse from too much traveling around? When would the Third Avenue "L" rust away? I miss him, but he is lucky not to be alive and worrying today. I don't think he could have handled all the terrors that keep testing my sanity; he might even have surrendered and become an optimist, thus forfeiting the hobby he loved.

⁴ He was my inspiration when I was a boy—a worrier to look up to. He used to visit me in my room, where he would examine my homework and then shake his head and say, "You'll never get through medical school with spelling like this."

⁵ "But these are brand-new words," I would tell him in a worried way. "Spelling is harder this year than it was in the second grade."

⁶ He would sigh and say, "I don't know. I'm not even sure you should be a doctor at all. I just read that they have the highest rate for dropping dead."

⁷ My grandfather's quaint worries about me and Mel Ott and Eleanor Roosevelt are enough to make a contemporary worrier weep with envy. I wonder what he would have done if he had read a recent prediction by Gunnar Myrdal that the American economy could utterly collapse within five years—just before the Eastern tidal wave but shortly after the arrival of the bees. Probably he would have adopted something like my own advanced worrying posture and learned to make room for each new worry by letting it trump one of the old ones. For example, when I read about the inundation of the East I forgot about my overdue Bloomingdale's bill; when I read Gunnar Myrdal's warning I decided to stop worrying about what would happen if Connecticut ever ran out of antiques. When I heard about the bees I eased off my worry about a root canal of mine and let the Panama Canal replace it on the Top Twenty.

⁸ What a list! Something old and something new, something cosmic yet something trivial too, for the creative worrier must forever blend the pedestrian with the immemorial. If the sun burns out, will the Mets be able to play their entire schedule at night? If cryogenically frozen human beings are ever

revived, will they have to re-register to vote? And if the little toe disappears, will field goals play a smaller part in the National Football League?

[9] Actually, I've never had a worry as worrisome as the universe-destroying black holes. I mean, the universe is where I do all my worrying, and if it suddenly disappears I may not be able to relocate. My only hope comes from a first principle of worry that I have learned in a lifetime of anxiety; i.e., some of the biggest problems are half of a self-cancelling pair. A nice example is that dreaded polar ice cap, which some scientists say isn't starting to melt at all but instead will shortly begin to enlarge rapidly, giving birth to a new ice age that soon will cover the entire United States. I worried about this ice layer from last February 9th until about Labor Day, by which time my worry about the price of bottom round had reduced it to the size of a rink. Lately, however, I have turned my mind back to the ice again, and I have been worrying about the fact that you cannot have ice that is growing and melting at the same time. One of these terrors is a dud, and the job of the dedicated worrier is to find out which one it is.

[10] Applying this principle to the black holes, I wonder if there may not be some white holes in space as well—pretty, glowing things that won't digest a universe but may prefer to spit it out again. All I need is a new flash from the Institute about one of these, and then perhaps I will be able to start worrying about chinch bugs and the male menopause and all the other gentle terrors my grandfather could endorse.

[11] Is that the right way to spell "chinch bugs"?

ANALYTICAL READING

1. What "how-to" suggestions for worrying does Schoenstein offer? How do these contribute to the overall tone?

2. How does the last paragraph contribute to the effectiveness of the essay?

REFLECTING

Point: Do you think the writer is advocating that we all should worry, or that we worry too much, or what? Discuss. Is there any suggestion about "the good old days" as opposed to the present?

Organization: Outline the organization of the personal essay by summarizing the main point of each paragraph. How do these relate to the focusing statement?

Support: Recall some of the specific things that Schoenstein and his grandfather worry about. How do these contribute to the organization?

Synthesis: Does this essay touch on your own experiences? Do you tend to worry needlessly? Would it help to be able to scoff at your own worries? Do you know people who always worry? What real worries have been omitted from the essay? Why?

Evaluation: Do you think the writer effectively sustains the point of view throughout? Discuss. What contribution does the character of the grandfather make to the account?

FROM READING TO WRITING

1. Make a list of your own persistent worries, categorize them into different types, and then write a humorous personal essay about them for your classmates. Remember to avoid a heavy touch; choose words carefully to maintain a gentle sarcasm.

2. Choose an annoying or puzzling habit that you or someone close to you has. Summarize it in one sentence that can serve as the focusing statement and write a brief personal essay about it for a general audience. Try for an amused but affectionate tone.

THE MAGIC POWER OF WORDS
Thomas H. Middleton

BIOGRAPHICAL SKETCH

Thomas Middleton (1926–   ), after his graduation from Princeton, became an actor and has appeared in both film and stage plays. During rehearsals he began to work Double-Crostic puzzles to kill time; later he started to create them himself. For the last ten years his Double-Crostic has been a regular feature of the Saturday Review. *In addition, he writes a regular column, "Light Refractions," which reflects his fascination with word meanings and usage.*

PRE-READING

1. What does the word "magic" conjure up in your mind? Can you think of words that have had "magic power" for you?

2. From the opening paragraph, what kind of words do you expect the essay to deal with?

[1] There was a distressing story in the newspaper a few months ago. I wish I'd clipped it out and saved it. As it is, I can only hope I remember it fairly accurately. There was a group of people who wanted a particular dictionary removed from the shelves of the local library because it contained a lot of obscenity. I think they said there were sixty-five or so dirty words in it. Some poor woman who was acting as a spokesman for the group had a list of the offending words, which she started to read aloud at a hearing. She managed to read about twenty of them before she started sobbing uncontrollably and couldn't continue.

[2] I'm sure I could have read off the entire list. I'm equally sure I'd have been somewhat embarrassed at reading some of the words out loud at a hearing. Today, there are undoubtedly many people—both men and women—who

could have managed the whole thing without a trace of a qualm. But the fact is that we'd not all be doing the same thing. For me, it would mean enunciating words whose connotations might range from the completely inoffensive to the quite unpleasant, with a good sprinkling of the ludicrous in between.

3 For those who could read the list with no feeling of uneasiness, the words would be "only words."

4 While I don't like anything about the idea of removing any dictionaries from any libraries, I can sympathize with the woman who broke down. For her, the words were not "only words": they were horrifying things with their own terrible power, and they were too much for her.

5 There is power in spoken words. Some of the power is not unlike magic. The fact that the power may (or may not) be all in our minds does not diminish its effect.

6 Most people probably don't know that if you tell someone your dream before breakfast, it will come true, but my mother told me that almost as soon as I was old enough to put my dreams into words. So all my life I've been telling my good dreams before breakfast and saving the nightmares for later. It wasn't until I was well into my twenties that I finally realized that this superstition was not at all widespread. In fact, I haven't met anyone outside of my immediate family who has ever heard of it. Maybe my mother made it up. It is, nevertheless, a minor instance of the magic power of the spoken word.

7 One of the major instances of this power is the widely held belief in the efficacy of knocking wood. If, for example, the old heap hasn't had to go to the garage for repairs in almost a year, you'd better not mention the fact out loud, or you'll need a new clutch and a new set of rings that evening—unless you knock wood.

8 When I was in college, one of the psychology professors told us, in a lecture on superstition, that even among men of science who knew that superstitions were only superstitions and should not be taken seriously, knocking wood was a very common practice. He made me feel better, because though I may fool around with other superstitions (dreams before breakfast, etc.), "knock wood" is one superstition I take absolutely seriously. I've walked under ladders; I ignore black cats; I've put a hat on a bed; even as a child, I stepped on many a crack, smug in the conviction that I would not thus break my mother's back; I've even spilled salt without tossing some over my shoulder; but if I were to say something like, "I haven't had a bad cold in over three years," I wouldn't be able to breathe regularly until I'd knocked wood.

9 Obviously, it's all right to *think* about how well things have been going. Just don't express your thoughts in words, where there is magic.

10 Countless generations have been taught, practically as soon as they could speak, that enunciating certain words constitutes a giant step toward hell and that speaking or chanting other words or combinations of words is a big help along the road to salvation or spiritual bliss; one man's nonsense syllable is another's path to peace.

11 While the power of traditionally shocking words to shock is at an all-

time low, at least in the United States, and many of us have decided that words are only words and are not in themselves either good or bad, it is still hard for me to imagine anyone for whom there are not some words with almost supernatural connotations, whether the words be Om, O Lord, Our Father, Holy Mary, Hare Krishna, or a simple statement of faith in one's carburetor.

[12] As one who has to find wood to knock in order to minimize the negative effects of his own words, I certainly can't fault someone who is overpowered by a collection of—to her—hideous taboos taken from a dictionary.

ANALYTICAL READING

1. Where does Middleton place his focusing statement?

2. Do you think Middleton intended to instruct his audience about words or simply to comment on some superstitions concerning them? Discuss. How does he feel about the people attacking the dictionary?

3. As you read, were you aware of the devices Middleton used to hold the essay together? Review the essay, noting how he moves from one paragraph to the next and how he repeats words that have to do with his subject.

REFLECTING

Point: Does Middleton's point have to do with what words mean or with what people *think* they mean? Explain.

Organization: How does Middleton use the final paragraph to pull the essay together? What does the opening anecdote contribute to the organization?

Support: What examples does Middleton use to support his statements? How effective are the examples in sustaining interest in the essay?

Synthesis: Does the essay relate to some situations you recalled from the title at the pre-reading stage? Do you know any magic words employed in folk tales, comic strips, movie cartoons, transcendental meditation? Should a dictionary list all words, or should certain kinds of words be omitted?

Evaluation: Compare this personal essay with Schoenstein's. Which do you find more effective? Why? Has Middleton given you any new understanding about language? If so, what?

FROM READING TO WRITING

1. For your college newspaper, write an essay about some superstitions you developed as a young child that are still with you. Try opening the essay with an anecdote.

2. For your classmates, write an essay that recounts how you learned that certain words were unacceptable in some social situations.

3. In J. D. Salinger's novel *Catcher in the Rye,* young Holden Caulfield tries to erase a dirty word written on a wall. Relate this action to Middleton's essay in a paper for a general audience.

4. Write a personal essay for your classmates recounting times when you have noticed that masculine gender words, such as *spokesman* or *chairman,* seemed to exert the "magical" effect of stereotyping.

5. For your classmates, write a personal essay about words that you use frequently, explaining why you find them so helpful.

TERRY PICKENS, NEWSBOY

Studs Terkel

BIOGRAPHICAL SKETCH

Studs Terkel (1912–   ), born in New York City, has a law degree from the Chicago Law School but has always worked in the communication field. He has been an actor in soap operas, a sports commentator, and a disc jockey, and has conducted on-the-spot interviews all over the world. These interviews have been collected in several best-selling books: Working *(1974),* Talking to Myself *(1977), and* American Dreams: Lost and Found *(1980).*

PRE-READING

1. Does the word *newsboy* in the title suggest any irritating experiences that might be common to all people who deliver papers? List a few before reading.

2. Does the first paragraph give an indication of the newsboy's attitude toward his job?

¹ I've been having trouble collecting. I had one woman hid from me once. I had another woman tell her kids to tell me she wasn't home. He says, "Mom, newsboy," She says (whispers), "Tell him I'm not home." I could hear it from the door. I came back in half an hour and she paid me. She's not a deadbeat. They'll pay you if you get 'em. Sometimes you have to wait . . .

² If I don't catch 'em at home, I get pretty mad. That means I gotta come back and come back and come back and come back until I catch 'em. Go around about nine o'clock at night and seven o'clock in the morning. This one guy owed me four dollars. He got real mad at me for comin' around at ten o'clock. Why'd I come around so late? He probably was mad 'cause I caught him home. But he paid me. I don't care whether he gets mad at me, just so I get paid.

³ I like to have money. It's nice to have money once in a while instead of being flat broke all the time. Most of my friends are usually flat broke. I spent $150 this summer. On nothing—candy, cokes, games of pool, games of pin-

ball. We went to McDonald's a couple of times. I just bought anything I wanted. I wonder where the money went. I have nothing to show for it. I'm like a gambler, the more I have, the more I want to spend. That's just the way I am.

⁴ It's supposed to be such a great deal. The guy, when he came over and asked me if I wanted a route, he made it sound so great. Seven dollars a week for hardly any work at all. And then you find out the guy told you a bunch of bull. You mistrust the people. You mistrust your customers because they don't pay you sometimes.

⁵ Then you get mad at the people at the printing corporation. You're supposed to get fifty-seven papers. They'll send me forty-seven or else they'll send me sixty-seven. Sunday mornings they get mixed up. Cliff'll have ten or eleven extras and I'll be ten or eleven short. That happens all the time. The printers, I don't think they care. They make all these stupid mistakes at least once a week. I think they're half-asleep or something. I do my job, I don't see why they can't do theirs. I don't like my job any more than they do.

⁶ Sunday mornings at three—that's when I get up. I stay up later so I'm tired. But the dark doesn't bother me. I run into things sometimes, though. Somebody's dog'll come out and about give you a heart attack. There's this one woman, she had two big German shepherds, great big old things, like three or four feet tall. One of 'em won't bite you. He'll just run up, charging, bark at you, and then he'll go away. The other one, I didn't know she had another one—when it bit me. This dog came around the bush. (Imitates barking.) When I turned around, he was at me. He bit me right there (indicates scar on leg). It was bleeding a little. I gave him a real dirty look.

⁷ He ran over to the other neighbor's lawn and tried to keep me from gettin' in there. I walked up and delivered the paper. I was about ready to beat the thing's head in or kill it. Or something with it. I was so mad. I called up that woman and she said the dog had all its shots and "I don't believe he bit you." I said, "Lady, he bit me." Her daughter started giving me the third degree. "What color was the dog?" "How big was it?" "Are you sure it was our yard and our dog?" Then they saw the dogs weren't in the pen.

⁸ First they told me they didn't think I needed any shots. Then they said they'd pay for the doctor. I never went to the doctor. It wasn't bleeding a whole lot. But I told her if I ever see that dog again, she's gonna have to get her papers from somebody else. Now they keep the dog penned up and it barks at me and everything. And I give it a dirty look.

⁹ There's a lot of dogs around here. I got this other dog, a little black one, it tried to bite me too. It lunged at me, ripped my pants, and missed me. (With the glee of W.C. Fields) I kicked it *good*. It still chases me. There are two black dogs. The other one I've kicked so many times that it just doesn't bother me any more. I've kicked his face in once when he was biting my leg. Now he just stays under the bushes and growls at me. I don't bother to give him a dirty look.

¹⁰ There was these two other dogs. They'd always run out in the street and chase me. I kicked them. They'd come back and I'd kick 'em again. I don't

have any problems with 'em any more, because they got hit chasin' cars. They're both dead.

¹¹ I don't like many of my customers, 'cause they'll cuss me if they don't get their papers just exactly in the right place. This one guy cussed me up and down for about fifteen minutes. I don't want to repeat what he called me. All the words, just up and down. He told me he drives past all those blank drugstores on his blank way home and he could stop off at one of 'em and get a blank newspaper. And I'm just a blank convenience.

¹² I was so mad at him. I hated his guts. I felt like taking a lead pipe to him or something. But I kept my mouth shut, 'cause I didn't know if the press guy'd get mad at me and I'd lose my route. You see, this guy could help or he could hurt me. So I kept my mouth shut.

¹³ A lot of customers are considerate but a lot of 'em aren't. Lot of 'em act like they're doing you such a favor taking the paper from you. It costs the same dime at a drugstore. Every time they want you to do something they threaten you: (imitates nasty, nasal voice) "Or I'll quit."

¹⁴ What I really can't stand: you'll be collecting and somebody'll come out and start telling you all their problems. "I'm going to visit my daughter today, yes, I am. She's twenty-two, you know." "Look here, I got all my sons home, see the army uniforms?" They'll stand for like half an hour. I got two or three like that, and they always got something to say to me. I'll have like two hours wasted listening to these people blabbin' before they pay me. Mmm, I don't know. Maybe they're lonely. But they've got a daughter and a son, why do they have to blab in my ear?

¹⁵ A lot of the younger customers have had routes and they know how hard it is, how mean people are. They'll be nicer to you. They tend to tip you more. And they don't blab all day long. They'll just pay you and smile at you. The younger people frequently offer me a coke or something.

¹⁶ Older people are afraid of me, a lot of them. The first three, four weeks—(muses) they seemed so afraid of me. They think I'm gonna rob 'em or something. It's funny. You wouldn't think it'd be like this in a small town, would you? They're afraid I'm gonna beat 'em up, take their money. They'd just reach through the door and give me the money. Now they know you so well, they invite you in and blab in your ear for half an hour. It's one or the other. I really don't know why they're afraid. I'm not old, so I wouldn't know how old people feel.

¹⁷ Once in a while I come home angry, most of the time just crabby. Sometimes kids steal the paper out of people's boxes. I lose my profits. It costs me a dime. The company isn't responsible, I am. The company wouldn't believe you probably that somebody stole the paper.

¹⁸ I don't see where being a newsboy and learning that people are pretty mean or that people don't have enough money to buy things with is gonna make you a better person or anything. If anything, it's gonna make a worse person out of you, 'cause you're not gonna like people that don't pay you. And you're not gonna like people who act like they're doing you a big favor paying

you. Yeah, it sort of molds your character, but I don't think for the better. If anybody told me being a newsboy builds character, I'd know he was a liar.

[19] I don't see where people get all this bull about the kid who's gonna be President and being a newsboy made a President out of him. It taught him how to handle his money and this bull. You know what it did? It taught him how to hate the people on his route. And the printers. And dogs.

ANALYTICAL READING

1. This account was recorded by Studs Terkel on a tape recorder. Is there anything about the language and sentence structure that indicates its oral nature? Why are some comments in parentheses?

2. What characteristics of autobiographical narrative did you find? Why is this selection closer in form to a personal essay?

3. Do the examples contribute to Pickens' conclusion?

4. How old do you think Pickens is? On what evidence do you base your guess?

REFLECTING

Point: What is the message? Where is it expressed? What is its purpose?

Organization: Even though it is an interview, the essay does have unity and structure. Trace the kinds of experiences Pickens talks about and point out how they are related. How does he move from one to the next?

Support: Outline the main points made and the devices that support and embellish them.

Synthesis: Have you had a job in which you had contact with the public? Were your experiences similar to Pickens'? Compare this essay with Sylvia Plath's account of her experiences as a waitress (pages 22-24). What did you know previously about being a newsboy? What did you learn about it from this essay?

Evaluation: Do you think the use of dialogue adds interest? Does the essay hold your interest? Why? Does the voice of the narrator seem authentic? Is he convincing? How typical do you think his experience is?

FROM READING TO WRITING

1. Add an opening paragraph to the interview to give it a suitable focusing statement. Be sure to imitate the voice of the narrator.

2. Write an essay for a general audience about the irritations or satisfactions you experienced in a job you have had.

3. For your classmates, write an essay about a disappointing experience, either in meeting some previously respected person or in attending some event you had eagerly anticipated.

WAKE UP TO AN EYE OPENER
Daniel Asa Rose

BIOGRAPHICAL SKETCH

Daniel Asa Rose (1950–   ) was born in New York City and grew up in Rowayton, Connecticut. His short story "The Goodbye Present" won an O. Henry Prize and was reprinted in *Prize Stories 1980: The O. Henry Awards*. Other stories have appeared in *The New Yorker, New American Review, Partisan Review,* and *Southern Review.* He lives with his wife and two children in a small Massachusetts village where he is working on his first novel, an "antiwestern."

PRE-READING

1. Does the title necessarily mean that the article will deal with eyes? Consider the multiple meanings possible in the title.

2. What words in the opening sentence indicate what the subject of the essay might be?

3. From reading the opening paragraph, what do you think the tone of the essay is?

[1] It may be true that to be a young man in his late 20's and never to have discovered eye contact until last weekend is to be a little slow. I will not make any excuses; I have been a little slow. Not that I was shifty-eyed—I did not glance, avert my eyes, then glance again; I simply did not look at all. But the point is that a number of good things have been happening in my life recently, so I felt good enough about myself and about where I happened to be at the moment—Third Avenue between 54th and 55th—to suddenly begin looking strangers in the eye and allowing them to look back into mine. It happened on the sidewalk and in stores with, I would say, about half the people I passed; salesclerks, parking attendants, mothers with babies, even a security guard. Half of us were not initiated; half of us were.

[2] Since this discovery I have enjoyed remembering all those new eyes, all the writhing warmth that was right there just waiting to be acknowledged. It is hard for me to grasp the fact that such intimacy is available between any pair of eyes that has courage enough to encounter another pair of eyes. Discovering eye contact ranks as one of the major thrills of my life, right up there with learning to tell time in a flash of comprehension one day in second grade; staying up all night for the first time and seeing how short it really is; flying the Atlantic for the first time and seeing how small it really is; having a girl touch me for the first time; beating my uncle at chess for the first (and last) time; watching my child being born at 4 A.M. then, all day, understanding that

nearly everyone has children; buying a house in the morning and walking the land in the afternoon and skating by myself on my own pond for hours under a full moon that night; putting on a snorkel and mask and discovering that beneath the black tabletop surface of the ocean there are vast, unending tea parties of activity, or trying on a pair of contact lenses and for the first time glimpsing in sharp focus what my adult self looks like without glasses.

[3] It has made my week. I have been in a great mood the whole time, thinking about the word "eye." I have enjoyed writing it down and seeing how stirring it looks on the page, and "oeil," too—it is even more open and unblinking in French. All week I have enjoyed realizing that certain types of art and music and writing have eye contact and certain types do not, and that I will be looking for the difference now. I have enjoyed acknowledging how much common beauty there is in eye contact, especially when walking across Third Avenue with the sun behind me so that the approaching irises are lit up in different colors and take on the texture of lion fur. I have enjoyed thinking that establishing eye contact with strangers from now on will bring a certain amount of peace to my daily encounters, whereas previously there has been a certain amount of chaos, a certain amount of thrashing about for the simple reason that I did not know eyes felt at home looking at other eyes, that that was where eyes *belonged*. And for the first time I feel ready to meet my mother's eyes, to hold her gaze, to see what I already know somehow: that her eyes are greyish-blue and small and have grown old and want to lean on me and partake of my strength. The funny thing is that this does not make me sad; it makes me almost so excited that I can't stand it. I cannot wait to see her and give her strength. I cannot wait to get out and see some more salesclerks and find out what they are up to and walk the sidewalk again and share whatever this thing is that is going on.

ANALYTICAL READING

1. What is the "eye opener" that the writer has wakened up to?

2. In the second paragraph, what is the effect of the listing of significant happenings?

3. What does "eye contact" mean to the writer? Why do you think he refers to the arts in paragraph 3?

4. How does the essay illustrate that he has "fallen in love" with eye contact?

REFLECTING

Point: What is the focusing idea in the article?

Organization: Explain the chronological aspects of the essay. Do they serve the same purposes as in a narrative? Do the three paragraphs represent the organizational scheme of the essay? How?

Support: How do the examples and details support the main point of the essay? What is the effect of the balanced sentence at the end of the first paragraph?

The long sentence with parallelism in the second paragraph? The use of *and's* in the final sentence?

Synthesis: Are you uncomfortable making eye contact with other people? Do you think eye avoidance is an aspect of our culture? Discuss.

Evaluation: Do you think Rose exaggerates the experience or that it effectively communicates his feelings? Discuss. Does the essay encourage you to experiment with eye contact? Why or why not?

FROM READING TO WRITING

1.   Experiment for a day or two by making eye contact with strangers and write a personal essay for your classmates, summarizing your experiences.

2.   For readers from a foreign country, write an essay discussing some aspects of eye contact that they might expect to encounter in our culture.

3.   For a general audience, write an essay about a similar discovery that you have made about bettering your relationship with other people, such as smiling, nodding a greeting, waving a hand. Use details as Rose did—to show the emotional impact the discovery had on you.

Assessment of Reading and Writing Skills: Personal Writing

Step 1

Read the essay that follows with the aim of understanding and recalling the important ideas. When you finish, note how long it took you to read the selection. Then close your book and write a summary of the important information without referring again to the essay. Indicate also your impression of the tone and word choice of the writer. You will be allowed 7 to 10 minutes to write; your instructor will establish the limit and tell you when the time is up.

A BOSTON TERRIER

E. B. White

I would like to hand down a dissenting opinion in the case of the Camel ad which shows a Boston terrier relaxing. I can string along with cigarette manufacturers to a certain degree, but when it comes to the temperament and habits of terriers, I shall stand my ground.

The ad says: "A dog's nervous system resembles our own." I don't think a dog's nervous system resembles my own in the least. A dog's nervous system is in a class by itself. If it resembles anything at all, it resembles the New York Edison Company's power plant. This is particularly true of Boston terriers, and if the Camel people don't know that, they have never been around dogs.

The ad says: "But when a dog's nerves tire, he obeys his instincts—he relaxes." This, I admit, is true. But I should like to call attention to the fact that it sometimes takes days, even weeks, before a dog's nerves tire. In the case of terriers it can run into months.

I knew a Boston terrier once (he is now dead and, so far as I know, relaxed) whose nerves stayed keyed up from the twenty-fifth of one June to the

FROM E. B. White, *One Man's Meat* (New York and London: Harper & Brothers, 1944), pp. 69–70.

sixth of the following July, without one minute's peace for anybody in the family. He was an old dog and he was blind in one eye, but his infirmities caused no diminution in his nervous power. During the period of which I speak, the famous period of his greatest excitation, he not only raised a type of general hell which startled even his closest friends and observers, but he gave a mighty clever excuse. He said it was love.

"I'm in love," he would scream. (He could scream just like a hurt child.) "I'm in love and I'm going *crazy*."

Day and night it was all the same. I tried everything to soothe him. I tried darkness, cold water dashed in the face, the lash, long quiet talks, warm milk administered internally, threats, promises and close confinement in remote locations. At last, after about a week of it, I went down the road and had a chat with the lady who owned the object of our terrier's affection. It was she who finally cleared up the situation.

"Oh," she said, wearily, "if it's that bad, let him out."

I hadn't thought of anything as simple as that myself, but I am a creature of infinite reserve. As a matter of record, it turned out to be not so simple—the terrier got run over by a motor car one night while returning from his amorous adventures, suffering a complete paralysis of the hip but no assuagement of the nervous system; and the little Scotty bitch returned to Washington, D. C., and a Caesarian.

I am not through with the Camel people yet. Love is not the only thing that can keep a dog's nerves in a state of perpetual jangle. A dog, more than any other creature, it seems to me, gets interested in one subject, theme, or object, in life, and pursues it with a fixity of purpose which would be inspiring to Man if it weren't so troublesome. One dog gets absorbed in one thing, another dog in another. When I was a boy there was a smooth-haired fox terrier (in those days nobody ever heard of a fox terrier that *wasn't* smooth-haired) who became interested, rather late in life, in a certain stone. The stone was about the size of an egg. As far as I could see, it was like a million other stones—but to him it was the Stone Supreme.

He kept it with him day and night, slept with it, ate with it, played with it, analyzed it, took it on little trips (you would often see him three blocks from home, trotting along on some shady errand, his stone safe in his jaws). He used to lie by the hour on the porch of his house, chewing the stone with an expression half tender, half petulant. When he slept, he merely enjoyed a muscular suspension: his nerves were still up and around, adjusting the bed clothes, tossing and turning.

He permitted people to throw the stone for him and people would. But if the stone lodged somewhere he couldn't get to he raised such an uproar that it was absolutely necessary that the stone be returned, for the public peace. His absorption was so great it brought wrinkles to his face, and he grew old before his time. I think he used to worry that somebody was going to pitch the stone into a lake or a bog, where it would be irretrievable. He wore off every tooth in his jaw, wore them right down to the gums, and they became mere brown vestigial bumps. His breath was awful (he panted night and day) and his eyes were alight with an unearthly zeal. He died in a fight with another dog. I have always suspected it was because he tried to hold the stone in his mouth all through the battle. The Camel people will just have to take my word for it: that dog was a living denial of the whole theory of relaxation. He was a paragon of nervous tension, from the moment he first laid eyes on his slimy little stone till the hour of his death.

The advertisement speaks of the way humans "prod" themselves to endeavor—so that they keep on and on working long after they should quit. The inference is that a dog never does that. But I have a dog right now that can prod himself harder and drive himself longer than any human I ever saw. This animal is a dachshund, and I shall spare you the long dull inanities of his innumerable obsessions. His particular study (or mania) at the moment is a black-and-white kitten that my wife gave me for Christmas, thinking that what my life needed was something else that could move quickly from one place in the room to another. The dachshund began his research on Christmas eve when the kitten arrived "secretly" in the cellar, and now, five months later, is taking his Ph.D. still working late at night on it, every night. If he could write a book about that cat, it would make *Middletown* look like the work of a backward child.

I'll be glad to have the Camel people study this animal in one of his relaxed moods, but they will have to bring their own seismograph. Even curled up cozily in a chair, dreaming of his cat, he quivers like an aspen.

Step 2

Read the following essay as quickly as you can without sacrificing your comprehension of the material. You will have a maximum of 2 minutes, 20 seconds (200 words per minute) to glean as much information as you can. If you finish before time is called, note how long it took you to read the selection. Again, close your book and write a summary of the essay, including a statement about the tone and word choice. You will have 7 to 10 minutes for this task.

A PROPERLY TRAINED MAN
IS DOG'S BEST FRIEND

Erma Bombeck

My name is Murray Bombeck and I'm a guest columnist.
I'm a 3½-month-old Yorkshire Terrier.
There are a lot of dogs who are wondering whether they want to own a

FROM Erma Bombeck, "At Wit's End," *Louisville Courier-Journal*, September 24, 1976, p. B6. Copyright 1976 by Field Enterprises, Inc. Courtesy of Field Newspaper Syndicate.

person. They like people. They're fun to be around, but are they worth all the fuss and bother?

I felt the same way when a few months ago I observed this couple. Their dog (another Yorkshire) had just been killed and, frankly, they were a psychological mess. During the interview, they kept calling me "Harry" (the deceased dog's name) and the woman kept swooping me off the floor and crying in my fur. They would take a lot of training.

First nights are generally a disaster. At 11 o'clock at night, just when things are beginning to cook, they turn off the lights and go to bed. (I had been warned by other person owners that this would happen.) I tried to keep them on their feet all night but things like this happen. Old habits are hard to break.

Another thing you have to know about people is that you have to keep them busy or they drive you crazy. Every time I ate a houseplant, they were there. When I chewed on shoes, they were there. They were smothering me. Once, when I went into the white living room to go to the bathroom, she came in, swooped me up, ran around hysterically finding a key to the back door, opened it up and heaved me out onto the grass.

You cannot imagine what turned her on.

When I "performed" she jumped up and down and clapped her hands while summoning three other people from the house to observe. I felt like a fool.

The hardest part of training a person, however, is discipline. You have to be firm with people or they'll run all over you. When they want to play by grabbing your nose, at first you just walk off, but when they pursue it, you just sink your teeth into their hands. They may look shocked and hurt at first, but you'll eventually have a person you don't have to be ashamed to take places.

And, lastly, be careful the first time you take them out in public. They wander away from you. I don't recommend a leash, but leave them in the car a few times and they'll shape up.

Everything you've heard about people is true. They're messy. They're tempermental and they're hard to train.

But in the evening when you're tired and they scratch behind your ears . . . or when you're beat from the sun and they let you play in the garden hose . . . or when you're sick and they put you on the sofa . . . they're worth it. People make great pets.

Step 3

Without looking back at the two essays, write a paragraph or two in which you evaluate them and explain how their ideas or issues are related. You may refer to your summaries, but not to the essays. Time: 10 minutes.

2 DESCRIPTIVE WRITING

In many ways, writing description is like painting a picture. The writer must approach the task with the same skills of perception that the artist has—the ability to look at an object, a person, or a scene and to reproduce it in vivid detail. There is, however, one notable difference in the two media. A painting appeals to the physical eye; written description to the mind's eye. Thus, while painters can often create the illusion of a tree or a building with a single brush stroke, writers must rely upon a number of well-chosen words that not only depict the image they wish to project but often convey an emotional response as well. Although the two media are different in many ways, both painting and descriptive writing share the need for detail—specific, concrete, colorful particulars. Where the artist paints with tints and strokes, the writer paints with words and phrases.

Therefore, to be most effective, descriptive writing demands that the writer select words carefully, being sensitive to all their subtle variations of meaning and to the way words sound together. Just as a painting can be marred by combining jarring colors or brushing too bold a stroke, so too can descriptive writing be flawed by a word that violates the imagery or the tone.

Another way that writers create descriptive pictures is by using comparison or analogy. An extended comparison is especially helpful when the writer is describing something that may be outside the reader's experience. Comparing the subject to something familiar can help the audience "see" it better. However, comparisons need not be lengthy to accomplish this. Figurative language devices such as simile, metaphor, and personification can make lively, effective comparisons with a single word or a short phrase. Remember, a simile uses *like* or *as;* a metaphor implies a comparison; personification ascribes human characteristics to nonhuman objects. For example:

Simile: ". . . the very grand old elms *like gray broomstraws."* (Edmund Wilson, *Upstate*)
Metaphor: "I drove across the *upraised thumb* of Idaho." (John Steinbeck, *Travels with Charley*)
Personification: "Lying in my bed under the *weeping night . . ."* (John Steinbeck, *Travels with Charley*)

Creating word pictures, then, is the primary aim of descriptive writing. It can be as objective, factual, and impersonal as a scientist's report or a view under a microscope, designed primarily to give the reader specific information about an object, a place, or a person. Or it can be subjective, impressionistic, and personal, fashioned as much to reflect the writer's feelings about the object being described as to supply information. These two approaches can be compared in the Schneirla and Dillard articles. Schneirla's description of the female carpenter ants' death by predators (page 115) is matter-of-fact and objective. Dillard's description of a frog's death by a giant water bug (page 121), although factual, reflects also her horror and revulsion.

Writers can employ these sensory possibilities in many ways. Complete articles or essays can be purely descriptive, with the main purpose to describe something in vivid detail. This is the case with most of the selections included in Part Two. Descriptive passages may also be used to add to the setting or atmosphere in narrative, to help explain a situation in expository writing, or to provide a vivid proof in argument. They can even introduce an explanatory or persuasive essay, as does Marilyn Kluger's article "A Time of Plenty." Regardless of its purpose, descriptive writing has distinctive characteristics that should be considered whether you are reading or writing it.

KINDS OF DESCRIPTIVE WRITING

PERSONAL DESCRIPTION

Personal description strives to be subjective. Words are chosen for their emotive qualities; the writer's voice bears the mark of the distinctive individual behind the pen—a person who is angry, sympathetic, amused, or awed about the subject. Addressing a less specialized audience than factual description reaches, writers of personal description usually seek some opening device to attract the reader's attention. Anne Rivers Siddons *hooks* her readers with a child's provocative question; Tom Wolfe's "A Sunday Kind of Love" starts with one of the most attention-grabbing words in the language—*love.*

FACTUAL DESCRIPTION

Assuming that readers have an established interest in the subject, writers of factual description, unlike writers of personal description, do not feel compelled to provide an attention-arousing device—a hook to attract the reader. Already interested in the subject, the reader wants a no-nonsense, complete, factual description that supplies all the pertinent information. The reader usually does not expect or even want the writer's personal impressions about the subject. Thus, the voice of the writer tends to be matter-of-fact and serious, using vocabulary that may be scientific or technical and aimed at a specialized audience.

MIXED DESCRIPTION

Often, description cannot be categorized exclusively as personal or factual, but combines features of both. The resulting mixed description frequently includes impressionistic and subjective passages. Writers may also tailor the factual descriptions to highlight a desired mood or tone that they wish to create, or to illustrate a judgment being made. Saul Bellow's factual description of the Illinois landscape in "Illinois Journey," for instance, adds to the mood of monotony he creates. Rachel Carson's objective descriptions of beaches in "Our Ever-Changing Shore" heightens her expression of concern for the preservation of the environment.

CHARACTER SKETCH

Descriptions of people are called character sketches and can be as varied as any other description. A character sketch can be entirely factual, as in a police description of a wanted criminal; it can be subjective—the writer's impressions of another person; or, as is frequently the case, it can be a mixture of the two. In addition, a sketch can either describe a particular person or a personality type. As you might expect, a character sketch of a *person* limits the writer to the physical and personality traits of that individual. A character sketch of a *type,* however, demands that the writer search for traits shared by the people who exemplify the type. Leo Durocher's description of Babe Ruth's physical appearance, for example, is appropriate in a character sketch of this particular baseball hero, but would not be suitable in a character sketch of the baseball hero as a type.

TACTICS FOR READING DESCRIPTIVE WRITING

PRE-READING

Many of the techniques you practiced in reading the personal writing in Part One will apply as well to reading descriptive writing. Certainly, you can profit from the habit of analyzing the title, reading any background material supplied, and skimming the opening paragraphs. But with description, you can follow our suggestion in the Introduction to the book that you also skim the closing paragraph. Knowing the ending of a description, unlike knowing how a narrative ends, will not detract from your satisfaction; on the contrary, you may gain added insight into the writer's attitudes toward the subject. You can note, for instance, that Roger Angell's factual description of a baseball ends with a statement about wanting to throw a ball and reveals his love for the baseball as a prop of the game (pages 112–13). Or when you realize from the last paragraph in the Rachel Carson selection (pages 126–30) that she considers the sea "the last outpost," you are prepared, before a full reading, for the tone of awe and concern that pervades the description and accounts for its main point and its subjectivity.

ANALYTICAL READING

In reading description, you can add to the skills emphasized in reading personal writing. Certainly you want to maintain a perception of the writer's voice and of the subtle shades of meaning in the words used. As you read, underline or mark descriptive passages that are especially effective, noting fresh, image-evoking adjectives or metaphors. Look for statements throughout that may reveal the writer's purpose in writing the description—to inform, to share a beloved person or place with others, or to record an image of a person or a place for posterity. Sentences that shed light on such questions can help you to gain a sense of the purpose and organization of the essay, if you relate them to the opening or focusing statement.

Sentence structure may demand more concentration from you in description than in personal narrative. You should become aware of the more complex sentences used to convey numerous descriptive details; however, this consciousness of sentence strategy need not interfere with your train of thought as you read.

Most important, remember that descriptive writing is meant to be sensory. So let yourself go and enjoy to the fullest the vicarious experience the writer sets up for you: see the details of the setting, smell the odors, and hear the sounds. If you are able to project yourself into the description, then you will be reading effectively and meaningfully.

REFLECTING

Point. Like personal essays, descriptions often begin with a statement indicating the writer's purpose. This is often a summary of the main point the writer wishes to make. It should be supported throughout the essay and is often reinforced, restated, or rephrased in the closing paragraph. Leo Durocher uses this device in "The Great Babe" (pages 132–34) to make his point that Babe Ruth was a superstar. The opening phrase, "everything about him was bigger than life," is reinforced by Durocher's opinion in the last paragraph that Ruth was the greatest instinctive ballplayer "who ever lived."

Organization. Like narrative writing, description can be arranged chronologically; however, the most frequent organizational device is spatial. A writer must describe a bird's plumage, for instance, by moving from one area of the body to another. The description moves in space (left to right, front to back), not in time. Occasionally, a description will have both chronological and spatial organization, as in Anne Rivers Siddon's essay on fall (pages 99–102). Time moves from October to Christmas, but the description is spatial—the objects of fall are strewn on the ground, hang on trees and vines; they are arranged in space.

Support. Support in description is achieved almost exclusively by word painting—the piling up of descriptive words and phrases. Obviously, some sentence structures are better suited to this kind of stockpiling than others.

The short, simple sentences often used in personal narrative dialogue would be inefficient, resulting in needless repetition of information. Compound sentences, strung across the page like beads by *and,* could create a monotonous style, one that would be likely to intrude on the reader's consciousness and interfere with the reading process.

Many modern writers find that a useful sentence type for handling a multitude of detail is the cumulative sentence, in which most of the basic information is given first, followed by a string of specific details. This basic sentence structure permits an amazing amount of variety. Here are three examples from John Steinbeck's *Travels with Charley* illustrating just a few of the possibilities. The basic information (main clause) is italicized in each:

> *The bed was lumpy,* the walls dirty yellow, the curtains like the undershirt of a slattern. (All details added after the main clause; all treated in similar sentence structures.)
>
> His dark, shining *hair was a masterpiece of overcombing,* the top hair laid back and criss-crossed with long side strands that just cleared the ears. (Details added before the subject *hair* and at the end of the main clause in random structures.)
>
> Just under the ridge of a pass, *I stopped for gasoline in a little* puttogether, do-it yourself *group of cabins,* square boxes, each with a stoop, a door, and one window, and no vestige of a garden or gravel paths. (Details added before the main clause, before the phrase *group of cabins,* and at the end of the main clause.)

Useful as the cumulative sentence is, it is certainly not the only sentence device employed by writers to present many details. Any sentence structure repeated over and over results in poor writing style. But used with care, the cumulative sentence does permit readers to follow easily the flow of the sentence, and does enable writers to add many vivid supporting details.

Synthesis. Effective description, like effective personal narrative, should strike some responsive chord in each reader. A well-written description of a favorite duck pond or a memorable teacher should remind you of the same or similar experience or memory against which a comparison or contrast can be made. In order to assimilate a written work completely, you should also be able to compare and contrast it with other essays you have read so that you can become aware of the organizational strategies and the word choices that make a description a unique, individual piece of work.

Evaluation. As with personal writing, your emotional response will be uniquely yours. You will react most strongly when reading descriptions of places or people that evoke your own experiences. But to be the kind of critical reader we outlined in the Introduction to the book, you should also be able to support your emotional response by citing specific traits that a work has—traits that are characteristic of that particular kind of writing. Is Gordon A. Reims' description of Maine lobstermen (pages 142–45), for instance, effective simply because he admires these colorful people, or does his organization, his word pictures of the trappings of the trade, his description of the hard sea life that they share contribute to the reader's response? When you can state in detail the reasons why you like or dislike a descriptive essay, you have become a critical evaluator of description.

FROM READING TO WRITING

Points that we have stressed about reading description can be utilized in your own writing assignments:

1. *Organization.* Somewhere in your opening paragraph, include a focusing statement that signals your reader what your subject is and how you feel about it. Then, before you write, think about how you wish to handle the organization and point of view. If it is a static description of a place or person, spatial arrangement is necessary, but where should you start? If your essay involves an incident or passage of time, how should you combine chronological and spatial organization? Also, do you need to attract the reader's interest in the opening paragraphs? And should your description be factual, personal, or mixed?

2. *Voice and language.* Decide in your early paragraphs which voice you wish to assume and try to keep it consistent throughout. You might remember that establishing a consistent voice is difficult even for experienced writers and may require adjustment in revision. As you look over your first draft, be alert for shifts in tone or in levels of usage. Experiment with words. Of all the forms of prose writing, description usually allows you the greatest freedom and creativity in language. Don't be satisfied until you have found the best combination of words to portray precisely what you wish to describe. Remember, you are not just *telling about* your subject, but *recreating* it—with all its sights, sounds, odors, tastes, and tactile feelings. As you play with the words, experiment also with sentence structure; try your hand at various cumulative sentences to include additional details. Remember, writing can be dull or it can be fun; it is fun only when you experiment and create.

Personal Description

FALL COMES IN ON ROLLER SKATES
Anne Rivers Siddons

BIOGRAPHICAL SKETCH

Anne Rivers Siddons, who was born in Atlanta, Georgia, has a B.A. degree in commercial art, with a minor in English, from Auburn University. She has been a senior editor of Atlanta Magazine *and a contributing editor to* Georgia Magazine. *She has published three books,* Heartbreak Hotel *(available in paperback),* John Chancellor Makes Me Cry *(1975), and* The House Next Door *(1978). In addition, she has contributed articles to such magazines as* Redbook, House Beautiful, *and* Gentlemen's Quarterly.

PRE-READING

1.   What is your reaction to the title? What tone is established by the title?

2.   After skimming the first five paragraphs, what statement can you make about the use of the title in the opening section?

[1] "How do you know when fall gets here?" a five-year-old of my acquaintance asked her mother and me on a Sunday afternoon last year. We were sitting on the edge of her parents' pocket-sized swimming pool, dangling our feet in the exhausted September water. The temperature was 92 degrees.

[2] "Fall is when the leaves are red and the air is nippy and you get to wear your new wool clothes," said her mother. "In fact, fall starts officially next week."

[3] The child, taking in the used-green leaves and the heat miasma uncoiling from the patio, clearly regarded this as another piece of adult propaganda and rewarded us with the level stare children reserve for kittenish adult excesses. Wool was a patent insanity in anybody's book, and bright foliage and tart mornings were light-years away from her back yard.

[4] It was most probably a rhetorical question. Children know when autumn comes, almost to the hour. Some small signal forever lost to adults trips the delicate interior alarm clock that is built into children somewhere behind

FROM *Atlanta Magazine*, October 1969. Reprinted by permission of Atlanta Magazine and the author.

their ribs. It isn't leaves going bright, or cool mornings. Those come later. Fall comes when you stop doing the summer things and start doing the fall ones.

⁵ When I was small, fall came in on roller skates. Somewhere in the last burning days of August, a morning came when we met under the oak tree in my front yard—as we had every morning that summer—and the skates were there. Jangling in bicycle baskets. Thumping over skinny shoulders like outsized epaulettes. Skate keys sprouted amulet-like around reedy necks, on shoelaces or grimy twine. There had been no previous agreement to put away the rubber-tire slingshots and the gut-spilling softballs. The alarm clock had simply, for each of us, gone off sometime in the dreamless night.

⁶ For the rest of fall, up until the lowering winter met us on the way home from school and robbed us of the light, skating was the autumn thing that we did. We went in swooping flights down sidewalks and streets, always with our parents' "Be *careful!*" thrumming in our ears, drunk on our own momentum, giddy on wind and wheels. The very small ones of us, restricted to front walks, windmilled on treacherous feet and looked with awe and hate at the flying phalanxes of big kids streaming by, trailing immortality like a bright comet's tail. The more accomplished of us were allowed to skate as far as the shuffleboard court on the high school playground—smooth, seamless, utopian skating.

⁷ We came to know every street, every sidewalk, by the burring skirr our skates made on them; they spoke to us in a hundred voices, through the soles of our feet. Each of us, every fall, ruined a pair of shoes with too-tight skate clamps. Knees were scabbed until Christmas.

⁸ School started somewhere in the yellowing days, and we went back to the rows of scarred desks that left forearms perpetually bruised with the ghosts of last year's ink. We were strange to each other for a little while in those first days, even though we'd been together like litters of kittens for a whole summer. Reluctant to be laid by, the jealous summer still tugged at our hair and tickled behind closed eyelids.

⁹ But soon we were the spawn of chalk and cloakrooms again, creatures of a thousand rituals, and the wild summer children were gone. Tans went mustardy and flaked under an onslaught of starch. Big colts' feet, bare and winged like Hermes's all summer, were earthbound as Clydesdales' in clunking new saddle oxfords. Rasping new sweaters began to feel good in the mornings as we jostled and quarreled to school, flanked by an honor guard of trotting dogs. But the sweaters were shed in the still-hot noons and left to grieve in balls, stuffed into our desks. By the time the real cold set in, and the hated coats and leggings were brought out of cedar chests, the sweaters were frail and used, forgotten until spring behind Blue Horse notebooks.

¹⁰ Summer was a time of good things to eat, of course, but it is the taste of autumn that I remember. Wild, smoky, bittersweet things ripened in the bronze afternoons, and the glazed mornings bit them to exotic sharpness. Preposterous yellow persimmons grew on a tree in the schoolyard, and if you got a good one, the taste was incredible, wonderful, like a topaz melting on your

tongue. Too-ripe ones were truly dreadful, tasting just like their overripe peers which had burst and gone to yellow slime on the ground looked, sly and sickened. Too-green ones would pucker your mouth to acid flannel for the rest of the day.

[11] Scuppernongs hung on an old broken arbor on my grandfather's farm; huge, green, gold-dusted things that were surely the sweetest fruits autumn ever gave a greedy child. Flinty little Yates apples lay on the ground under the old trees in the ruined orchard, each one worth one bite of pure, winy nectar before you noticed half a worm. Sweet potatoes, newly dug from their sand hills and roasted in my grandmother's black coal stove, were honey and smoke, too rich to finish.

[12] But pomegranates were the Grail.

[13] It seems that pomegranates always hung over my childhood autumns. And they were always forbidden fruit. Just as Persephone was imprisoned six months in the underworld for eating pomegranates, so I was regularly placed under house arrest for stealing Mrs. Word's next-door pomegranates. On the outside, Mrs. Word's pomegranates were tough and leathery and rosy and enormous. On the inside, when you broke them open, the rows of rose-quartz crystals were Kubla Khan's toys. I don't think I ever really liked the strange Persian taste to them, but I stole enough of them to keep a Bronx fruit stand in business. Like Everest, they were there. One of the worst moments in my life to this day was the time my mother apprehended me at my black business and marched me, mewling like a cornered kitten, into Mrs. Word's impeccable parlor to confess and seek forgiveness. It was, of course, granted.

[14] As the fall wore on, mornings were born silver, and bleeding sunsets came earlier, and rumbling furnaces came alive in basements. We melted, with a winter-long stench, the soles of our saddle oxfords, standing over hot-air registers. The Southeastern Fair wheeled by in a technicolor blur of sawdust and cotton candy and forbidden midway shows where, the big kids said, ladies took their clothes off. Halloween smelled of the wet, burnt insides of pumpkins and was terrible with an atavistic terror in front of the fire in our living room, where my father read me the witches' speech from *Macbeth*. I remember one magic night in October when I was plucked up out of sleep, wrapped in a quilt, and taken outside in our back yard to watch a meteor shower. Warm on my father's shoulder, but with everything strange and too big and not like our back yard at all, I watched as the very sky above me wheeled and arced and bloomed. It was, I thought, something God arranged for me because He knew my father.

[15] Soon ice crystals bristled in red clay, waiting to be scrunched under the loathsome galoshes. Saturdays and Sundays, which had been vast blue bowls to whoop and tumble in, so full of joy that little gold specks pin-wheeled behind your eyelids when you closed them, turned gray and howled. We did smeary things with stubbly, useless scissors and paste—does anyone remember the forbidden peppermint taste of library paste?—and drove our parents wild, whining plaintively about the eternities of our heavy days.

[16] We listened, with much the same look as my young friend beside the swimming pool, to their patient recounting of the fun we'd have next spring, when we could go outside again. But that was next year, a different digit on a new calendar. And between us and spring, as the fall came down like a black window shade, was a long, whirling winter place where anything could happen.

[17] Even Christmas. But that's another story.

ANALYTICAL READING

1. What purpose do you think the first four paragraphs serve? Do the last two paragraphs relate to that purpose?

2. What part is played by the definition of "fall" in paragraph 4?

3. Point out descriptive phrases that you found especially effective. Can you analyze the devices used by the writer?

4. Find examples of metaphor and simile in the essay. Can you say that the use of figurative language is a strong element of Siddons' style of writing?

5. Find examples of cumulative sentences that you found especially effective in providing vivid details.

6. Explain the following words and phrases: "heat miasma," "amulet-like," "flying phalanxes," "winged like Hermes's," "earthbound as Clydesdales'," "scuppernongs," "pomegranates."

7. How does the writer use color imagery to contrast summer, fall, and winter?

REFLECTING

Point: How does the title tie in with the focusing statement of the essay? What do you think the writer's point is? Does it have anything to do with a contrast between the viewpoints of adults and children?

Organization: Is the organization chronological, spatial, or a combination of the two? How important is time in the essay? How is it handled?

Support: How do the descriptions of children's activities help to reinforce the association of roller-skating with fall? How do the figurative language and the color imagery in the essay help to support the main idea? What senses are appealed to besides sight?

Synthesis: As you read, did you recall activities in your own life that have seasonal significance—sports, childhood games, farm or yard chores, hiking? Discuss. Do you know Keats' "Ode to Autumn"? If so, compare its description with the essay's.

Evaluation: How effective did you find the essay? Were you able to re-create in your own mind the things described in the essay? If so, what writing tactics contributed to that?

FROM READING TO WRITING

1. Using the form of Siddons' title as a focusing point, write a short essay for your classmates that vividly describes an activity which has seasonal importance, or did when you were a child: Fall (summer, spring, winter) came (comes) in on _____.

2. For a general audience, write a description of an activity that you as a child viewed in a different way than did your parents. It could be an activity that you considered exciting, but that your parents thought dangerous, such as swimming in a forbidden swimming hole or hitching sled rides on cars; or something you did that your parents simply found maddening, such as the way you ate mashed potatoes or waded through mud puddles.

A SUNDAY KIND OF LOVE
Tom Wolfe

BIOGRAPHICAL SKETCH

Tom Wolfe was born in Richmond, Virginia, in 1931, earned a B.A. degree (cum laude) *from Washington and Lee University and a Ph.D. from Yale University in 1957. He has written for a number of newspapers, among them the* Washington Post, *the* New York Herald Tribune, *and* New York *magazine. He has been a contributing editor of* New York *since 1968. The journalistic style he pioneered, "new journalism," has won him two Washington Newspaper Guild awards. Wolfe defines "new journalism" as a "nonfiction form that combines the emotional impact" of fiction, the "analytical insights" of scholarly writing, and the "deep factual foundation of 'hard reporting.' " His published works include:* The Kandy-Kolored Tangerine-Flake Streamline Baby *(1965),* The Painted Word *(1975),* Mauve Gloves and Madmen, Clutter and Vine *(1977), and* In Our Time *(1980).*

PRE-READING

1. What does the title suggest? Would the omission of the words "kind of" make any difference?

2. Skim the first paragraph. What direction is suggested in the opening sentences, particularly by the fragment, "Still, the odds!"?

[1] Love! Attar of libido in the air! It is 8:45 A.M. Thursday morning in the IRT subway station at 50th Street and Broadway and already two kids are hung

FROM Tom Wolfe, *The Kandy-Kolored Tangerine-Flake Streamline Baby* (New York: Farrar, Straus & Giroux, 1965), pp. 256–61. Copyright © 1963, 1964, 1965, by Thomas K. Wolfe, Jr. Copyright © 1963, 1964, 1965 by New York Herald Tribune, Inc. Reprinted with the permission of Farrar, Straus & Giroux, Inc.

up in a kind of herringbone weave of arms and legs, which proves, one has to admit, that love is not *confined* to Sunday in New York. Still, the odds! All the faces come popping in clots out of the Seventh Avenue local, past the King Size Ice Cream machine, and the turnstiles start whacking away as if the world were breaking up on the reefs. Four steps past the turnstiles everybody is already backed up haunch to paunch for the climb up the ramp and the stairs to the surface, a great funnel of flesh, wool, felt, leather, rubber and steaming alumicron, with the blood squeezing through everybody's old sclerotic arteries in hopped-up spurts from too much coffee and the effort of surfacing from the subway at the rush hour. Yet there on the landing are a boy and a girl, both about eighteen, in one of those utter, My Sin, backbreaking embraces.

² He envelops her not only with his arms but with his chest, which has the American teen-ager concave shape to it. She has her head cocked at a 90-degree angle and they have their eyes pressed shut for all they are worth and some incredibly feverish action going with each other's mouths. All round them, tens, scores, it seems like hundreds, of faces and bodies are perspiring, trooping and bellying up the stairs with arteriosclerotic grimaces past a showcase full of such novel items as Joy Buzzers, Squirting Nickels, Finger Rats, Scary Tarantulas and spoons with realistic dead flies on them, past Fred's barbershop, which is just off the landing and has glossy photographs of young men with the kind of baroque haircuts one can get in there, and up onto 50th Street into a madhouse of traffic and shops with weird lingerie and gray hair-dyeing displays in the windows, signs for free teacup readings and a pool-playing match between the Playboy Bunnies and Downey's Showgirls, and then everybody pounds on toward the Time-Life Building, the Brill Building or NBC.

³ The boy and the girl just keep on writhing in their embroilment. Her hand is sliding up the back of his neck, which he turns when her fingers wander into the intricate formal gardens of his Chicago Boxcar hairdo at the base of the skull. The turn causes his face to start to mash in the ciliated hull of her beehive hairdo, and so she rolls her head 180 degrees to the other side, using their mouths for the pivot. But aside from good hair grooming, they are oblivious to everything but each other. Everybody gives them a once-over. Disgusting! Amusing! How touching! A few kids pass by and say things like "Swing it, baby." But the great majority in that heaving funnel up the stairs seem to be as much astounded as anything else. The vision of love at rush hour cannot strike anyone exactly as romance. It is a feat, like a fat man crossing the English Channel in a barrel. It is an earnest accomplishment against the tide. It is a piece of slightly gross heroics, after the manner of those knobby, varicose old men who come out from some place in baggy shorts every year and run through the streets of Boston in the Marathon race. And somehow that is the gaffe against love all week long in New York, for everybody, not just two kids writhing under their coiffures in the 50th Street subway station; too hurried, too crowded, too hard, and no time for dalliance. Which explains why the real thing in New York is, as it says in the song, a Sunday kind of love.

⁴ There is Saturday, but Saturday is not much better than Monday through Friday. Saturday is the day for errands in New York. More millions of shoppers are pouring in to keep the place jammed up. Everybody is bobbing around, running up to Yorkville to pick up these arty cheeses for this evening, or down to Fourth Avenue to try to find this Van Vechten book, *Parties*, to complete the set for somebody, or off to the cleaner's, the dentist's, the hairdresser's, or some guy's who is going to loan you his station wagon to pick up two flush doors to make tables out of, or over to some place somebody mentioned that is supposed to have fabulous cuts of meat and the butcher wears a straw hat and arm garters and is colorfully rude.

⁵ True, there is Saturday night, and Friday night. They are fine for dates and good times in New York. But for the dalliance of love, they are just as stupefying and wound up as the rest of the week. On Friday and Saturday nights everybody is making some kind of scene. It may be a cellar cabaret in the Village where five guys from some place talk "Jamaican" and pound steel drums and the Connecticut teenagers wear plaid ponchos and knee-high boots and drink such things as Passion Climax cocktails, which are made of apple cider with watermelon balls thrown in. Or it may be some cellar in the East 50's, a discotheque, where the alabaster kids come on in sleeveless minksides jackets, tweed evening dresses and cool-it Modernismus hairdos. But either way, it's a scene, a production, and soon the evening begins to whirl, like the whole world with the bed-spins, in a montage of taxis, slithery legs slithering in, slithery legs slithering out, worsted, piqué, grins, eye teeth, glissandos, buffoondos, tips, par lamps, doormen, lines, magenta ropes, white dickies, mirrors and bar bottles, pink men and shawl-collared coats, hatcheck girls and neon peach fingernails, taxis, keys, broken lamps and no coat hangers. . . .

⁶ And, then, an unbelievable dawning; Sunday, in New York.

⁷ George G., who writes "Z" ads for a department store, keeps saying that all it takes for him is to smell coffee being made at a certain point in the percolation. It doesn't matter where. It could be the worst death-ball hamburger dive. All he has to do is smell it, and suddenly he finds himself swimming, drowning, dissolving in his own reverie of New York's Sunday kind of love.

Anne A.'s apartment was nothing, he keeps saying, and that was the funny thing. She lived in Chelsea. It was this one room with a cameo-style carving of a bored Medusa on the facing of the mantelpiece, this one room plus a kitchen, in a brownstone sunk down behind a lot of loft buildings and truck terminals and so forth. Beautiful Chelsea. But on Sunday morning by 10:30 the sun would be hitting cleanly between two rearview buildings and making it through the old no man's land of gas effluvia ducts, restaurant vents, aerials, fire escapes, stairwell doors, clotheslines, chimneys, skylights, vestigial lightning rods, mansard slopes, and those peculiarly bleak, filthy and misshapen backsides of New York buildings, into Anne's kitchen.

⁸ George would be sitting at this rickety little table with an oilcloth over it. How he goes on about it! The place was grimy. You couldn't keep the soot out.

The place was beautiful. Anne is at the stove making coffee. The smell of the coffee being made, just the smell . . . already he is turned on. She had on a great terrycloth bathrobe with a sash belt. The way she moved around inside that bathrobe with the sun shining in the window always got him. It was the atmosphere of the thing. There she was, moving around in that great fluffy bathrobe with the sun hitting her hair, and they had all the time in the world. There wasn't even one flatulent truck horn out on Eighth Avenue. Nobody was clobbering their way down the stairs in high heels out in the hall at 10 minutes to 9.

⁹ Anne would make scrambled eggs, plain scrambled eggs, but it was a feast. It was incredible. She would bring out a couple of these little smoked fish with golden skin and some smoked oysters that always came in a little can with ornate lettering and royal colors and flourishes and some Kissebrot bread and black cherry preserves, and then the coffee. They had about a million cups of coffee apiece, until the warmth seemed to seep through your whole viscera. And then cigarettes. The cigarettes were like some soothing incense. The radiator was always making a hissing sound and then a clunk. The sun was shining in and the fire escapes and effluvia ducts were just silhouettes out there someplace. George would tear off another slice of Kissebrot and pile on some black cherry preserves and drink some more coffee and have another cigarette, and Anne crossed her legs under her terrycloth bathrobe and crossed her arms and drew on her cigarette, and that was the way it went.

¹⁰ "It was the *torpor*, boy," he says. "It was beautiful. Torpor is a beautiful, underrated thing. Torpor is a luxury. Especially in this stupid town. There in that kitchen it was like being in a perfect cocoon of love. Everything was beautiful, a perfect cocoon."

¹¹ By and by they would get dressed, always in as shiftless a getup as possible. She would put on a big heavy sweater, a raincoat and a pair of faded slacks that gripped her like neoprene rubber. He would put on a pair of corduroy pants, a crew sweater with moth holes and a raincoat. Then they would go out and walk down to 14th Street for the Sunday paper.

¹² All of a sudden it was great out there on the street in New York. All those damnable millions who come careening into Manhattan all week weren't there. The town was empty. To a man and woman shuffling along there, torpid, in the cocoon of love, it was as if all of rotten Gotham had improved overnight. Even the people looked better. There would be one of those old dolls with little flabby arms all bunched up in a coat of pastel oatmeal texture, the kind whose lumpy old legs you keep seeing as she heaves her way up the subway stairs ahead of you and holds everybody up because she is so flabby and decrepit . . . and today, Sunday, on good, clean, empty 14th Street, she just looked like a nice old lady. There was no one around to make her look slow, stupid, unfit, unhip, expendable. That was the thing about Sunday. The weasel millions were absent. And Anne walking along beside him with a thready old pair of slacks gripping her like neoprene rubber looked like possibly the most

marvelous vision the world had ever come up with, and the cocoon of love was perfect. It was like having your cake and eating it, too. On the one hand, here it was, boy, the prize: New York. All the buildings, the Gotham spires, were sitting up all over the landscape in silhouette like ikons representing all that was great, glorious and triumphant in New York. And, on the other hand, there were no weasel millions bellying past you and eating crullers on the run with the crumbs flaking off the corners of their mouths as a reminder of how much *Angst* and *Welthustle* you had to put into the town to get any of that out of it for yourself. All there was was the cocoon of love, which was complete. It was like being inside a scenic Easter Egg where you look in and the Gotham spires are just standing there like a little gemlike backdrop.

[13] By and by the two of them would be back in the apartment sprawled out on the floor rustling through the Sunday paper, all that even black ink appliquéd on big fat fronds of paper. Anne would put an E. Power Biggs organ record on the hi-fi, and pretty soon the old trammeler's bass chords would be vibrating through you as if he had clamped a diathermy machine on your solar plexus. So there they would be, sprawled out on the floor, rustling through the Sunday paper, getting bathed and massaged by E. Power Biggs' sonic waves. It was like taking peyote or something. This marvelously high feeling would come over them, as though they were psychedelic, and the most commonplace objects took on this great radiance and significance. It was like old Aldous Huxley in his drug experiments, sitting there hooking down peyote buttons and staring at a clay geranium pot on a table, which gradually became the most fabulous geranium pot in God's world. The way it curved . . . why, it curved 360 d-e-g-r-e-e-s! And the clay . . . why, it was the color of the earth itself! And the top . . . It had a r-i-m on it! George had the same feeling. Anne's apartment . . . it was hung all over the place with the usual New York working girl's modern prints, the Picasso scrawls, the Mondrians curling at the corners . . . somehow nobody ever gets even a mat for a Mondrian print . . . the Toulouse-Lautrecs with that guy with the chin kicking his silhouette leg, the Klees, that Paul Klee is cute . . . why, all of a sudden these were the most beautiful things in the whole hagiology of art . . . the way that guy with the chin k-i-c-k-s t-h-a-t l-e-g, the way that Paul Klee h-i-t-s t-h-a-t b-a-l-l . . . the way that apartment just wrapped around them like a cocoon, with lint under the couch like angel's hair, and the plum cover on the bed lying halfway on the floor in folds like the folds in a Tiepolo cherub's silks, and the bored Medusa on the mantelpiece looking like the most splendidly, gloriously b-o-r-e-d Medusa in the face of time!

[14] "Now, that was love," says George, "and there has never been anything like it. I don't know what happens to it. Unless it's Monday. Monday sort of happens to it in New York."

ANALYTICAL READING

1. What sentence did you underline that might serve as the focusing sentence for the essay? How does the title help to determine the focusing idea?

2. What is the setting for the first part of the essay? What is its importance?

3. What appears to be the narrator's attitude toward the young lovers?

4. Why do you think there is no specific mention of Tuesday or Wednesday?

5. What details did you find most descriptive?

6. At the beginning, Anne's apartment is described in one way; at the end, in another. Are these factual or personal descriptions? Explain.

7. Is "cocoon of love" an apt metaphor? Why? What other figures of speech help to create a vivid description? What passages did you mark as being especially effective?

8. Does "real love" occur only on Sunday? Explain.

REFLECTING

Point: Is Wolfe describing New York, love, young and middle-aged lovers, or what?

Organization: The essay is organized chronologically; but what other rhetorical devices provide the basic organizational pattern? Would it have been more effective to have started with Sunday and then moved on through the other days? And to have explicitly described George and Anne's love instead of describing how they spent their Sundays?

Support: Point out several cumulative sentences and show how they contribute to describing the scene. How does Wolfe use only Thursday morning, Friday night, and Saturday to convey a sense of the entire week besides Sunday?

Synthesis: Is the subway scene anything like some comparable scene in a high school or on a college campus? Is "torpor" a luxury to people everywhere? To young as well as middle-aged people? Could you guess from context what *torpor* means?

Evaluation: Was Wolfe effective in portraying the peace and beauty and completeness of a Sunday kind of love? Why? Is the essay too limited in scope, pertaining only to New York City? Does the selection fit Wolfe's definition of the "new journalism" quoted in the biographical sketch? Discuss. How effective are the introductory and closing paragraphs?

FROM READING TO WRITING

1. Write a paper for your college newspaper comparing a description of the real and the artificial, for example, in restaurants, churches, classes, homes. Try to emulate Wolfe's style of writing.

2. For your classmates, write about different manifestations of teenage love in real life, films, books, or television shows, presenting the settings and actions vividly.

A TIME OF PLENTY
Marilyn Kluger

BIOGRAPHICAL SKETCH

Marilyn Kluger and her husband run a successful mail-order business—The Country Store—in Newburgh, Indiana. Although their home is in Newburgh, they and their teen-aged sons spend part of each year in Vermont. A regular contributor to Gourmet *magazine, she also teaches classes on food and herbs at the University of Evansville. Her three books are on food and crafts:* The Joy of Spinning *(1971),* The Wild Flavor *(1973), and* Preserving Summer's Bounty *(1979).*

PRE-READING

1. Could the title be misleading today and, if so, in what way? How do the first two sentences establish the scene and the subject of the essay?

2. The essay appeared in the magazine *Gourmet.* What does this indicate the subject might be?

[1] Thanksgiving Day on our Indiana farm has always meant an epic of cookery for the women, a day of quail hunting for the men, and unstinted feasting for all who sit at our table to partake of the bountiful meal that symbolizes the end of another growing season and the gathering in of the year's crops. In my childhood the Thanksgiving feast was not an occasion for a full-scale reunion with our many relatives, although we were never without company for dinner. Extra places were laid at the table for my maternal grandparents and perhaps for an aunt and uncle, some cousins, or visiting hunters. And usually among our guests were the hired hands who worked steadily, sometimes even on Thanksgiving Day, to complete my father's harvest before the end of Indian summer and the advent of bad weather.

[2] It was my parents' custom year round to rise before dawn, as soon as the roosters began their crowing. On ordinary days I was only dreamily aware of the hen house cacophony and the muffled sounds of morning activity that drifted up to my bedroom under the eaves. But on such a special day as Thanksgiving the scents arising from below the stairway were especially tantalizing and the louder noises from the kitchen were different from the everyday sounds of breakfast preparation. It was not a day when Mother tiptoed in the kitchen so that the rest of the household could sleep. Was that the rattling of the turkey roaster? Would the enormous bird vanish into the oven while I drowsed? The impending activities of the day and the lure of the kitchen were enough to rouse even the most incurable sleepyhead from a featherbed.

[3] On the last Thursday in November I could stay in bed only until the

night chill left the house, hearing first the clash of the heavy gates in the huge black iron range, with its flowery scrolls and nickeled decorations, as Mother shook down the ashes. Then, in their proper sequence, came the sounds of the fire being made—the rustle of newspaper, the snap of kindling, the rush of smoke up the chimney when Mother opened the damper, slid the regulator wide open, and struck a match to the kerosene-soaked corncobs that started a quick hot fire. I listened for the bang of the cast-iron lid dropping back into place and for the tick of the stovepipe as fierce flames sent up their first heat, then the sound of the lid being lifted again as Mother fed more dry wood and lumps of coal to the greedy new fire. The duties of the kitchen on Thanksgiving were a thousandfold, and I could tell that Mother was bustling about with a quicker step than usual.

⁴ Outside beneath my window my father whistled for Queen, our English setter. At the sound of his whistle, my brothers, who were sleeping in the next room, would begin to mumble and stir. Their ears were as acutely attuned to my father's whistle as mine were to the kitchen noises. Jim and Harold did not want to be left behind, tardily finishing their chores, when Dad strode out across the fields with the gun on his shoulder and Queen at his side. And I did not want to miss the goings-on in the kitchen, where Mother, Grandmother, and Aunt Emma would cook and visit all morning, telling interesting stories and creating delicious foods for the harvest feast.

.   .   .

ANALYTICAL READING

1. For this family, in what ways is Thanksgiving Day different from other days?

2. About how old is the narrator?

3. About how many people would you guess are at the dinner table? Explain.

4. How do the activities of the women differ from those of the men?

5. Which senses are appealed to in the essay? Refer to specific sentences.

REFLECTING

Point: Does the writer merely describe Thanksgiving morning, or does she also provide some symbolic element? These paragraphs provide background for a longer article. What would you expect the rest of the article to deal with?

Organization: How does the opening paragraph fit into the organization of the rest of the selection? How are the second and third paragraphs related?

Support: How are cumulative sentences used to re-create the Thanksgiving Day? What sentence or sentences—cumulative or not—do you think provide a vivid description of the morning? Is the language used that of an adult, a child, or a mixture of both? Cite examples.

Synthesis: Can you compare the essay with some childhood festive occasion or family tradition of your own? What memories do the descriptions bring to mind?

Evaluation: Does the lengthy opening sentence detract from the essay? Does the final paragraph about the writer's brothers violate the unity of the kitchen scene? Is the writer successful in making you feel part of the household, in experiencing what the day meant to her? If so, to what writing devices do you attribute this success?

FROM READING TO WRITING

1. For a general audience, write a similar essay describing an eventful occasion in your family, perhaps Christmas dinner, a Passover seder, or an annual reunion. Be certain not to focus on your personal feelings but on the sights, sounds, odors, tastes, and tactile (touch) sensations that you recall.

2. In the same vein, describe a past or present ordinary day, perhaps early morning in your household, with every member of the family following a set routine. Write the essay as though you plan to read it at a family reunion.

Factual Description

ON THE BALL
Roger Angell

BIOGRAPHICAL SKETCH

Born in New York City in 1920, Roger Angell earned a B.A. degree from Harvard University in 1942. He has written for and been editor of a number of magazines, including Holiday *and* The New Yorker. *He has also found time to be active in community affairs, serving as a trustee of Sydenham Hospital and as a leading administrator of the New York Civil Liberties Union. His numerous articles and books include* The Stone Arbor *(1961),* The Summer Game *(1972), and* Five Seasons: A Baseball Companion *(1977). Since 1956 he has been a general contributor to* The New Yorker.

PRE-READING

1. In what way does the title aptly describe this selection and in what way does it gain your attention?

2. At what point in the opening sentences do you fully realize the subject of the piece?

¹ It weighs just over five ounces and measures between 2.86 and 2.94 inches in diameter. It is made of a composition-cork nucleus encased in two thin layers of rubber, one black and one red, surrounded by a hundred and twenty-one yards of tightly wrapped blue-gray wool yarn, forty-five yards of white wool yarn, fifty-three more yards of blue-gray wool yarn, a hundred and fifty yards of fine cotton yarn, a coat of rubber cement, and a cowhide (formerly horsehide) exterior, which is held together with two hundred and sixteen slightly raised red cotton stitches. Printed certifications, endorsements, and outdoor advertising spherically attest to its authenticity. Like most institutions, it is considered inferior in its present form to its ancient archetypes, and in this case the complaint is probably justified; on occasion in recent years it has actually been known to come apart under the demands of its brief but rigorous active career. Baseballs are assembled and hand-stitched in Taiwan (before this

FROM "On the Ball," *The New Yorker*, October 4, 1976, p. 90. Copyright © 1972, 1973, 1974, 1975, 1976, 1977 by Roger Angell. This article first appeared in *The New Yorker*. Reprinted by permission of Simon & Schuster, a Division of Gulf & Western Corporation.

year the work was done in Haiti, and before 1973 in Chicopee, Massachusetts), and contemporary pitchers claim that there is a tangible variation in the size and feel of the balls that now come into play in a single game; a true peewee is treasured by hurlers, and its departure from the premises, by fair means or foul, is secretly mourned. But never mind: any baseball is beautiful. No other small package comes as close to the ideal in design and utility. It is a perfect object for a man's hand. Pick it up and it instantly suggests its purpose; it is meant to be thrown a considerable distance—thrown hard and with precision. Its feel and heft are the beginning of the sport's critical dimensions; if it were a fraction of an inch larger or smaller, a few centigrams heavier or lighter, the game of baseball would be utterly different. Hold a baseball in your hand. As it happens, this one is not brand new. Here, just to one side of the curved surgical welt of stitches, there is a pale-green grass smudge, darkening on one edge almost to black—the mark of an old infield play, a tough grounder now lost in memory. Feel the ball, turn it over in your hand; hold it across the seam or the other way, with the seam just to the side of your middle finger. Speculation stirs. You want to get outdoors and throw this spare and sensual object to somebody, or, at the very least, watch somebody else throw it. The game has begun. . . .

ANALYTICAL READING

1. Is this description personal, factual, or both? Explain, using specific references to the selection.

2. Discuss the statement: "Like most institutions, it is considered inferior in its present form to its ancient archetypes."

3. What is the purpose of including the sentence about "a true peewee"? Explain fully the phrase "by fair means or foul."

4. This excerpt from a longer article is not divided into paragraphs. Where might the author have started a new paragraph or new paragraphs?

5. What is the author's tone? Explain your answer.

REFLECTING

Point: What is the purpose of the initial sentences? Which sentence did you underline as the focusing sentence?

Organization: Analyze the selection, showing the relationship of the parts.

Support: Do the details provide reasonably sufficient evidence for the writer's conclusion about a baseball? Point out where a cumulative sentence has been used to present numerous facts. Do the details about baseballs suggest to you that the author is an authority? If so, why is that important?

Synthesis: Is the selection sexist, appealing only to men and failing to interest women? Have you ever looked hard at or thought much about a baseball before? Did you gain a new or fresh insight from reading the selection?

Evaluation: Is Angell's viewpoint and attitude contagious? Do you feel as he does in the closing line, or can you at least understand how he would feel this way? If so, how has he enabled you to share his attitude? This paragraph introduces an article about types of players and their attitudes toward baseball. In light of that knowledge, what do you think of the approach used?

FROM READING TO WRITING

1. Write a factual description of common subject or object such as one side of a penny, the palm of your hand, a matchbook, a shoe, or a watch. Then write a personal description of it, bringing out your feelings and thoughts. It need not be something you like; you might select your alarm clock and describe first objectively and then subjectively how the clock appears to you and your reaction to its raucous ring early in the morning.

2. For your classmates, write a paper similar to Angell's piece, describing an object, such as a basketball, tennis ball, backpack, bicycle, or stereo. Avoiding a revelation about your emotional reactions to the subject, give as many factual details as possible. You may wish to obtain some information from the library.

CARPENTER ANTS
T. C. Schneirla

BIOGRAPHICAL SKETCH

T(heodore) C(hristian) Schneirla (1902–68) was born in Bay City, Michigan, and received the B.S., M.S., and Sc.D. degrees from the University of Michigan. An authority on Eciton, or army ants, he explored their habits in the jungles of Mexico, Trinidad, and the Panama Canal Zone. From 1947 to 1968 he was curator of the department of animal behavior of the American Museum of Natural History in New York. He was the author of Animal Psychology, *the co-author, with L. C. Craft, of* Experiments in Psychology, *and a contributor to* Encyclopaedia Britannica, Twentieth Century Psychology, *and* Philosophy for the Future. *Schneirla's numerous articles appeared in such periodicals as* Natural History, Scientific American, *and* Psychological Review.

PRE-READING

1. From skimming the first and last paragraphs, what particular activity of the carpenter ants do you expect to be described?

2. Is the tone personal or impersonal? Explain. What kind of description does this suggest?

FROM "Carpenter Ants," in *Ants, Indians, and Little Dinosaurs,* edited by Alan Ternes (New York: Charles Scribner's Sons, 1975), pp. 85–87. Copyright © 1975 by The American Museum of Natural History. Reprinted by permission of Charles Scribner's Sons.

3. Is any special attempt made in the introductory paragraph to interest readers, to arouse their curiosity, or to attract their attention?

[1] The colonies of the black species C. *pennsylvannicus* and its subspecies C. *ferrugineus* of the American temperate zone may grow to be fairly large. There may be as many as a few thousand workers, a single reproductive female (the queen), a brood of varying make-up, according to the season, and at certain times of year a considerable number of young winged males and queens. As with many other species of *Camponotus,* the workers (or neuter females) are polymorphic; that is, they range in size and type from the large and robust workers-major to the smallest, the workers-minor. The queen is readily distinguished from the workers by her great size, her large head and bulging thorax, and by the high polish she generally acquires from the almost incessant licking and stroking of her body by workers.

[2] Colonies that have weathered the hazard of their first two or three years are usually able to produce reproductive individuals—the large winged males and females. The late summer brood of males and females, after emerging from their large cocoons, usually remain in their parent nests through the winter, huddled in clusters with the hibernating workers within the inner recesses of their catacomb-like shelter. They make their exodus early in the following warm season, in late spring or early summer as a rule. If the occupants of a house have been unaware of a flourishing *Camponotus* colony within the foundation beams, the discovery is likely to come on some warm day in late spring, when from some chink in the molding a whole host of males and numerous females may come out into the room.

[3] In the open, the winged males and females spill out of their home nests on the warm and bright days from May into July and soon take to the air in a mating flight. This results in the fertilization of many of the females. In contrast to the large-eyed but tiny-headed males, which cannot survive long as solitary individuals after the flight, many of the inseminated queens return to some woody surface or to the earth and are able to establish themselves. Fascinating and unsolved problems are presented both by their behavior and their physiology, which seem to change markedly after fertilization has taken place.

[4] When a fertilized queen descends from her flight, she drops or bites off her wings, then soon becomes photo-negative. That is to say, she is markedly light-shy, whereas before fertilization she was light-positive, as indicated by upward spiraling toward light in the mating flight. As a result of this change, when the newly fertilized queen reaches a sheltered dark place, she settles down. If accidentally exposed to light, she again promptly disappears from view. In the northern states, if you pull strips of bark from logs and stumps in the late spring, you are likely to expose one or more newly established *Camponotus* queens. Each is in a little cell ringed around with a wall of wood fibers set up by the queen herself. Or she may find her way into the deserted burrow of a tunneling wood beetle in which she comes to rest at some turning. She may perish through seasonal vissicitudes or through the invasion of her cell by ants

or other predatory insects. Otherwise, however, the young queen can survive by living on her own tissues and can found a colony through her own resources.

⁵ Her now degenerating wing muscles and the fat bodies with which she is abundantly equipped provide nourishment for her and her first brood. For, unlike the colony-founding queen of some Australian ants of primitive ponerine species, which leave their cells and forage about, thereby procuring food for themselves and for their first brood, the *Camponotus* queens remain sequestered and have no food except what is available from their own bodies. On this special "reducing diet," the queen soon begins to lay eggs, and with this substance she can feed the larvae which presently appear.

⁶ That the first brood is not lavishly fed by the queen is evident from the very small stature of the few workers that appear in the first lot. They are all of the worker-minor caste. However, these diminutive workers may succeed in consolidating the young colony by slowly extending the nest and by foraging in the environs, bringing in food that is used to replenish the queen's reserves and feed the additional brood. If the first pygmy workers do not carry out such work effectively, the colony is likely to perish. If they work well, the population grows and the nest is extended into wood and earth. As soon as the first workers have appeared and are busy in the nest, the queen turns to producing eggs as her exclusive task. Thereafter she labors no more except in this important capacity as egg-making machine.

ANALYTICAL READING

1. On the basis of the first paragraph, do you think Schneirla is writing to a general or a specific audience? Why or why not? Why are Latin terms used?

2. In what sentence in paragraph 3 does the writer's tone change? Explain the function of this sentence in relation to the paragraphs that follow it.

3. Where does Schneirla indicate he is interested not only in describing the carpenter ants but also in alerting readers to their possible presence? Explain why you think he does this.

4. What are the two main problems confronting the queen and her new colony?

REFLECTING

Point: What is the main activity that Schneirla describes in this selection? Summarize this activity in a sentence or two.

Organization: What organizational plan is followed? Does this plan start with the second or third paragraph? Justify your answer.

Support: How does Schneirla define terms that may be too technical for his readers? Point to examples. Why is the information about the males subordinated in the third sentence of paragraph 3? What is the function of the final sentence in paragraph 4? What purpose does the contrast in paragraph 5 serve?

Synthesis: What did you find most interesting in the selection? Is there any relationship between the queen's first offspring and the child of a human family? Has
reading the selection affected your attitude toward ants? Is there any possible
analogy between the queen and her workers, and some husbands and wives?

Evaluation: Although you may not have been interested in carpenter ants, did you
find the selection well organized, clearly written, and informative? Were sufficient details provided? Was the author's voice appropriate, authoritative, objective?

FROM READING TO WRITING

1. For a general audience, write a factual description of some animals, such as ants
    or birds building a nest, fish swimming in a tank, birds at a feeder or tugging a
    worm out of the ground, dogs getting acquainted, or cats fighting.

2. For your classmates, write a factual description of some advertisement, such as
    one about cars, liquor or beer, apparel, or some food or other product. Submit
    the advertisement with your paper.

3. For high-school students, describe some routine campus activity, such as stu-
    dents leaving a class, entering the library, chaining their bicycles. Be factual and
    objective.

Mixed Description

THE VIEW FROM THE CASTLE

S. Dillon Ripley

BIOGRAPHICAL SKETCH

S. Dillon Ripley was born in New York City in 1913. Besides a Ph.D. from Harvard University and an LL.D. from Yale University, he has received honorary degrees from many universities, including Cambridge University and Brown University. As a director of various corporations, foundations, and museums, Ripley has headed many scientific expeditions to the South Pacific, Southeast Asia, India, and Nepal. He has been president of the International Council of Bird Preservation and Chairman of the World Wildlife Fund. Currently, he is a professor at Yale University and Secretary of the Smithsonian Institution. Among his many works on birds and wildlife is his most recent, Paradox of the Human Condition *(1975).*

PRE-READING

1. What does the title suggest to you?

2. From the biographical sketch, what would you expect Ripley to write about? Would you consider him an authority on the subject? Why?

3.. Skim the opening paragraph. Which sentence best indicates what is to follow?

[1] After sunset, these fall evenings, there is a time of twilight on the ponds when the senses are quickened as the light fails. Hearing sharpens, one smells more keenly, the eyes seem to adjust to reduced light reflection even as pools of darkness gather between the trees. I used to love this time on our duck ponds, for then imagination wakens and one senses again the life of the hunter. But now our feelings are mixed with dread, for a new predator has been added to the roster of mink, raccoon, fox and stray dog that our fences guard against.

[2] Beyond the first ponds is a bench, and here I can sit and watch in the gloaming. Ducks and geese coursing over the water leave behind a variety of v-shaped ripples and deliquescing colors, pinks to reds to mauves to purples. Some v's are narrow—a single wood duck on an errand of its own; others are

FROM *Smithsonian*, November 1976, p. 6. Copyright 1976 by the Smithsonian Institution.

a series of expanding trails—a family group of small geese, sailing effortlessly in line. Two larger geese junket by, tails higher, necks lower, sleepily pushing along.

³ But suddenly the spell is broken, drowsiness is gone. We are alert, all of us. Why? No sound, no smell, but distant motion—or is it? It's hard to tell; birds are all on the water now, all looking in one direction, beginning a slow drifting movement, as if mesmerized. At the end of the pond there is a big boulder sticking out of the water, gray against the limpid purple. And, yes, there's a shape on top, quite still—no darting mink or deliberate raccoon, just still and tall. It can only be a great owl, silent, motionless, come on velvet wings like a wraith. I dare not move, for the owl's eyes are five to ten times more light-receptive than my own.

⁴ The ducks and geese seem riveted on the owl, as I am. Like some cloaked Mephistophelian figure the predator decoys his prey, for they are drifting toward the boulder, seemingly spellbound. The owl does not move. I cannot see if it even blinks. As we all watch, a blurred movement comes from behind. Without a sound a second owl sweeps low over the water, strikes with outstreched feet at a duck, and glides away, its talons locked in the back of the helpless bird.

⁵ It is over in an instant and I am powerless. With cries of alarm, ducks and geese dart in all directions in panic. The hypnotist flies off to join its mate, and I can only marvel at the drama which has deprived us of one of our small supply of breeding canvasback ducks. From being very uncommon a generation ago, great horned owls have become locally more visible on the East Coast, perhaps because with the spread of the suburbs have come untended woodland, town dumps and a plethora of rats and skunks to feed upon. Now our ducks are threatened in a manner that fences cannot cure. The subsiding ripples of the pond seem like wavelets in a mirage as our rare birds disappear—canvasbacks, ring-necks, Hawaiian ducks, teal, all carefully nurtured on our ponds and formerly secure.

⁶ The succession of life itself, the changes in the ratio of predator to prey, the ebb and flow of species—all this is a marvel in nature, no matter how painful in the eye of the beholder. Like life itself, change is the only surety. And so who will win? Perhaps the owls will, for their power is great, their adaptability more breathtaking than anyone could know.

ANALYTICAL READING

1. Why did the author formerly love this time of year on the duck ponds? What does he mean by "then imagination wakens and one senses again the life of the hunter" (paragraph 1)? Is this statement ironic? Why?

2. At the end of paragraph 3, why does Ripley "dare not move"?

3. How does the author account for the presence of the great horned owls?

4. Explain the final paragraph, discussing the ideas and implications in each sentence.

REFLECTING

Point: This selection mainly uses description but includes narration and exposition. Identify uses of each method and explain how all relate to the author's main idea.

Organization: How is the essay organized? Be certain to account for the function of the opening and closing paragraphs.

Support: Point out the many appeals to the senses. Discuss the following verbs or verbals in paragraph 2: *coursing, sailing, junket by.* Is there a contrast between the author's vocabulary and his voice (note "*deliquescing* colors" in paragraph 2)? How do the questions in paragraph 3 enhance the effect of tension? Point out effective figures of speech that you think add support to the essay—for example, "like a wraith" in paragraph 3 and "Like some cloaked Mephistophelian figure" in paragraph 4. Explain your choices.

Synthesis: Can you relate some experience of your own to this one: a cat attacking a bird, or a dog a cat? Do you share the author's view that such things are "a marvel in nature"?

Evaluation: Can you understand the reasons for the author's views in the final paragraph? What has contributed to his conclusion that the owls may win? What makes the episode so vivid and dramatic?

FROM READING TO WRITING

1. Describe vividly some natural change that has occurred around your home, such as drought, an invasion of blackbirds or squirrels, or environmental pollution that threatens wildlife. If you wish, you may include the description in a letter to your local newspaper, supporting some environmental cause.

2. Write a before-and-after description of the changes that take place in a scene with the arrival of an intruder. You might consider writing about the quiet on a street before the touring ice cream truck arrives, the locker room before and after players arrive, a dorm on a weekday and then on the weekend.

TERROR AT TINKER CREEK
Annie Dillard

BIOGRAPHICAL SKETCH

Annie Dillard grew up in Pittsburgh, Pennsylvania, and attended Hollins College. After living in Roanoke Valley, Virginia, the location of Tinker Creek, she moved to the state of Washington, where she teaches at Western Washington State

FROM Annie Dillard, *Pilgrim at Tinker Creek* (New York: Harper's Magazine Press, Harper & Row, 1974), pp. 5–6. Reprinted by permission of the author.

College. A journalist and a poet, she has been a contributing editor to Harper's *magazine and a columnist for the* Wilderness Society. *In addition to her Pulitzer Prize winning,* Pilgrim at Tinker Creek, *from which this selection is taken, she has published a book of poems,* Tickets for a Prayer Wheel, *and the recent* Holy the Firm.

PRE-READING

1. What word in the title of her book from which this selection is taken gives a clue as to Dillard's attitude toward the Tinker Creek area? Explain.

2. From the biographical sketch, what kind of attitude would you expect her to have about nature?

3. What does the first paragraph reveal about the kind of person Dillard is? What appears to be the subject of this chapter?

¹ A couple of summers ago I was walking along the edge of the island to see what I could see in the water, and mainly to scare frogs. Frogs have an inelegant way of taking off from invisible positions on the bank just ahead of your feet, in dire panic, emitting a froggy "Yike!" and splashing into the water. Incredibly, this amused me, and incredibly, it amuses me still. As I walked along the grassy edge of the island, I got better and better at seeing frogs both in and out of the water. I learned to recognize, slowing down, the difference in texture of the light reflected from mudbank, water, grass, or frog. Frogs were flying all around me. At the end of the island I noticed a small green frog. He was exactly half in and half out of the water, looking like a schematic diagram of an amphibian, and he didn't jump.

² He didn't jump; I crept closer. At least I knelt on the island's winter-killed grass, lost, dumbstruck, staring at the frog in the creek just four feet away. He was a very small frog with wide, dull eyes. And just as I looked at him, he slowly crumpled and began to sag. The spirit vanished from his eyes as if snuffed. His skin emptied and drooped; his very skull seemed to collapse and settle like a kicked tent. He was shrinking before my eyes like a deflating football. I watched the taut, glistening skin on his shoulders ruck, and rumple, and fall. Soon, part of his skin, formless as a pricked balloon, lay in floating folds like bright scum on top of the water: it was a monstrous and terrifying thing. I gaped bewildered, appalled. An oval shadow hung in the water behind the drained frog; then the shadow glided away. The frog skin bag started to sink.

³ I had read about the giant water bug, but never seen one. "Giant water bug" is really the name of the creature, which is an enormous, heavy-bodied brown beetle. It eats insects, tadpoles, fish, and frogs. Its grasping forelegs are mighty and hooked inward. It seizes a victim with these legs, hugs it tight, and paralyzes it with enzymes injected during a vicious bite. That one bite is the only bite it ever takes. Through the puncture shoot the poisons that dissolve the victim's muscles and bones and organs—all but the skin—and through it the giant water bug sucks out the victim's body, reduced to a juice. This event

is quite common in warm fresh water. The frog I saw was being sucked by a giant water bug. I had been kneeling on the island grass; when the unrecognizable flap of frog skin settled on the creek bottom, swaying, I stood up and brushed the knees of my pants. I couldn't catch my breath.

⁴ Of course, many carnivorous animals devour their prey alive. The usual method seems to be to subdue the victim by downing or grasping it so it can't flee, then eating it whole or in a series of bloody bites. Frogs eat everything whole, stuffing prey into their mouths with their thumbs. People have seen frogs with their wide jaws so full of live dragonflies they couldn't close them. Ants don't even have to catch their prey: in the spring they swarm over newly hatched, featherless birds in the nest and eat them tiny bite by bite.

ANALYTICAL READING

1. What initially attracted Dillard to the "small green frog"? Why was she so horrified? What effect does the repetition of "he didn't jump" have?

2. Is there any indication that the frog feels pain? What explanation for this does Dillard offer?

3. Do you think the contrast in tone between the first paragraph and the second adds to the horror? Explain. How does Dillard achieve that contrast through the content of the two paragraphs?

4. Does the last paragraph help relieve the horror the author establishes? Why or why not?

REFLECTING

Point: State in one sentence what you think Dillard tries to illustrate in this vivid description.

Organization: Discuss the organization. Why is it effective for Dillard to describe the event exactly as it happened before she explains about the water beetle?

Support: Pick out images and comparisons that you find especially effective and that you think help to support the writer's purpose or point.

Synthesis: Did you share the experience with Dillard? Have you too witnessed natural phenomena about which you could say "I couldn't catch my breath"? Discuss.

Evaluation: Although this is essentially a factual description, Dillard is able to inject her own emotional reaction to the phenomenon. Select some words and phrases that reveal her attitudes. Discuss the various techniques—language, organization, content—that you found contributed most to your emotional reaction to the description.

FROM READING TO WRITING

1. For a general audience, describe in detail a natural phenomenon that you have observed and that affected you. As Dillard does, let the straight, factual description express your reaction to the situation.

2.   Write a factual description of your pet or of a plant you have in your room. Try to let your classmates see it vividly enough to be able to draw a reasonably accurate sketch of it.

3.   Go to a quiet spot on campus or near your home—a wooded area or a pond—and observe an encounter between two bird, dogs, fish, squirrels, or other creatures. Describe the incident, using the kind of vivid detail that Dillard does.

ILLINOIS JOURNEY
Saul Bellow

BIOGRAPHICAL SKETCH

Saul Bellow was born in a suburb of Montreal, Canada, in 1915. Nine years later his family, immigrants from Russia, moved to Chicago. Bellow first attended the University of Chicago, then transferred to and graduated from Northwestern University with honors in sociology and anthropology; he did graduate work in anthropology at the University of Wisconsin. Currently Professor of the Committee on Social Thought at the University of Chicago, he received the Nobel Prize for Literature in 1976. The best known of Bellow's many written works, which include stories, one-act plays, essays, reviews, translations, are his major novels: The Adventures of Augie March *(winner of the National Book Award for Fiction, 1953);* Henderson the Rain King; Herzog *(winner of the National Book Award, 1964);* Mr. Sammler's Planet *(winner of the National Book Award, 1970); and* Humboldt's Gift *(winner of the Pulitzer Prize, 1975).*

PRE-READING

1.   What do the title and first sentence suggest about what Bellow plans to discuss? What does the phrase "at first appear monotonous" imply?

2.   How helpful is the first sentence of the last paragraph?

3.   From the biographical sketch, would you expect Bellow to be interested in the scenery from the standpoint of its beauty or as a human environment? Explain.

¹ The features of Illinois are not striking; they do not leap to the eye but lie flat and at first appear monotonous. The roads are wide, hard, perfect, sometimes of a shallow depth in the far distance but so nearly level as to make you feel that the earth really is flat. From east and west, travelers dart across these prairies into the huge horizons and through cornfields that go on forever; giant skies, giant clouds, an eternal nearly featureless sameness. You find it hard to travel slowly. The endless miles pressed flat by the ancient glacier

FROM *Holiday,* March 1976, pp. 31, 62. Copyright © 1957 by Saul Bellow. Reprinted by permission of Russell & Volkening, Inc. as agents for the author.

seduce you into speeding. As the car eats into the distances you begin gradually to feel that you are riding upon the floor of the continent, the very bottom of it, low and flat, and an impatient spirit of movement, of overtaking and urgency passes into your heart.

[2] Miles and miles of prairie, slowly rising and falling, sometimes give you a sense that something is in the process of becoming, or that the liberation of a great force is imminent, some power, like Michelangelo's slave only half released from the block of stone. Conceivably the mound-building Indians believed their resurrection would coincide with some such liberation, and built their graves in imitation of the low moraines deposited by the departing glaciers. But they have not yet been released and remain drowned in their waves of earth. They have left their bones, their flints and pots, their place names and tribal names and little besides except a stain, seldom vivid, on the consciousness of their white successors.

[3] The soil of the Illinois prairies is fat, rich and thick. After spring plowing it looks oil-blackened or colored by the soft coal which occurs in great veins throughout the state. In the fields you frequently see a small tipple, or a crazy-looking device that pumps oil and nods like the neck of a horse at a quick walk. . . . Along the roads, with intervals between them as neat and even as buttons on the cuff, sit steel storage bins, in form like the tents of Mongolia. They are filled with grain. And the elevators and tanks, trucks and machines that crawl over the fields and blunder over the highways—whatever you see is productive. It creates wealth, it stores wealth, it is wealth.

[4] As you pass the fields, you see signs the farmers have posted telling in short code what sort of seed they have planted. The farmhouses are seldom at the roadside, but far within the fields. The solitude and silence are deep and wide. Then, when you have gone ten or twenty miles through cornfields without having seen a living thing, no cow, no dog, scarcely even a bird under the hot sky, suddenly you come upon a noisy contraption at the roadside, a system of contraptions, rather, for husking the corn and stripping the grain. It burns and bangs away, and the conveyor belts rattle. . . .

[5] When you leave, this noise and activity are cut off at one stroke: you are once more in the deaf, hot solitude of trembling air, alone in the cornfields.

[6] North, south, east and west, there is no end to them. They line roads and streams and hem in the woods and surround towns, and they crowd into back yards and edge up to gas stations. An exotic stranger might assume he had come upon a race of corn worshipers who had created a corn ocean; or that he was among a people who had fallen in love with infinite repetition of the same details, like the builders of skyscrapers in New York and Chicago who have raised up bricks and windows by the thousands, and all alike. From corn you can derive notions of equality, or uniformity, massed democracy. You can, if you are given to that form of mental play, recall Joseph's brethren in the lean years, and think how famine has been conquered here and superabundance itself become such a danger that the Government has to take measures against it.

⁷ The power, the monotony, the oceanic extent of the cornfields do indeed shrink up and dwarf the past. How are you to think of the small bands of Illini, Ottawas, Cahokians, Shawnee, Miamis who camped in the turkey grass, and the French Jesuits who descended the Mississippi and found them. When you force your mind to summon them, the Indians appear rather doll-like in the radiance of the present moment. They are covered in the corn, swamped in the oil, hidden in the coal of Franklin County, run over by the trains, turned phantom by the stockyards. There are monuments to them . . . throughout the state, but they are only historical ornaments to the pride of the present. . . .

ANALYTICAL READING

1. What main impressions about Illinois do you derive from the description?

2. What sense perceptions has Bellow primarily relied on?

3. What is the purpose of referring to the Indian tribes?

4. What is the writer's attitude toward the changed landscape? Does it represent progress to him? How does he seem to feel about New York and Chicago?

REFLECTING

Point: Which sentence best summarizes the essay? How would you express the author's dominant impression of and attitude toward Illinois?

Organization: Can you discern an overall pattern? What is the specific subject of paragraph 4 and how is it organized? What function does paragraph 5 serve? How is paragraph 6 organized?

Support: How well educated an audience is Bellow writing to? Explain with references to particular passages. What figures of speech are particularly effective? Discuss some, such as, "nods like the neck of a horse at a quick walk" (paragraph 3); "like the builders of skyscrapers" (paragraph 6); "the Indians appear rather doll-like" (paragraph 7).

Synthesis: Have your views about Illinois been changed? If so, how? Do you share the author's views about the Indians of Illinois? Do his descriptions reflect your answer to question 3 under "Pre-reading" (page 123)?

Evaluation: How clear and convincing is Bellow's description of his Illinois journey? How complete is it? Does it gain or lose by the inclusion of references to Indians? What specific features of the selection help to make it effective or ineffective?

FROM READING TO WRITING

1. Describe your own city or state, giving general readers your personal impression but being careful to support it with many details.

2. Describe your college to a high school student who would like to see it and learn about its campus atmosphere but who is unable to visit it.

OUR EVER-CHANGING SHORE
Rachel Carson

BIOGRAPHICAL SKETCH

Rachel Carson (1907–1964), an author and scientist with an M.A. from Johns Hopkins University, worked with the United States Fish and Wildlife Service from 1936 to 1952. Her second book, The Sea Around Us *(1951), earned her a worldwide reputation as a naturalist. In the 1960s she became very concerned about the effect of DDT and other pesticides on fish and bird life. Her book on the subject,* Silent Spring *(1962), created an international controversy and was instrumental in the subsequent banning of DDT.*

PRE-READING

1. What does the title suggest? Have you ever heard of conservationist Rachel Carson and her work? If so, what attitude toward nature might you expect to find in the selection?

2. What words or phrases in the first and last paragraphs provide clues to the subject?

   ¹ The shore means many things to many people. Of its varied moods the one usually considered typical is not so at all. The true spirit of the sea does not reside in the gentle surf that laps a sun-drenched bathing beach on a summer day. Instead, it is on a lonely shore at dawn or twilight, or in storm or midnight darkness that we sense a mysterious something we recognize as the reality of the sea. For the ocean has nothing to do with humanity. It is supremely unaware of man, and when we carry too many of the trappings of human existence with us to the threshold of the sea world our ears are dulled and we do not hear the accents of sublimity in which it speaks.

   ² Sometimes the shore speaks of the earth and its own creation; sometimes it speaks of life. If we are lucky in choosing our time and place, we may witness a spectacle that echoes of vast and elemental things. On a summer night when the moon is full, the sea and the swelling tide and a creature of the ancient shore conspire to work primeval magic on many of the beaches from Maine to Florida. On such a night the horseshoe crabs move in, just as they did under a Paleozoic moon—just as they have been doing through all the hundreds of millions of years since then—coming out of the sea to dig their nests in the wet sand and deposit their spawn.

   ³ As the tide nears its flood dark shapes appear in the surf line. They gleam with the wetness of the sea as the moon shines on the smooth curves of their massive shells. The first to arrive linger in the foaming water below the advancing front of the tide. These are the waiting males. At last other forms

FROM Rachel Carson, "Our Ever-Changing Shore," in Paul Brooks, *The House of Life: Rachel Carson at Work* (Boston: Houghton Mifflin, 1972), pp. 218–24. Copyright © 1972 by Paul Brooks. Reprinted by permission of Houghton Mifflin Company.

emerge out of the darkness offshore, swimming easily in the deeper water but crawling awkwardly and hesitantly as the sea shallows beneath them. They make their way to the beach through the crowd of jostling males. In thinning water each female digs her nest and sheds her burden of eggs, hundreds of tiny balls of potential life. An attending male fertilizes them. Then the pair moves on, leaving the eggs to the sea, which gently stirs them and packs the sand about them, grain by grain.

[4] Not all of the high tides of the next moon cycle will reach this spot, for the water movements vary in strength and at the moon's quarters are weakest of all. A month after the egg laying the embryos will be ready for life; then the high tides of another full moon will wash away the sand of the nest. The turbulence of the rising tide will cause the egg membranes to split, releasing the young crabs to a life of their own over their shallow shores of bays and sounds.

[5] But how do the parent crabs foresee these events? What is there in this primitive, lumbering creature that tells it that the moon is full and the tides are running high? And what tells it that the security of its eggs will somehow be enhanced if the nests are dug and the eggs deposited on these stronger tides of the moon's cycle?

[6] Tonight, in this setting of full moon and pressing tide, the shore speaks of life in a mysterious and magical way. Here is the sea and land's edge. Here is a creature that has known such seas and shores for eons of time, while the stream of evolution swept on, leaving it almost untouched since the days of the trilobites. The horseshoe crabs in their being obliterate the barrier of time. Our thoughts become uncertain: is it really today? or is it a million—or a hundred million years ago?

[7] Or sometimes when the place and mood are right, and time is of no account, it is the early sea itself that we glimpse. I remember feeling, once, that I had actually sensed what the young earth was like. We had come down through spruce woods to the sea—woods that were dim with drifting mists and the first light of day. As we passed beyond the last line of trees onto the rocks of the shore a curtain of fog dropped silently but instantly behind us, shutting out all sights and sounds of the land. Suddenly our world was only the dripping rocks and the gray sea that swirled against them and occasionally exploded in a muted roar. These, and the gray mists—nothing more. For all one could tell the time might have been Paleozoic, when the world was in very fact only rocks and sea.

[8] We stood quietly, speaking few words. There was nothing, really, for human words to say in the presence of something so vast, mysterious, and immensely powerful. Perhaps only in music of deep inspiration and grandeur could the message of that morning be translated by the human spirit, as in the opening bars of Beethoven's Ninth Symphony—music that echoes across vast distances and down long corridors of time, bringing the sense of what was and of what is to come—music of swelling power that swirls and explodes even as the sea surged against the rocks below us.

[9] But that morning all that was worth saying was being said by the sea. It

is only in wild and solitary places that it speaks so clearly. Another such place that I like to remember is that wilderness of beach and high dunes where Cape Cod, after its thirty-mile thrust into the Atlantic, bends back toward the mainland. Over the thousands of years the sea and the wind have worked together to build this world out of sand. The wide beach is serene, like the ocean that stretches away to a far-off horizon. Offshore the dangerous shoals of Peaked Hill Bars lie just beneath the surface, holding within themselves the remains of many ships. Behind the beach the dunes begin to rise, moving inland like a vast sea of sand waves caught in a moment of immobility as they sweep over the land.

10 The dunes are a place of silence, to which even the sound of the sea comes as a distant whisper; a place where, if you listen closely, you can hear the hissing of the ever mobile sand grains that leap and slide in every breath of wind, or the dry swish of the beach grass, writing its endless symbols in the sand.

11 Few people come out through that solitude of dune and sky into the vaster solitude of beach and sea. A bird could fly from the highway to the beach in a matter of minutes, its shadow gliding easily and swiftly up one great desert ridge and down another. But such easy passage is not for the human traveler, who must make his slow way on foot. The thin line of his footprints, toiling up slopes and plunging down into valleys, is soon erased by the shifting, sliding sands. So indifferent are these dunes to man, so quickly do they obliterate the signs of his presence, that they might never have known him at all.

12 I remember my own first visit to the beach at Peaked Hill Bars. From the highway a sandy track led off through thickets of pine. The horizon lay high on the crest of a near dune. Soon the track was lost, the trees thinned out, the world was all sand and sky.

13 From the crest of the first hill I hoped for a view of the sea. Instead there was another hill, across a wide valley. Everything in this dune world spoke of the forces that had created it, of the wind that had shifted and molded the materials it received from the sea, here throwing the surface of a dune into firm ridges, there smoothing it into swelling curves. At last I came to a break in the seaward line of dunes and saw before me the beach and the sea.

14 On the shore below me there was at first no sign of any living thing. Then perhaps half a mile down the beach I saw a party of gulls resting near the water's edge. They were silent and intent, facing the wind. Whatever communion they had at that moment was with the sea rather than with each other. They seemed almost to have forgotten their own kind and the ways of gulls. When once a white, feathered form drifted down from the dunes and dropped to the sand beside them none of the group challenged him. I approached them slowly. Each time I crossed that invisible line beyond which no human trespasser might come, the gulls rose in a silent flock and moved to a more distant part of the sands. Everything in that scene caused me to feel apart, remembering that the relation of birds to the sea is rooted in millions of years, that man came but yesterday.

[15] And there have been other shores where time stood still. On Buzzards Bay there is a beach studded with rocks left by the glaciers. Barnacles grow on them now, and a curtain of rockweeds drapes them below the tide line. The bay shore of mud and sand is crossed by the winding trails of many periwinkles. On the beach at every high tide are cast the shells and empty husks of all that live offshore: the gold and silver shells of the rock oysters of jingles, the curious little half decks or slipper shells, the brown, fernlike remains of Bugula, the moss animal, the bones of fishes and the egg strings of whelks.

[16] Behind the beach is a narrow rim of low dunes, then a wide salt marsh. This marsh, when I visited it on an evening toward the end of summer, had filled with shore birds since the previous night; and their voices were a faint, continuous twittering. Green herons fished along the creek banks, creeping at the edge of the tall grasses, placing one foot at a time with infinite care, then with a quick forward lunge attempting to seize some small fish or other prey. Farther back in the marsh a score of night herons stood motionless. From the bordering woods across the marsh a mother deer and her two fawns came down to drink silently, then melted back into their forest world.

[17] The salt marsh that evening was like a calm, green sea—only a little calmer, a little greener than the wide sheet of the bay on the other side of the dunes. The same breeze that rippled the surface of the bay set the tips of the marsh grasses to swaying in long undulations. Within its depths the marsh concealed the lurking bittern, the foraging heron, the meadow mouse running down long trails of overarching grass stems, even as the watery sea concealed the lurking squids and fishes and their prey. Like the foam on the beach when the wind had whipped the surface waters into a light froth, the even more delicate foam of the sea lavender flecked the dune barrier and ran to the edge of the marsh. Already the fiery red of the glasswort or marsh samphire flickered over the higher ground of the marsh, while offshore mysterious lights flared in the waters of the bay at night. These were signs of approaching autumn, which may be found at the sea's edge before even the first leaf shows a splash of red or yellow.

[18] The sea's phosphorescence is never so striking alongshore as in late summer. Then some of the chief light producers of the water world have their fall gatherings in bays and coves. Just where and when their constellations will form no one can predict. And the identity of these wheeling stars of the night sea varies. Usually the tiny glittering sparks are exceedingly minute, one-celled creatures, called dinoflagellates. Larger forms, flaring with a ghostly blue-white phosphorescence, may be comb jellies, crystal clear and about the size of a small plum.

[19] On beach and dune and over the flat vistas of salt marsh, too, the advancing seasons cast their shadows; the time of change is at hand. Mornings, a light mist lies over the marshes and rises from the creeks. The nights begin to hint of frost; the stars take on a wintry sparkle; Orion and his dogs hunt in the sky. It is a time, too, of color—red of berries in the dune thickets, rich yellow of the goldenrod, purple and lacy white of the wild asters in the fields. In the dunes and on the ocean beach the colors are softer, more subtle. There may be

a curious purple shading over the sand. It shifts with the wind, piles up in little ridges of deeper color like the ripple marks of waves. When first I saw this sand on the northern Massachusetts coast, I wondered about it. According to local belief the purple color comes from some seaweed, left on the shore, dried, and reduced to a thin film of powder over the coarser particles of sand. Years later I found the answer. I discovered drifts of the same purple color amid the coarse sand of my own shore in Maine—sand largely made up of broken shell and rock, fragments of sea urchin spines, opercula of snails. I brought some of the purple sand to the house. When I put a pinch of it under the microscope I knew at once that this came from no plant—what I saw was an array of gems, clear as crystal, returning a lovely amethyst light to my eyes. It was pure garnet.

[20] The sand grains scattered on the stage of my microscope spoke in their own way of the timeless, unhurried spirit of earth and sea. They were the end product of a process that began eons ago deep inside the earth, continued when the buried mineral was brought at last to the surface, and went on through millennia of time and, it may be, through thousands of miles of transport over land and sea until, tiny, exquisite gems of purest color, they came temporarily to rest at the foot of a glacier-scarred rock.

[21] Perhaps something of the strength and serenity and endurance of the sea—of this spirit beyond time and place—transfers itself to us of the land world as we confront its vast and lonely expanse from the shore, our last outpost.

ANALYTICAL READING

1. What common misconception about the sea does the author try to change?

2. What is significant about the horseshoe crabs?

3. What is memorable about the early morning sea?

4. What essential characteristics do the beaches of Cape Cod, Peaked Hill Bars, and Buzzards Bay have in common, and why are these characteristics important?

5. What does the phrase "time stood still" at the end of the first sentence in paragraph 15 mean to you?

6. What point does Carson make about the purple color of the sand at the end of the selection? What does this incident reveal about her?

REFLECTING

Point: What purpose do all the descriptions of the various shores serve? Try to state in one sentence the central idea of the selection.

Organization: Outline the main sections. Do you find an organizational pattern, or just a series of loose associations?

Support: Which paragraph did you find most vivid and why? Which words or phrases were most suggestive? Discuss the effect of the following: "a spectacle that echoes" (paragraph 2); "primeval magic" (paragraph 2); "a curtain of fog" (paragraph 7); "communion" (paragraph 14). Explain the impact of the series of questions in paragraph 5.

Synthesis: In paragraph 8, Carson states that perhaps only Beethoven's Ninth Symphony could do justice to her experience. Do you sometimes share that feeling about the inadequacy of words and the superiority of music? Do you think that Carson does convey her feelings effectively in words, thus perhaps contradicting herself? Has your feeling about the sea changed as a result of having read the selection? On the basis of this selection, why do you think that Carson became a conservationist?

Evaluation: Do you experience the author's feelings and relive them with her? How clearly has she conveyed her ideas about something that she found difficult to express in words? How convincing has she been about the sea? What are the strengths of her writing? The weaknesses?

FROM READING TO WRITING

1. Describe some natural setting that has stirred you, awaking you in some manner to a new understanding of nature and your place in it. Try to help your classmates who read the description to see and feel the place as much as you did.

2. Write a letter to your college or local newspaper about some building, painting, outdoor sign, advertisement, or other object that has attracted or repelled you, being careful to describe it clearly.

Character Sketch—
An Individual

THE GREAT BABE

Leo Durocher

BIOGRAPHICAL SKETCH

Leo Durocher was born in 1906 in West Springfield, Massachusetts. He played with the New York Yankees in the late 1920s, but he was better known as the scrappy captain of the St. Louis Cardinals' "Gashouse Gang," where he starred in the mid-1930s after two years with the Cincinnati Reds. Traded to the Brooklyn Dodgers in 1937, Durocher was their manager from 1939 to 1946. He returned to the Dodgers in 1948, but soon afterward became manager of their archrivals, the New York Giants, and remained there until the early 1950s. Among the many highlights of his colorful career were playing in several World Series, receiving a Manager of the Year award, and piloting the 1952 Giants into a World Series victory. Few baseball players and managers were as capable and controversial, or were associated with as many famous players, as Durocher.

PRE-READING

1. How does the first line indicate the writer's thesis? In the opening paragraph, what sentence shows the relationship between Ruth and Durocher at this time?

2. Which sentence in the first paragraph most clearly suggests how discussion of the subject, Babe Ruth, will be restricted or limited to one view or aspect of his life?

3. From the biographical sketch, would you expect Durocher to be a good judge of baseball players? Explain.

[1] Babe Ruth dominated that team totally. He dominated it on the field, and he dominated it even more off the field. He made more money by far than anybody else, and nobody resented it, because we knew he was putting money

in all of our pockets. There has never been anything like Babe Ruth, because everything about him was bigger than life.

² As far as I am concerned, there is only one all-time home-run champ and that's Babe Ruth. All right, Henry Aaron went to bat 2,890 more times in order to hit one more home run. All you have to do is use your common sense. I'm not trying to take anything away from Henry Aaron. Long before anybody even thought he had a shot at the record I had been saying that they ought to put Henry Aaron in the Hall of Fame right now. While he was still playing. Henry Aaron is a great all-around ballplayer who, among his other accomplishments, hit a lot of home runs. It you appreciate baseball in all its finer aspects, he has been a pleasure to watch.

³ Babe Ruth was *** The Sultan of Swat ***

⁴ Babe Ruth was *** THE BAMBINO ***

⁵ Babe Ruth was what you came to see!!!!

⁶ It was like going to a carnival, with Babe as both the star performer and the side-show attraction. Hell, that's what we called him: "You big ape." He was what a home-run hitter was supposed to look like. Wide, flat nose. Big feet. Little ankles. Belly hanging over his belt. All he had to do was walk on to the field and everybody would applaud. The air became charged with electricity. You just felt that something great was going to happen.

⁷ He'd twirl that big 48-ounce bat around in little circles up at the plate as if he were cranking it up for the Biggest Home Run Ever Hit—*you felt that*—and when he'd hit one he would hit it like nobody has hit it before or since. A mile high and a mile out. I can see him now, as I did so many times, just look up, drop the bat and start to trot, the little pitter-patter pigeon-toed, high-bellied trot that seemed to say, I've done it before and I'll do it again, but this one was for you. (Henry Aaron has a good home-run trot too, it's probably the most colorful thing about him. He holds his elbows up high, if you've ever noticed, and kind of swaggers from the waist up while he's kind of shuffling from the waist down.)

⁸ The Babe didn't even have to hit a home run to thrill you. He would hit infield flies that were worth the price of admission. The fielder would holler, "I got it," and he'd wait . . . and wait . . . and then he'd begin to stagger and finally he'd make a wild lunge. The ball would land fifteen feet away from him, and the Babe would be standing on second base with a big grin on his face.

⁹ You'll think I'm exaggerating when I say that it was a thrill to see him strike out. But not if you ever saw him. He would take that big swing of his and you could hear the whole stands go *Whooooossshhhh!* And then break out into wild applause as he was walking back to the bench.

¹⁰ Charisma counts. Charisma is what takes a superstar and turns him into a super-superstar. I've never seen a charismatic ballplayer who didn't make the team better than it figured to be, for the same reason that a charismatic actor makes any play he is in better than it should be. There is just something about these people that carries everybody else along with them.

[11] There's no question about it, Babe Ruth was the greatest instinctive baseball player who ever lived. He was a great hitter, and he had been a great pitcher. The only thing he couldn't really do was run, but when he went from first to third—or stole a base for you—he invariably made it because he instinctively did the right thing.

ANALYTICAL READING

1. What does the author mean in paragraph 1 when he says that Ruth was not resented because "he was putting money in all our pockets"?

2. Why does Durocher compare Ruth with Henry Aaron? What is the point about Aaron's having gone to bat many more times than Ruth? Does Durocher belittle Aaron while glorifying Ruth?

3. Explain the statement in paragraph 6 that Ruth was "both the star performer and the side-show attraction."

4. In what ways was it thrilling to watch Ruth bat even if he didn't hit a home run?

5. Why does Durocher discuss charisma?

6. What seldom-mentioned but important fact about Babe Ruth is mentioned in the last paragraph?

7. What does Durocher mean when he refers to Ruth as an "instinctive" player?

REFLECTING

Point: Which sentence best indicates Durocher's thesis?

Organization: How does each paragraph contribute to that thesis? Do you find any organizational pattern?

Support: What facts are used and what is their purpose? How do descriptions make this character sketch more interesting and vivid? What is the effect of the three parallel sentences in paragraphs 3, 4, and 5? Do the sentence fragments in paragraph 6 serve some purpose? Do you approve of the coinage "super-superstar" in paragraph 10? Discuss the voice and tone of the writer.

Synthesis: Can you understand after reading the excerpt why some older fans rave about the Babe? Are there modern players with charisma? Do you think another Babe Ruth is likely to appear one of these days, or has big-league baseball changed too much?

Evaluation: Has the author shown how Ruth "dominated" the team "even more off the field" and explained how "everything about him was bigger than life" (paragraph 1)? Is there too much discussion of Henry Aaron, resulting in an unnecessary digression? Is Ruth's charisma sufficiently explained?

FROM READING TO WRITING

1. For your classmates, write a character sketch about a college or professional athlete, trying to explain what makes him or her so exciting.

2. For a general audience, write a character sketch about a celebrity other than an athlete, trying to account for the person's charisma.

3. Write a character sketch about some charismatic person you have known personally, concentrating on those personality traits and accomplishments that contribute to the person's appeal.

THE WILD BOY AND THE CIVILIZED TEACHER

Harlan L. Lane

BIOGRAPHICAL SKETCH

Born in Brooklyn, New York, in 1936 Harlan Lane received degrees from Columbia University and a doctorate in psychology from Harvard; he also holds the Doctorat d'Etat, a French degree. Before accepting his present position at Northeastern University, he taught psychology at the University of Michigan, the Sorbonne, and the University of California at San Diego. He has also served as a consultant to the U.S. Office of Education and to UNESCO. He has received several honors for his research in linguistics and psychology, and his publications number more than seventy articles. His interest in the education of deaf children led him to write The Wild Boy of Aveyron, *from which this selection is taken.*

PRE-READING

This introduction to the book presupposes that the reader knows it is about an experiment to educate a boy found in the wilderness. But the opening paragraph suggests something more about the subject of the book. What is it, and which sentence best states it?

¹ The Luxembourg Gardens are an island of calm, of lawns, gravel paths, fountains, and statues, in the heart of left-bank Paris. On a summer's day in 1800, two young Frenchmen from the provinces met there for the first time and joined together their lives and futures. Although neither could have said so, each was engaged in a search whose success required the other.

² The first young man was well but not elegantly dressed in a long coat, drawn in at the waist, with full lapels. His curly hair fell in locks over a slanting forehead; his aquiline nose extended the plane almost as far as his jutting chin. Tightly drawn wide lips and large, dark brown eyes completed the Mediterranean features, set off by a broad white collar that rose funnel-like from his frilly white shirt. Jean-Marc-Gaspard Itard was twenty-six and had just be-

FROM Harlan L. Lane, *The Wild Boy of Aveyron* (Cambridge, Mass.: Harvard University Press, 1976), pp. 3–5. Copyright © 1976 by Harlan Lane. Reprinted by permission of the author and publishers.

come a doctor. He had left the barren village at the foot of the French Alps where he was raised and had come to Paris in search of a place for himself in the new social order that had emerged from the chaos of the Revolution. Paris at this time was vibrant: painting, theater, music, and literature were flourishing, abetted by the glittering salons of the very rich, the rendezvous of the intellectual and social elite. Medicine was surging ahead; it had become possible to protect people against disease by giving them some of the disease itself, although no one really knew why. One of Itard's teachers, Philippe Pinel, had just written the first book of psychiatric diagnosis, and had dramatically ordered inmates of the city's insane asylums to be unchained. The first anthropological society was formed, while expeditions returned with the flora, fauna, and inhabitants of Africa, Indonesia, and the New World, to the delight and fascination of naturalists, anatomists, and, above all, philosophers. Itard had left the relative isolation of the provinces in search of this excitement of senses and mind, to share in it, even to contribute to it if he could. His alliance with the strange boy rocking back and forth in front of him would surely bring him public attention; it might admit him to the ranks of the great doctors and philosophers of his time, or it might destroy his career right at its beginning.

³ The boy was twelve or thirteen years old, but only four-and-a-half feet tall. Light-complexioned, his face was spotted with traces of smallpox and marked with several small scars, on his eyebrow, on his chin, on both cheeks. Like Itard, he had dark deep-set eyes, long eyelashes, chestnut brown hair, and a long pointed nose; unlike Itard, the boy's hair was straight, his chin receding, his face round and childlike. His head jutted forward on a long graceful neck, which was disfigured by a thick scar slashed across his voice box. He was clothed in only a loose-fitting gray robe resembling a nightshirt, belted with a large leather strap. The boy said nothing; he appeared to be deaf. He gazed distantly across the open spaces of the gardens, without focusing on Itard or, for that matter, on anything else. That same day, he had ended a grueling week-long journey. By order of the Minister of the Interior, Napoleon Bonaparte's brother, Lucien, the boy had come to Paris from a forest region in the province of Aveyron in southern France. This journey was the latest development in his search, which began a year before when he clambered out of the forests, worked his way across an elevated plateau in the bitterest winter in recent memory, and entered a farmhouse on the edge of a hamlet. He exchanged the freedom and isolation of his life in the forests of Aveyron, where he had run wild, for captivity and the company of men in society. He came without a name, so he was called the Wild Boy of Aveyron.

⁴ Perhaps Itard knew better than the savants of his time, who expected to see in the boy the incarnation of Rousseau's "noble savage," man in the pure state of nature; perhaps he did not. What he saw, he wrote later, was "a disgustingly dirty child affected with spasmodic movements, and often convulsions, who swayed back and forth ceaselessly like certain animals in a zoo, who bit and scratched those who opposed him, who showed no affection for those who took care of him; and who was, in short, indifferent to everything

and attentive to nothing." The society of the eighteenth century had held both young men at bay, depriving the first of the best it had to offer, depriving the second of everything. Itard sought to master the ultimate skills of his culture— trained observation, persuasive language, social grace—the boy, their rudiments. So be it: they would help each other. Educating the boy would be a test of the new science of mental medicine and a proof of philosophy's new empiricist theory of knowledge. It would give still more justification for social reform by showing how utterly man depends on society for all that he is and can be. If the effort succeeded, the nineteenth century would give them their proper place, where the eighteenth had not.

ANALYTICAL READING

1. What was Itard's background? What does this information contribute to your understanding of the relationship between him and the boy?

2. What purpose is served by the description of Paris?

3. In what way was the influence of Pinel, Itard's teacher, important?

4. Compare and contrast the general appearance of Itard and the boy.

5. Are you familiar with the reference in paragraph 4 to Rousseau's "noble savage," or can you guess from the context what it means?

6. In what ways were both young men deprived by the society of their time?

7. What was Itard attempting to prove? If his work was successful, what implications would it have?

8. What pattern of comparison and contrast is used?

REFLECTING

Point: How do the first and final paragraphs present the thesis of the selection? How do the character sketches of Itard and the boy show their differences and yet establish a basic similarity?

Organization: Indicate the general organization of the selection. Point out where and why the second paragraph might have been divided into two parts.

Support: Indicate, by referring to words, phrases, allusions, and ideas, the kind of readers Lane is addressing. Explain the use of the colon in the middle of paragraph 2 after the statement that "Paris at this time was vibrant." Illustrate how the sentence in paragraph 3 about the boy's journey exemplifies the cumulative structure. Can you find several others?

Synthesis: Can you compare the challenge faced by Itard with the educational problems of today? Can you sense what motivated Itard? Was it self-interest or the desire to contribute to science or a combination of the two? Can you understand why the boy reacted as he did to those taking care of him? Is there some relationship between Itard and young people who today leave their home towns to seek success in New York, Hollywood, Nashville, or other places?

Evaluation: Are Lane's brief character sketches of the two young men effective? Is there more information about the wild boy than about Itard? Is this a weakness or not? Why? Has the writer pictured Paris of 1800 adequately? How successful has the writer been in introducing his book about the "wild boy"? What specifically contributes to his success or lack of it?

FROM READING TO WRITING

1. For your classmates, write a character sketch comparing and contrasting two friends or other people you know, such as your mother and father, two uncles or aunts, teachers, coaches, or clergy.

2. Write a paper for a general audience comparing and contrasting the family black sheep with some other relative.

3. For your classmates, write a character sketch of a high school, hometown, or college acquaintance who has some outstanding characteristic that makes him or her unique.

Character Sketch—A Type

A BOOK REVIEWER

George Orwell

BIOGRAPHICAL SKETCH

George Orwell (1903–1950) was born in Motihari, Bengal, educated in England at Eton, and joined the Indian Imperial Police in Burma. Resigning in protest against British imperialism, he then worked as a dishwasher, private tutor, teacher, and bookstore assistant. As a communist, he fought and was wounded in the Spanish Civil War, but later became disillusioned with communism. He is well known for his essays—particularly "Politics and the English Language" and "Shooting an Elephant," which are among the most anthologized prose writings—and for his novels, particularly Animal Farm *and* Nineteen Eighty-Four.

PRE-READING

1. What is a book reviewer?

2. Do you know anything about or have you read George Orwell's most famous books? Could he be writing about his early writing days? Should his views about the subject be considered authoritative? Why?

[1] In a cold but stuffy bed-sitting room littered with cigarette ends and half-empty cups of tea, a man in a moth-eaten dressing-gown sits at a rickety table, trying to find room for his typewriter among the piles of dusty papers that surround it. He cannot throw the papers away because the wastepaper basket is already overflowing, and besides, somewhere among the unanswered letters and unpaid bills it is possible that there is a cheque for two guineas which he is nearly certain he forgot to pay into the bank. There are also letters with addresses which ought to be entered in his address book. He has lost his address book, and the thought of looking for it, or indeed of looking for anything, afflicts him with acute suicidal impulses.

[2] He is a man of 35, but looks 50. He is bald, has varicose veins and wears spectacles, or would wear them if his only pair were not chronically lost. If

FROM George Orwell, "Confessions of a Book Reviewer," in *The Collected Essays, Journalism and Criticism of George Orwell*, vol. 4, ed. Sonia Orwell and Ian Angus (New York: Harcourt Brace Jovanovich, 1968). Copyright © by Sonia Brownell Orwell. Reprinted by permission of Harcourt Brace Jovanovich, Inc.

things are normal with him he will be suffering from malnutrition, but if he has recently had a lucky streak he will be suffering from a hangover. At present it is half-past eleven in the morning, and according to his schedule he should have started work two hours ago; but even if he had made any serious effort to start he would have been frustrated by the almost continuous ringing of the telephone bell, the yells of the baby, the rattle of an electric drill out in the street, and the heavy boots of his creditors clumping up and down the stairs. The most recent interruption was the arrival of the second post, which brought him two circulars and an income-tax demand printed in red.

3 Needless to say this person is a writer. He might be a poet, a novelist, or a writer of film scripts or radio features, for all literary people are very much alike, but let us say that he is a book reviewer. Half hidden among the pile of papers is a bulky parcel containing five volumes which his editor has sent with a note suggesting that they "ought to go well together". They arrived four days ago, but for 48 hours the reviewer was prevented by moral paralysis from opening the parcel. Yesterday in a resolute moment he ripped the string off it and found the five volumes to be *Palestine at the Cross Roads, Scientific Dairy Farming, A Short History of European Democracy* (this one is 680 pages and weighs four pounds), *Tribal Customs in Portuguese East Africa,* and a novel, *It's Nicer Lying Down,* probably included by mistake. His review—800 words, say—has got to be "in" by midday tomorrow.

4 Three of these books deal with subjects of which he is so ignorant that he will have to read at least 50 pages if he is to avoid making some howler which will betray him not merely to the author (who of course knows all about the habits of book reviewers), but even to the general reader. By four in the afternoon he will have taken the books out of their wrapping paper but will still be suffering from a nervous inability to open them. The prospect of having to read them, and even the smell of the paper, affects him like the prospect of eating cold ground-rice pudding flavoured with castor oil. And yet curiously enough his copy will get to the office in time. Somehow it always does get there in time. At about nine pm his mind will grow relatively clear, and until the small hours he will sit in a room which grows colder and colder, while the cigarette smoke grows thicker and thicker, skipping expertly through one book after another and laying each down with the final comment, "God, what tripe!" In the morning, blear-eyed, surly and unshaven, he will gaze for an hour or two at a blank sheet of paper until the menacing finger of the clock frightens him into action. Then suddenly he will snap into it. All the stale old phrases— "a book that no one should miss", "something memorable on every page", "of special value are the chapters dealing with, etc etc"—will jump into their places like iron filings obeying the magnet, and the review will end up at exactly the right length and with just about three minutes to go. Meanwhile another wad of ill-assorted, unappetising books will have arrived by post. So it goes on. And yet with what high hopes this downtrodden, nerve-racked creature started his career, only a few years ago.

⁵ Do I seem to exaggerate? I ask any regular reviewer—anyone who reviews, say, a minimum of 100 books a year—whether he can deny in honesty that his habits and character are such as I have described. Every writer, in any case, is rather that kind of person, but the prolonged, indiscriminate reviewing of books is a quite exceptionally thankless, irritating and exhausting job. It not only involves praising trash—though it does involve that, as I will show in a moment—but constantly *inventing* reactions towards books about which one has no spontaneous feelings whatever. The reviewer, jaded though he may be, is professionally interested in books, and out of the thousands that appear annually, there are probably fifty or a hundred that he would enjoy writing about. If he is a top-notcher in his profession he may get hold of ten or twenty of them: more probably he gets hold of two or three. The rest of his work, however conscientious he may be in praising or damning, is in essence humbug. He is pouring his immortal spirit down the drain, half a pint at a time.

ANALYTICAL READING

1. From the first two paragraphs, what overall impression do you get of the man being described?

2. Discuss the implications of Orwell's statement at the beginning of paragraph 3: "Needless to say this person is a writer."

3. What is the "howler" that the book reviewer might commit (paragraph 4)? What American word would you use as a synonym for this British one?

4. What does the book reviewer rely on to meet his deadline? How honest, reliable, and thorough will his reviews probably be?

5. What does Orwell think is the most miserable part of being a book reviewer?

REFLECTING

Point: To what extent has Orwell written a character sketch of a book reviewer and to what extent is he concerned with some broader issue? Discuss the main idea in the selection and several of the secondary ones.

Organization: What are the main sections of this character sketch? What does the last paragraph contribute?

Support: List the specific sights, sounds, and odors in the first two paragraphs. Select several of the British words in the essay and give their American synonyms or counterparts. Point out several figures of speech, such as the simile in paragraph 4 and the image in the last sentence. Select what you consider to be the most vivid sentence, the one that most aptly conveys the plight of the book reviewer.

Synthesis: Does Orwell make you sympathize with the reviewer, or do you feel that this man has sold out? Is there any relationship between the reviewer's attempt to meet his deadline and your own efforts to meet deadlines for your college papers and other assignments?

Evalution: Have you gained any new insight into reviewers? How would you extend the reviewer's predicament to that of other writers? What makes Orwell's character sketch particularly effective? Do you think that much of the material is autobiographical? Why or why not?

FROM READING TO WRITING

1. Write a character sketch for a general audience about someone in a job or position that seems interesting or exciting, but expose how boring and frustrating it really is. You might draw upon your own job or high school experiences, or the experiences of your parents or friends.

2. For a general audience, write just the opposite kind of character sketch, showing how a person in an apparently dull job or position finds it to be more challenging and stimulating than most people think it is.

3. For your classmates, write a character sketch of a high-school or college type: the cheerleader, the jock, the rock star, the social butterfly, the electronic or automobile freak. You may treat the type favorably or unfavorably; but let your word choice establish your attitude toward its characteristics.

AN INDIVIDUALIST: THE MAINE LOBSTERMAN

Gordon A. Reims

BIOGRAPHICAL SKETCH

Gordon A. Reims was born in New York City in 1918 and spent most of his life in the Long Island suburbs before moving to Maine in 1968. He studied creative writing at New York University and then pursued a career in publishing, working twenty-two years for Doubleday & Company and seven for the International Marine Publishing Company in Camden, Maine. Reims has written some forty magazine articles, chiefly about Maine and marine subjects, and many of his photographs of Maine have also been published.

PRE-READING

1. There are two parts to the title; what does each suggest?

2. What do the first two paragraphs tell you about what this character sketch will focus on?

[1] The lobsterman is an indelible part of the atmosphere, flavor and mystique of the Maine coastal town. When travelers go "down" to the coast of

FROM *Travel*, September 1976, pp. 41–44. Reprinted by permission of the author and *Travel* Magazine.

Maine they are invariably attracted and intrigued by those special sights and articles that pertain to lobstering. To those who have never seen them, or to those who have been away for a time, the sight of many white lobster boats scattered at moorings across a cove, all neatly facing in the same direction at the dictate of tide or wind, never fails to enthrall. There is an austerity, tenacity, and innate love for things marine evident in the character of the old wharves bedecked with traps and pails and other gear, or in the long-unpainted bait sheds, reeking with fish odors in their dark interiors, their outer walls gayly festooned with brightly colored lobster buoys drying in the sun.

[2] The lobsterman himself is a symbol, a mystery person to many who do not know him. He is a man who must pilot a seagoing truck from dawn until mid-afternoon, work hard and fast through lonely hours on the open water, and constantly wend his way through chains of rocky islets, past dangerous ledges, and across narrow tidal rips, ever-watchful of weather, wind and current.

[3] The colorful implements of the lobsterman are, of course, simply the basic necessities of his trade. The brightly colored buoys are the floating markers of which each lobsterman must have at least one or two hundred—and their colors are not decorative but dictated by law.

[4] When a lobsterman scatters a hundred or more traps into the sea, dropping each to the bottom, he has to be able to find them again a day or two later. The obvious way, of course, is by fastening one end of a line to the trap, and the other to an object floating on the surface. The buoys are the floating objects, and in order that a lobsterman may recognize his own, he colors it with his personal color-scheme—usually a bright, two-color combination. These color combinations are registered with the state, so that each lobsterman has official right to the use of his colors. A painted insignia on his boat displays the color-scheme, so that all may see he hauls his own traps.

[5] The lobsterman's other conspicuous items are his traps, and again each lobsterman has need of hundreds. His spares are usually stacked on or near the wharves, and add measurably to the distinctive atmosphere of a lobster port. Virtually all lobster traps (or "pots," as they were once invariably called) are alike. Basically a slatted wooden cage with a rope net in the entrance, the traps are about a yard long and much stronger than they look. The wood is heavy and seasoned, not only to withstand constant submersion, but frequent hard blows against rocks, wharves, and the sides of boats. The rope netting, frequently a hemp product called "pot warp," is simply but ingeniously devised so that a lobster can easily enter the trap, but will become hopelessly entangled if he attempts to leave. Weights are added to keep the traps anchored to the bottom.

[6] The lobster boats themselves are distinctive, and certainly recognizable once you've seen a few of them. Riding at their moorings in many a Maine cove and bay, they are very much a part of the pictorial lobster scene. Almost universally white, the lobster boats are usually 30 feet or a little more in length, and are low and broad with a high prow. The lobsterman operates the boat

standing up in a half-cabin just forward of center. His winch, his gaff hook and his bait pails, along with other paraphernalia, are all close beside him in this half-cabin, so that he may work entirely alone if need be.

[7] The lobsterman's task is not an easy one, and he's a hard worker. He must find his marker buoy, bobbing in the waves; maneuver the boat close alongside it, and then let go of the boat's controls in order to grasp the gaff hook and proceed with the hauling operation. While the lobster boat begins to bob and pitch and turn, with momentum and master gone, the lobsterman catches his rope line with the hook, loops it over a winch pulley, and hauls the trap up from the deep. While the bobbing boat, by now perhaps drifting broadside to the waves, tries best to hinder him, he must balance the trap on the rail, remove and peg legal-length lobsters, toss back crabs and "shorts," and then re-bait the trap and return it to the sea. All of these things he does as fast as his hands can move, the slowest chore being perhaps the pegging—the placing of a short peg in the joint of the lobster's claw, to prevent him from damaging lobsters or humans during the course of his captivity. Finally, the lobsterman grips the wheel again, roars the throttle, and surges forward to seek the next marker. The problem of pausing in choppy waters for a least a full minute or two is the reason most lobstermen, particularly those who work alone, stay in port when seas are rough or the wind rises.

[8] Lobstermen do fall overboard and drown in cold waters—usually because a slipper trap pulls a lone man from a pitching boat, or he becomes too daring in attempts to free a trap line that has fouled his propeller. Lobstermen also founder in stormy seas and freeze to death in blizzards when engines fail and cold winds force them seaward, but the tragedies are thankfully few and far between, limited generally to a comparatively reckless and mechanically unprepared few. The average lobsterman is capable but careful, heeds weather warnings and keeps his boat in shape, and will not place himself in danger.

[9] In the movies and on television, the lobsterman is sometimes pictured as a taciturn individual, speaking to strangers in dry monosyllables, and living in a hermit-like shanty. In books he is often a rugged and fearless man who constantly battles storm and fog to bring back the coveted lobster. Actually, he's rarely either of these, and lobstermen differ from each other as greatly as in other walks of life. Some are quiet old men, clinging tenaciously to ways of the past; some are young, restless, and employ every modern device in an effort to bring in the largest hauls, and some are kids just out of high school, pulling traps by hand from an outboard launch. All who are experienced and work at lobstering steadily make a decent income from it.

[10] If the various types of lobstermen do have any attributes in common, they are sharp eyes, deeply tanned and weather-beaten faces, strong arms and wrists, and a tendency to be gruff-voiced from repeatedly shouting across water. Psychologically, they are individuals—men for whom the pride of being one's own boss, in one's own boat, far outweighs the discomforts of the job. To rise before dawn and wrestle with pails and traps and rowing dinghies in the raw damp of a March morning is not always pleasant—but many a lobsterman

does it, month after month, year after year, sometimes until he is 80 or 90 years old.

[11] You can see the wharves and traps and bright buoys, along with lobstermen and their boats, at a hundred small towns and coves along Maine's coast. At New Harbor you can eat on the "upper deck" of a harborside restaurant and watch lobster boats come and go. At Friendship, where the sloops race each summer, there is a succession of weathered lobster wharves set against a backdrop of quiet water and green shores. At Tenants Harbor, Port Clyde, and Stonington there are similar views. Even at edges of the open sea, one may observe lobstermen at work. One or two lobstermen sink traps only a few yards from the granite ledges at Pemaquid Point, carefully maneuvering to keep the swells of the Atlantic from sweeping them to destruction. You can also see them lobstering close to shore at Camden Hills State Park, and along the bases of the cliffs at Acadia National Park. Wherever the colorful buoys dot the surface of bay or sea, a lobster boat will eventually come chugging along.

[12] The 1970s race along. Although new problems beset the lobsterman in these days of rising costs and sophisticated equipment, he still follows his traditional ways pretty much in the same manner—and if he has his way he'll never really change. The colorful sight of distinctive traps, buoys, boats and wharves will remain an important ingredient in the Down East scene.

ANALYTICAL READING

1.   What does Reims mean by the "mystique of the Maine coastal town" in the first sentence?

2.   What are the main tools of the lobsterman's trade? Describe each and explain its use and purpose. How do the descriptions of them contribute to Reims' characterization of the lobsterman?

3.   What makes the lobsterman's job so difficult?

4.   How do lobstermen differ from the way they are usually portrayed in books, television, and movies? Why do you think they have been stereotyped in this way? How does the author account for their individualism?

5.   According to the author, how can a vacationer in Maine spot lobstering waters?

REFLECTING

Point: What particular point does the author make about lobstermen? What is its significance? Which sentence best expresses it?

Organization: Point out the main sections of the essay. What do the first and last paragraphs contribute? What is the point of paragraph 11? In view of the probable readers of the magazine, could it have been omitted?

Support: How much does the writer assume his audience knows about the subject? In answering, refer to particular passages. Illustrate how the last sentence in paragraph 1 is a cumulative sentence; point out several others. Select other sentences that you find especially effective. Pick out several colorful words or phrases that enhance this character sketch.

Synthesis: Does the essay enable you to experience and understand the Maine lobsterman's life? Does it offer an insight into other occupations that attract individualists?

Evaluation: Should the thesis idea have been stated and developed earlier? Should paragraphs 3 and 4 have been combined—why or why not? Is the opening paragraph too long and too difficult, perhaps appealing to people familiar with the coast but not to inlanders? Can you understand the lure of lobstering as a life's occupation and the nature of the men who pursue it? If so, what specific features of the essay are noteworthy?

FROM READING TO WRITING

1. For a general audience, write a character sketch about a type of individualist you know, describing the routine activities and, if you wish, account for the desire for individualism.

2. For your classmates, write about a person engaged in some little-known occupation or hobby, describing the individual and the work in detail.

3. For the college newspaper, write about a fanatical fan: of some sport, of chamber music, of rock music, of poker, of soap operas, or of cars.

LIBRARIANS TODAY AND IN THE FUTURE
Richard Armour

BIOGRAPHICAL SKETCH

Richard Armour was born in San Pedro, California, in 1906. He completed his undergraduate work at Pomona College and received an M.A. and a Ph.D. from Harvard University. He has taught at several universities, including Texas and Northwestern, but has spent most of his academic career as an English professor and dean at Claremont College. Among his awards are a Ford Foundation Faculty Fellowship and a Harvard Research Scholarship. A popular lecturer and columnist, he has contributed more than 6,000 poems and prose pieces, most of them short and humorous, to over a hundred magazines in America and England. Among the more than fifty books that he has written or edited are Gold Is a Four Letter Word, American Lit Relit, *and* Going Around in Academic Circles.

PRE-READING

1. From the name of the book containing this selection, what approach do you suspect that the author will take toward his subject?

FROM Richard Armour, *The Happy Bookers* (New York: McGraw-Hill, 1976), pp. 123–32. Copyright © 1976 by Richard Armour. Used with permission of McGraw-Hill Book Company.

2. How is this inference confirmed in the opening paragraphs and the footnotes?

3. Does the information in the biographical sketch suggest the voice that you could expect to encounter in the essay?

[1] Librarians have come a long way since stone and baked clay tablets, hieroglyphics, Ashurbanipal, rolls of papyrus, parchment codices, Pisistratus, Tyrannion, the *scriptorium*, Gutenberg (or Gänsefleisch), Caxton, Manutius, incunabula, Benjamin Franklin, Andrew Carnegie, the founding of the A.L.A., and everything else treated so thoroughly[1] in the previous chapters. As Melvil Dewey would put it, "Hyly important chanjes hav been numerus."

[2] Of recent years, the image of the librarian as a little old lady in tennis shoes has changed drastically. She has come a long way. Now she wears shoes with high heels that enable her to reach the topmost shelf. Or, if she is really "with it," she may wear sandals.[2] More men are librarians and some are in subordinate positions, though not insubordinate. It is not enough to be merely a librarian, but one must be a reference librarian, a cataloger, a children's librarian, or an audio-visual specialist. Also a librarian can be in a university library, a law library, a public library, a medical library, an armed services library, a prison library, and on and on or, for the part-time librarian, on and off.

[3] As with paramedical personnel, there are more and more paralibrarians, not to be confused with a pair of librarians. The paralibrarian has no library degree and, just as her medical counterpart is not permitted to perform surgery, should be careful about doing any reader's advisory or reference work. Presumably giving wrong advice might lead to a malpractice suit.

[4] The work of librarians has necessarily changed because of changes in libraries. College and university libraries, for example, now have carrels. These are unlike Christmas carrels in that they are used the year around.[3] There are also rooms for showing films and slides as well as soundproof recording booths and darkrooms for developing photographs. Some of these rooms have dual-purpose uses, a room for showing films also being useful for lectures and for putting on plays and puppet shows for children. However, the darkroom is not recommended as a place for reading.

[5] Extended services of some school and public libraries necessitate that librarians handle many items in addition to books: motion picture films, filmstrips, slides, transparencies, overlays, disc and tape recordings, projectors, record players, tape recorders, cassettes, viewers for individual use, multimedia kits, etc. Whereas formerly nothing could upset a librarian more than loss of a book, now there could be such disasters as breakdown of a film projector, finding a crack in a record, or discovering a gap or erasure in a tape.

[1] If not exhaustively, then exhaustingly.

[2] Secretly she may imagine herself in an ancient Roman library, hoping the Emperor will drop in and she can get his autograph.

[3] The word "carrel" for a small enclosure or alcove is also spelled "carol" by architects, and "carol" comes from the Middle English word for dancing accompanied by singing. In fact it goes back to the Latin *choraules*, a flute player who accompanied the choral dance. Librarians would, I am sure, discourage singing, dancing, and flute playing in the modern carrel.

⁶ All of this means that a librarian is no longer fully prepared by Library School courses such as "Bibliography and Reference Sources," "Basic Cataloging and Classification," and "Administration of Libraries." Now the librarian must also take work in "How to Splice a Broken Film," "The Operation and Care of Tape Recorders," and "The Underlying Benefits of Overlays." Some librarians, proud of their open-mindedness, who were never shocked by a book, are shocked by a short circuit in the electronic equipment.

⁷ Many librarians have been unionized. They may have joined the union of a library staff, or government employees, or of plumbers, carpenters, or electricians. They had long used the union catalog, but now they carry a union card as well.⁴

⁸ Indeed the change has been so great of recent years that some libraries are no longer called libraries but are known as Learning Resource Centers or Media Centers. Librarians, however, are still generally known as librarians and not yet as Learning Resourcists or Media Centerists, though this may be only a matter of time.

⁹ A twentieth-century development has been the bookmobile, which permits librarians to take books to those who are unable to get to the library. The bookmobile also makes it possible to get outdoors and go for a spin into rural areas, especially enjoyable in the spring and fall. Though I have been searching the police records, I have been unable to find the driver of a bookmobile booked (an appropriate term) for speeding or drunken driving. There must be something about that precious cargo that keeps librarians on the straight and narrow and, when necessary, on the curved and narrow.

¹⁰ So much for librarians of today, though no reference has been made, among other things, to the interlibrary loan, the *Library Journal,* or the *Horn Book.*⁵ Let us now turn briefly to libraries and librarians of the future. This, it must be confessed, is purely speculative, since even the most thoroughly researched reference books give no clear picture of what conditions will be like in another fifty or one hundred years.⁶ Even the foreseeable future is hard to foresee.

¹¹ The way things are going, however, it would seem that microfilms will become micro-micro-microfilms, and a page can be reduced to the size of the head of a pin. According to John David Marshall,⁷ an important service of the librarian will be to direct the library patron, before he peers at the micro-micro-microfilm screen, to the resident optometrist (or ophthalmologist) to secure the proper glasses. On leaving, the reader will be provided with a seeing-eye dog to help him home.

---

⁴ They joined a union either by choice or by being outvoted. "In the union there is strength," they were told by union officials.

⁵ This last will be a disappointment to anyone wishing information about the trumpet or the tuba.

⁶ One book in this field that seems accurate and soundly based is John David Marshall's *A Fable of Tomorrow's Library,* Peacock Press, 1965. This scholarly work runs to seven pages, including the title page and copyright page.

⁷ *Op. cit.*

[12] But what will the librarian of the future be like? In order to cope with the minuscule microfilm books that have been forecast, the librarian also may have to be reduced to a comparable size, at least during working hours. This might be accomplished by scientific means or, more literarily, by using the technique Alice learned from the caterpillar in *Alice in Wonderland.* Thus the librarian before starting work would eat a piece of mushroom held in the right hand to become smaller, and at quitting time would eat a piece held in the left hand to become larger. Just who on the library staff or the Library Board would be identified with the White Rabbit, the March Hare, the Mad Hatter, and others will perhaps vary with the library.

[13] This is assuming, however, that there will still be flesh-and-blood librarians amidst the microfilmed books in the computerized library or Center for Storage and Retrieval. It is possible that librarians will be robots, controlled by Master Minds having mastery of a master computer at the Library of Congress.[8]

[14] Or there will be no libraries and no librarians, flesh-and-blood or otherwise. The onetime library patron will press a button and turn a dial on his TV, whereupon the requested book, in the desired language, will appear on the screen, the pages turning at the designated speed. The only interruptions will be commercials in which authors plug their latest books. These they will have produced with electronic typewriters that, when set to WRITE, will produce overnight a novel, biography, juvenile, or whatever the author has programmed.

[15] Then again, as some old-fashioned members of the literary community hope, authors will write much as they do now, books will be books, libraries will be libraries, and librarians will be librarians.

[16] Then science, helping but not taking over, can concentrate on finding a cure for the common cold, which sometimes keeps librarians away for a day or two from the work they love.

ANALYTICAL READING

1. In what respects has the image of librarians changed drastically, as Armour indicates?

2. Is it that librarians have changed or that libraries have changed, or both? Explain.

3. Is the author merely joking about such new courses as "The Underlying Benefits of Overlays," or is there an element of seriousness in his discussion of the new curriculum for library students? Explain.

4. Is there such a thing as a "union catalog" (paragraph 7)? What about the *Horn Book* (paragraph 10)? Check your dictionary.

5. In his discussion of micro-micro-microfilm (paragraph 11), Armour relies on a device called *reductio ad absurdum* that is used frequently in argument when

---

[8] These Master Minds may, of course, also be robots, operated by a superior race on a distant planet.

someone attacks something by showing how absurd it would be if carried to its logical conclusion. Explain how Armour uses this device humorously.

6. What fun does the author have with science and mechanization?

7. Do you think that Armour is in favor of the many changes that have occurred and may occur, or would he like libraries and librarians to remain just about as they are today? Justify your answer.

REFLECTING

Point: Can you formulate the main idea in this character sketch about librarians? Does any such statement fail to do justice to the essay? Why?

Organization: What are the main divisions of the selection? Where do these divisions occur? Show how Armour moves easily back and forth from writing about librarians to discussing libraries.

Support: What purpose do the footnotes provide? Armour uses puns to supply humor. Puns are not necessarily the lowest form of humor, but often a clever play on words in which a word is used to mean several things at once. Point out several puns and discuss how they help support an idea he is discussing. Is there any pattern in the use of humor—does it appear at the end of paragraphs that begin with relatively serious information? What language tendency is Armour satirizing when he states that libraries are often called Learning Resource Centers? To what kind of audience is Armour writing—a general or specialized one? If specialized, what educational background do the readers probably have? Explain. Which sentences or concepts did you find most amusing?

Synthesis: What is your general impression of librarians? Have you seen changes in your school, community, or college library? What changes do you foresee in the future? Is there a possibility that television will be used in some fashion? Are computers being used in libraries? Is it possible that librarians will be replaced by robots? Do you approve of the new libraries, or do you prefer the old ones? Explain. What experiences have you had with librarians?

Evaluation: Has the author been successful in writing an amusing but informative account of librarians today and in the future, or is the humor too extreme? Is there too much about libraries instead of librarians? If so, is that justified?

FROM READING TO WRITING

1. For your classmates, write a humorous character sketch of a type whose job may change because of future technology, such as the garbage collector, farmer, secretary, truckdriver, or supermarket checker. Let your imagination run rampant.

2. For a general audience, write a sketch of the future parent, showing how roles may change, how raising children may differ, and what the effects might be.

3. For your classmates, write a serious character sketch of a type that you know from your parents' acquaintances, from your own work, or from your experience. Suggestions: the school's bus driver, the high school basketball coach, the substitute teacher, the car salesperson, the barber or beautician, the carpenter.

THE WATCHER AT THE GATES
Gail Godwin

BIOGRAPHICAL SKETCH

Gail Godwin, a native of Birmingham, Alabama, graduated from the University of North Carolina, and received her master's and doctor's degrees from the University of Iowa. She has been a reporter for the Miami Herald *and has taught at the University of Iowa, Vassar College, and Columbia University. A contributor to* Harper's, McCall's, Cosmopolitan, Esquire, *and other periodicals, she has written four novels—*The Glass People, The Perfectionists, The Odd Woman, *and* Violet Clay*— and a collection of short stories,* Dream Children.

PRE-READING

1. Are titles always helpful in discerning the subject of an essay? Should they be? Is there another purpose they might serve?

2. What words in the opening sentence suggest the subject of the essay?

3. What point does the author seem to be making about the subject in the first sentences of each paragraph?

[1] I first realized I was not the only writer who had a restraining critic who lived inside me and sapped the juice from green inspirations when I was leafing through Freud's "Interpretation of Dreams" a few years ago. Ironically, it was my "inner critic" who had sent me to Freud. I was writing a novel, and my heroine was in the middle of a dream, and then I lost faith in my own invention and rushed to "an authority" to check whether she could have such a dream. In the chapter on dream interpretation, I came upon the following passage that has helped me free myself, in some measure, from my critic and has led to many pleasant and interesting exchanges with other writers.

[2] Freud quotes Schiller, who is writing a letter to a friend. The friend complains of his lack of creative power. Schiller replies with an allegory. He says it is not good if the intellect examines too closely the ideas pouring in at the gates. "In isolation, an idea may be quite insignificant, and venturesome in the extreme, but it may acquire importance from an idea which follows it. . . . In the case of a creative mind, it seems to me, the intellect has withdrawn its watchers from the gates, and the ideas rush in pell-mell, and only then does it review and inspect the multitude. You are ashamed or afraid of the momentary and passing madness which is found in all real creators, the longer or shorter duration of which distinguishes the thinking artist from the dreamer . . . you reject too soon and discriminate too severely."

[3] So that's what I had: a Watcher at the Gates. I decided to get to know

him better. I discussed him with other writers, who told me some of the quirks and habits of their Watchers, each of whom was as individual as his host, and all of whom seemed passionately dedicated to one goal: rejecting too soon and discriminating too severely.

⁴ It is amazing the lengths a Watcher will go to to keep you from pursuing the flow of your imagination. Watchers are notorious pencil sharpeners, ribbon changers, plant waterers, home repairers and abhorrers of messy rooms or messy pages. They are compulsive looker-uppers. They are superstitious scaredy-cats. They cultivate self-important eccentricities they think are suitable for "writers." And they'd rather die (and kill your inspiration with them) then risk making a fool of themselves.

⁵ My Watcher has a wasteful penchant for 20-pound bond paper above and below the carbon of the first draft. "What's the good of writing out a whole page," he whispers begrudgingly, "if you just have to write it over again later? Get it perfect the first time!" My Watcher adores stopping in the middle of a morning's work to drive down to the library to check on the name of a flower or a World War II battle or a line of metaphysical poetry. "You can't possibly go on till you've got this right!" he admonishes. I go and get the car keys.

⁶ Other Watchers have informed their writers that:

⁷ "Whenever you get a really good sentence you should stop in the middle of it and go on tomorrow. Otherwise you might run dry."

⁸ "Don't try and continue with your book till your dental appointment is over. When you're worried about your teeth, you can't think about art."

⁹ Another Watcher makes his owner pin his finished pages to a clothesline and read them through binoculars "to see how they look from a distance." Countless other Watchers demand "bribes" for taking the day off: lethal doses of caffeine, alcoholic doses of Scotch or vodka or wine.

¹⁰ There are various ways to outsmart, pacify or coexist with your Watcher. Here are some I have tried, or my writer-friends have tried, with success:

¹¹ Look for situations when he's likely to be off-guard. Write too fast for him in an unexpected place, at an unexpected time. (Virginia Woolf captured the "diamonds in the dustheap" by writing at a "rapid haphazard gallop" in her diary.) Write when very tired. Write in purple ink on the back of a Master Charge statement. Write whatever comes into your mind while the kettle is boiling and make the steam whistle your deadline. (Deadlines are a great way to outdistance the Watcher.)

¹² Disguise what you are writing. If your Watcher refuses to let you get on with your story or novel, write a "letter" instead, telling your "correspondent" what you are going to write in your story or next chapter. Dash off a "review" of your own unfinished opus. It will stand up like a bully to your Watcher the next time he throws obstacles in your path. If you write yourself a good one.

¹³ Get to know your Watcher. He's yours. Do a drawing of him (or her). Pin it to the wall of your study and turn it gently to the wall when necessary.

Let your Watcher feel needed. Watchers are excellent critics after inspriation has been captured; they are dependable, sharp-eyed readers of things already set down. Keep your Watcher in shape and he'll have less time to keep you from shaping. If he's really ruining your whole working day sit down, as Jung did with his personal demons, and write him a letter. On a very bad day I once wrote my Watcher a letter. "Dear Watcher," I wrote, "What is it you're so afraid I'll do?" Then I held his pen for him, and he replied instantly with a candor that has kept me from truly despising him.

   [14] "Fail," he wrote back.

ANALYTICAL READING

1. What does the Freud reference contribute to the essay? Who are Freud, Schiller, and Jung? How can you find out quickly?

2. Explain Schiller's allegory, stating exactly what "The Watcher at the Gates" is.

3. What's wrong with getting it "perfect the first time" or checking on a fact at the library?

4. What does Godwin mean in paragraph 9 about the Watchers demanding "bribes"?

5. Explain why deadlines are "a great way to outdistance the Watcher."

6. At what stage in the writing process can Watchers be helpful? Explain.

7. Why does the Watcher say "Fail" in the last paragraph?

REFLECTING

Point: What statement is Godwin making about the writing process?

Organization: Divide the essay into three sections, providing a heading for each. Discuss the techniques used to begin and end the essay. What is personification? How is it used here?

Support: Are sufficient examples provided? Are they specific or general or a combination of each? Explain. Do any seem exaggerated?

Synthesis.   To what lengths does your Watcher go? What stories have you heard about the Watchers of your friends or of professional writers? Do you have any advice for handling a Watcher?

Evaluation: What audience is Godwin writing to? In terms of this audience, what does Godwin contribute to their understanding of writing? How important is this? How effective is the opening sentence and paragraph? The closing paragraph? The tone? Has the use of personification contributed to or detracted from the essay? Why?

FROM READING TO WRITING

1. Write a similar essay personifying some force that keeps you from cleaning your room, doing your homework promptly, staying within your budget, sticking to your diet, or doing something else.

2. Write a letter to Gail Godwin, thanking her for making you more aware of your own Watcher and describing it.

3. Write an essay for a general audience personifying some object, like a car, a computer, or a programmed elevator that seems to have a life and personality of its own.

Assessment of
Reading and Writing Skills:
Descriptive Writing

Step 1

Read the essay that follows with the aim of understanding and recalling the important ideas. When you finish, note how long it took you to read the selection. Then close your book and write a summary of the important information without referring again to the essay. Indicate also your impression of the tone and word choice of the writer. You will be allowed 7 to 10 minutes to write; your instructor will establish the limit and tell you when the time is up.

BEAUTIFUL DAY
Dave Kindred

The snow was the packing kind. Just reach down with a gloved hand and there you had it: a wonderful, marvelous, round and firm, throw-it-at-his-head, take-me-back-to-my-childhood SNOWBALL. On a hill across the street, the enemy waited: Dale and Steve, both about 15, both right-handers. They had the faces of angels, but I knew better.

The barrage of snowballs was remarkable on several counts. Dale and Steve threw hard and straight. So did my son, Jeff, 14, who was allied with The Old Man. For reasons I prefer not to think about, my throws described gentle arcs and tended to sail to the right of the target.

Soon enough Dale and Steve scored the victory they sought. As I turned my back to scoop up ammunition, an artillery round collided with my cap, knocking it off my head. Everybody thought that was pretty funny, even my blood ally, who was laughing his thermal underwear off.

Those gentle arcs I mentioned—they became rainbows. If in the days of Frankie Avalon and Annette Funicello a kid could throw snowballs all day—

FROM *Louisville Courier-Journal*, 25 January 1977, p. C1. Copyright © 1977, The Courier-Journal, Louisville, Kentucky. Reprinted with permission.

throw them at trees, mailboxes, cars, wandering dogs—the same kid in Elton John's time has maybe 30 or 40 throws before paralysis sets in. So I moved on, leaving the three boys.

Mary Kay is 7 years old. She wore a red snow suit and was on her knees. In front of her were the beginnings of two snowmen.

"I'm going to make BIG snowmen," she said.

"As big as you?"

"Real big."

"How big?" I said.

"No, no, not THAT big. I'm going to make them kinda big and kinda little."

I passed Mary Kay's house on the way to the little creek that runs behind our subdivision. It was a beautiful day. New snow covered the old. The sun shone. One of the charms of this city is that you can be a part of it, yet be apart from it. Hardly 15 minutes from my office, the world was white velvet and silence. . . . This [day] was for snowballs and snowmen and walking in the snow.

It was a foot and a half deep in the woods behind Mary Kay's house. No one had walked there recently enough to leave footprints. I felt like an explorer, moving into uncharted land. The new snow gave way under my feet with the gentle sound of old paper tearing. Then, coming over a knoll, I saw the creek at the bottom of the hill, a black ribbon lying across the velvet.

From a distance came the bark of a dog. A boy somewhere shouted to a friend, "Hey, Tom, c'mon." Then it was quiet again. The creek isn't much. Maybe five feet wide, never deeper than a foot or so. It winds through the woods, past the ash trees, the maples, wild cherries, the tall cedars and beautiful white birches. Snow lay on branches, disturbed only by an occasional rush of air that caused a puff of powder to float down to the creek.

Water moved in the creek. Where the snow hit the water, ripples were born, the circles finally touching snow on the creek banks. I saw a squirrel a hundred feet away, my only company, and I wondered if he minded this heavy-footed intruder.

The ducks did. I'd walked on, toward the squirrel, when an incomprehensible noise broke the silence. Then I saw the ducks, a dozen of them, making a hurried take-off from an island of ice in the creek. Wings flapping, quacking, the ducks flew away, nine of them to the left of a clump of trees, the other three going to the right. They joined forces again on the other side of the trees.

On the way back home, I walked past Mary Kay's again.

The two snowmen were gone.

"What happened?" I said.

"I ruined them," she said brightly.

"Did you make them too big?"

"One got bigger than the other one, and the other one got ruined."

She was on her knees, having a grand time pushing snow with her red gloves. "Are you going to make another one?"

"Yes, I am. I'm going to start right now."

Dale and Steve, the flame-throwing snowballers, were shoveling snow out of a driveway. "Got you working." I said, probably unable to hide my Old Man intimation of it's-about-time.

I was 50 feet away, my back turned, when I heard a snowball land next to my feet. I turned. Dale, smiling, pointed to Steve.

Step 2

Read the following essay as quickly as you can without sacrificing your comprehension of the material. You will have a maximum of 3 minutes, 25 seconds (200 words per minute) to glean as much information as you can. If you finish before time is called, note how long it took you to read the selection.

Again, close your book and write a summary of the essay, including a statement about the tone and word choice. You will have 7 to 10 minutes for this task.

THOUGH UNOFFICIAL, SPRING COMES EARLY IN SPOTS
James Kilpatrick

It is a well-known fact—at least it is well-known here in Rappahannock County—that spring lives in a small swampy area just east of the Shade Road; about a quarter mile south of the apple packing plant. On the evening of Friday, March 11, spring made her first appearance.

The event is especially worth marking this year, for many discouraged Rappahannockers had begun to think the lady had moved away.

Under the heading of Mean and Dirty Winters, our winter certainly was small potatoes compared to the winter in Buffalo, Fargo and Brainerd, but it was a mean and dirty one all the same.

The winter went on and on. It would not stop. Our whole country froze up like a tray of ice. Pipes burst and water pumps froze, and it was a back-breaking effort to get hay to the cattle. Nobody could remember anything like it.

But a few days into March, things began to thaw; and on this particular Friday evening, driving home from Washington, there was spring beside the Shade Road. How do I know? Because you could hear the peepers. They are the certain heralds of April on its way.

If you have never met a peeper, you should know that a peeper is a tree frog. He is not bigger than a minute—maybe three-quarters of an inch, greenish-brown, pop-eyed. His sole function is annually to announce the entrance of spring. This he does by puffing up his tiny throat, thrusting his head forward, and crying PEEP-er, PEEP-er, PEEP, PEEP, PEEP-er. The note is somewhere

FROM *Lexington (Ky.) Herald-Leader,* 19 March 1977, p. A4. Reprinted by permission of the Washington Star Syndicate, Inc.

around B-natural above middle C; and after a winter like ours, it is the most welcome note ever sounded.

Spring turned up the next day, Saturday, in the great willow tree down at Woodville. Twenty-four hours earlier, the branches were bare. Now they had become a green cascade, a fountain of leaves as tiny as tears. People came to the Woodville Rural Independent Post Office to get their mail, and they looked at the willow across the road, and they all said the same thing: Spring!

After that, the lady turned up everywhere. The crocuses popped up, lavender and orange, and in the rock garden all kinds of tiny things began to lift their heads: Hepatica, aconite, dwarf daffodils.

The heather that had been given up for dead came back to life. The wild iris shouldered its sturdy frame above the ground. By Thursday, St. Patrick's Day, the fields were unmistakably green.

We hadn't seen a groundhog since October. Now, driving down the Rudasill's Mill Road, we saw four of them lumbering along: Four fat men out for a morning jog. They were sweating and complaining and saying, "Man, am I out of shape!" A dozen rabbits were on the lawn Wednesday evening, practicing sprints and hurdles. Chipmunks and squirrels appeared out of nowhere.

The past Tuesday, a pair of newly-wed bluebirds arrived, took one look at Apartment 4–D, our very best bluebird box, and promptly moved in. This is a truly elegant apartment, if you will forgive a little bragging, equipped with washer, drier, two ovens, air conditioning and wall-to-wall carpeting throughout. It rents promptly every spring.

A flock of 50 robins arrived. The killdeer is back, foolish bird, building a nest in a perilous spot right next to the driveway. Most of the juncos have gone, and the grosbeaks also, but we have a new visitor not registered before: A fox sparrow, and a handsome fellow he is.

With spring looking on, everyone has started plowing and planting and getting gardens ready. On the 12th, we planted onion sets and lettuce, and we raked up the backyard around the great chestnut oak that rules our hill. Once again we marveled at the sheer fecundity of nature. In an area perhaps 15 × 30 feet, we must have raked up—or pulled up—5,000 acorns. Half of them were trying to take root and turn into oak trees.

Down on your hands and knees, digging out these seedlings, you wonder what the chestnut oak knew what we didn't. A year ago, that tree saw the bitter winter coming; it produced more acorns that we ever have seen before, each fruitful with the germ of life. The winds of November scattered them, and the snow and ice watered them, and now spring warms them, and the wonder and the mystery all begin anew. Peepers and willows and bluebirds and groundhogs! The shut-in spirit opens like a crocus, lifting fragile petals to a welcome sun.

Step 3

Without looking back at the two essays, write a paragraph or two in which you evaluate them and explain how their ideas or issues are related. You may refer to your summaries, but not to the essays. Time: 10 minutes.

3 EXPOSITORY WRITING

The main purpose of exposition is to explain. Unlike personal and some descriptive writing, in exposition the writer usually tries to suppress strong personal or emotional involvement. The aim is to write objectively and clearly so that every reader understands exactly what the writer is saying. Even when expressing an opinion, the writer uses a rational approach, rather than strong emotional appeal. Thus, the emphasis changes from the writer-centered approach of personal writing to a reader-centered one. The audience is viewed not as a group of sympathetic, homogeneous friends sharing common interests and backgrounds, but as strangers, not necessarily hostile, but unknown and mixed— a conglomerate of many different people of all ages and of varying interests and backgrounds. Therefore, the writer is more formal, more precise, and more careful to choose words and grammatical usages that are generally approved. The personality of the writer may still be evident, but the voice used is businesslike, matter-of-fact, rather than folksy or intimate.

Because clarity is a main concern, form is significant in expository writing. Chronological or spatial organization is not always suitable for writing that explains *why* a certain phenomenon happens, *how* an operation works, precisely *what* a word or term means, or *why* a certain opinion is held. These writing problems require logical techniques: explaining cause-and-effect relationships, making comparisons and contrasts, dividing items into their component parts, supporting a thesis or main idea. These rhetorical tactics are used not only in the essay's overall organization but also in individual paragraphs throughout. In the most effective expository writing, form and meaning work together—one enhances the other. To illustrate, let us look at the four major forms of exposition: process description, classification, definition, analysis.

KINDS OF EXPOSITORY WRITING

PROCESS DESCRIPTION

Like other kinds of description, process description is informational, providing a detailed account of not only how something looks, but also *how* it works. Process writing traces the steps involved in an operation or task; consequently the writer should usually move chronologically from the first step to the last. In writing directions for starting a car, for instance, if a writer advises stepping on the accelerator before turning on the ignition, the readers who are novice drivers will never get the car started.

Although process descriptions are normally factual and informative, they can occasionally be as personal in nature as a personal description or essay. For instance, L. Rust Hills' "How to Eat an Ice-Cream Cone" (pages 167–73) outlines the step-by-step process of eating an ice-cream cone, but captures the fun of the activity as well. In his description, as in the more matter-of-fact ones included in this section, Hills follows an organizational pattern common to all process descriptions: presenting the essential steps in chronological order, indicating the purpose of each, showing any relationships between steps, and describing the end result.

CLASSIFICATION

Like process description, classification, definition, and analysis involve a sorting-out process. But instead of determining steps and their chronological sequence, these latter three divide an item into its component parts. In classification, the main purpose is to subclassify an item whose general category has already been established. The writer does not need to define the term, but does need to find a basis for classifying it. For instance, an article about concert bands can assume that all readers will have similar definitions of the term *concert band,* but one writer might subclassify the band on the basis of instrument families—woodwinds, brass, tympani, and so on. Another writer might choose to subdivide it into "voices"—tenor, baritone, bass. Or tone quality might serve as a third basis for classification. But once the basic criterion for classification is established, it must be used consistently throughout the paper. In "Letter Writers" (pages 184–86), this consistency is clearly exemplified as John Ciardi, a columnist for the *Saturday Review,* restricts his subclasses to those letter writers whom he does not answer.

DEFINITION

Although closely related to classification, definition must establish the general category (class) of an item before subdivision begins. As you know, a particular word may have many connotations, or shades of meaning. To define an item precisely, writers must sort out their particular meaning from other possible meanings. Sometimes definition can be handled simply; a one-word synonym or a short descriptive phrase following the word may suffice. At other times the kind of sentence definition found in dictionaries is sufficient. Often terms require extensive discussion: one then not only sorts out the meaning of the word from other meanings, but also subclassifies the term into its component parts, using the skills of classification. Definition then becomes an aim in itself. For instance, if the intent is to define the word *Republican* and then to subclassify it into various kinds or subclasses of Republicans, the writer must first pinpoint an exact meaning. *Republican* can refer to a form of government, to a political party or its members, to a set of political beliefs and ideals, or to a particular social stance. So you can see the need to provide a basis for subclassifying.

Before any discussion of subclasses can begin, the writer must establish a precise definition of the term, sorting out the intended meaning by revealing the features that distinguish it from other possible meanings. For instance, in a definition of *Republican* as one of the two major political parties in the United States, the writer would have to separate first that connotation of the word from the others and then would need to describe those distinguishing features of Republicanism that separate it from other political parties in the country. At that point the subclassification of *types* of Republicans could begin and the same procedures involved in writing classification would apply. A lengthy, well-developed definition is usually called an *extended definition*. Warren Boroson's "The Workaholic in You" (pages 195–200) is an extended definition that follows the pattern just outlined in defining *Republican*.

ANALYSIS

A third expository form that subdivides a subject into its component parts is analysis. In this process, the writer's purpose goes beyond dividing a whole into parts; the aim also is to examine and weigh the relationships of the parts to one another and to the whole.

There are several ways these relationships can be shown: one is by exploring causes and effects—what causes a certain phenomenon or what effect a situation has. In his "Prohibition and Drugs" (pages 222–24), Milton Friedman concentrates on effects: prohibition of alcohol and drugs causes or intensifies certain social ills.

Another analytical device is comparison and contrast. Theodore I. Rubin in "Competition" (pages 238–42) compares the cooperative attitudes of Swiss medical schools with the competitive ones of American schools to support his opinion that competition is destructive.

In analyzing a subject, writers also use examples or statistics to show relationships, as several essays in this section illustrate. Or writers may choose to use a combination of the techniques outlined here to explain *why* they feel or think as they do about a topic.

TACTICS FOR READING
EXPOSITORY WRITING

PRE-READING

Pre-reading expository writing requires rather specialized skills in addition to the suggestions offered earlier. In pre-reading process papers, search the opening and closing paragraphs for the initial and final steps in the process, so that you develop an overview of the situation. In reading through the first and last few paragraphs of a classification or a definition, try to determine not only the general subject of the paper but also the writer's basis for subdividing the subject as a whole into its component parts.

In pre-reading all explanatory papers, search the opening and closing paragraphs for the thesis statement—the sentence containing what seems to be the main idea. Remember also to use the title as a clue. Determining the thesis idea before you start to read gives you all the advantages that the writer had before writing—a focusing point for the discussion, a revelation of the purpose for writing, and an expression of the writer's attitude toward the subject.

ANALYTICAL READING

As we said in the Introduction to the book, form is extremely important in expository writing. Therefore, to understand explanatory material thoroughly, you should be generally aware of structure as you read. For instance, the demands of the processes involved in writing classification and definition almost automatically dictate their organizational scheme. The brief outline below indicates the kind of organization you might expect in each:

DEFINITION
- Discussion of other possible meanings (historical or current)
- A brief, "dictionary"-type definition that clearly defines the limits of meaning to be used in the paper
- Subclassification of a *class* into parts } CLASSIFICATION

REFLECTING

This step in reading exposition involves close analysis of the relationship between form and meaning. The following series of questions to ask yourself will be useful:

Point. Is the writer's main idea the one that you had arrived at in the pre-reading stage? Where in the essay is the best single statement of the main idea?

Organization. Can you easily outline the essay? If so, is it effectively organized? You might profit from trying to analyze what transitional devices the writer used to link the ideas together.

Support. What kinds of support did the writer rely on—examples, comparison and contrast, cause-and-effect relationships? Which did you find most effective?

Synthesis. Did the essay express some of the ideas that you hold about the subject or its parts? Do you have similar or conflicting views on the subject? Did you find ideas that relate to other works that you have read?

Evaluation. How effectively was information given? Did the writer's organizational scheme, word choice, and paragraph structure aid you in understanding the material? Did you have to reread sections, or did the style sometimes interfere—confusing rather than clarifying? Also, was the explanation complete, or did it omit some important material?

FROM READING TO WRITING

If you follow the reading suggestions, you will become aware of how writers use form in achieving clarity in expository writing. As a writer of exposition, you have the same responsibility. Learning from the organizational schemes, the paragraph structure, sentence devices, and word choice of the models you read, you can adapt those insights to your own writing.

Because most writers don't begin until they have devised some organizational format, you should follow that practice. Prepare some kind of outline before you start to write: know the basis you will use in subdividing processes; the point you wish to make; and the ideas you will use to support it. Work out the logical relationships you intend to reveal before you start to write the first draft. You will find that preliminary planning, rather than hindering your writing, frees you for the creative aspects of writing—designing effective sentence structure, making decisions about word choice, experimenting with paragraph devices.

But the organization of analysis papers follows different patterns. Generally, writers place the main idea or thesis of the paper early in the opening paragraphs; a discussion of the relationships of parts then follows. Occasionally, however, a writer may prefer the climactic effect of waiting until the end of the article to reveal the central point.

Following our suggestion in the Introduction to read both the opening and closing paragraphs in the pre-reading stage can help you to determine not only the writer's thesis, but often the method of analysis planned as well. In cause-and-effect analysis, for example, the thesis is often an *effect:* Drug prohibition has created drug abuse. What follows such a thesis is a series of main supporting ideas that serve as *causes* of the effect. As you read, make yourself aware of the underlying organizational scheme of the writer. A cause and effect treatment might look like this:

Thesis: Effect of a condition

(Because) I. ⎤
(Because) II. ⎬   Supporting ideas—component
(Because) III. ⎦   causes of the effect

Or if the writer is using comparison and contrast, one of the two following organizational patterns may be involved:

ITEM PLAN		POINT PLAN	
THESIS:	SETS UP BASIS FOR THE COMPARISON AND CONTRAST	THESIS:	SETS UP BASIS FOR THE COMPARISON AND CONTRAST
	ITEM I		POINT I
	SERIES OF POINTS		ITEM I ITEM II
	ITEM II		POINT II
	SERIES OF POINTS		ITEM I ITEM II

By making yourself sensitive to the subject of the paper, the restriction the writer imposes on the subject (thesis), and the method of analysis used in its illustration (body of the paper), you can make your reading skills more efficient, and also acquire an understanding of how writers solve complex organizational problems.

Process Description

HOW TO EAT AN ICE-CREAM CONE
L. Rust Hills

BIOGRAPHICAL SKETCH

L. (Lawrence) Rust Hills was born in Brooklyn, New York, in 1924. He received a B.S. degree from the Merchant Marine Academy, then earned B.A. and M.A. degrees from Wesleyan University. He has taught at several colleges, including Carleton, Columbia, and the New School for Social Research. In addition to being a former editor of Esquire, the Saturday Evening Post, *and* Audience *magazines, Hills has edited several anthologies, the best known being* How We Live (*with Malcolm Cowley*). *Currently a freelance writer, his articles, reviews, interviews, and humorous sketches have appeared in* The New Yorker, Esquire, McCall's, Harper's, *and other magazines.*

PRE-READING

1. What words in the title indicate the purpose of the essay?

2. What tone is established in the opening and closing paragraphs? Do you expect it to be a serious discussion? What might you expect from the fact that the article was first published in *The New Yorker?*

3. To what readers is the essay directed? Explain.

[1] Before you even get the cone, you have to do a lot of planning about it. We'll assume that you lost the argument in the car and that the family has decided to break the automobile journey and stop at an ice-cream stand for cones. Get things straight with them right from the start. Tell them that after they have their cones there will be an imaginary circle six feet away from the car and that no one—man, woman, or especially child—will be allowed to cross the line and reënter the car until his ice-cream cone has been entirely consumed and he has cleaned himself up. Emphasize: Automobiles and ice-cream cones don't mix. Explain: Melted ice cream, children, is a fluid that is eternally sticky. One drop of it on a car door handle spreads to the seat covers, to trousers, to hands, and thence to the steering wheel, the gearshift, the rear-

FROM L. Rust Hills, *How to Do Things Right* (New York: Doubleday, 1972), pp. 76–86. Reprinted by permission of Doubleday and Company, Inc. The article first appeared in *The New Yorker*, copyright © 1968 by The New Yorker Magazine, Inc.

view mirror, all the knobs of the dashboard—spreads *everywhere* and lasts *forever*, spreads from a nice old car like this, which might have to be abandoned because of stickiness, right into a nasty new car, in secret ways that even scientists don't understand. If necessary, even make a joke: "The family that eats ice-cream cones together sticks together." Then let their mother explain the joke and tell them you don't mean half of what you say, and no, we won't be getting a new car.

2 Blessed are the children who always eat the same flavor of ice cream or always know beforehand what kind they will want. Such good children should be quarantined from those who want to "wait and see what flavors there are." It's a sad thing to observe a beautiful young child who has always been perfectly happy with a plain vanilla ice-cream cone being subverted by a young schoolmate who has been invited along for the weekend—a pleasant and polite visitor, perhaps, but spoiled by permissive parents and scarred by an overactive imagination. This schoolmate has a flair for contingency planning: "Well, I'll have banana if they have banana, but if they don't have banana then I'll have peach, if it's fresh peach, and if they don't have banana or fresh peach I'll see what else they have that's like that, like maybe fresh strawberry or something, and if they don't have that or anything like that that's good I'll just have chocolate marshmallow chip or chocolate ripple or something like that." Then—turning to one's own once simple and innocent child, now already corrupt and thinking fast—the schoolmate invites a similar rigmarole. "What kind are *you* going to have?"

3 I'm a great believer in contingency planning, but none of this is realistic. Few adults, and even fewer children, are able to make up their minds beforehand what kind of ice-cream cone they'll want. It would be nice if they could all be lined up in front of the man who is making up the cones and just snap smartly when their turn came, "Strawberry, please," "Vanilla, please," "Chocolate, please." But of course it never happens like that. There is always a great discussion, a great jostling and craning of necks and leaning over the counter to see down into the tubs of ice cream, and much interpersonal consultation—"What kind are *you* having"—back and forth, as if that should make any difference. Until finally the first child's turn comes and he asks the man, "What kinds do you have?"

4 Now, this is the stupidest question in the world, because there is always a sign posted saying what kinds of ice cream they have. As I tell the children, that's what they put the sign up there for—so you won't have to ask what kinds of ice cream they have. The man gets sick of telling everybody all the different kinds of ice cream they have, so they put a sign up there that *says.* You're supposed to read it, not ask the man.

5 "All right, but the sign doesn't say strawberry."

6 "Well, that means they don't have strawberry."

7 "But there *is* strawberry, right there."

8 "That must be raspberry or something." (Look again at the sign. Raspberry isn't there, either.)

⁹ When the child's turn actually comes, he says, "Do you have straw-berry?"

¹⁰ "Sure."

¹¹ "What other kinds do you have?"

¹² The trouble is, of course, that they put up that sign saying what flavors they have, with little cardboard inserts to put in or take out flavors, way back when they first opened the store. But they never change the sign—or not often enough. They always have flavors that aren't on the list, and often they don't have flavors that *are* on the list. Children know this—whether innately or from earliest experience it would be hard to say. The ice-cream man knows it, too. Even grownups learn it eventually. There will always be chaos and confusion and mind-changing and general uproar when ice-cream cones are being ordered, and there has not been, is not, and will never be any way to avoid it.

¹³ Human beings are incorrigibly restless and dissatisfied, always in search of new experiences and sensations, seldom content with the familiar. It is this, I think, that accounts for people wanting to have a taste of your cone, and wanting you to have a taste of theirs. *"Do* have a taste of this fresh peach—it's delicious," my wife used to say to me, very much (I suppose) the way Eve wanted Adam to taste her delicious apple. An insinuating look of calculating curiosity would film my wife's eyes—the same look those beatiful scary women in those depraved Italian films give a man they're interested in. "How's *yours?"* she would say. For this reason, I always order chocolate chip now. Down through the years, all those close enough to me to feel entitled to ask for a taste of my cone—namely my wife and children—have learned what chocolate chip tastes like, so they have no legitimate reason to ask me for a taste. As for testing other people's cones, never do it. The reasoning here is that if it tastes good, you'll wish you'd had it; if it tastes bad, you'll have had a taste of something that tastes bad; if it doesn't taste either good or bad, then you won't have missed anything. Of course no person in his right mind ever *would* want to taste anyone else's cone, but it is useful to have good, logical reasons for hating the thought of it.

¹⁴ Another important thing. Never let the man hand you the ice-cream cones for the whole group. There is no sight more pathetic than some bumbling disorganized papa holding four ice-cream cones in two hands, with his money still in his pocket, when the man says, "Eighty cents." What does he do then? He can't hand the cones back to the man to hold while he fishes in his pocket for the money, for the man has just given them to *him.* He can start passing them out to the kids, but at least one of them will have gone back to the car to see how the dog is doing, or have been sent round in back by his mother to wash his hands or something. And even if papa does get them distributed, he's still going to be left with his own cone in one hand while he tries to get his money with the other. Meanwhile, of course, the man is very impatient, and the next group is asking him, "What flavors do you have?"

¹⁵ No, never let the man hand you the cones of others. Make him hand them out to each kid in turn. That way, too, you won't get those disgusting

blobs of butter pecan and black raspberry on your own chocolate chip. And insist that he tell you how much it all costs and settle with him *before* he hands you your own cone. Make sure everyone has got paper napkins and everything *before* he hands you your own cone. Get *everything* straight before he hands you your own cone. Then, as he hands you your own cone, reach out and take it from him. Strange, magical, dangerous moment? It shares something of the mysterious, sick thrill that soldiers are said to feel on the eve of a great battle.

[16] Now, consider for a moment just exactly what it is that you are about to be handed. It is a huge, irregular mass of ice cream, faintly domed at the top from the metal scoop, which has first produced it and then insecurely balanced it on the uneven top edge of a hollow inverted cone made out of the most brittle and fragile of materials. Clumps of ice cream hang over the side, very loosely attached to the main body. There is always much more ice cream than the cone could hold, even if the ice cream were tamped down into the cone, which of course it isn't. And the essence of ice cream is that it melts. It doesn't just stay there teetering in this irregular, top-heavy mass; it also melts. And it melts *fast*. And it doesn't just melt—it melts into a sticky fluid that *cannot* be wiped off. The only thing one person could hand to another that might possibly be more dangerous is a live hand grenade from which the pin had been pulled five seconds earlier. And of course if anybody offered you that, you could say, "Oh. Uh, well—no thanks."

[17] Ice-cream men handle cones routinely, and are inured. They are like professionals who are used to handling sticks of TNT; their movements are quick and skillful. An ice-cream man will pass a cone to you casually, almost carelessly. Never accept a cone on this basis! Too many brittle sugar cones (the only good kind) are crushed or chipped or their ice-cream tops knocked askew, by this casual sort of transfer from hand to hand. If the ice-cream man is attempting this kind of brusque transfer, keep your hands at your side, no matter what effort it may cost you to overcome the instinct by which everyone's hand goes out, almost automatically, whenever he is proffered something delicious and expected. Keep your hands at your side, and the ice-cream man will look up at you, startled, questioning. Lock his eyes with your own, and *then*, slowly, calmly, and above all deliberately, take the cone from him.

[18] Grasp the cone with the right hand firmly but gently between thumb and at least one but not more than three fingers, two-thirds of the way up the cone. Then dart swiftly away to an open area, away from the jostling crowd at the stand. Now take up the classic ice-cream-cone-eating stance: feet from one to two feet apart, body bent forward from the waist at a twenty-five-degree angle, right elbow well up, right forearm horizontal, at a level with your collarbone and about twelve inches from it. But don't start eating yet! Check first to see what emergency repairs may be necessary. Sometimes a sugar cone will be so crushed or broken or cracked that all one can do is gulp at the thing like a savage, getting what he can of it and letting the rest drop to the ground, and then evacuating the area of catastrophe as quickly as possible. Checking the cone for possible trouble can be done in a second or two, if one knows where

to look and does it systematically. A trouble spot some people overlook is the bottom tip of the cone. This may have been broken off. Or the flap of the cone material at the bottom, usually wrapped over itself in that funny spiral construction, may be folded in a way that is imperfect and leaves an opening. No need to say that through this opening—in a matter of perhaps thirty or, at most, ninety seconds—will begin to pour hundreds of thousands of sticky molecules of melted ice cream. You know in this case that you must instantly get the paper napkin in your left hand under and around the bottom of the cone to stem the forthcoming flow, or else be doomed to eat the cone far too rapidly. It is a grim moment. No one wants to eat a cone under that kind of pressure, but neither does anyone want to end up with the bottom of the cone stuck to a messy napkin. There's one other alternative—one that takes both skill and courage: Forgoing any cradling action, grasp the cone more firmly between thumb and forefinger and extend the other fingers so that they are out of the way of the dripping from the bottom, then increase the waist-bend angle from twenty-five degrees to thirty-five degrees, and then eat the cone, *allowing* it to drip out of the bottom onto the ground in front of you! Experienced and thoughtful cone-eaters enjoy facing up to this kind of sudden challenge.

[19] So far, we have been concentrating on cone problems, but of course there is the ice cream to worry about, too. In this area, immediate action is sometimes needed on three fronts at once. Frequently the ice cream will be mounted on the cone in a way that is perilously lopsided. This requires immediate corrective action to move it back into balance—a slight pressure downward with the teeth and lips to seat the ice cream more firmly in and on the cone, but not so hard, of course, as to break the cone. On other occasions, gobs of ice cream will be hanging loosely from the main body, about to fall to the ground (bad) or onto one's hand (far, far worse). This requires instant action, too; one must snap at the gobs like a frog in a swarm of flies. Sometimes, trickles of ice cream will already (already!) be running down the cone toward one's fingers, and one must quickly raise the cone, tilting one's face skyward, and lick with an upward motion that pushes the trickles away from the fingers and (as much as possible) into one's mouth. Every ice-cream cone is like every other ice-cream cone in that it potentially can present all of these problems, but each ice-cream cone is paradoxically unique in that it will present the problems in a different order of emergency and degree of sensitivity. It is, thank God, a rare ice-cream cone that will present all three kinds of problems in exactly the same degree of emergency. With each cone, it is necessary to make an instantaneous judgment as to where the greatest danger is, and to *act!* A moment's delay, and the whole thing will be a mess before you've even tasted it (*Figure 1*). If it isn't possible to decide between any two of the three basic emergency problems (i.e., lopsided mount, dangling gobs, running trickles), allow yourself to make an arbitrary adjudication; assign a "heads" value to one and a "tails" value to the other, then flip a coin to decide which is to be tended to first. Don't, for heaven's sake, *actually* flip a coin—you'd have to dig in your pockets for it, or else have it ready in your hand before you were

handed the cone. There isn't remotely enough time for anything like that. Just decide *in your mind* which came up, heads or tails, and then try to remember as fast as you can which of the problems you had assigned to the winning side of the coin. Probably, though, there isn't time for any of this. Just do something, however, arbitrary. Act! *Eat!*

Figure 1   Figure 2

[20] In trying to make wise and correct decisions about the ice-cream cone in your hand, you should always keep the objectives in mind. The main objective, of course, is to get the cone under control. Secondarily, one will want to eat the cone calmly and with pleasure. Real pleasure lies not simply in eating the cone but in eating it *right.* Let us assume that you have darted to your open space and made your necessary emergency repairs. The cone is still dangerous—still, so to speak, "live." But you can now proceed with it in an orderly fashion. First, revolve the cone through the full three hundred and sixty degrees, snapping at the loose gobs of ice cream; turn the cone by moving the thumb away from you and the forefinger toward you, so the cone moves counterclockwise. Then, with the cone still "wound," which will require the wrist to be bent at the full right angle toward you, apply pressure with the mouth and tongue to accomplish overall realignment, straightening and settling the whole mess. Then, unwinding the cone back through the full three hundred and sixty degrees, remove any trickles of ice cream. From here on, some supplementary repairs may be necessary, but the cone is now defused.

[21] At this point, you can risk a glance around you. How badly the others are doing with their cones! Now you can settle down to eat yours. This is done by eating the ice cream off the top. At each bite you must press down cautiously, so that the ice-cream settles farther and farther into the cone. Be very careful not to break the cone. Of course, you never take so much ice cream into your mouth at once that it hurts your teeth; for the same reason, you never let unmelted ice cream into the back of your mouth. If all these procedures are followed correctly, you should shortly arrive at the ideal—the way an ice-cream cone is always pictured but never actually is when it is handed to you *(Figure 2).* The ice cream should now form a small dome whose circumference exactly coincides with the large circumference of the cone itself—a small skull-cap that fits exactly on top of a larger, inverted dunce cap. You have made order out of chaos; you are an artist. You have taken an unnatural, abhorrent,

irregular, chaotic form, and from it you have sculpted an ordered, ideal shape that might be envied by Praxiteles or even Euclid.

²²Now at last you can begin to take little nibbles of the cone itself, being very careful not to crack it. Revolve the cone so that its rim remains smooth and level as you eat both ice cream and cone in the same ratio. Because of the geometrical nature of things, a constantly reduced inverted cone still remains a perfect inverted cone no matter how small it grows, just as a constantly reduced dome held within a cone retains *its* shape. Because you are constantly reshaping the dome of ice cream with your tongue and nibbling at the cone, it follows in logic—and in actual practice, if you are skillful and careful—that the cone will continue to look exactly the same, except for its size, as you eat it down, so that at the very end you will hold between your thumb and forefinger a tiny, idealized replica of an ice-cream cone, a thing perhaps one inch high. Then, while the others are licking their sticky fingers, preparatory to wiping them on their clothes, or going back to the ice-cream stand for more paper napkins to try to clean themselves up—*then* you can hold the miniature cone up for everyone to see, and pop it gently into your mouth.

ANALYTICAL READING

1. In most process descriptions, the paper starts with the first step in the actual process. What advantage does Hills gain by starting at the planning stage? Would you recommend this for every process description? Why or why not?

2. How does Hills use cause-and-effect reasoning in the essay? Cite examples.

3. Point out places where you noticed effective uses of metaphor.

4. Where does Hills use exaggeration (hyperbole) to create humor?

5. Does Hills show the relationship of one step of tackling an ice-cream cone to the next? Discuss.

6. Where does he describe the process in terms of playing a game?

7. Do we get any hint of Hills' family relationships? Or his personality? How?

REFLECTING

Point: Why do you think Hills wrote the article (other than for money!)? Does it contain serious advice, or is it just an amusing account?

Organization: Make a topic outline of the process as he describes it. Is the organization chronological or spatial? Explain.

Support: Point out how the writer's descriptions and analogies help to support his steps in the process. Why is dialogue handled differently in paragraph 3 and paragraphs 5—11?

Synthesis: Did this remind you of times you have gone for ice-cream cones with your own family? Did you take the family dog with you? If so, what steps could you add to Hills' process description?

Evaluation: Did you enjoy reading the article? Why or why not? Discuss word choices that you found especially delightful. Does Hills forget about the children late in the essay?

FROM READING TO WRITING

1.   Hills is able to see the ritual in ice-cream eating. What other food did you eat as a child that became a ritual—milkshakes, popcorn, watermelon, cotton candy, pizzas? Write a similar humorous process description explaining to a student from a foreign country how to eat a typical American food.

2.   Write a process description explaining how to do something that you have done so often that it has become a ritual, such as how to get permission to use the family car; how to walk in the rain; how to go camping or picnicking; how to skip a day of high school; or how to use a skateboard. Try to make the paper entertaining: one that would interest a general audience.

3.   Describe to someone who did not grow up in this country the steps in a game you played as a child. Be sure to avoid unnecessary or irrelevant information.

GO TIE A FLY
J. A. Maxtone Graham

BIOGRAPHICAL SKETCH

J. A. Maxtone Graham is a native of Streatley, England, a town on the Thames River about fifty miles west of London, but he spends much of his time at his fishing cottage in southern Scotland. He describes himself as a "free-lance fisherman" who must work as a free-lance writer to support his true vocation. His articles have appeared in such magazines as Signature, Sports Afield, McCall's, *and* Lithopinion. *This article is a segment of a longer piece that appeared in the latter publication.*

PRE-READING

1.   If you knew nothing about fishing, would you be able to tell from the title what the article is about? Would the final paragraph give you a clue? What word play is possible on the imperative structure of the title?

2.   What tone is established in the first paragraph of this selection? What kind of person is revealed? Do you expect serious, objective instructions?

 [1] . . . I drifted into fly-tying by mistake. While at school, I studied the clarinet and at some concert or other won first prize in the clarinet division—not surprising, since I was the only entrant. They gave me a bookshop certificate worth 10 shillings and sixpence, doubtless imagining I would buy an ad-

FROM *Lithopinion*, Spring 1975, pp. 43–45. Reprinted by permission. Original drawings by Betty Fraser.

vanced book on clarinet-playing with it. What I bought was L. Vernon Bates's *Tackle-making for Anglers.* Bates taught his readers to make rods, reels, bobbers, nets, sinkers, spinning-reels—and flies. I couldn't afford to buy all the proper materials, so I simply stole: My younger brother and sister still haven't forgiven me my assaults on their possessions when I was inventing the Red Indian and Golliwog, a somewhat gaudy fly that did indeed catch a trout or two. Through the goodwill of farmers, poulterers, drapers, and older friends of mine who had guns, I built up a fair stock of birds and animals.

[2] Then, during some wartime move, I somehow lost my precious box of materials and it wasn't until 20 years later, when a horse-racing acquaintance gave me four tips for that afternoon at the local track, that I resumed my interest in fly-tying. I hadn't bet for years, but I lashed out in a complicated parlay of mixed doubles. Three of the horses won, and I was the richer by nearly $40. I didn't want to do anything foolish with that windfall, like save it; so the next day I went to the tackle shop, bought a vise and quite a good basic lot of materials. I found the old skill nearly gone, but I struggled through the making of one fly, and pretty awful it was. I took it to the river, tied it to the nylon leader, cast it to a rising trout, which ate it first shot. The fish weighed nearly two pounds. I knew that every fisherman in the area had been after it for weeks—and I can only suppose that it had never seen anything quite like the terrible concoction I threw at it.

[3] Since then, I haven't bought a single fly; but, of course, I found the original $40 went nowhere. I have to stock thousands of hooks in three-dozen shapes and sizes; over 30 colors of wires and tinsels; feathers from 40 or 50 different types of birds; furs and skins from seal, deer, rabbit, squirrel and mole. A junk dealer wouldn't give me a dollar for the lot, yet I suppose they must have cost me the price of a third-hand car. By the end of my life, I might be showing a small profit.

[4] Many materials are just not to be bought. A farmer I know owns a rooster whose neck feathers (which provide the hackle, the fibers flaring out around the eye of the hook) are of a delicate and desirable greenish-olive shade. He has promised them to me, but the wretched bird seems destined to live forever.

[5] One day, I read of an ancient fly-dressing which demanded, for the body of the fly, some pinkish fur obtained from the underbelly of a half-grown hedgehog, a material that sounds like what suitors of princesses in fairy tales have to dig up. No one—not surprisingly—in the fly-material trade seemed to stock it. Then, my attention was caught by the words of the barmaid in the local pub. Her children had found this baby hedgehog, she said, and were trying to raise it at home, on milk and stuff. "Listen, Valerie," I whispered to her when I got her alone in the corner of the bar. "Valerie, I've got to speak to you . . . Please remember, if anything should happen to that animal . . ." Knowing about my hobby, she looked at me suspiciously. "Listen you," she said through clenched teeth for all to hear, "you keep your hands off my hedgehog!"

⁶ The experienced flytier is characterized by constant dissatisfaction with his past efforts. You manufacture a superb imitation of the Blue-Winged Olive: Its three tails, its brown-olive body, its slate-blue hackles and wings look just right, and you catch your limit of fish on Wednesday. On Thursday, perhaps through some subtle change in the sun's light, or a difference in the clarity of the water, the trout ignore it. Back to the drawing board: Friday's fly has a touch more orange than olive, and the hackles are enriched by a few fibers of brown. Come Saturday, when the fish won't look at either, the flytier feels he may have been on the wrong track after all. A few months later, after his formal release from the mental home, he starts all over again.

⁷ There is little doubt that some thoughtful psychiatrist will have advised him to take up some therapeutic hobby, something skilled but relaxing, like maybe tying flies . . .

⁸ Want to try fly-tying? Except for the hook, the materials are at hand in every household. The instructions that follow will enable you to make a very simple fly that is certainly capable of catching a trout: your child, or parent or spouse cannot fail to be impressed.

⁹ You need: a fishhook, with a ring or eye at the blunt end (which can be bought at any tackle shop—ask for size 8), about three-quarters of an inch long; a foot of sewing thread, silk preferred; the stub of a candle; a small piece of aluminum foil, about three-eighths by one-half inches; a feather from a pillow, one of those long ones with fibers about half-an-inch long, a pair of small sharp scissors; and nail polish.

¹⁰ Wax the thread by drawing it through the candle several times. Hold the hook at the bend, in the fingers of the left hand.

¹¹ Lay a short length of the thread along the shank, or straight part, of the hook. Starting about one-eighth inch from the eye, wind the rest of the thread over the short length, making each successive turn farther to your *left*.

¹² Continue winding to your *left* until you reach the start of the hook's bend.

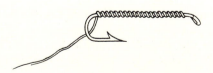

¹³ Tie a half-hitch (the simplest form of knot) around the shank. This gives the thread a firm grip and provides a surface on which you can build the rest of the fly.

¹⁴ Take the aluminum foil and wrap it as best you can round the now thread-covered shank, leaving the loose end of the thread uncovered. Wind the thread in spaced turns (about six times) around the aluminum, to form a ribbing that protects the aluminum from the teeth of the innumerable trout that will soon be irresistibly drawn to your new lure. Make another half-hitch at the right-hand end of the aluminum, about an eighth-inch from the eye of the hook.

¹⁵ Strip from the feather any fluffy bits at the stem's thick end. Hold the tip of the thin end between forefinger and thumb of the left hand. With the fingers of the right hand, brush back the remaining fibers of the feather until they stick out at right angles to the stem. This will form a "neck" between the brushed and unbrushed fibers.

¹⁶ With the stem of the feather pointing to your left, apply the "neck" to the place of your last half-hitch. Tie in place with four turns of thread; tie a half-hitch.

[17] Cut off the extreme tip of the feather, which should be protuding over the eye of the hook. Next, holding the shank with your left hand, start winding the feather round the hook, making sure that each turn is to the *right* of the previous one. The fibers will splay outward, at right angles, to the shank. Give the feather three turns round the hook, then tie it down with four turns of thread. (This is the part where you wish you had three hands.)

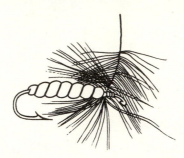

[18] Make one more half-hitch. Cut off any surplus stem of the feather. Then make two or three more half-hitches near the eye of the hook. (There is a more professional way of finishing off, but it's quite difficult, and you may have suffered enough already.) Paint a little nail polish over the last visible turns of thread and allow to dry. Trim thread.

[19] You have now made a basic trout-fly. Tell someone to go catch a fish with it.

ANALYTICAL READING

1. What information about fly-tying does the reader gain from the first seven paragraphs? What can the reader infer about the availability of materials? What would be lost if these paragraphs were omitted?

2. Why is paragraph 9 a good device for a process description paper?

3. Could you follow each step without its accompanying illustration? Why or why not?

4. Where is irony used in the article? Does it have a use other than revealing the writer's personality?

REFLECTING

Point: What does the reader learn besides how to tie a fly? Does the essay say something about hobbies?

Organization: Is the process arranged chronologically? How does the sentence structure help to reveal the organization?

Support: How do the very specific instructions dealing with direction help the reader in duplicating the process? Refer to a particular example.

Synthesis: Were you reminded of an unusual hobby you have? How does this essay relate to Hills' "How to Eat an Ice-Cream Cone" (pages 167–73)? Even if you don't fish, did you enjoy the essay?

Evaluation: Did you find the article entertaining as well as informative? Why or why not? Are the instructions clear and simple enough for anyone to follow? Why or why not?

FROM READING TO WRITING

1.   For your classmates, write a paper about an unusual skill you have, giving instructions that will enable another person to repeat the process. Examples: making kites, blowing glass, making ceramic pots, knotting macramé, cooking crêpes. If you like, you might write a few paragraphs explaining how you became interested in this hobby. Note that Graham's article is restricted to one kind of fly.

2.   Write an objective process description, telling a general audience how to perform some sequential task, such as fixing a carburetor; planting a garden; making pickles; changing a flat tire; restringing a tennis racquet. Either avoid using jargon or be sure to define terms with specialized meanings.

BIRD PHOTOGRAPHY IN YOUR OWN BACK YARD

The Editors of *Changing Times*

PRE-READING

1.   What do the opening paragraphs contribute to your knowledge of the essay's subject, which is stated in the title?

2.   What tone is established in these paragraphs?

[1] Surely, shooting a charging rhino with a camera must be a terrific thrill, although both the suspense and the expense might be unbearable.

FROM *Changing Times*, September, 1980, pp. 16, 19. Reprinted with permission from *Changing Times* Magazine. ©1981 Kiplinger Washington Editors, Inc., December 1981.

² There's excitement, too, in catching a nuthatch coming headfirst down a tree and into your viewfinder. And when it sets its head just so and you fire at precisely the right split second, that little nuthatch provides as lovely a color portrait as any other wild thing in this wide, wild world.

² Every bird that comes to pose in your backyard—or would come, if invited—could make its own interesting, attractive picture, too.

⁴ So why leave wildlife photography to the safari crowd when the fun of it awaits you, economically and conveniently, right at home?

⁵ Throngs of people are ready for this sport. The birds are at hand even in large cities, where 20% or more of all households actively lure birds to their yards by putting out free lunch. Nationally we spend an estimated $40,000,000 a year for birdhouses and bird feeders, another $100,000,000 or so on birdseed, just to bring birds within eyeshot. And where the eye can see, the camera can record.

⁶ You can't photograph a bird to good effect with just any fixed-focus snapshooter, of course. Bird photography does call for equipment more sophisticated than that, but nothing particularly unusual. If you do enough picture taking to consider photography a hobby rather than a mere adjunct to your memory book, your accessory bag may already hold all the gear you need.

⁷ Photographically, the challenge is this. A bird comes into your yard a wild creature, wary of people and all sudden movements, elusive, swift in motion, a thing of beauty at rest or in flight, and often quite small—in the case of the chickadee only four inches stem to stern.

⁸ You wish to photograph this tiny subject in its natural, sheltering surroundings. Getting close enough for so small a bird to fill an entire frame may be out of the question; getting close enough to reveal the bird in detail and to distinguish it from its background is perfectly possible and practical.

⁹ This is the equipment you need:

¹⁰ A good 35mm single-lens reflex camera. A built-in light meter isn't necessary; in fact, you won't need a light meter at all when you're working with a flash. Be aware that the new automatic 35mm SLRs also have disadvantages: The need to override their automatic features complicates what a bird photographer has to do.

¹¹ A telephoto lens of at least 250mm focal length, plus a set of extension tubes that go between the camera body and the lens to increase magnification and get you in tight for closeups. The powerful, expensive mirror-reflex telephoto lenses aren't particularly satisfactory for bird work. Depth of field is shallow, giving distorted backgrounds.

¹² A tripod sturdy enough to hold your camera steady when the telephoto lens is attached. Birds are fast-moving subjects, and a high-magnification lens magnifies any camera movement. Successful unsupported hand-held shots of birds are rare.

¹³ A strobe-light flash attachment, preferably with a second, or "slave," unit. The first unit provides primary illumination while the slave fills in backlight and eliminates the heavy shadows that one-source lighting produces.

Flash also permits you to use the slower films, which give better color with less graininess than fast ones. For many bird photographers Kodachrome 64 is the film of choice.

[14] A cable release, preferably a long one, to minimize the movement required to snap the shutter.

And that's it, enough to put you in business—except for one more item, which you can't pick up at the camera store: concealment for yourself.

[15] You could set up your tripod, focus on a favorite perch or feeder, position the strobes halfway between camera and subject, run the release cable through the kitchen door and retire there in shadowy, relaxing comfort to await action. Purposeful bird photographers, however, generally provide field concealment for themselves, usually in the form of a portable screening shelter called a "blind" unless you're from England, in which case it's a "hide."

[16] Pup tents can be used as blinds, but they are hot and cramped, especially if you spend several hours in one, as is likely. John Trott, a wildlife photographer who has taught at the Smithsonian Institution and whose bird portraits have appeared in National Audubon Society and the National Geographic Society publications, knows exactly what a blind should be: porous, portable and sufficiently capacious to accommodate the photographer plus tripod, camera and chair. If you're to have the patience to wait out a good shot, comfort counts.

[17] Blinds can be improvised. The early ones were umbrellalike contraptions, draped to the ground like Victorian ladies. A parked car may do; birds quickly grow accustomed to cars. An inverted refrigerator carton once served Trott as a blind from which to make his portrait of the Belding ground squirrel for the U.S. Forest Service. His favorite blind, though, is a dome-shaped frame of aluminum tubing covered with burlap fastened with those big, plastic-headed safety pins sold for diapers. This blind works fine, he reports, provided the frame is firmly planted in the ground and the covering is tightly pinned to prevent flapping.

[18] Snapping shots of birds at the seed feeder is the natural way for a neophyte bird photographer to, shall we say, try his wings. At that location you at least know just where the birds will perch, which birds will drop in and what time of day they are likely to visit. You can get set up and be ready with a reasonable expectation of success.

[19] Taking pictures at the feeder is fun, and it is gratifying to build an album or a slide show featuring your regular clientele. You will soon note, though, that there is much more bird activity afoot than just plucking seeds from the feeder. Some birds prefer dining off seed spilled on the ground rather than at your hanging snack bar. And still others simply prefer fare other than seeds. The colorful woodpecker's appetite, for example, runs more to wood-boring insects, whereas the bossy mockingbird favors berries.

[20] Besides, you tire of seeing that same old feeder in every shot you print. So you begin thinking of ways to photograph a wider variety of birds and to picture them in more natural settings. You strew more seed on the ground for

the ground feeders and a suet ball brings in both the woodpecker and the mockingbird. A bit later you stuff suet into a hole in a section of tree trunk and get the same birds in settings that are less backyardy and more photogenic.

²¹ Water is another dependable attraction, and not just in a dry spell. A birdbath placed on the ground can be easily masked by vegetation. It should be shallow, hold clear water and have a rough surface. Birds will drink from a smooth basin but not bathe in it; you'll miss all the lively action shots. The sound of falling water makes a birdbath particularly irresistible. Let a hose drip slowly on leaves around the bath, or position a lawn sprinkler so that the spray wets leaves above the bath.

²² Probably you can invent other enticements, too. How good the resulting pictures are depends on how well you observe the behavior of the birds you attract. They are creatures of habit and will use the same approach patterns to get to food or water over and over again. Notice how they descend from the treetops by moving from one favorite perch to another in the same sequence. Take good advantage of those behavior patterns and you'll get some good pictures.

²³ Know your subject. Know its ways. And wait. When the moment comes, focus on the bird's eye if you can.

²⁴ Bird photography is not entirely a matter of f-stops and shutter speeds. There is a conscience factor, too. Consider what you are doing with your bird-seed, suet and free water. To put it plainly, you are baiting wild creatures for your own esthetic and photographic pleasure. And what you do holds some potential dangers for your subjects.

²⁵ There is the dependence question. If you teach birds to depend upon you for food and drink, then you must be dependable in return. Don't stop providing it just because you run out of film or enthusiasm.

²⁶ Then there is the cat problem. Attract birds and you also attract their enemies. Explore ways you might protect your birds from predators. It is not difficult, for example, to place a feeder out of cat's reach or to surround a feeding or bathing area with an inconspicuous, cat-foiling barrier of chicken wire. You can shoot over the wire. It won't spoil your pictures.

²⁷ Finally, if temptation arises, resist photographing nestlings. Leave nests completely alone. Ordinarily birds nest in concealment, so you can't photograph an undisturbed nest. If you tie back foliage or cut branches away so that your camera can peek, you also tip predators to the nest's location. So keep away. A nestling's chances are slim enough without having them made worse by thoughtless interference.

ANALYTICAL READING

1. What audience is the article written for? Explain the meaning of this statement in paragraph 6: "If you do enough picture taking to consider photography a hobby rather than a mere adjunct to your memory book, your accessory bag may already hold all the gear you need."

2. Why is so much of the article devoted to the discussion of a blind?

3. Explain what the author means by "a conscience factor" in photographing birds (paragaph 24).

4. What are the main steps in taking backyard bird pictures?

5. Why is information about f-stops and shutter speeds omitted?

REFLECTING

Point: Does the article describe how professionals take pictures of backyard birds or does it inform readers how to take these pictures? Explain. What else does the reader learn about birds besides photographing them?

Organization: How long is the introduction? What is its purpose? What are the main divisions of the article? How might their order have been changed? Which order is the most effective?

Support: Which specific details are most helpful? Why are the new 35mm SLRs mentioned in paragraph 10?

Synthesis: Do you agree that the required equipment is "nothing particularly un-usual" for most serious photographers? Is the article written for people who want to take occasional pictures of birds or for would-be bird photographers? Do people have to know or learn much about birds to follow the instructions provided?

Evaluation: How interesting and informative is the article? Does it seem to provide all the necessary details and practical advice about taking bird photos? Does it explain not only what bird photographers have to do but why they should do it?

FROM READING TO WRITING

1. For the audience of *Changing Times,* write an article about taking photos of children, family members, sporting events, or some similar subject. Try to make it interesting as well as informative.

2. For a college newspaper, write a process description about changing oil in a car, starting a car with jumper cables, registering for a class, baking bread, getting a date, dieting, or starting a jogging routine.

Classification

LETTER WRITERS
John Ciardi

BIOGRAPHICAL SKETCH

John Ciardi was born in Boston, Massachusetts, in 1916 and educated at the University of Michigan, where he received an M.A. degree. After teaching at Harvard, Rutgers, and several other universities, he became poetry editor of Saturday Review *from 1956 to 1972. Since then he has served as one of the magazine's contributing editors. Ciardi is known mainly for his many books of poetry, for which he has received numerous awards, but he has also written books of literary criticism, books for children, and an excellent translation of Dante's* Inferno.

PRE-READING

1. From the title and the opening lines, what is the item or class you expect to be subclassified in this essay?

2. What kind of voice is projected in the opening and closing paragraphs? Is the tone serious or sardonic, formal or informal, angry or slightly annoyed?

3. From the biographical sketch, what kind of letters would you expect John Ciardi to receive?

[1] Readers of this magazine [*Saturday Review*], as I have long since discovered, are Herculean letter writers. Whether to confirm or confound, the subscription list makes itself felt. Three qualified cheers for them! What is more disappointing for a writer than to drop his published words into a bottomless well of silence from which no echo is ever to be heard? But if only a man could wish for an echo without wishing-up a roar. I dare not count how many letters are at this moment spilling over my desk unanswered. They are unanswered for the good reason that to answer them would not be a chore but a career. And because I have other work to do.

[2] One good reason, of course, for answering mail is that it is fun to receive it. But there are even better reasons for not answering, and certainly the first among them is the fact that many letters ought not to have been written in

FROM John Ciardi, *Manner of Speaking* (New Brunswick, N.J.: Rutgers University Press, 1972), pp. 118–21. Copyright © 1972, Rutgers, The State University. Reprinted by permission of the author.

the first place. In terms of any reasonable social contract, the writer should have known better.

³ In the first rank of such social misdemeanors I certainly place the scores of letters I have received from misguided students fumbling at a term paper, who have blandly asked me in effect to write it for them. At first—because I have myself put in too many years as a teacher—I used to reply with a mild avuncular scolding, along with a brief summary of basic reference works available in any good library, and the assurance that the writer would neither lose social standing nor be shot down by the librarian were he to pass quietly through the front door and look for himself.

⁴ But no more. I am persuaded we have reared an unmannerly generation unto ourselves. Not one of the young whelps I wrote to took the trouble to say thanks. (One mother did write to thank me for the scolding I had given her young whippersnapper.) Not one enclosed a self-addressed stamped envelope. And not one knew enough to frame a considered (which is to say answerable) question, but only such hopelessly hopeful casts as "Please tell me what you think of William Butler Yeats. I am doing my term paper on him." I must insist on assuming that one is absolved when bad manners are added to ignorance, and that there need be no social debt to answer such letters.

⁵ The second rank of letters that must be discarded at once is made up of those that come along with a batch of bad poems (they are always bad) and a request for a personal critique.

⁶ Certainly I understand why a writer wants someone else to read his work and to comment on it. I have sought such reading and comment all my life. "Well, isn't that a debt?" one hears the letter writer thinking. Yes it is, and I do my best to repay it to my students. I try to repay it there because, there, repayment is more or less possible. I *can* criticize their writing—for better or worse—but only after at least a month of setting forth principles, rules of thumb, and a vocabulary of criticism.

⁷ What happens, on the other hand, when the editor confuses himself with the teacher? If a student passes in a poem whose diction is random I can say, "Show me how the overtones of your words bear any relation to one another." Or in another case I can say, "Break the poem down into its mechanical and meaningful stresses and show me what you think happens between the two." The student—at least the good one—will understand because he has been to the lectures that set up those criteria and because he has done supervised exercises in analyzing those elements of the poem.

⁸ But suppose I mention overtones to a reader? Or mechanical and meaningful stresses? I have not answered the mail, I have only multiplied it. Back comes another letter saying, "What is an overtone? And what is a mechanical and a meaningful stress?"

⁹ By that point the hour has struck. Nothing less than 10,000 words could begin to make sense. I compute that I am offered daily the opportunity to write roughly 500,000 such words, and I leave simple addition to attest that the answer must be no. Sorry, but no. And since that is the only possible answer, why answer at all?

[10] The third rank in the army of the pestiferous carries a banner that reads "Chatty Pals." Between Bangor and San Diego there must be millions of literate and semiliterate people with nothing to do, and the itch to write long soul-searching single-spaced letters. To engage in two such correspondences would be a life work for an unfastidious Lord Chesterfield. Forgive me, dear leisured friends, but once again, the rest is silence.

[11] I suspect we are all overcivilized these days, and it does in fact cause an uneasy feeling (at first) to leave letters unanswered. But in time the callouses grow. And in the name of reason, is everyman's mistake a duty upon me once any given writer has bought a postage stamp?

[12] But to ask that question is a way of wheedling toward an easy self-justification. A writer has purer grounds within his own need. The Age of Public Relations is upon us all, and where is the executive, however majestic in his banker's eye, who has not established a routine for making some sort of acknowledgement of every scrap of mail? He has heard the legend that the busiest and most important men always find time to answer, and since he is obviously busy and obviously important, he will not disappoint his own legend of himself. After all, it takes only a standard-forms book and a secretary who knows her business—both of them deductible items.

[13] No thanks. I shall rest with the writer's purer refusal. What need he care about the legends of importance? He has the holy right of his own selfishness. His attention belongs to himself and to his writing. He owes no private pieces of his mind to junior college students in Minnesota, to hopefully hopeless young writers on Long Island, or to chatty housewives in Tuscaloosa. What he has to say is best said within the formalities of his writing. Whatever he has written well is there to be received by anyone able to read it, and nothing he might scribble out of a misplaced sense of public relations will take its place.

[14] In the name of that indispensable selfishness, therefore, and to ask of such readers as are willing to grant it, their mercy upon selfish need, I hereby sweep the desk clean of all letters I have lacked the courage to chuck out before, and for such amends as it may offer, I begin this column in which I shall try to answer, among other things, some of the questions that crop up in the mailbag, at least such as involve matters of general interest. I have some thought of getting down to occasional specific discussion of poetic techniques. And obviously—along with every other columnist—I must take a shot at saving the world now and then. At saving it or damning it.

[15] My plans are no more definite than that. Except to look at the mail when there is time, and to give most letter writers the fullest assurance that unless their letters are answered here they will not be answered at all.

ANALYTICAL READING

1. Is classification the main purpose of the paper, or does Ciardi have another aim? If so, what?

2. How does Ciardi use cause-and-effect reasoning in the article?

3. How many kinds of letter writers does Ciardi describe? Where does he include himself?

4. What devices in the opening and closing paragraphs help to establish the tone of the article? By what devices is the tone sustained throughout?

5. What kind of readers is Ciardi addressing? Discuss their age, schooling, and so on, referring to the article to support your conclusions.

6. Indicate word choices that you found especially effective.

REFLECTING

Point: What is the point of the article? Is classification the primary purpose, or is it secondary to something else? Discuss.

Organization: Can you construct an organizational scheme showing the subclasses Ciardi outlines? Is there any pattern in his ranking of letter writers?

Support: How do examples serve as support?

Synthesis: Could you sympathize with Ciardi's aversion to answering letters? What kinds of letters do you find particularly unrewarding to answer? Do you expect letters that you write to magazines and businesses to be answered?

Evaluation: If you had not already known from the biographical sketch, would you have found evidence in the writing style that Ciardi is a poet? Did you respond favorably or unfavorably to his sarcastic humor? Why? Does Ciardi make a convincing case for not answering letters?

FROM READING TO WRITING

1. If you have dealt with the public serving in a restaurant, clerking at a supermarket or department store, delivering papers, and so on, classify customers according to their behavior. Write to a general audience, emulating Ciardi's approach of expressing a strong opinion about the people being classified.

2. Write a humorous or satirical classification paper for your classmates in which you subclassify the kinds of people you have telephone conversations with.

3. As you walk on campus for several days, jot down the insignia that adorn T-shirts. Grouping these "messages" into types or subclasses (sexist, athletic, and so on), write an essay for the college newspaper. Your tone can be serious or humorous; just keep it consistent.

SLEEPING BAGS

The Editors of *Consumer's Research Magazine*

PRE-READING

1. From the title and type of publication this article appeared in, what would you expect the writer's purpose to be?

2. What tone is projected in the opening paragraph?

FROM *Consumer's Research Magazine*, June 1979, pp. 11–12. Copyright © 1979 Consumers' Research Inc. P.O. Box 168, Washington, N.J. Reprinted by persmission.

¹ Over the past few years, all forms of camping, whether backpacking, trailer camping, or just sleeping out in the backyard, have increased tremendously in popularity. The experienced camping enthusiast knows all too well the importance of proper equipment, but even the backyard camper should not take this subject lightly. Of all the types of equipment available, the sleeping bag is one of the most important.

² In purchasing a sleeping bag, it is important to consider the type of filler material suitable for your particular needs. That material is what determines how warm you will be. Good thermal qualities of the bag and its ability to retain body warmth can ensure a good night's sleep. The lining and outer shell of the bag may be 100 percent cotton or any one of a variety of synthetic fibers. The filler materials can also be of several kinds. Goose down is generally used for cold-weather camping and is considered the best insulator against the cold; polyester and other synthetic-fiber fills are widely used for warm-weather bags.

³ Down has two advantages. Pound for pound, it can keep you warmer than a synthetic-fiber fill. The function of a sleeping bag is to retain whatever heat is generated by the body. The ability of the bag to do this is determined by the amount of air it can trap. A given quantity of down can hold more dead air than any other fiber, natural or man-made; thus, a little down can go a long way.

⁴ A second advantage of down is its ability to "fluff-out" or spring back after being tightly compressed (referred to as its "loft"). Because of its resilience, a down bag is a must for backpackers who are concerned with maximum warmth as well as weight.

⁵ With the advantages of down come certain disadvantages. Since down can hold more dead air, it can also hold more moisture. A wet down bag can be heavy and very difficult to launder; it may often require drycleaning. When wet, it takes a long time to dry completely. A sleeping bag loses its good insulating properties when wet. Therefore, special care is needed to keep a down-filled bag dry at all times.

⁶ An alternative which is growing fast among sleeping bag manufacturers is the use of man-made fibers. Some synthetic-fiber fills have been developed to the point of being only one step away from down. A decade ago, synthetic-fiber fill was usually about 2-½ times heavier than down, but constant research and development in the chemical industry have led to the production of fibers that permit the construction of fiber-fill bags which are substantially lighter than comparable down bags. Since polyester (a synthetic) fiber retains almost no moisture, bags using this material are easy to wash and dry quickly. However, as synthetics tend to offer more resistance to compression, the bag will be bulkier.

⁷ DuPont, one of the three major manufacturers of polyester, developed a hollow tubular fiber called *Hollofil 808*. The individual fibers are larger than in most of the competitors' brands, and the hollow centers help to increase the dead air space. There is considerable confidence among engineers that, in the

future, they can make the hollow centers larger without enlarging the fibers themselves and, thus, make more expensive down obsolete as sleeping bag filler.

[8] Sleeping bag manufacturers produce a variety of differently shaped sleeping bags to fulfill most campers' needs. The conventional bag of rectangular shape is probably the most popular for warm-weather camping. Of the thirteen bags tested, twelve were of the rectangular shape. A tapered bag is constructed so as to fit somewhat closer to the camper's body, allowing for more warmth.

[9] With the increase in camping, a bag more suitable for cold temperatures, the mummy bag, was developed. The mummy bag is tapered to fit snugly around the body and generally has an attached hood to enclose the camper's head and retain more body heat. Because the present test was confined to comparatively warm-weather bags, mummy bags were not included.

[10] Manufacturers also use many different types of construction. Among the bags tested, sewn-through construction was the most common. The sewn-through design is judged to be the least desirable of the major types. The filler material is held in place by stitching *all the way through* the outer shell, filler, and inner lining. Since there is no filler at the stitching, the cold can penetrate more readily there than at other spots in the bag. The insulating quality of the bag is thus not uniform, and the sewn-through bags are, for this reason, not suggested for cold-weather camping.

[11] A few sleeping bags can be found with added features for comfort as well as practical reasons. Several bags tested had a pillow sewn into the bag for extra comfort. One bag had a flap of material which extended under the camper's head to protect him from moisture and dampness. One had a drawstring at the head opening of the bag to minimize drafts. For easy storage, several bags can be purchased with protective "stuff sacks" included.

[12] Although sizes of sleeping bags can vary slightly, the average dimensions are approximately 30 to 35 inches wide and 75 inches long. Larger bags can be purchased from most manufacturers. Many makers offer rectangular bags which can be zipped together, making a double bag.

[13] Sleeping bags may have a full-length zipper (one that runs the entire length of the bag and along one end), a partial-length zipper, or none at all. Some mummy bags have no zipper but have instead a drawstring at the head opening. The drawstring allows for maximum heat retention and eliminates the excess weight of the zipper—something with which most backpackers will be concerned. A partial zipper (one that runs only part of the way down one side of the bag) will allow some air to enter the bag but will make it somewhat easier to get into and out of the bag. Full-length zippers have three chief advantages. If two bags have the same dimensions and the same type of zipper, they can be zipped together to make a double bag. Also, since the bag can be completely opened, it can easily be aired out after each use. Furthermore, when the weather is warm, a full-length zipper can be opened to allow warm air trapped inside to escape.

[14] No matter what type of zipper a sleeping bag has, that fastener should be covered on the inside of the bag with some sort of insulated flap. Air seeping in would be kept to a minimum and cold spots would be prevented from developing along the inside line of the zipper.

[15] One very important factor to consider when purchasing a sleeping bag is the type of fabric of the outer shell. Dampness or high humidity, not to mention snow or rain, can severely chill a camper, particularly when one is sleeping on the ground. It is important to choose a sleeping bag that will guard against moisture passing through the bag. At first thought, one might be inclined to seek out a waterproof bag, one which would not allow moisture to pass in or out. But the body gives off moisture (about 2 pints each night), and this moisture must escape or the sleeper will become damp and chilled. A water-repellent or water-resistant bag is therefore needed. Such a bag allows moisture to escape from inside but, at the same time, keeps water out with a minimal amount of absorption. A bag that is neither water repellent nor water resistant will allow water from any source to pass freely through the outer shell with very little resistance.

ANALYTICAL READING

1.   How does the writer subdivide the subject?

2.   What weather conditions are taken into account?

3.   What types of fillers are discussed? For what purposes?

4.   Why does the writer advise against waterproof materials?

5.   Does the writer recommend anything or merely discuss alternatives?

REFLECTING

Point: Is the main purpose of the article merely to evaluate sleeping bags? Explain.

Organization: Outline the classification scheme used. What advantages can you see in beginning with types of fillers?

Support: What devices does the writer employ in supporting the points made about sleeping bags? How is comparison and contrast used?

Synthesis: Have you experienced any of the conditions the writer describes? How could you have benefited from reading such an article before making a recent purchase? Do you disagree with the author? Can you add anything?

Evaluation: Is it necessary for an article such as this to be humorous and entertaining? Why do people read such articles?

FROM READING TO WRITING

1.   Making your target audience the readers of a consumer magazine, write a paper classifying jeans, T-shirts, sweaters, pens, or some other item regularly purchased by college students. As in this article, show advantages according to the intended use of the item.

2. Write a similar classification paper about some item that you know a lot about—tennis racquets, guns, violin strings, guitars, racing cars, boats—using examples as in the article. The paper should serve as a source of information for a reader trying to decide what to buy.

THE SCIENCE OF GETTING A CAT OUT OF A TREE

The Editors of *Changing Times*

PRE-READING

1. From the title what do you think the purpose of the article will be?

2. What tone is established in the first three paragraphs? How does the last paragraph sustain that tone?

[1] Usually you can tell when a cat is up a tree.

[2] You can tell by the distraught children, anxious owners, sympathetic neighbors and excited dogs who surround the tree.

[3] Furthermore, those involved—which include all of the above plus the cat—will themselves be surrounded by controversy.

[4] Several controversies, in fact.

[5] The first controversy is about what the cat is doing up there in the tree in the first place.

[6] One school of thought holds that what sends a cat up a tree is its intent to carry out certain malign and slanty-eyed designs of its own. These are best known to the cat itself but are commonly believed to be bad news for songbirds.

[7] An opposing school maintains that a cat goes up a tree only to escape pursuit and with the sole object of saving its own pelt. And a cat's pelt, need it be said, covers just about everything a cat has worth saving.

[8] The conflict between those two theories almost always goes unresolved for lack of witnesses. Treed cats generally are discovered only when treed, so nobody really knows how they got up there, much less why.

[9] Nevertheless, there is unanimity among the disputants on one point: However and whyever the cat went up the tree, it certainly chose an inconvenient time to do so.

[10] Don't let accord on this tangential matter fool you. There is more controversy to come on the main issue, which is: How shall the cat be got out of the tree?

[11] On this question there are worse than two schools of thought. There are three.

[12] **The activists.** The first school holds that the most agile person in attendance should climb the tree, seize the cat and carry it down to safety and wild acclaim.

[13] No sensible person should fall for this scenario. The plan won't work. Very few trees are capable of being climbed extemporaneously. And even in the unlikely event that puss picked a tree that a person could climb, only two outcomes could result, neither of them very desirable.

[14] One outcome is that the climber never reaches the cat because, as rescue nears, the cat climbs ever higher. It will be shown that it is a law of nature—or at least a law of relative mass—that a cat can climb higher in any given tree than any given human being can.

[15] In the other possible outcome, the climber against all odds succeeds in grabbing the cat, whereupon the cat does just what you would do if another species tried prying you loose from a frighteningly lofty, swaying and insecure perch. You would resist, fight back tusk and claw. Thus does the cat, and its would-be rescuer must back down—repulsed, maybe bloodied and certainly bowed.

[16] **The technologists.** Adherents of this second persuasion also believe that the cat must be got out of the tree but hold that high technology should be brought to bear.

[17] In this context, for "high technology" read "a ladder." Where you get the ladder really doesn't matter. The ladder won't be long enough, not unless it belongs to your local fire department. Don't expect a leaping response from the fire laddies to your cat alarm, either. Most modern fire companies rank fires far ahead of treed cats. The dogma is that cats come last, if at all.

[18] So the high-tech game plan winds down to essentially the same dissatisfying result obtained in the shinny-up-the-tree plan. That is, either the cat will refuse to be had or it will have at its savior first.

[19] **The pragmatists.** This brings us to the third philosophy. The method it espouses is inglorious, unimaginative, time-consuming and unpopular. There is very little to be said for this program except that it is safe, sane, humane and effective. In short, it works.

[20] The central idea is to go away and let the cat come down the tree by itself when it is good and ready.

[21] Granted, this may take some time. A cat may not be ready to come down until dinnertime, perhaps somewhat later.

[22] But down it will come. Voluntarily. And in good working order, for as Guinness is our witness, there is no record of any cat anywhere damaging itself by falling out of a tree or starving itself by staying up one. Such things just do not happen, not to so eminently sensible an animal as a cat.

[23] The correct procedure, therefore, is to disperse the thronging persons and animals below, head off the fire department if it comes anywhere near the neighborhood and act the part of nonchalance personified.

²⁴ Saunter off to some secluded nook, there to reflect on the moral to be drawn from the certain unraveling of the affair. And, as always in encounters with a cat, there is a moral to be drawn.

²⁵ In fact, there are two.

²⁶ One moral is that if a cat goes up a tree, getting down is the cat's problem, not yours. The other is that in the end, Newton was right.

ANALYTICAL READING

1. Why do you think the writer uses the word *science* in the title? Why not just "How to Get a Cat Out of a Tree"?

2. What controversies does the writer discuss in the article? How are they related?

3. What devices are used to maintain the tone set in the opening paragraphs? Point out examples of how language contributes?

4. The writer occasionally uses vocabulary that shows an awareness of the kind of person who reads *Changing Times: tangential, unanimity, scenario, extemporaneously, espouses, nonchalance.* What words could you substitute for these in writing to a more general audience?

5. Is it necessary to have so many short paragraphs? How could they be combined?

REFLECTING

Point: What is the main purpose of the article? What opinion does the writer reveal about the subject?

Organization: How does the "class" established in the article explain the title? How many items are subclassified in the article? Make an outline, showing the organizational scheme. What keeps this article from being a process description?

Support: Why do you think the writer relies heavily on description? What kinds of examples might have been used? Statistics?

Synthesis: Have you ever tried or seen someone else try to rescue a cat from a tree? How does your experience relate to the article?

Evaluation: Do you think the article succeeded in its purpose? In what ways does the subject matter control the writing approach? (Compare with "Sleeping Bags," pages 187–90).

FROM READING TO WRITING

1. Using an experience that you have had in rescuing an animal, such as a dog from a storm sewer, a bird from a chimney, a chipmunk from the jaws of a cat, write an entertaining paper, classifying the methods you tried.

2. For a campus publication, write an article that divides a certain type of popular music into various subtypes. Examples of such types are country, rock, folk, progressive jazz, and so on. Be sure to include specific performers or recordings that are representative examples of the different subtypes.

3. For your campus newspaper, write an article that follows the organizational scheme of the *Changing Times* article, using as your title "The Science of _____." Likely subjects might include dealing with a stalled car in traffic, getting good tickets to a popular athletic or musical event, finding a parking place on campus. Be sure that it does not become a "how to" process description; concentrate on classifying the *methods* employed in the process.

Definition

THE WORKAHOLIC IN YOU
Warren Boroson

BIOGRAPHICAL SKETCH

Warren Boroson was born in New York City in 1935. He completed his under-graduate studies at Columbia University and did graduate work there, at the New School for Social Research, and at New York University, mainly in writing and edit-ing. He has worked as a reporter and editor for several publications, including Trans-Action, *a social science periodical, and he has contributed articles to numerous magazines.*

PRE-READING

1. What is the basis for the coined word in the title?

2. After reading the opening paragraph, can you find Boroson's "dictionary" defini-tion of *workaholic?*

3. This article appeared in *Money* magazine. What audience is it aimed at?

[1] Lots of Americans work hard and play hard. But some just work, either from the unquenchable love of it or from a compulsion beyond their control. Work lovers—the unquenchables—provide society with many leaders in busi-ness, politics, science and the arts. Those who overwork out of compulsion—the work addicts, or workaholics, of this world—are in trouble. Their addiction can lead to dead-end careers, to poor health, even to early death. They are so emotionally dependent on work that without it they start coming unglued. Though the purebred workaholic is rare, there is a little of him in almost everyone. It is well to know the warning signals and how to cope with them.

[2] Confusing workaholics with work lovers is a bit like confusing winos with oenophiles. Mark Twain was a work lover. In 1908, when he was nearly 73, he said he hadn't done a lick of work in over 50 years. Wrote Twain: "I have always been able to gain my living without doing any work; for the writing of books and magazine matter was always play, not work. I enjoyed it; it was merely billiards to me."

FROM *Money*, June 1976, pp. 32–35. Reprinted from *Money* Magazine by special permission. © 1976 by Time Inc. All rights reserved.

³ Psychiatrist Carl Jung once said that the difference between the recondite prose of James Joyce and the poetry of Joyce's insane daughter was that he was diving and she was falling. The work lover is diving. He works hard and long by choice. When he wants to, he can stop without suffering acute withdrawal pains. When work addicts go on vacation, however, it is not the natives but the tourists who are restless.

⁴ The work lover's work is also his play. The work addict's motives are mixed. In many cases, he is seeking the admiration of other people because he doesn't approve of himself. As Dr. Alan McLean, an IBM psychiatrist, points out, the healthiest people usually have various sources of satisfaction: they are lawyers, say, but they are also spouses, parents, friends, citizens, churchgoers, art lovers, stamp collectors, golfers and so forth. If such people lose their jobs, or if their work becomes less satisfying or its quality starts deteriorating, they have not lost their sole interest in life, the only prop to their self-esteem. Many compulsive workers, according to cardiologist Meyer Friedman of San Francisco, co-author of the bestselling book *Type A Behavior and Your Heart* (1974), "want status, and their status depends on what other people think of them." Eventually, many addicts manage to labor under the delusion that they are indispensable.

⁵ Guilt propels some workaholics. Several years ago, a theological seminary in the East had a problem with guilt-ridden students who kept working even when the school closed for vacations. To get them out, the school was finally forced to turn off the electricity and water and change all the locks during vacation periods.

⁶ Because of their diligence, work addicts in corporations tend to keep getting promoted; but a lack of imagination keeps them from reaching the top rungs. They make great salesmen and terrible corporation presidents. "Workaholics rarely become famous," says Dr. Frederic Flach, a New York psychiatrist who has treated many people with work problems. "Because they lack creativity, they rarely make an original contribution to the welfare of mankind. They usually end up in upper-middle management, giving grief to everyone around them."

⁷ Continual work, Dr. Flach notes, "violates one of the basic rules for coming up with original solutions—to move into another area and let the problem simmer." He adds that one reason workaholics work ten to twelve hours a day is that "they are not good at finding ways to think about something in a new fashion." Work addicts, says Robert F. Medina, an industrial psychologist in Chicago, like "the sureness and safety of processing endless details. Creativity is a little too scary. It looks like idleness to them."

⁸ As employees of large corporations, work addicts can have a hard time of it. The staff psychiatrist at a huge national manufacturing firm tells of an executive in the New York headquarters who came to him for help. Discussion brought out that the executive felt best when things were "impossible"—when he was being seriously tested and overworked. Free time made him uneasy

and anxious. Many addicts like him end up self-employed so they can have expandable working time. (But even blue-collar workers can manage to become work addicts by taking second jobs or constantly volunteering for overtime.)

⁹ Wherever he earns his living, the workaholic is likely to work hard not just on the job but off duty too. "When his back is to the wall," says Dr. Howard Hess, a Western Electric corporate psychiatrist, "he may cut the lawn with a vengeance or play a murderous game of tennis." A Chicago psychiatrist, Dr. Saul M. Siegel, recalls a work addict who had an extramarital affair. He kept working as hard as ever, though, and "wound up with both a nagging wife and a nagging mistress."

¹⁰ While work addicts work hard, they tend to die easily. Time and again, researchers have found that the compulsively hard-working person is particularly prone to heart disease in middle age. Dr. Friedman and his cardiologist co-author, Dr. Ray H. Rosenman, divide the world into two working types. Hard-driving people are classified as Type A and low-pressure people as Type B. Both types can become workaholics, but in different ways. The Type-A person is excessively ambitious and competitive, and frequently hostile; he feels pressured by deadlines. Cardiologists have found that he is two or three times as likely to have a premature heart attack as a Type B, who is not so competitive and hard driving.

¹¹ Type-B workaholics are civil service types who lose themselves in dull paperwork or other routine activities. Wayne Oates, a Louisville psychologist, thinks that a Type-B work addict, unlike the individualistic Type A, tends to identify with the company he works for and "not have any selfhood of his own. The company is a flat earth to him. Everything beyond it is dragons and disaster."

¹² The domestic life of the workaholic is likely to be troubled. In some cases, addicts marry each other and go their own unmerry ways. More typically, the wife is a non-addict, resentful that her husband has so little time and energy to expend on the family. The addict himself may nonetheless expect his wife and children to be robotlike perfectionists. Although the typical work addict doesn't like to help around the house, he "may be a busybody poking into his wife's household affairs and telling her how inefficient she is with the cooking and the housecleaning," reports Dr. Nelson J. Bradley, a psychiatrist in Park Ridge, Ill. "He's too preoccupied with his own work goals to be sensitive to the needs of others" in the family.

¹³ Going on a family vacation with a workaholic can be a hellish ordeal. Robert Medina, the Chicago psychologist, tells of the president of a midwestern company whose wife and daughter shanghaied him to Hawaii for three weeks on the beach. The man hadn't taken a vacation in 13 years. He made everybody so miserable by his compulsion to keep phoning the office that after four days his family was as frantic to get home as he was.

¹⁴ A housewife can be a workaholic too. She may insist on doing so much

that her children never learn everyday household skills. The daughters of such women "often grow up without knowing how to cook, sew, clean and decorate the home," says psychologist Wayne Oates.

¹⁵ Sometimes a work addict can persuade himself as well as other people that he is really a work lover, the way an alcoholic can persuade himself and others that he doesn't have a drinking problem because all he drinks is vintage cognac. Reading someone's basic motives can be difficult. But it's very likely that a work lover—unlike a work addict—has a job that offers freedom and diversity; he is well recognized and amply rewarded for his efforts. An obscure middle-aged heart surgeon or social reformer who works as hard as Dr. Denton Cooley or Ralph Nader is more likely to be a self-destructive work addict than those two men are. Nader scoffs at the notion that his ceaseless toil makes him a workaholic. "You wouldn't ask an Olympic swimmer or chess player why he works 20 hours a day," Nader says. People don't understand Nader "because we haven't a tradition which explains me."

¹⁶ Without being workaholics, most people experience the addict's symptoms from time to time. "Anyone who's been busy and active," says Dr. Flach, the New York psychiatrist, "has a tendency to get locked in, to become dependent on his work." Examples are accountants in March and April, salesclerks during the Christmas rush, air traffic controllers all the time. When they are no longer so busy, they may suffer from a mild version of "postpartum depression," like women who have just given birth.

¹⁷ Some people work too long and hard at times because they fear being fired or are bucking for promotion or cannot do their jobs as well as they know they should. Other people sometimes lose themselves in work to escape emotional problems—the loss of a loved one, a financial setback or some other worry. They use work to keep from breaking down completely. Occupational therapy is, after all, one of the very best painkillers and tranquilizers.

¹⁸ These people differ from chronic addicts in that once they have stopped working for a while, their pain begins to ebb, their spirits perk up, and they are back to normal. But someone who has been temporarily habituated to hard work would be best advised to unwind slowly. People who suddenly switch from hard work to idleness tend to develop a variety of physical and psychological illnesses, heart disease in particular. Social psychologist Jerome E. Singer of the National Research Council in Washington, D.C. mentions how people often die shortly after retiring from important posts.

¹⁹ For some work addicts, the realization that something is amiss comes only when they develop health problems. For Wayne Oates, author of *Confessions of a Workaholic* (1971), recognition came when his five-year-old son asked for an appointment to see him. (Oates probably coined the term "workaholic," though the editors of the Merriam-Webster dictionaries give the Wall Street Journal of Feb. 2, 1971 as the first source.) Someone who suspects he may be growing psychologically dependent on work should ask himself whether he can unwind readily over a weekend or during a vacation.

[20] Jerome Singer recommends that hard-working people generally avoid making abrupt major changes in their work habits. People who work frenetically all year long may suffer if they suddenly flop down on a beach in Hawaii for a few weeks. Instead, Singer suggests that hard workers would be better off taking frequent short vacations or easing into long vacations by cutting down gradually on their work.

[21] Recognizing the value of vacations, many companies (General Motors, for one) now require all employees to take the vacations they are entitled to instead of accumulating them from year to year. Dr. Nicholas A. Pace, medical director of GM's New York executive offices, adds that employees who try not to take vacations "don't get brownie points any more. They're just looked upon as damn fools." But a vacation need not be long to be therapeutic. Dr. John P. McCann of the Life Extension Institute in New York, which gives physicals to executives, points out that for many people even a one-day vacation may constitute a refreshing change of pace.

[22] The ideal vacation, in the opinion of Dr. Ari Kiev, a New York psychiatrist and author of *A Strategy for Handling Executive Stress* (1974), is a foil to a person's occupation. Someone who does close, detailed work all year long, like an accountant, might take up something less exacting, like sailing. (Says Dr. Howard Hess: "A Caribbean vacation is not the solution to everyone's problems. Just mine and yours.") A person who sees in himself symptoms of workaholism should try developing interests outside of his job. Dr. Flach recommends returning to the hobbies of your adolescence—photography, stamp collecting or what have you. "Your early interests," he believes, "are perhaps the closest expression of you as a person." Wayne Oates suggests renewing old acquaintances, making new friends and reading books you don't have to read, like mysteries. It may be easier for those further along the path to addiction to switch to hobbies that, like work, have well-defined goals, such as woodworking or sports.

[23] To suppress temptations to expand your work load, Oates cautions, take a wary look at offers of promotions that would keep you from doing the things you like best about your present job. Lest he try to do two jobs at once, a salesman who enjoys selling might be best off turning down a promotion to sales manager; a teacher who loves teaching might refuse a department chairmanship. In his own case, to keep from taking on so much extra work, Oates put a ceiling on the extra income he wanted each month, and he has stuck to it—with periodic adjustments for inflation.

[24] Sometimes workaholism is thrust on people. There are workaholic companies, which may expect everyone to be at work early, to skip lunch, to work late and to think about office problems on weekends. Work addicts tend to wind up in such places; incipient addicts should escape while they easily can. Dr. Flach, for one, doesn't think the workaholic organization has a special edge over its competitors. Like work addicts themselves, such outfits may lack imagination. "The typical workaholic organization," he says, "may set up the

most carefully thought-out way to distribute money into a project, for example, and miss the obvious point—like how all that money is going to get ripped off."

[25] The incipient addict with the hard-driving personality of a Type A should consider slowing down the general pace of his life. Dr. Friedman, a Type A himself (complete with heart attack), deliberately began dressing informally. He spent lunch hours examining the stained glass windows in a nearby cathedral; he began rereading the seven parts of Marcel Proust's interminable *Remembrance of Things Past.* He now avoids cocktail parties: "I found that all you do at them is shout, and no one cares whether you leave or stay." And he keeps away from "people who readily bring out my free-floating hostility, because I've never been able to convince those sons of bitches about anything and they've never been able to convince me."

[26] To get advice from other well-known people who are reputed to work very hard, I wrote Harold S. Geneen, president of ITT, actor Elliot Gould, film director Robert Altman, Governor Jerry Brown of California and Dr. DeBakey, among others. A spokesman for ITT apologetically reported that Geneen could not reply because he had been very busy with management meetings recently and was out on the golf course. The others did not respond at all. Presumably they were too busy working.

ANALYTICAL READING

1. How does Boroson establish *workaholic* as a class in paragraphs 1–6? What features set workaholics apart from work lovers? What is the danger of being a workaholic?

2. How many subclasses does Boroson set up? What authoritative source does he use to set up the subclasses?

3. What are the distinguishing features of each of the subclasses? How does he present them?

4. How does he capitalize throughout the article on the analogy set up in the title? Does he refer only to men? Distinguish between temporary and chronic work addicts.

5. What is meant by "incipient addicts" (paragraphs 24–25)?

6. Discuss several paragraphs that you found effective in making comparisons and contrasts.

7. Point out some of the devices that Boroson uses to keep the definition from becoming too dry and technical.

REFLECTING

Point: Did you find another purpose in the article besides that of defining *workaholic?* If so, what?

Organization: Does the organizational pattern follow the one suggested in the Introduction to this section of the book? Demonstrate.

Support: How does the author use examples to support his subclassification? How does he use authority?

Synthesis: Do you know anyone who fits the definition? Do you think that you or one of your parents might be an "incipient workaholic"?

Evaluation: Did you find the article interesting? If so, what devices made it so? Is it merely a book review of *Type A Behavior and Your Heart?* Do you think you could identify a workaholic now?

FROM READING TO WRITING

1. Write an extended definition for a general audience of a type of person you know who exhibits some compulsive behavior, such as addiction to tennis (tennisholic), bridge (bridgaholic), or fishing (fishaholic). Following Boroson's example, establish class by separating compulsive behavior from normal.

2. Do you know any students who are compulsive about their studies? If so, construct an extended definition of the study addict for readers not attending college.

3. For an audience of business people, write a reply to the maxim, "Hard work never hurt anyone."

WHITE LIES
Sissela Bok

BIOGRAPHICAL SKETCH

Sissela Bok, born in 1934, was educated at the Sorbonne and George Washington University before receiving a Ph.D. from Harvard. Winner of the Orwell Award in 1976 for her book Lying: Moral Choice in Private and Public Life, *she had previously coauthored and edited* The Dilemmas of Euthanasia. *Her articles on ethics in medical and governmental affairs have appeared in numerous publications. Currently, she is a lecturer in medical ethics at Harvard-MIT and coeditor of* The Teaching of Ethics, *a book that will soon be published.*

PRE-READING

1. Basing your answer on the title of the book from which the selection was taken, what stand toward the subject would you expect the author to take?

2. What does Sissela Bok do in the opening paragraph?

   [1] White lies are at the other end of the spectrum of deception from lies in a serious crisis. They are the most common and the most trivial forms that

FROM Sissela Bok, *Lying: Moral Choice in Public and Private Life (New York:* Pantheon, 1978), pp. 60–63. Copyright © 1978 by Sissela Bok. Reprinted by permission of Pantheon Books, a Division of Random House Inc.

duplicity can take. The fact that they are so common provides their protective coloring. And their very triviality, when compared to more threatening lies, makes it seem unnecessary or even absurd to condemn them. Some consider *all* well-intentioned lies, however momentous, to be white; in this book, I shall adhere to the narrower usage: a white lie, in this sense, is a falsehood not meant to injure anyone, and of little moral import. I want to ask whether there *are* such lies; and if there are, whether their cumulative consequences are still without harm; and, finally, whether many lies are not defended as "white" which are in fact harmful in their own right.

[2] Many small subterfuges may not even be intended to mislead. They are only "white lies" in the most marginal sense. Take, for example, the many social exchanges: "How nice to see you!" or "Cordially Yours." These and a thousand other polite expressions are so much taken for granted that if someone decided, in the name of total honesty, not to employ them, he might well give the impression of an indifference he did not possess. The justification for continuing to use such accepted formulations is that they deceive no one, except possibly those unfamiliar with the language.

[3] A social practice more clearly deceptive is that of giving a false excuse so as not to hurt the feelings of someone making an invitation or request: to say one "can't" do what in reality one may not *want* to do. Once again, the false excuse may prevent unwarranted inferences of greater hostility to the undertaking than one may well feel. Merely to say that one can't do something, moreover, is not deceptive in the sense that an elaborately concocted story can be.

[4] Still other white lies are told in an effort to flatter, to throw a cheerful interpretation on depressing circumstances, or to show gratitude for unwanted gifts. In the eyes of many, such white lies do no harm, provide needed support and cheer, and help dispel gloom and boredom. They preserve the equilibrium and often the humaneness of social relationships, and are usually accepted as excusable so long as they do not become excessive. Many argue, moreover, that such deception is so helpful and at times so necessary that it must be tolerated as an exception to a general policy against lying. Thus Bacon observed:

> Doth any man doubt, that if there were taken out of men's minds vain opinions, flattering hopes, false valuations, imaginations as one would, and the like, but it would leave the minds of a number of men poor shrunken things, full of melancholy and indisposition, and unpleasing to themselves?

[5] Another kind of lie may actually be advocated as bringing a more substantial benefit, or avoiding a real harm, while seeming quite innocuous to those who tell the lies. Such are the placebos given for innumerable common ailments, and the pervasive use of inflated grades and recommendations for employment and promotion.

[6] A large number of lies without such redeeming features are nevertheless often regarded as so trivial that they should be grouped with white lies. They are the lies told on the spur of the moment, for want of reflection, or to get out of a scrape, or even simply to pass the time. Such are the lies told to boast or exaggerate, or on the contrary to deprecate and understate; the many lies told or repeated in gossip; Rousseau's lies told simply "in order to say something"; the embroidering on facts that seem too tedious in their own right; and the substitution of a quick lie for the lengthly explanations one might otherwise have to provide for something not worth spending time on.

[7] Utilitarians often cite white lies as the *kind* of deception where their theory shows the benefits of common sense and clear thinking. A white lie, they hold, is trivial; it is either completely harmless, or so marginally harmful that the cost of detecting and evaluating the harm is much greater than the minute harm itself. In addition, the white lie can often actually be beneficial, thus further tipping the scales of utility. In a world with so many difficult problems, utilitiarians might ask: Why take the time to weigh the minute pros and cons in telling someone that his tie is attractive when it is an abomination, or of saying to a guest that a broken vase was worthless? Why bother even to define such insignificant distortions or make mountains out of molehills by seeking to justify them?

[8] Triviality surely does set limits to when moral inquiry is reasonable. But when we look more closely at practices such as placebo-giving, it becomes clear that all lies defended as "white' cannot be so easily dismissed. In the first place, the harmlessness of lies is notoriously disputable. What the liar perceives as harmless or even beneficial may not be so in the eyes of the deceived. Second, the failure to look at an entire practice rather than at their own isolated case often blinds liars to cumulative harm and expanding deceptive activities. Those who begin with white lies can come to resort to more frequent and more serious ones. Where some tell a few white lies, others may tell more. Because lines are so hard to draw, the indiscriminate use of such lies can lead to other deceptive practices. The aggregate harm from a large number of marginally harmful instances may, therefore, be highly undesirable in the end—for liars, those deceived, and honesty and trust more generally.

ANALYTICAL READING

1. To what does Sissela Bok restrict her definition of "white" lies?

2. What justifications do people give for telling white lies?

3. What is a "placebo"(paragraph 8)? Why does Bok consider the giving of placebos similar to the telling of white lies?

4. Explain the position of the utilitarians (paragraph 7).

5. What does Bok perceive as the moral dangers in telling white lies?

6. Do you think the writer would accept any kind of white lies? If so, what kind? Cite evidence from the selection.

REFLECTING

Point: What is the writer's opinion of white lies?

Organization: Does the selection follow the outline given for definition on page 164? Outline the subclasses Bok deals with.

Support: How does the author use examples? How does she use authority?

Synthesis: Have you ever hurt another person or been hurt yourself by a white lie? What kinds of white lies do you feel are justified?

Evaluation: Did the article make you think about the subject in a different way? If so, in what way? Are there any types of white lies that you feel Bok left out of her discussion?

FROM READING TO WRITING

1.   Restrict white lies to a smaller class—social white lies, family white lies, classroom white lies, business white lies, for example—and write an extended definition, breaking the topic into subtypes as Bok did. Decide on a specific audience before writing.

2.   For a campus publication, define *cheating* or *plagiarism*. Formulate an opinion to serve as the purpose for writing the definition.

3.   For a teacher's publication, write a definition of a *good teacher* or a *bad teacher*. Be sure to deal with different subtypes, which should come from your own experience with teachers.

4.   Many graduating seniors ask professors to write letters of recommendation for them. The professors are often torn between their desire to help students find jobs and their moral obligation to write the truth. Should professors omit unfavorable comments? Should they be overgenerous in their remarks? For your college newspaper, write a definition of *a good recommendation* that also deals with the problems suggested above.

INTRODUCTION TO *SPORTSWORLD*
Robert Lipsyte

BIOGRAPHICAL SKETCH

Robert Lipsyte was born in New York City in 1938 and graduated from Columbia University. For about fourteen years he wrote an internationally syndicated column, "Sports of the Times." During this period, he won several awards for distinguished reporting. Since he retired from journalism, Lipsyte has written three novels and

FROM Robert Lipsyte, *SportsWorld* (New York: Quadrangle/The New York Times Book Co., 1975), pp. ix–xv. Copyright © 1975 by Robert Lipsyte. Reprinted by permission of Times Books, a division of Quadrangle/The New York Times Book Co.

three nonfiction works, including Nigger *(with Dick Gregory),* The Masculine Mystique, *and* SportsWorld: An American Dreamland.

PRE-READING

1. From the biographical sketch, what would you expect Lipsyte's attitude toward sports to be?

2. Before reading the opening paragraphs, try to explain what SportsWorld means to you.

3. Skim the first two paragraphs and the last one. What do you think Lipsyte's attitude toward SportsWorld is?

[1] For the past one hundred years most Americans have believed that playing and watching competitive games are not only healthful activities, but represent a positive force on our national psyche. In sports, they believe, children will learn courage and self-control, old people will find blissful nostalgia, and families will discover new ways to communicate among themselves. Immigrants will find shortcuts to recognition as Americans. Rich and poor, black and white, educated and unskilled, we will all find a unifying language. The melting pot may be a myth, but we will all come together in the ballpark.

[2] This faith in sports has been vigorously promoted by industry, the military, government, the media. The values of the arena and the locker room have been imposed upon our national life. Coaches and sportswriters are speaking for generals and businessmen, too, when they tell us that a man must be physically and psychologically "tough" to succeed, that he must be clean and punctual and honest, that he must bear pain, bad luck, and defeat without whimpering or making excuses. A man must prove his faith in sports and the American Way by whipping himself into shape, playing by the rules, being part of the team, and putting out all the way. If his faith is strong enough, he will triumph. It's his own fault if he loses, fails, remains poor.

[3] Even for ballgames, these values, with their implicit definitions of manhood, courage, and success, are not necessarily in the individual's best interests. But for daily life they tend to create a dangerous and grotesque web of ethics and attitudes, an amorphous infrastructure that acts to contain our energies, divert our passions, and socialize us for work or war or depression.

[4] I call this infrastructure SportsWorld. For most of my adult life, as a professional observer, I've explored SportsWorld and marveled at its incredible power and pervasiveness. SportsWorld touches everyone and everything. We elect our politicians, judge our children, fight our wars, plan our vacations, oppress our minorities by SportsWorld standards that somehow justify our foulest and freakiest deeds, or at least camouflage them with jargon. We get stoned on such SportsWorld spectaculars as the Super Bowl, the space shots, the Kentucky Derby, the presidential conventions, the Indianapolis 500, all of whose absurd excesses reassure us that we're okay.

[5] SportsWorld is a sweaty Oz you'll never find in a geography book, but

since the end of the Civil War it has been promoted and sold to us like Rancho real estate, an ultimate sanctuary, a university for the body, a community for the spirit, a place to hide that glows with that time of innocence when we believed that rules and boundaries were honored, that good triumphed over evil, and that the loose ends of experience could be caught and bound and delivered in an explanation as final and as comforting as a goodnight kiss.

[6] Sometime in the last fifty years the sports experience was perverted into a SportsWorld state of mind in which the winner was good because he won; the loser, if not actually bad, was at least reduced, and had to prove himself over again, through competition. As each new immigrant crop was milled through the American system, a pick of the harvest was displayed in the SportsWorld showcase, a male preserve of national athletic entertainment traditionally enacted by the working class for the middle class, much as the performing arts are played by the middle class for the amusement of the upper class.

[7] By the 1950s, when SportsWorld was dominated by what are now called "white ethnics," the black American was perceived as a challenging force and was encouraged to find outlets in the national sports arena. Although most specific laws against black participation had already been erased, it took cautious, humiliating experiments with such superstars as Jackie Robinson and Larry Doby to prove that spectator prejudice could be deconditioned by a winning team. Within a few years, pools of cheap, eager black and dark Latin labor were channeled into mainstream clubs.

[8] So pervasive are the myths of SportsWorld that the recruitment of blacks has been regarded as a gift of true citizenship bestowed upon the Negro when he was ready. It has been conventional wisdom for twenty years that the black exposure in sports has speeded the integration of American society, that white Americans, having seen that blacks are beautiful and strong, became "liberalized."

[9] This is one of the crueler hoaxes of SportsWorld. Sports success probably has been detrimental to black progress. By publicizing the material success of a few hundred athletes, thousands, perhaps millions, of bright young blacks have been swept toward sports when they should have been guided toward careers in medicine or engineering or business. For every black star celebrated in SportsWorld, a thousand of his little brothers were neutralized, kept busy shooting baskets until it was too late for them to qualify beyond marginal work.

[10] The white male spectator who knew few ordinary black men to measure himself against may have had his awareness raised by watching such superior human beings as Frank Robinson, Jim Brown, Bill Russell, O. J. Simpson, and other highly merchandised SportsWorld heroes, but it also doubled his worst fears about blacks: added to the black junkie who would rip out his throat was the black superstud who could replace him as a man—in bed, on the job, as a model for his children.

¹¹ By the middle of the 1970s it seemed as though the black experience in SportsWorld might be recapitulated by women. SportsWorld seemed on the verge of becoming the arena in which women would discover and exploit their new "equality." It would be a complex test of adaptability for SportsWorld. The major sports were created by men for the superior muscles, size, and endurance of the male body. Those sports in which balance, flexibility, and dexterity are the crucial elements have never been mass-promoted in America. When a woman beats a man at a man's game, she has to play like a man.

¹² There were signs, however, that women may not embrace SportsWorld as eagerly as did the blacks, profiting from that sorry lesson as well as from their own greater leverage in American society. It is no accident that Billie Jean King, while still an active player, became an entrepreneur and an important voice in American cultural consciousness while Jackie Robinson was a Rockefeller courtier almost to the end of his life.

¹³ A great deal of the angry energy generated in America through the coming apart of the 1960s was absorbed by SportsWorld in its various roles as socializer, pacifier, safety valve; as a concentration camp for adolescents and an emotional Disneyland for their parents; as a laboratory for human engineering and a reflector of current moral postures; and as a running commercial for Our Way of Life. SportsWorld is a buffer, a DMZ, between people and the economic and political systems that direct their lives; women, so long denied this particular playland, may just avoid this trap altogether.

¹⁴ But SportsWorld's greatest power has always been its flexibility. Even as we are told of SportsWorld's proud traditions, immutable laws, ultimate security from the capriciousness of "real life," SportsWorld is busy changing its rules, readjusting its alliances, checking the trends. SportsWorld is nothing if not responsive. Hockey interest lagging, how about a little more blood on the ice? Speed up baseball with a designated hitter. Move the football goal posts. A three-point shot in basketball. Women agitating at the college arena gates? Let 'em in. Give 'em athletic scholarships, "jock" dorms, and Minnie Mouse courses. How about a Professional Women's Power Volleyball League?

¹⁵ Stars, teams, leagues, even entire sports may rise or fall or never get off the ground, but SportsWorld as a force in American life orbits on.

¹⁶ Ah, baseball. Our National Pastime. An incredibly complex contrivance that seems to have been created by a chauvinistic mathematician intent upon giving America a game so idiosyncratic that it would be at least a century before any other country could beat us at it. And indeed it was. After a century in which baseball was celebrated as a unique product of the American character, Chinese boys began winning Little League championships, and young men from Latin America and the Caribbean began making a significant impact upon the major leagues. The highly organized Japanese, who had taken up the game during the postwar occupation of their country (perhaps as penance for yelling "To Hell with Babe Ruth" during banzai charges) were almost ready to attack again.

[17] But SportsWorld had spun on. That other peculiarly American game, football, declared itself the New National Pastime. Baseball and God were announced dead at about the same time, but the decision against baseball apparently is taking longer to reverse, thanks in the main to pro football's colossal public relations machine. The National Football League played its scheduled games on Sunday, November 24, 1963, because its historic television deal was pending and Commissioner Pete Rozelle was determined to prove that nothing, *nothing*, could cancel the show. But that winter, NFL sportscasters infiltrated the banquet circuit with the engaging theory—quintessential SportsWorld—that America had been at the brink of a nervous breakdown after President Kennedy's assassination and that only The Sport of the Sixties' business-as-usual attitude had held the country together until Monday's National Day of Mourning unified us all in public grief.

[18] Ten years later, though hopefully still grateful, America had grown bored with the cartoon brutality of pro football. America was boogieing to the magic moves and hip, sly rhythms of basketball, The Sport of the Seventies. We've had enough of pure violence, simulated or otherwise, went the SportsWorld wisdom, now we need something smooooooooth.

[19] There is no end to SportsWorld theories—of the past, the present, the future—especially now that a new generation of commentators, athletes, coaches, and fans feels free to reform and recast sports, to knock it off the pedestal and slide it under the microscope, giving it more importance than ever. SportsWorld newspapermen dare to describe to us action that we have seen more clearly on television than they have from the press box, and SportsWorld telecasters, isolated from the world in their glass booths, dare to explain to us what the players are *really* thinking. SportsWorld analysts were once merely "pigskin prognosticators" predicting the weekend football scores; now they may be as heavy as any RAND Corporation futurist. Is hockey an art form or is it a paradigm of anarchy, in which case are we obligated as concerned citizens to watch it? Is tennis more than just a convenient new market for clothes and building materials and nondurable goods? What will be The Sport of the Eighties? Will no sport ever again have its own decade? Will cable television and government-regulated sports gambling and the institutionalized fragmenting of society balkanize us into dozens of jealous Fandoms?

[20] SportsWorld, once determinedly anti-intellectual, has become a hotbed of psychologists, physicians, and sociologists questioning premises as well as specific techniques. Should lacrosse players really be eating steak before games, or pancakes? Why are the lockers of defensive linemen neater than those of offensive linemen? Does athletic participation truly "build character" or does it merely reinforce otherwise unacceptable traits? Should communities rather than corporations own teams?

[21] But very few people seem to be questioning SportsWorld itself, exploring the possibility that if sports could be separated from SportsWorld we could take a major step toward liberation from the false values, the stereotypes, the idols of the arena that have burdened us all since childhood.

²² SportsWorld is not a conspiracy in the classic sense, but rather an expression of a community of interest. In the Soviet Union, for example, where world-class athletes are the diplomat-soldiers of ideology, and where factory girls are forced to exercise to reduce fatigue and increase production, the entire athletic apparatus is part of government. Here in America, SportsWorld's insidious power is imposed upon athletics by the banks that decide which arenas and recreational facilities shall be built, by the television networks that decide which sports shall be sponsored and viewed, by the press that decides which individuals and teams shall be celebrated, by the municipal governments that decide which clubs shall be subsidized, and by the federal government, which has, through favorable tax rulings and exemptions from law, allowed sports entertainment to grow until it has become the most influential form of mass culture in America.

²³ SportsWorld is a grotesque distortion of sports. It has limited the pleasures of play for most Americans while concentrating on turning our best athletes into clowns. It has made the finish more important than the race, and extolled the game as that William Jamesian absurdity, a moral equivalent to war, and the hero of the game as that Henry Jamesian absurdity, a "muscular Christian." It has surpassed patriotism and piety as a currency of communication, while exploiting them both. By the end of the 1960s, SportsWorld wisdom had it that religion was a spectator sport while professional and college athletic contests were the only events Americans held sacred.

²⁴ SportsWorld is neither an American nor a modern phenomenon. Those glorified Olympics of ancient Greece were manipulated for political and commercial purposes; at the end, they held a cracked mirror to a decaying civilization. The modern Olympics were revived at the end of the nineteenth century in an attempt to whip French youth into shape for a battlefield rematch with Germany. Each country of Europe, then the United States, the Soviet Union, the "emerging" nations of Africa and Asia, used the Olympics as political display windows. The 1972 Arab massacre of Israeli athletes was a hideously logical extension of SportsWorld philosophy.

²⁵ SportsWorld begins in elementary school, where the boys are separated from the girls. In *Sixties Going on Seventies*, Nora Sayre recounts the poignant confrontation of a gay man and a gay woman at a meeting. She is banging the floor with a baseball bat, and he asks her to stop; the bat symbolizes to him the oppression of sports in his childhood. But to her the bat symbolizes liberation from the restraint that had kept her from aggression, from sports, in her childhood.

²⁶ By puberty, most American children have been classified as failed athletes and assigned to watch and cheer for those who have survived the first of several major "cuts." Those who have been discarded to the grandstands and to the television sets are not necessarily worse off than those tapped for higher levels of competition. SportsWorld heroes exist at sufferance, and the path of glory is often an emotional minefield trapped with pressures to perform and fears of failure. There is no escape from SportsWorld, for player or spectator

or even reporter, that watcher in the shadows who pretends to be in the arena but above the fray.

ANALYTICAL READING

1. This article is an extended definition. Formulate a one-sentence "dictionary" definition of SportsWorld from the material in the first three paragraphs.

2. The following sentences from the essay contain elements that appear to be short definitions. Discuss the weaknesses of each as a logical definition that could serve as the basis for the essay.
   a. "SportsWorld is a sweaty Oz. . . . " (paragraph 5)
   b. "SportsWorld is not a conspiracy in the classic sense, but rather an expression of a community of interest." (paragraph 22)
   c. "SportsWorld is a grotesque distortion of sports." (paragraph 23)
   d. "SportsWorld is neither an American nor a modern phenomenon." (paragraph 24)

3. According to Lipsyte, what aspects of the ethic of SportsWorld have invaded our society?

4. What are the "myths" and characteristics of SportsWorld that Lipsyte finds especially dangerous? Why?

5. How does Lipsyte subclassify the various sports? To what causes does he attribute the changing of the "National Pastime" every decade? Is basketball displaying any of the traits he claims for football? What sport do you think is the most likely candidate for the sport of the 1980s?

6. Did you have trouble with the word *infrastructure* (paragraph 3)? Does the meaning become clear in context as you read, or would a brief definition help? If so, formulate a synonym or short definition for *infrastructure.*

7. Where does Lipsyte use words that might be classified as slang? What is their effect?

8. What tone of voice is projected? Is it sincere? Is sentence structure important in establishing the tone? Illustrate.

REFLECTING

Point: Lipsyte wrote this introduction as a definition of *SportsWorld,* a term he coined for his book. Do you also find an opinion expressed? If so, what?

Organization: Outline the article so that the "infrastructure" of Lipsyte's definition is revealed. Note how he uses the historical background.

Support: Discuss how Lipsyte uses example, cause-and-effect relationships, and analogy to support his subclassifications. Cite specific examples of each technique.

Synthesis: Do you agree or disagree with many of his ideas about sports? Do some of the attitudes you encountered in Leo Durocher's essay (pages 132–34) illustrate or contradict any of Lipsyte's convictions? Can you provide examples for any of the claims made in paragraph 4?

Evaluation: How do you react to the article? Do you think it is effective and thoughtful, or do you think Lipsyte exaggerates the sports situation? Defend your answer by citing examples from the essay. How effectively has he stated and supported his points?

FROM READING TO WRITING

1. For a general audience, write an extended definition of a term that you create, such as *DormWorld, RockWorld, SpectatorWorld.* Be sure that you follow the form given for definition on page 164.

2. For your classmates, write an extended definition about a subject that is surrounded with a number of myths—the freshman English grading system, childbirth, marijuana, for example.

3. Choose a term or idiom from a sports activity or a game that has made its way into the general language and write an extended definition of it for foreign students: for instance, *throw a curve, behind the eightball, two strikes against you, stalemate, hazard, take a swan dive, touché, hold the line.*

IN BED
Joan Didion

BIOGRAPHICAL SKETCH

Joan Didion, who was born in Sacramento, California, in 1934, graduated from the University of California at Berkeley. She has been an associate feature editor for Vogue, *and is currently a contributing editor for* Esquire, *the* Saturday Evening Post, *and the* National Review. *Among her written works are a screenplay for* A Star Is Born; *three novels,* Run, River; Play It As It Lays; *and* A Book of Common Prayer; *and two essay collections,* Slouching Toward Bethlehem *and* The White Album. *In many of her articles and stories, Didion has written vividly and trenchantly about West Coast culture and society, particularly during the turbulent 60s.*

PRE-READING

1. From the opening paragraph, what do you think the subject of the essay will be?

2. Explain how the author's attitude toward migraines in the first paragraph differs from the one expressed in the last paragraph.

[1] Three, four, sometimes five times a month, I spend the day in bed with a migraine headache, insensible to the world around me. Almost every day of every month, between these attacks, I feel the sudden irrational irritation and the flush of blood into the cerebral arteries which tell me that migraine is on its

FROM *The White Album* (New York: Simon and Shuster, 1979), pp. 168–72. Copyright © 1979 by Joan Didion. Reprinted by Simon & Schuster, a Division of Gulf & Western Corporation.

way, and I take certain drugs to avert its arrival. If I did not take the drugs, I would be able to function perhaps one day in four. The physiological error called migraine is, in brief, central to the given of my life. When I was 15, 16, even 25, I used to think that I could rid myself of this error by simply denying it, character over chemistry. "Do you have headaches *sometimes! frequently! never!*" the application forms would demand. "Check one." Wary of the trap, wanting whatever it was that the successful circumnavigation of that particular form could bring (a job, a scholarship, the respect of mankind and the grace of God), I would check one. *"Sometimes,"* I would lie. That in fact I spent one or two days a week almost unconscious with pain seemed a shameful secret, evidence not merely of some chemical inferiority but of all my bad attitudes, unpleasant tempers, wrongthink.

² For I had no brain tumor, no eyestrain, no high blood pressure, nothing wrong with me at all: I simply had migraine headaches, and migraine headaches were, as everyone who did not have them knew, imaginary. I fought migraine then, ignored the warnings it sent, went to school and later to work in spite of it, sat through lectures in Middle English and presentations to advertisers with involuntary tears running down the right side of my face, threw up in washrooms, stumbled home by instinct, emptied ice trays onto my bed and tried to freeze the pain in my right temple, wished only for a neurosurgeon who would do a lobotomy on house call, and cursed my imagination.

³ It was a long time before I began thinking mechanistically enough to accept migraine for what it was: something with which I would be living, the way some people live with diabetes. Migraine is something more than the fancy of a neurotic imagination. It is an essentially hereditary complex of symptoms, the most frequently noted but by no means the most unpleasant of which is a vascular headache of blinding severity, suffered by a surprising number of women, a fair number of men (Thomas Jefferson had migraine, and so did Ulysses S. Grant, the day he accepted Lee's surrender), and by some unfortunate children as young as two years old. (I had my first when I was eight. It came on during a fire drill at the Columbia School in Colorado Springs, Colorado. I was taken first home and then to the infirmary at Peterson Field, where my father was stationed. The Air Corps doctor prescribed an enema.) Almost anything can trigger a specific attack of migraine: stress, allergy, fatigue, an abrupt change in barometric pressure, a contretemps over a parking ticket. A flashing light. A fire drill. One inherits, of course, only the predisposition. In other words I spent yesterday in bed with a headache not merely because of my bad attitudes, unpleasant tempers and wrongthink, but because both my grandmothers had migraine, my father has migraine and my mother has migraine.

⁴ No one knows precisely what it is that is inherited. The chemistry of migraine, however, seems to have some connection with the nerve hormone named serotonin, which is naturally present in the brain. The amount of serotonin in the blood falls sharply at the onset of migraine, and one migraine drug, methysergide, or Sansert, seems to have some effect on serotonin.

Methysergide is a derivative of lysergic acid (in fact Sandoz Pharmaceuticals first synthesized LSD-25 while looking for a migraine cure), and its use is hemmed about with so many contraindications and side effects that most doctors prescribe it only in the most incapacitating cases. Methysergide, when it is prescribed, is taken daily, as a preventive; another preventive which works for some people is old-fashioned ergotamine tartrate, which helps to constrict the swelling blood vessels during the "aura," the period which in most cases precedes the actual headache.

⁵ Once an attack is under way, however, no drug touches it. Migraine gives some people mild hallucinations, temporarily blinds others, shows up not only as a headache but as a gastrointestinal disturbance, a painful sensitivity to all sensory stimuli, an abrupt overpowering fatigue, a strokelike aphasia, and a crippling inability to make even the most routine connections. When I am in a migraine aura (for some people the aura lasts fifteen minutes, for others several hours), I will drive through red lights, lose the house keys, spill whatever I am holding, lose the ability to focus my eyes or frame coherent sentences, and generally give the appearance of being on drugs, or drunk. The actual headache, when it comes, brings with it chills, sweating, nausea, a debility that seems to stretch the very limits of endurance. That no one dies of migraine seems, to someone deep into an attack, an ambiguous blessing.

⁶ My husband also has migraine, which is unfortunate for him but fortunate for me: perhaps nothing so tends to prolong an attack as the accusing eye of someone who has never had a headache. "Why not take a couple of aspirin," the unafflicted will say from the doorway, or "I'd have a headache, too, spending a beautiful day like this inside with all the shades drawn." All of us who have migraine suffer not only from the attacks themselves but from this common conviction that we are perversely refusing to cure ourselves by taking a couple of aspirin, that we are making ourselves sick, that we "bring it on ourselves." And in the most immediate sense, the sense of why we have a headache this Tuesday and not last Thursday, of course we often do. There certainly is what doctors call a "migraine personality," and that personality tends to be ambitious, inward, intolerant of error, rather rigidly organized, perfectionist. "You don't look like a migraine personality," a doctor once said to me. "Your hair's messy. But I suppose you're a compulsive housekeeper." Actually my house is kept even more negligently than my hair, but the doctor was right nonetheless: perfectionism can also take the form of spending most of a week writing and rewriting and not writing a single paragraph.

⁷ But not all perfectionists have migraine, and not all migrainous people have migraine personalities. We do not escape heredity. I have tried in most of the available ways to escape my own migrainous heredity (at one point I learned to give myself two daily injections of histamine with a hypodermic needle, even though the needle so frightened me that I had to close my eyes when I did it), but I still have migraine. And I have learned now to live with it, learned when to expect it, how to outwit it, even how to regard it, when it does come, as more friend than lodger. We have reached a certain understanding,

my migraine and I. It never comes when I am in real trouble. Tell me that my house is burned down, my husband has left me, that there is gunfighting in the streets and panic in the banks, and I will not respond by getting a headache. It comes instead when I am fighting not an open but a guerrilla war with my own life, during weeks of small household confusions, lost laundry, unhappy help, canceled appointments, on days when the telephone rings too much and I get no work done and the wind is coming up. On days like that my friend comes uninvited.

[8] And once it comes, now that I am wise in its ways, I no longer fight it. I lie down and let it happen. At first every small apprehension is magnified, every anxiety a pounding terror. Then the pain comes, and I concentrate only on that. Right there is the usefulness of migraine, there in that imposed yoga, the concentration on the pain. For when the pain recedes, ten or twelve hours later, everything goes with it, all the hidden resentments, all the vain anxieties. The migraine has acted as a circuit breaker, and the fuses have emerged intact. There is a pleasant convalescent euphoria. I open the windows and feel the air, eat gratefully, sleep well. I notice the particular nature of a flower in a glass on the stair landing. I count my blessings.

ANALYTICAL READING

1. What misconceptions about migraines does Joan Didion discuss?

2. How does she distinguish migraine from other types of headaches? What symptons are peculiar to migraine?

3. What do you think the author's real purpose is in defining migraines?

4. Which sentences contain advice that could be followed by any person with a chronic health condition?

5. What advantages has Didion learned to glean from migraine attacks?

6. Didion uses a number of short descriptive phrases. For your classmates, explain: "lobotomy on house call" (paragraph 2); "wrongthink," "strokelike aphasia" (paragraph 5); "imposed yoga," "circuit breaker," "convalescent euphoria" (paragraph 8).

7. Didion skillfully relies on parallelism to pack her sentences with vivid details. Point out several examples.

REFLECTING

Point: What is the twofold purpose of the article?

Organization: Although in narrative form, the article is essentially a definition. Outline the organizational structure, using the scheme on page 164.

Support: How does the author's own experience with migraine lend support to the definition? How does the chronological narrative provide support for some of the features of migraine that she uses in the definition?

Synthesis: Have you ever had a recurring or chronic health problem that you had to learn to deal with? If so, explain its relationship to Didion's experience. How do Didion's actions relate to Sissela Bok's discussion of the kind of white lies that people tell (see pages 201–03)?

Evaluation: Does the article do more for the reader than simply define a medical term? Did you find the title and opening paragraph misleading? Do you think the author's narrative form adds to or detracts from her purpose? Explain.

FROM READING TO WRITING

1.   Write an essay for a college audience telling about your experience with some medical or health condition that you found embarrasing or that curtailed your activities for a period of time. Define the condition, as Joan Didion does in the article, indicating how you learned to live with the situation. Possible topics: braces for your teeth, severe acne, a trick knee or back, a bout with warts, asthma attacks, overweight, and so on.

2.   Using the information from Didion's "In Bed," write an article for your college newspaper defining migraine headaches and appealing for sympathy and understanding for students suffering from them.

Analysis
Analysis Using Cause and Effect

THE STAGES OF DYING
Elisabeth Kübler-Ross

BIOGRAPHICAL SKETCH

Elisabeth Kübler-Ross was born in Zurich, Switzerland, in 1926. A doctor of psychiatry, she has received degrees from a number of universities, including the University of Zurich, Smith College, and Albany College of Medicine. She has been a practitioner, a teacher, and a consultant in psychiatry since 1959. Although her professional interests include children's emotional problems and psychosomatic medicine, her main concern has been with the psychological adjustment to dying. Besides On Death and Dying, *from which this selection is taken, her publications include* Death: The Final Stage of Growth, Questions and Answers on Death and Dying, *and* Living with Death and Dying.

PRE-READING

1. From the title of the book and the opening paragraph, what do you think will be the author's attitude toward dying?

2. Does the opening paragraph help to allay your aversion to reading aboout death? If so, how?

3. From the biographical sketch, what do you assume about Kübler-Ross as an authority on the subject?

[1] In a time of uncertainty, of the hydrogen bomb, of the big rush and the masses, the little small, personal gift may again become meaningful. The gift is on both sides: from the [dying] patient in the form of the help, inspiration, and encouragement he may give to others with a similar predicament; from us in the form of our care, our time, and our wish to share with others what they have taught us at the end of their lives.

[2] One reason perhaps for patients' good response is the need of the dying person to leave something behind, to give a little gift, to create an illusion of

FROM Elisabeth Kübler-Ross, *On Death and Dying* (New York: Macmillan, 1969), pp. 233–47. Copyright © 1969 by Elisabeth Kübler-Ross. Reprinted with permission of Macmillan Publishing Co., Inc.

immortality perhaps. We acknowledge our appreciation for their sharing with us their thoughts about this taboo topic, we tell them that their role is to *teach* us, to help those who follow them later on, thus creating an idea that something will live perhaps after their death, an idea, a seminar in which their suggestions, their fantasies, their thoughts continue to live, to be discussed, become immortal in a little way.

[3] A communication has been established by the dying patient who attempts to separate himself from human relationships in order to face the last separation with the fewest possible ties, yet is unable to do this without help from an outsider who shares some of these conflicts with him.

[4] We are talking about death—the subject of social repression—in a frank, uncomplicated manner, thus opening the door for a wide variety of discussions, allowing complete denial if this seems to be necessary or open talk about the patient's fears and concerns if the patient so chooses. The fact that *we* don't use denial, that we are willing to use the words death and dying, is perhaps the most welcomed communication for many of our patients.

[5] If we attempt to summarize briefly what these patients have taught us, the outstanding fact, to my mind, is that they are all aware of the seriousness of their illness whether they are told or not. They do not always share this knowledge with their doctor or next of kin. The reason for this is that is it painful to think of such a reality, and any implicit or explicit message not to talk about it is usually perceived by the patient and—for the moment—gladly accepted. There came a time, however, when all of our patients had a need to share some of their concerns, to lift the mask, to face reality, and to take care of vital matters while there was still time. They welcomed a breakthrough in their defenses, they appreciated our willingness to talk with them about their impending death and unfinished tasks. They wished to share with an understanding person some of their feelings, especially the ones of anger, rage, envy, guilt, and isolation. They clearly indicated that they used denial when the doctor or family member expected denial because of their dependency on them and their need to maintain a relationship.

[6] The patients did not mind so much when the staff did not confront them with the facts directly, but they resented being treated like children and not being considered when important decisions were made. They all sensed a change in attitude and behavior when the diagnosis of a malignancy was made and became aware of the seriousness of their condition because of the changed behavior of the people in their environment. In other words, those who were not told explicitly knew it anyway from the implicit messages or altered behavior of relatives or staff. Those who were told explicitly appreciated the opportunity almost unanimously except for those who were told either crudely in hallways and without preparation or follow-up, or in a manner that left no hope.

[7] All of our patients reacted to the bad news in almost identical ways, which is typical not only of the news of fatal illness but seems to be a human reaction to great and unexpected stress: namely, with shock and disbelief. De-

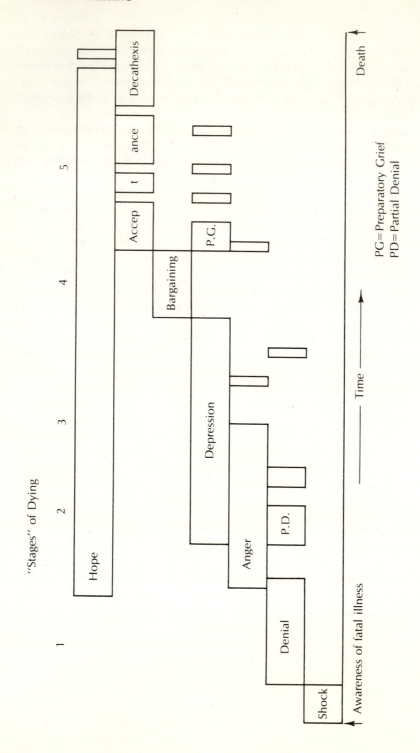

nial was used by most of our patients and lasted from a few seconds to many months. . . . This denial is never a total denial. After the denial, anger and rage predominated. It expressed itself in a multitude of ways as an envy of those who were able to live and function. This anger was partially justified and enforced by the reactions of staff and family, at times almost irrational and a repetition of earlier experiences. . . . When the environment was able to tolerate this anger without taking it personally, the patient was greatly helped in reaching a stage of temporary bargaining followed by depression, which is a stepping-stone towards final acceptance. The following diagram demonstrates how these stages do not replace each other but can exist next to each other and overlap at times. The final acceptance has been reached by many patients without any external help, others needed assistance in working through these different stages in order to die in peace and dignity.

[8] No matter the stage of illness or coping mechanisms used, all our patients maintained some form of hope until the last moment. Those patients who were told of their fatal diagnosis without a chance, without a sense of hope, reacted the worst and never quite reconciled themselves with the person who presented the news to them in this cruel manner. As far as our patients are concerned, all of them maintained some hope and it is well for us to remember this! It may come in the form of a new discovery, a new finding in a research laboratory, a new drug or serum, it may come as a miracle from God or by the discovery that the X-ray or pathological slide really belongs to another patient. It may come in the form of a naturally occurring remission, . . . but it is this hope that should always be maintained whether we can agree with the form or not.

[9] Though our patients greatly appreciated sharing their concerns with us and talked freely about death and dying, they, too, gave their signals when to change the topic, when to turn to more cheerful things again. They all acknowledged that it was good to ventilate their feelings; they also had the need to choose the time and the duration for this.

[10] Earlier conflicts and defense mechanisms allow us to predict to a certain degree what defense mechanisms a patient will use more extensively at the time of this crisis. Simple people with less education, sophistication, social ties, and professional obligations seem in general to have somewhat less difficulty in facing this final crisis than people of affluence who lose a great deal more in terms of material luxuries, comfort, and number of interpersonal relationships. It appears that people who have gone through a life of suffering, hard work, and labor, who have raised their children and been gratified in their work, have shown greater ease in accepting death with peace and dignity compared to those who have been ambitiously controlling their environment, accumulating material goods, and a great number of social relationships but few meaningful interpersonal relationships which would have been available at the end of life. . . .

[11] Religious patients seemed to differ little from those without a religion. The difference may be hard to determine, since we have not clearly defined

what we mean by a religious person. We can say here, however, that we found very few truly religious people with an intrinsic faith. Those few have been helped by their faith and are best comparable with those few patients who were true atheists. The majority of patients were in between, with some form of religious belief but not enough to relieve them of conflict and fear.

[12] When our patients reached the stage of acceptance and final decathexis, interference from outside was regarded as the greatest turmoil and prevented several patients from dying in peace and dignity. It is the signal of imminent death and has allowed us to predict the oncoming death in several patients where there was little or no indication for it from a medical point of view. The patient responds to an intrinsic signal system which tells him of his impending death. We are able to pick up these cues without really knowing what psycho-physiological signals the patient perceives. When the patient is asked, he is able to acknowledge his awareness and often communicates it to us by asking us to to sit down *now*, since he knows that tomorrow will be too late. We should be keenly aware of such insistence on the part of our patients, as we may miss a unique chance to listen to them while there is still time.

. . .

[13] At this time in a patient's life the pain ceases to be, when the mind slips off into a dreamless state, when the need for food becomes minimal and the awareness of the environment all but disappears into darkness. This is the time when the relatives walk up and down the hospital hallways, tormented by the waiting, not knowing if they should leave to attend the living or stay to be around for the moment of death. This is the time when it is too late for words, and yet the time when the relatives cry the loudest for help—with or without words. It is too late for medical interventions (and too cruel, though well meant, when they do occur), but is is also too early for a final separation from the dying. Is is the hardest time for the next of kin as he either wishes to take off, to get it over with; or he desperately clings to something that he is in the process of losing forever. It is the time for the therapy of silence with the patient and availability for the relatives.

[14] The doctor, nurse, social worker, or chaplain can be of great help during these final moments if they can understand the family's conflicts at this time and help select the one person who feels most comfortable staying with the dying patient. This person then becomes in effect the patient's therapist. Those who feel too uncomfortable can be assisted by alleviating their guilt and by the reassurance that someone will stay with the dying until his death has occurred. They can then return home knowing that the patient did not die alone, yet not feeling ashamed or guilty for having avoided this moment which for many people is so difficult to face.

[15] Those who have the strength and the love to sit with a dying patient in the *silence that goes beyond words* will know that this moment is neither frightening nor painful, but a peaceful cessation of the functioning of the body. Watching a peaceful death of a human being reminds us of a falling star; one of a

million lights in a vast sky that flares up for a brief moment only to disappear into the endless night forever. To be a therapist to a dying patient makes us aware of the uniqueness of each individual in this vast sea of humanity. It makes us aware of our finiteness, our limited lifespan. Few of us live beyond our three score and ten years and yet in that brief time most of us create and live a unique biography and weave ourselves into the fabric of human history.

The water in a vessel is sparkling; the water in the sea is dark.
The small truth has words that are clear; the great truth has great silence.
—Rabindranath Tagore, from *Stray Birds*, CLXXVI*

ANALYTICAL READING

1. What relationship has the mention of the "small, personal gift" in paragraph 1 to the discussion of dying that follows?

2. What reasons does Kübler-Ross give for dealing openly with dying patients?

3. How does the author use classification in her discussion of the stages of dying? What are they?

4. What recommendations does she make about the initial informing of patients that they have a terminal illness? What personality characteristics should a doctor develop?

5. What does she have to say about religious beliefs? Did this surprise you? Why?

6. How would you define the *silence that goes beyond words* (paragraph 15) and *decathexis* (paragraph 12)?

7. What philosophy about human life is revealed in the last paragraph? Does it appear in other parts of the essay? Where?

REFLECTING

Point: State in one sentence the thesis of the selection. Where is it first stated? What opinion or point of view does it express?

Organization: Outline the organizational scheme of the selection.

Support: How does the author's classification of the stages of dying help to support her thesis idea?

Synthesis: What have been your own experiences with death? Have you been shielded from family deaths? Do you agree with Kübler-Ross that we should become more open about dying and death? If so, what are some means of achieving that aim? Do you think a terminal cancer patient should be informed? Why or why not?

Evaluation: Did you find the essay effective and thought-provoking? How would you characterize the writer's voice? Does the voice contribute to the effectiveness of the selection? Discuss.

*Copyright 1916 by Macmillan Publishing Co., Inc. Renewed 1944 by Rathindranath Tagore.

FROM READING TO WRITING

1. For a general audience, write an article in which you formulate a thesis statement concerning whether or not children should be exposed to death in other ways than by watching violent television programs and movies. Use cause-and-effect relationships in support of your thesis as Kübler-Ross does.

2. For a general audience, write an article relating sex education to the attitude toward dying reflected in Kübler-Ross' essay.

PROHIBITION AND DRUGS
Milton Friedman

BIOGRAPHICAL SKETCH

Milton Friedman was born in New York City in 1912. He received a Ph.D. from Columbia University and holds seven honorary degrees. Awarded the Nobel Prize for economics, he has a distinguished career as a columnist (currently for Newsweek), government advisor to Republican Presidents, and scholar and teacher of economics at the University of Chicago. He has been president of the American Economic Association and is a member of the National Academy of Sciences. Best known as the founder of the monetarist "Chicago School" of economics, Friedman has written about a wide variety of social and political subjects, crusading tirelessly and vigorously for freedom from government controls in all fields. Among his countless articles and sixteen books is the 1980 best-seller Free to Choose, *which was co-authored by his wife and which served as the basis of his PBS television series.*

PRE-READING

1. Having read the biographical sketch, are you surprised to find Friedman writing about drugs? What position do you think he will take?

2. Skim the opening and closing paragraphs. What opinion do you expect Friedman to express in the essay?

[1] "The reign of tears is over. The slums will soon be only a memory. We will turn our prisons into factories and our jails into storehouses and corncribs. Men will walk upright now, women will smile, and the children will laugh. Hell will be forever for rent."

[2] This is how Billy Sunday, the noted evangelist and leading crusader against Demon Rum, greeted the onset of Prohibition in early 1920. We know now how tragically his hopes were doomed. New prisons and jails had to be built to house the criminals spawned by converting the drinking of spirits into

FROM Milton Friedman, *There's No Such Thing as a Free Lunch* (La Salle, Ill.: Open Court Publishing Co., 1975), pp. 227–29. The article was originally published in *Newsweek,* 1 May 1972. Copyright 1972 by Newsweek, Inc. Reprinted by permission.

a crime against the state. Prohibition undermined respect for the law, corrupted the minions of the law, created a decadent moral climate—but did not stop the consumption of alcohol.

³ Despite this tragic object lession, we seem bent on repeating precisely the same mistake in the handling of drugs.

⁴ On ethical grounds, do we have the right to use the machinery of government to prevent an individual from becoming an alcoholic or a drug addict? For children, almost everyone would answer at least a qualified yes. But for responsible adults, I, for one, would answer no. Reason with the potential addict, yes. Tell him the consequences, yes. Pray for and with him, yes. But I believe that we have no right to use force, directly or indirectly, to prevent a fellow man from committing suicide, let alone from drinking alcohol or taking drugs.

⁵ I readily grant that the ethical issue is difficult and that men of goodwill may well disagree. Fortunately, we need not resolve the ethical issue to agree on policy. *Prohibition is an attempted cure that makes matters worse—for both the addict and the rest of us.* Hence, even if you regard present policy toward drugs as ethically justified, considerations of expediency make that policy most unwise.

⁶ *Consider first the addict.* Legalizing drugs might increase the number of addicts, but it is not clear that it would. Forbidden fruit is attractive, particularly to the young. More important, many drug addicts are deliberately made by pushers, who give likely prospects their first few doses free. It pays the pusher to do so because, once hooked, the addict is a captive customer. If drugs were legally available, any possible profit from such inhumane activity would disappear, since the addict could buy from the cheapest source.

⁷ Whatever happens to the number of addicts, the individual addict would clearly be far better off if drugs were legal. Today, drugs are both incredibly expensive and highly uncertain in quality. Addicts are driven to associate with criminals to get the drugs, become criminals themselves to finance the habit, and risk constant danger of death and disease.

⁸ *Consider next the rest of us.* Here the situation is crystal-clear. The harm to us from the addiction of others arises almost wholly from the fact that drugs are illegal. A recent committee of the American Bar Association estimated that addicts commit one-third to one-half of all street crime in the U.S. Legalize drugs, and street crime would drop automatically.

⁹ Moreover, addicts and pushers are not the only ones corrupted. Immense sums are at stake. It is inevitable that some relatively low-paid police and other government officials—and some high-paid ones as well—will succumb to the temptation to pick up easy money.

¹⁰ Legalizing drugs would simultaneously reduce the amount of crime and raise the quality of law enforcement. Can you conceive of any other measure that would accomplish so much to promote law and order?

¹¹ But, you may say, must we accept defeat? Why not simply end the drug traffic? That is where experience under Prohibition is most relevant. We cannot

end the drug traffic. We may be able to cut off opium from Turkey—but there are innumerable other places where the opium poppy grows. With French cooperation, we may be able to make Marseilles an unhealthy place to manufacture heroin—but there are innumerable other places where the simple manufacturing operations involved can be carried out. So long as large sums of money are involved—and they are bound to be if drugs are illegal—it is literally hopeless to expect to end the traffic or even reduce seriously its scope.

[12] In drugs, as in other areas, persuasion and example are likely to be far more effective than the use of force to shape others in our image.

ANALYTICAL READING

1. Why is the quotation from Billy Sunday an effective way to open the paper?

2. Did you note the use of parallel structure in paragraph 4? What is the effect?

3. What effects does Friedman claim drug prohibition has had? How does he classify the effects?

4. What is his main reason for legalizing drugs? Is it a persuasive one? Does he attempt to present opinions other than his own?

5. What solutions does the author recommend? Has he examined all the possibilities? Is his solution practical? Would it be publicly and politically effective?

REFLECTING

Point: Did you underline the sentence that contains the thesis idea? Where does it occur?

Organization: How does Friedman indicate to the reader the pattern of his organization?

Support: How does the writer use cause-and-effect reasoning and the example of alcohol to support his ideas?

Synthesis: Do you agree with Friedman, or do you think he ignores other factors? Has ending alcohol prohibition eliminated all our problems with liquor? How does the information about the writer's economic philosophy given in the biographical sketch relate to the attitudes expressed in the article?

Evaluation: Do you find the article convincingly written? To what extent is it persuasive?

FROM READING TO WRITING

1. For an audience not familiar with this essay, write a paper in which you utilize cause-and-effect reasoning, agreeing or disagreeing with Friedman's thesis.

2. For a general audience, write a paper analyzing the possible advantages or disadvantages of decriminalizing (as distinct from outright legalizing) marijuana, heroin, or cocaine.

ARCHIE BUNKER, LENNY BRUCE, AND BEN CARTWRIGHT: TABOO-BREAKING AND CHARACTER IDENTIFICATION IN *ALL IN THE FAMILY*

Dennis E. Showalter

BIOGRAPHICAL SKETCH

Dennis E. Showalter was born in Delano, Minnesota, in 1942. He received an undergraduate degree from St. John's University and M.A. and Ph.D. degrees in history from the University of Minnesota. After teaching there, he joined the faculty at Colorado College, where he has remained since 1969. Showalter has received grants from the Ford Foundation and the National Endowment for the Humanities. His special area of interest is Prussian history, particularly its military aspects, about which he has published several scholarly articles.

PRE-READING

1. Sometimes the name of the periodical and the date of original publication can help in understanding an article. *The Journal of Popular Culture,* in which this essay first appeared, is written mainly by and for a scholarly audience; consequently it is carefully footnoted. The year of publication, 1975, is useful as a warning that some of the statements may be outdated. Do you think that the title is different in structure from many others in this book because of the readers it is addressed to? Explain.

2. Who was Lenny Bruce, and what is meant by "taboo-breaking"? Do the answers to these questions suggest what Showalter's essay is concerned with?

3. What main point about the essay is revealed in the first few sentences of the second paragraph?

4. From a reading of the final paragraph, what other major trend does the essay describe?

[1] Television's first family of five years' standing, Archie and Edith, Gloria and Mike, has evoked as much controversy as anything coming over the airwaves since Lucille Ball's advancing pregnancy regaled fans of "I Love Lucy" during the 1950s. In the first year of their existence the Bunkers received the accolade of a *Newsweek* cover story and were attacked in the columns of the *Ladies' Home Journal* by no less a pop authority figure than Doctor Theodore Rubin. "All in the Family" was described as an insult to blue-collar America and an accurate picture of the silent majority. It was called good clean fun and an insidious legitimation of bigotry. It established a model for series featuring

FROM *Journal of Popular Culture,* 9:3, Winter 1975, pp. 618–21. Reprinted by permission.

ethnic insults, right-on dialogue, and family infighting. Whether originally developed as spinoffs, counter-attacks, or imitations, programs such as "Maude" and "The Jeffersons," "Sanford and Son" and "Lotsa Luck," "Hot L Baltimore" and "Chico and The Man," are all part of Archie's extended family. And if discussion of the series' message and meaning no longer occupies a prominent place in the media's entertainment columns, "All in the Family" continues to attract attention from other sources. It is presented as a source of pop theology, with Edith as a "little Christ."[1] It has been linked with classical drama, with Mike described as descending from the glutton figure of the Greco-Roman stage.[2] It is even the subject of at least two doctoral dissertations.

[2] In the process of incorporating "All in the Family" into the intellectual establishment, it becomes increasingly easy to forget the fact that the show is a reflection of two major trends in American popular entertainment. The first is shock value: Archie Bunker is a legitimate successor to Lenny Bruce. Of course there are substantial differences between the stage personality of Bruce and the scriptwriters' creation animated by Carroll O'Connor—who from the beginning took careful and successful pains to separate himself from the role. Yet both Archie and Lenny utter the unspeakable, both contemplate the unthinkable, with relish. It may be truism to suggest that bigotry in all its forms has replaced sex as a taboo subject, yet the generalization is accurate. In the permissive 1970s accusations of an overt Oedipus complex became mere opening shots in a spirited political dialogue. The stage nudity of *Oh! Calcutta!* evolved into the multiple presentation of the sex act before increasingly jaded audiences. Yet at a time when exploiters of the new sexual freedom are increasingly concerned over what to do for an encore, what Michael Novak calls "the rise of the unmeltable ethnics" has created new forbidden fruits. "Black" is capitalized by journalists as well as militants. "Polish Power" is a slogan vital enough to have given ex-teen idol Bobby Vinton a second career. The women's movement has swept away much of the "take my wife—please!" genre of sexist humor, and the Gray Panthers attack Johnny Carson's Aunt Blabby as a tasteless slur on the elderly.

[3] Without debating the intrinsic merit of this new taboo, it is certain that like its predecessor, it exists to be broken. The delicious sense of participation in the forbidden as Lenny Bruce said "fuck" in a 1960 cabaret was felt by a new generation as Archie Bunker growled "nigger" on coast-to-coast television in 1971. But Archie's is taboo-breaking with a difference. The new age of militancy and permissiveness puts strains on the middle-class white American who sincerely wants to do the right thing and feel the right emotions. As the grandfather developed avoidance mechanisms to avert sexual response at the sight of an exposed ankle, so the grandson suppresses or sublimates negative

---

[1] Edward McNulty, "The Gospel According to Edith Bunker," *Christian Century,* March 27, 1974, 346–47.

[2] John L. Wright, "Tunie-In: The Focus of Television Criticism," *Journal of Popular Culture,* VII (1974), 891.

reactions to behavior patterns *he* finds obnoxious. Yet the commuter jostled by a black in the subway, the businessman involved in an acrimonious dispute with a Jewish associate, the professor who has had one too many relevant students, can find release as Carroll O'Connor echoes his own subconscious. On the other hand, Archie's blue-collar vulgarity prevents the kind of excessive identification which disturbs the viewer's equilibrium and incites him to change channels. Indeed Archie's character relates uniquely to the possibility of such identification. His incongruous command of ideas and phrases, his glib flights of verbal fancy, his "Bunkerisms," those made-up words and malapropisms which provide much of the show's ongoing humor, reflect pretension as well as prejudice.[3] They convey the idea of an ignoramus vainly trying to rise above himself. They are not necessary to the character; Redd Foxx and Jack Albertson play broadly similar roles without them. Bunkerisms are rather an educated person's image of the way someone like Archie *ought* to use words of more than two syllables. Archie is in fact an intellectual's *Doppelgänger*, an academician's Mr. Hyde. His degenerate verbalizations offer the opportunity to alleviate lingering guilt by indulging one's superior learning at Archie's expense and therefore, by extension, reaffirming one's superior moral sense as well.

[4] It is not necessary, however, to explain "All in the Family's" ambiguous appeal strictly in terms of pop psychology. Simply put, in five years Archie's character has mellowed and those of his family have developed. This pattern is common in American television, particularly in programs with several regularly-featured players. Such a series usually begins with sharply-delineated characters, and scripts emphasizing conflicts among them. If the show survives, a combination of changed script structure and growing familiarity of the actors with each other and the characters they portray often results in a softening of interpretations, a blurring of outlines.[4] The dominant pattern of interaction between Alan Alda's Hawkeye and Loretta Swit's Hot Lips in "M.A.S.H." has changed from hostility to affection since the initial episodes. In the western series "The High Chaparral," tensions among the partriarchal rancher, his ineffectual son, and his scapegrace brother dominated the first seasons' scripts. The relationship between the rancher and his Mexican wife was hardly less strained. By the time the show was cancelled the Cannons were one big happy family, with conflicts among them played as comedy rather than drama. But the best example of this process remains that longtime prime-time favorite, "Bonanza." It requires a real effort of memory to recall the days when Little Joe carried an epée, Ben Cartwright pronounced anathemas on wrongdoers, and there were three brothers who fought each other almost as fiercely as they battled external enemies. How many viewers even of syndicated reruns know

---

[3] Alfred F. Rosa and Paul A Eschholz, "Bunkerisms: Archie's Suppository Remarks in 'All in the Family,'" *ibid.*, VI (1972). 275.

[4] This can also be done by network or producer's fiat, as illustrated by the rapid mellowing of Jack Albertson's Ed Brown in response to Chicano criticism of "Chico and the Man."

that Adam's mother was a Yankee, Little Joe's a southern belle, and Hoss's a Swedish immigrant? And how many can remember when those distinctions were important to "Bonanza's" plots?

⁵ It is possible similarly to trace the evolution of Archie Bunker from a faintly malevolent embodiment of bigotry into an avuncular Chester Riley whose bark bears little relationship to his bite. Apart from the scripts, which generally show Archie as ridiculous or ineffectual in any role he tries to perform, the process was furthered by his appearance. Caroll O'Connor has never managed to make Archie *look* threatening or vicious, an important characteristic in a visual medium. The swaggering walk, the clenched teeth, and the ever present cigar are belied by the pudgy body and the perpetual expression of bewilderment at the complexities of present-day life. Moreover, as the secondary characters have become personalities in their own right, the series no longer focusses so strongly on Archie and his rhetoric. Indeed he vanished entirely from several recent episodes during a recent contract dispute. Gloria's increasing maturity, her search for an identity, Mike's male chauvinism, Edith's emerging assertiveness, are at least as interesting and amusing as Archie's undifferentiated prejudices—perhaps even more so, because there are only a limited number of ways to say "Hebe." To a new viewer, or an old one willing to suspend his sense of outrage, "All in the Family" can be seen as developing into just another situation comedy. Archie's racial and religious slurs fit the pattern of Felix Unger's fussiness in "The Odd Couple," or Maude Finley's stridently liberal rhetoric. They represent a method of character identification and an aid to comedy—nothing more. As "All in the Family" begins its new season, Lenny Bruce has given way to Ben Cartwright.

ANALYTICAL READING

1. How is Showalter's statement that "bigotry . . . has replaced sex as a taboo subject" (paragraph 2) important in his article?

2. What role does Archie's misuse of words or creation of new ones ("Malapropisms" or "Bunkerisms") play in the audience's response to his character?

3. What does Showalter mean by the "ambiguous appeal" of *All in the Family* (paragraph 4)?

4. What is the function of paragraph 4 in the development of Showalter's ideas?

5. What is the importance of the point that Showalter makes about Carroll O'Connor's physical appearance?

6. What does the last sentence do for the meaning and the organization of the essay?

7. In paragraph 5, replace the following words with appropriate synonyms: *malevolent, embodiment, avuncular, ineffectual, rhetoric, undifferentiated.* Try to find words more familiar to a general audience and note the difference in tone achieved by these substitutions.

REFLECTING

Point: What is the purpose of Showalter's historical approach to his subject? What two major trends embody his thesis? Write another title for the essay, indicating these two trends more clearly. Would you classify the essay as an argument? Why or why not?

Organization: What is the function of the opening paragraph? Would it make any difference if Showalter had discussed the trend involving Ben Cartwright before the one involving Lenny Bruce? Discuss the way that he organizes the comparison and contrast of Lenny Bruce and Archie Bunker (paragraphs 2 and 3).

Support: Should any statements have been footnoted besides the ones that are? Discuss. How does Showalter support his contention about the changes that take place in series like *All in the Family?* In what ways does the author reveal that he is writing to a highly educated audience, not to a general one? How does footnote 4 differ from the others?

Synthesis: How do you react to Archie—with annoyance, sympathy, or mixed feelings? Explain. To what do you attribute the success of the series? Do you agree with Showalter's point about the changes that occur in series with numerous characters? Discuss, referring to more recent programs. Is Showalter's criticism outdated? Would he have included *Dallas* in his article? According to his analysis, do you think that *All in the Family* will continue for years? Why or why not?

Evaluation: How knowledgeable does Showalter appear to be about television programs like *All in the Family?* Does he adequately suport his main points? Is his essay well organized, informative, and convincing? Is his analysis of Archie thorough, perceptive, and clear? How appropriate are the voice and tone of the writer? Has he overlooked anything significant about *All in the Family* or Archie that would weaken his thesis?

FROM READING TO WRITING

1. Write a review of examples of certain kinds of television programs, showing how their appeal may be attributed to taboo-breaking. For example, you might examine the popular "celebrity roasts," the late-evening "adult" or interview discussions, or a particular show such as Franco Zeffirelli's *Jesus of Nazareth* presented on Palm Sunday and Easter Sunday.

2. Write a critical review of a popular, long-running series other than *All in the Family,* showing how it has not changed over the years.

3. Compare and contrast the series originated by Norman Lear that are mentioned in paragraph 1 (and any more recent ones), paying particular attention to the reasons for their success or failure.

4. To what extent has violence replaced both sex and bigotry as the main attraction of television? Write a paper on this theme, referring to several television programs. Indicate what effects these programs have on adolescents.

Analysis
Analysis Using Comparison and Contrast

MARRIAGE IS NOT A PERSONAL MATTER
John Finley Scott

BIOGRAPHICAL SKETCH

John Finley Scott was born in California in 1934. He did his undergraduate work at Reed College and earned M.A. and Ph.D. degrees from Stanford University. Presently a professor of sociology at the University of California at Davis, he has written numerous articles and a book, Internalization of Norms.

PRE-READING

1. What do you think the rather enigmatic title means?

2. From skimming the first and last paragraphs, what would you guess the subject and the writer's opinion to be?

[1] The newest wrinkle in the old game of courtship is match-making by computer. It goes something like this: a young man lists in a "data bank" what he most desires in a prospective female companion and supplies information about his own characteristics. The computer compares the qualities and interests desired against those of an . . . inventory of candidates who have also put themselves on file. After some adjustment and compromise, our young man is presented with the name, address and telephone number of a "Miss Just-Right-and-very-nice-too." Since electronic match-making is not quite yet an exact science, he may also be informed of a few alternates . . . in case something goes wrong and he doesn't quite hit it off with Miss Just-Right.

[2] The fact that many "computerized introduction services" are pretty much fly-by-night operations does not mean that computer match-making is unworkable in principle. If marital felicity can be accurately defined, then it would seem that a compatible marriage partner would more likely be found

FROM *Women: Their Changing Roles*, ed. Elizabeth Janeway (New York: Arno Press, 1973), pp. 516–19. Originally printed in *The New York Times Magazine.* © 1966 by The New York Times Company. Reprinted by permission.

among the thousands of candidates to which a computer could refer than among the handful that any one person could ever meet face to face.

[3] But the problem is identifying "marital felicity"; what on earth *is* a successful marriage? Can any kind of successful matching be based on the verbal responses of the largely adolescent segment of the population that is on the verge of matrimony? Any programmer will tell you that a computer is no better than the information put into it. In many respects, the verbal professions of persons facing marriage are the last things on which to base predictions about the future condition of the families thus formed. That a number of marriages—a minority, to be sure, but a substantial one—will terminate in divorce within three years will hardly be revealed through polling the expectations of brides-to-be.

[4] Part of the problem is that marriage, though often regarded as an intensely personal affair, is one of the least individualistic of all social institutions. The family . . . has evolved not because it satisfies individual preferences but because it is socially useful. It combines the functions of reproduction, child care, sexual gratification and economic cooperation with an over-all efficiency that no alternative arrangement has so far been able to match. Since marriage is such a good thing from the society's point of view, it is convenient to make young people want to get married by teaching them that marriage satisfies their *own* needs, and to soft-pedal the demands of the larger society. This is why marriage . . . is easier to enter than to leave. Young people are recruited to matrimony, but at the same time their hopes come to depend on frequently unrealistic aspirations, and their ability to predict what lies ahead becomes limited.

Excerpts from the sort of questionnaire a person in search of a date or mate might fill out for processing by computer.

For Men

1. Which of the following activities most appeals to you?
   (1) *skindiving in Montego Bay*
   (2) *touring the Rijksmuseum in Amsterdam*
   (3) *watching a bullfight in Seville*
   (4) *mountain climbing in Lausanne*
   (5) *eating leberkase and drinking dark beer in a brauhaus in Munich*

2. With which of the following cars can you most readily identify?
   (1) *Rolls Royce*
   (2) *Mustang*
   (3) *Cadillac*
   (4) *Jaguar XKE*
   (5) *Maxwell (vintage)*
   (6) *Volkswagen*

For Women

1. In which of the following situations would you feel most comfortable?
   (1) *exploring Vesuvius and the ruins of Pompeii*
   (2) *sipping cappucino on the Via Veneto (Rome)*
   (3) *boating off the island of Mykonos (Greece)*
   (4) *conversing with peasants in Skoplje (Yugoslavia)*
   (5) *visiting the Uffizi Galleries (Florence)*

2. Of the following, which would you prefer?
   (1) *loving a man who did not love you*
   (2) *being loved by a man you could not love*
   (3) *neither loving nor being loved until the feeling was mutual, regardless of how long it took to come about*

For Men

3. You are at a party where you don't know anyone. You would very likely:
   (1) *leave early*
   (2) *find a comfortable chair in a corner*
   (3) *join a conversation about sports*
   (4) *introduce yourself to the women*
   (5) *introduce yourself to the men*

4. Which of the following fields are you most closely associated with or interested in?
   (1) *medicine and research*
   (2) *law*
   (3) *education*
   (4) *social services*
   (5) *advertising–public relations*
   (6) *science and technology*
   (7) *military service*
   (8) *sales*
   (9) *finance and industry*

5. Your fiancée informs you that she has had relations with another man. You would probably:
   (1) *break the engagement*
   (2) *marry her despite grave misgivings*
   (3) *tell her it doesn't matter*
   (4) *tell her of your own amorous adventures*
   (5) *feel that her experience would make for a more successful marriage*

6. Which of the following would probably give you the greatest personal satisfaction?
   (1) *working for the welfare of others*
   (2) *traveling extensively*
   (3) *being elected to public office*
   (4) *earning a fortune*
   (5) *raising a family*

7. You've taken her out to dinner three or four times, but when you ask her to prepare the next meal herself, she informs you that she can't cook. You would most likely feel:
   (1) *angry*
   (2) *dejected*
   (3) *relieved*
   (4) *indifferent*
   (5) *hungry*

For Women

3. How well can you cook?
   (1) *expertly, exotic dishes and proper wines*
   (2) *quite well, but nothing fancy*
   (3) *hit or miss*
   (4) *TV dinners and canned soup*
   (5) *can-openers are for picture-hanging*

4. Which of the following fields are you most closely associated with or interested in?
   (1) *nursing*
   (2) *secretarial*
   (3) *modeling or fashion*
   (4) *sales or purchasing*
   (5) *fine arts or design*
   (6) *education*
   (7) *business administration*

5. Your date has spent his money on an electronic fish-finder, but you had wanted him to escort you to a concert. You would most likely:
   (1) *pay your own way*
   (2) *lend him money*
   (3) *find another date and let him go fishing*
   (4) *treat him*
   (5) *go fishing with him*

6. You are with your friends when an argument develops about the evening's activity. You would:
   (1) *remain silent*
   (2) *compromise*
   (3) *go along with the majority*
   (4) *insist upon your choice*
   (5) *go off alone*

7. Which of the following date ideas most appeals to you?
   (1) *dining and dancing*
   (2) *horseback riding*
   (3) *a picnic in the country*
   (4) *watching TV*
   (5) *attending a concert*

8. How important is it that your match own and drive a car?
   (1) *very important*
   (2) *moderately important*
   (3) *he can borrow mine*

Questions reprinted courtesy of Data-Date, Inc.

[5] Here lies the problem with any scheme of matchmaking that relies solely on the expressed preferences of the young people involved. This is hardly anything new: many parents, and most professional matchmakers . . . have known it for years. It would be interesting to see what kind of matches a computer would arrange if it interviewed parents as well as their eligible children.

[6] We live in a society where unprecedented numbers of young people, aided by rapid social change, higher education, urbanization and widespread geographical and social mobility, negotiate marriages on their own, without the help of kith and kin. But the notion that the process as a whole is primarily an individual matter is a myth. When two people date who did not know each other beforehand, it is called a "blind date"—a name which stresses the fact that most dates are not blind. Wherever dating customs are studied closely—from church socials to Army barracks—intermediaries and "fixer-uppers" are found busily at work, pairing off the boys and girls in roughly the same way as the new computers. Considering the cost involved, it is economical for persons who date to rely on some outside help. For a young man, expected to take the initiative, dating is one of the most ruthless and unprotected forms of competition in which he can engage. He must put himself up for acceptance or rejection, and rejection can produce severe psychic wounds.

[7] For a young woman, masculine attention in dating and courtship is the greatest social reward she will ever receive, and she therefore desires it to an extreme degree. But for her to accept dates indiscriminately is to run a variety of risks from boredom to sexual assault. The services of intermediaries, who present young men with invitations already accepted and young women with escorts already screened, are therefore greatly appreciated and widely practiced. . . . When young people today talk in all sincerity about their freedom to date anybody they please, they simply are not describing the entire process, of whose many controls they are often artfully kept unaware.

[8] One very general answer can be given to the question of who marries whom: Most people marry someone pretty much like themselves. . . . But scientific and garden-variety curiosity alike concentrate on the unexpected and unlikely combinations. . . .

[9] Unexpected marriages . . . catch our attention when they deviate from social norms. The salient thing about marriage in this society—indeed, in any society with an organized system of kinship—is that it is regulated by the kinship-based groups which it affects. On the one hand, rules against incest drive young adults out of their own families; yet everywhere these young adults are expected to marry someone from a quite similar family. The anthropologist A. R. Radcliffe-Brown put the matter well when he referred to marriage as a "crisis."

[10] Norms of mate selection—as sociologists rather coarsely phrase it—can be looked at as a classification of social groups in some of which marriage is to be preferred and in others is to be avoided. The practice of marriage within a group is called endogamy. All large groups formed by inheritance—what we

call "ethnic groups"—will prefer endogamy to some degree. Since two parents who share the same ethnic traditions can pass them on more consistently than two whose backgrounds differ, endogamy makes a good deal of sense if one wishes to preserve traditions. And the more traditions are cherished, the stronger is the urge toward endogamy. American Jews, for example, voice great concern over the extent of Jewish exogamy—the opposite of endogamy—although, from a comparative point of view, it is amazingly small—probably less than 10 percent of all marriages involving a Jew. But it seems that the only way for Jewish traditions to survive is through lifelong training of persons born into the group. . . . Jewish control of endogamy is therefore remarkably strong, and the democracy and indulgence that seem characteristic of Jewish family life usually end abruptly when the prospect of intermarriage looms. Similar rules can be found among American Oriental population groups, the Mormons and, in weaker form, Roman Catholics (who more willingly accept converts).

.   .   .

[11] Predicting whether a certain proportion of marriages will be endogamous or exogamous actually depends on a few rather obvious variables. The relative numbers of the two sexes—the "sex ratio"—is one of the most obvious. It is historically important because men are more likely to migrate than women. This is largely why America, as a land of migrants, has been as much of a melting pot as it has. Many immigrant men who felt strongly about "marrying a nice (Jewish-Polish-Irish-Armenian, etc.) girl" found there wasn't enough of the kind they wanted to go around. Faced with the choices of marrying out or not marrying at all, many of them married out. The same thing goes on inside America today because men migrate to one place and women to another (there are usually more unmarried women than men in big cities, for example), so that rules for some sort of endogamous marriage get slighted in the competition for anyone to marry at all.

[12] Another factor is the degree of parental control. This is important because it is the older generation that most respects the traditional rules of endogamy, while young people are easily swayed by personal attractions. Here residence is important. A young lady who lives at home and receives her suitors there cannot easily entertain young men of whom her parents strongly disapprove. Even when she is given much freedom, the elders can still influence her choice. Daughters can hardly fall in love with unsuitable men they never meet, and the chances of their not meeting them are greatly increased if the parents happen to have moved (for the children's sake, of course) to a class-homogeneous suburb. When a girl becomes infatuated with a boy beneath her station, her parents can use the old strategem of inviting him to a rather formal dinner, the better that his incorrigible unfitness for symbolically important occasions will be forced on the daughter's attention.

[13] Today, however, parental control faces the peculiar threat of college education. When children live at home, parents can keep track daily of whom they are dating. But college often requires "dependent" and "irresponsible"

children to live away from home. To be sure, a few young people have been going away to college for generations. But three trends combine to make college today a major threat to endogamy: (1) More persons of college age are in college (currently about 40 per cent); (2) An increasing proportion of students are women; and (3) The average age at marriage has dropped (especially for women) to a point where it falls for many in the traditional undergraduate years.

[14] College and matrimony thus combine to render the campus the most active marriage market of modern times. Even when children live at home while attending college (a growing trend as new campuses and junior colleges are built), the dating situation on the campus is hard for parents to control. Student bodies tend to be large and heterogeneous, and almost any of the many campus activities can be used for making contacts and thus beginning the process of dating and courtship. Not that parents have not fought back. College fraternities, and especially sororities, embody many ingenious arrangements whereby the courtship of young persons is kept in line with the desires of an older generation. Yet it is safe to predict that an increasing number of American marriages will be between persons who meet in college, and they are likely to meet under conditions largely indifferent to older rules of endogamy.

[15] A third factor affecting the maintenance of endogamy is social mobility—the process by which members of a generation achieve a higher class position than that into which they were born. In America this movement is ultimately related to higher education, for we widely believe that upward mobility is a good thing and that higher education contributes to it. But to the extent that young people start moving up before they are married, and that boys move up in different ways, or at different rates, than girls, then the traditional ways of pairing them off endogamously no longer work.

[16] The most basic difference here is that a man gains his status mainly through his job, whereas a woman's status is mainly conferred on her by her husband. We often speak as if occupational success were equally inportant for both sexes, but actually it is much less important for women. Women *can* gain a tolerable status through work, but a better one can usually be gained more easily through marriage. Where men move up most directly by competing for good jobs, women move up mainly by marrying men who move up. Marriage thus becomes the means of mobility for women. Insofar as she responds to the American dream of upward mobility, every unmarried American girl has a bit of the gold-digger in her.

[17] Consider the situation of American Catholics. Catholic girls are expected to marry Catholic boys, but they also want to marry successful men. And it just so happens that, for most of the country, Protestant men on the average hold higher-ranked positions than do Catholic men. If the Catholic girl marries up, she is likely to marry out. And evidently this does occur, because more Catholic women marry outside their faith than do Catholic men. Among Jews, however, the situation is reversed. Men in this group are eminently suc-

cessful and are "good catches" for girls of any faith who want to marry up. Evidently they do get caught, for many more Jewish boys marry gentiles than do Jewish girls.

[18] The pressure for marrying up among women produces a kind of imbalance in marital bargaining, to the advantage of high-status men and low-status women and the disadvantage of low-status men and high-status women. A low-status man has little wealth or prestige to offer a wife. In addition, he must compete for a wife not only with others in his own station but with higher-ranked men as well.

[19] A well-born woman, if she is to maintain through marriage the status conferred on her by her parents, must marry a man at least equally well-born—but for such men she faces a deadly competition from lower-status female rivals who also regard them as desirable husbands. As a result, low-status men are more likely to remain bachelors, and high-status women are more likely to remain spinsters. . . .

[20] If a sociologist is so artlessly blunt as to ask young women whether they marry for money or for love, he will be lucky to escape with his questionnaire forms. Love, the girls indignantly tell us, conquers all. Lovable personal qualities eclipse Philistine wealth. But this is too simple by far.

[21] On the one hand, there is a strong statistical tendency for women to marry up. If our hypothetical sociologist returns, suitably chastened, with a subtler set of questions on what makes men lovable, he will receive a list of characteristics of which many—urbane good manners, sensitivity, sophisticated good taste, interesting conversation, and so on—depend on expensive education and are thus associated with wealth. . . .

[22] On the other hand, there probably never has been a society in which all lovable attributes were monopolized by one class. Love thus becomes a potentially random factor in marriage, one contrary to all rules of endogamy. In societies with stronger rules of endogamy than our own, love is not unknown, but it is strongly controlled and is regarded as irrelevant in the choice of marital partners.

[23] The emotions of love are strong, but they are also ambiguous and volatile, and are therefore subject to deception and fraud. This places an emphasis on sincerity, but sincerity in love is very hard to assess. Young women are besieged with professions of love which they suspect are voiced simply to facilitate a quick seduction—and this is not what "love" means to most of them.

[24] Especially where courtship tends to be individualistic, so that suitors cannot be effectively held to account for their promises, young women tend to measure the love of a young man not simply by what he says, but also by what he invests in the relationship. Often this is his money, but more often it is his time. Because any marriage market involves a wide age range of men competing for the smaller range of women in the years when they are young and pretty, the investment required in courtship gets bid up to a high level. Feminine nubility, thus rewarded, becomes a veritable institution in its own right.

The extravagance of attention that young girls expect, however, paradoxically limits their chances for marrying well. Regardless of his income, the *time* of a successful man is always dear, while the adult male who is "still finding himself" is the one with the leisure to invest in courtship.

²⁵ This applies also at the college level, where the pre-professional student who is going places occupationally has little time for dating and leaves most of the social life to the less ambitious campus playboys. This means that women who expect their suitors to spend a great deal of time in dating are likely to marry men of modest achievement in other areas.

²⁶ Now: How can all this be put in a matchmaking computer? It would be easy to specify the information that would be required, but awfully hard to find any way of digging it up. Getting it by simple interrogation—which is what the computers use now—would make the money-or-love question look like a masterpiece of diplomacy.

.   .   .

²⁷ The marriage practices of human society embody both ancient traditions and novel responses to changing times. The broad patterns of marriage—movement across class lines, the age at which it occurs, its impact on education and work—can be pretty well predicted, and in fact are predicted by sociologists, demographers and insurance actuaries. But the narrow practical questions—"Will he marry her?" or "Will they be happy together?"—are likely to remain inexplicable, at least to the people involved. And the mystery is what gives these questions their abiding appeal. Successful computer matching—unlikely, anyway—would only spoil the fun.

ANALYTICAL READING

1. What purpose does the opening discussion about computer courtship have? What is the function of the first sentence of paragraph 4?

2. What social reasons does Scott give for the evolution of marriage?

3. In what ways are young people programmed for marriage? Explain *endogamy* and the importance of a woman's residence.

4. How does Scott classify the "norms of mate selection" (paragraph 10)?

5. What reasons does he give for women using marriage as a device of "upward mobility" (paragraph 16)? This article was written in 1966; to what extent do you think women still do this?

6. What does Scott have to say about love as a basis for marriage?

7. Does the writer think computer selection could work? Why or why not? What are the difficulties?

REFLECTING

Point: What opinion is the writer expressing? Is he against love?

Organization: How does the writer employ classification in this article? Is it the main organizational scheme? Discuss.

Support: How are classification and comparison and contrast used to support the opinion expressed?

Synthesis: Have any societal attitudes changed since this article was written? Do the marriages in your own family reflect Scott's opinions about the way we select mates?

Evaluation: Did you find the essay effective? Why or why not? Did you disagree with any points the writer made? Why?

FROM READING TO WRITING

1. Fill in the questionnaire and compare answers with your classmates. Then for your classmates, write a paper in which you suggest an approach for collecting information from people for computer matchmaking. Be sure that you break down the approach into its component parts and show their relationships.

2. For a general audience, write a paper using comparison and contrast to analyze the role that sororities and fraternities play in mate selection.

3. Ask your classmates to answer all the questions on the questionnaire—not just those indicated for their particular sex. Write a paper to Scott, analyzing any differences in attitudes you found in a class of students in the 1980s.

COMPETITION
Theodore Isaac Rubin

BIOGRAPHICAL SKETCH

Born in Brooklyn, Theodore Isaac Rubin (1923–   ) earned a B.A. from Brooklyn College, an M.D. from the University of Lausanne (Switzerland), and a degree in Psychiatry from the American Institute of Psychoanalysis. He is President of the American Institute for Psychoanalysis, a teacher, and a practicing psychiatrist. In addition to writing a regular column for the Ladies Home Journal, *Dr. Rubin has published a number of books, both fiction and nonfiction. His most famous novel,* David and Lisa, *was made into a successful movie. His nonfiction works include* Compassion and Self Hate, Reflections in a Goldfish Tank, The Winner's Notebook, *and* Reconciliations: Inner Peace in an Age of Anxiety, *from which this selection is taken. Married, with three children, he resides in New York City.*

PRE-READING

1. After reading the opening paragraph, explain the author's attitude about competition.

2. How does the final paragraph reinforce this attitude?

FROM Chapter 5 in *Reconciliations: Inner Peace in an Age of Anxiety* by Theodore I. Rubin, M.D. Copyright © 1980 by El-Ted Rubin, Inc. Reprinted by permission of Viking Penguin Inc.

¹ In *Compassion and Self Hate* I wrote about how competition is a form of self-hate and how our culture has come to believe that competition "brings out the best" in people. I still believe that it brings out the worst. It is intimately linked to envy, jealousy, and paranoia, and blocks evolvement and development of self. It ultimately has a depleting and deadening effect on self as its unrelenting demands are met and self-realizing needs are ignored.

² In competition, the focus of one's life is essentially outside one's self. The use of our time and energy is determined by our competitors rather than by our own selves and our own real needs. This weakens our own sense of identity, and to compensate for this ever-increasing feeling of emptiness and vulnerability we compete still more, completing a self-depleting cycle. When enough depletion takes place to preclude further "successful" competition, we feel hopeless and futile and our lives seem purposeless.

³ Despite talk about good sportsmanship, competition is totally incompatible with the kind of easy aliveness that is the aim of this book. It flourishes in an atmosphere of high stimulation (tennis players' insistence on being "psyched up" reminds me of my patient who could only thrive on crisis) and vindictive triumph. Its rewards and goals are immediate and short-lived, and self-glorification guarantees virtual exclusion of self-realization. It destroys our inner sense of autonomy and stability and is also destructive to outside relationships and to real communication. Competitive friction is inimical to kindness, and without kindness a self-enriching philosophy is impossible. Despite protestations and reassurances about "friendly competition," antagonists are not friendly. The "feeling good" that competitors say comes from competition is based on someone else's feeling bad. And this "feeling good" doesn't last because it is based on putting the next fellow down rather than on a sustained strengthening of yourself through self-realization. So competition becomes addictive.

⁴ Competition is a residual of a primitive past, and it is *not* a genetic residual. It is passed on to us through training in our society from generation to generation. This training starts early and can usually be seen in very early sibling rivalry. I do not believe that rivalry among children of the same family is instinctual. I believe that it is engendered by parents who themselves were victims of victims: they may convey the competitive motif blatantly or so subtly that it is not readily perceived. They themselves are caught in the same trap—they spend enormous time and energy getting ahead of the Joneses. Small wonder so many children are pressured into Little League or equivalent competitive structures—all with rationalization that this will promote their self-development, well-being, and health. Actually these activities and organizations nearly always serve as vicarious vehicles designed to satisfy *parental* craving for competitive success. People brought up in this way feel lost if they are suddenly thrust into a situation of low competitive tension. They exist to compete and they've lost their *raison de'être*, so they invent hierarchies and games to provide the stimulation they need to "keep the motor running," even if these inventions are ultimately destructive to inner peace and personal health.

⁵ I am reminded of my own medical school experience in Lausanne, Switzerland. I was part of a group of about eighty Americans studying at the medical faculty of the university at that time. The system was noncompetitive. People who were qualified were accepted into the school. These consisted of people who received passing grades in the required premedical or foundation courses. Two series of examinations—one in the basic sciences one and one half years after admission, and the other after studies were completed—determined qualification for graduation. Students were allowed to postpone these examinations as long as they felt was necessary. To pass, students were required to demonstrate adequate knowledge of the material. The atmosphere was totally benevolent and without the presence of any coercion or intimidation whatsoever. There was no "curve" and students were not graded relative to each other.

⁶ The Swiss students exhibited great camaraderie among themselves, helped each other, and for the most part demonstrated great proficiency in grasping and integrating the material. There were no "tricks" whatsoever, no surprise quizzes or exams. Indeed there were no examinations at all, other than the two sets of standardized government exams. Requirements for passing the examinations were well defined for everyone. Instruction was superb.

⁷ We Americans arrived as graduates of a highly competitive system. Indeed, many of us arrived as refugee victims of that system. We were all qualified to attend medical school inasmuch as all of us had satisfactorily completed bachelor degrees in the premedical courses necessary for medical school. Some of us had fair grades in premedical courses, some good grades, and some excellent. None of us had been admitted to an American medical school. Some had been excluded because of the Jewish quota quite prevalent in our own country at that time; some because we had gone to the "wrong schools" (excellent schools academically but not held in high esteem socially or politically— these were usually the city colleges of New York); some of us for receiving good but not perfect grades; and some of us for all three reasons.

⁸ By the time we arrived in Switzerland our paranoia ran high. I suppose we suffered a kind of culture shock. Few of us could believe that medical school could be such a straightforward, noncompetitive activity, and that we would be required to learn only the material we were told to learn. (Some of us remembered too well taking competitive examinations that contained questions on the most abstruse reading, some of it "non-required.")

⁹ Stimulation addicts like ourselves found little motivation in the Swiss system—so we formed competitive cliques. Some people convinced themselves and others that the Swiss professors were tricky and that the two sets of exams could never be passed. Others stated that the school was not good, below standard, and that it would never be recognized in the United States. (This belief persisted, despite the fact that the school had been in existence for hundreds of years and was superb in all respects.) People kept secret from each other the ready availability of course notebooks. Bets were made as to who would and who would not get through. Scouts were secretly sent from various cliques to see if other European schools were better. People tried to convince

other people that they would never get through and should return home. There was much gossip about absences from classes and who was and who wasn't dedicated to medical school and his chosen field. Former friends who came to Switzerland together stopped talking to each other because they now saw each other as competitors.

[10] The Swiss went on as they always did. The Americans did also. They had re-created American competition in Switzerland. Some of them became so panicked and depressed that they packed up and went home, giving up their life's desire forever. Some adjusted to the benevolent society they found themselves in and became good doctors. But even now, after some thirty years, one of my former Lausanne classmates still feels he has to say that the Swiss medical schools were particularly tough to get through—he must exaggerate a sense of accomplishment by exaggerating the difficulty or if necessary inventing it. And after I graduated from medical school I heard that several suicides had occurred among students who came after me. I wondered about the role hysterical competition had played in these tragedies.

[11] When my son Jeff, now an M.D. and a psychiatrist, was taking a microbiology examination in premed school, he realized that most of the students were making sure that the microscopes they had used were out of focus before passing on to succeeding specimens—this to make it more difficult for their "colleagues" taking the exam. What effect can this kind of cutthroat competition to get into medical school, and to stay there, have on our future medical practitioners?

[12] Competition damages people other than students. It provides a stressful, isolating, and paranoid atmosphere that is the very antithesis of peace of mind. Competitive strivings are not felt directly or blatantly. They do not occur solely when we are locked in antagonistic embrace with adversaries—we have, after all, come a considerable distance from the dinosaurs. But the subtle influence of competitive standards to be met and our consciousness of how the next guy is doing—in terms of earnings, position, accomplishments, notoriety, possessions, or whatever—work their subtle and not-so-subtle corrosive effects. They provide constant pressure and undermine our efforts to build a self-realizing value system. This means that we are more involved with how the next fellow is doing than with knowing what *we* really want to do. We are more concerned with how *they* feel about us than how we feel.

[13] Competition also contributes to a mood of paranoia. Since anyone and everyone can be a potential or actual competitor, suspiciousness reigns supreme and openness is viewed with contempt. This makes it very difficult to accept and to feel the nourishing effects of give-and-take and often makes much-needed help from others impossible to accept. Our culture in large measure has made this paranoid closure to nourishment from others a virtue, especially a masculine virtue, often rationalized by ideas about independence and self-reliance. Independence and self-reliance are valuable assets but often they are actually cover-ups of fear of other people and are functions of sick pride invested in isolation and rejection of other people's much-needed help.

[14] Competition in this way also has a powerful fragmenting effect: it causes

us to be preoccupied with fragmented single areas rather than with integration and wholeness. Competitors almost inevitably become specialists, limiting the area of their endeavors and concentrating all their energy in the pursuit of one goal in order to beat the competition. Thus, the big "successes" in our culture are usually successful in their given areas but fail in all others.

ANALYTICAL READING

1. According to Rubin, what is wrong with competition? What does he suggest instead?

2. Why does he make the point that competition is "not a genetic residual" (paragraph 4)?

3. What purpose do his examples about sibling rivalry and Little League baseball serve?

4. Why does Rubin mention that there was no grading on a curve at Lausanne?

5. Explain what the author means in paragraph 7 when he states that many of the Americans were "refugee victims" of a highly competitive system?

6. Try to explain and account for the actions of the American students at Lausanne. How does Rubin suggest that such actions, which occurred in his generation, might take place today?

7. What does Rubin find wrong with such values as independence and self-reliance?

8. Explain, using examples, what Rubin means by the fragmenting effect of competition?

REFLECTING

Point: In your own words, write a one- or two-sentence statement of Rubin's central thesis.

Organization: Write a two-level outline of the essay. How might Rubin have changed the order for an article in a popular magazine like *Sports Illustrated?*

Support: Rubin devotes a lot of space to his medical school experiences. How effective is his use of comparison and contrast here? How else does he support his ideas?

Synthesis: Because American life is competitive, shouldn't young people be taught to compete? Compare Rubin's article with *SportsWorld* (pages 205–10). Is there much competition in high schools today? Do you agree with Rubin that parents are responsible for sibling rivalries and for making children fiercely competitive?

Evaluation: How convincing is Rubin? Would more examples have helped? Where? Is the example about the medical school outdated or too specialized to be representative? Should the author have discussed in some detail what he advocates instead of competition?

FROM READING TO WRITING

1. For *Parent's Magazine,* write an article about Little League baseball or some other organized sports activity, pointing out how it is beneficial or detrimental for children. Or, explain how parents influence their children's participation in such activities.

2. Write a letter to a teachers' group, showing how competition for grades may encourage cheating.

3. For a general audience, write a paper about whether there is more competition among students in high school or in college. You might want to talk to some college juniors or seniors before forming an opinion.

4. Are men more competitive than women? Write an article for *Ms.* magazine.

EQUALITY'S UNEVEN HAND
Thomas Griffith

BIOGRAPHICAL SKETCH

Thomas Griffith was born in New York in 1915 and graduated from the University of Washington. He has been an editor at Time *and* Life, *a writer for* Fortune, *and is currently a contributing editor for the* Atlantic Monthly. *A former Nieman Fellow, he is the author of two books,* How True: A Skeptic's Guide to Believing the News *and* Waist High Culture.

PRE-READING

1. From the opening paragraph, what position do you think that the author will take on equality?

2. How does the figure of speech in the opening paragraph contribute to the presentation of Griffith's views?

¹ There are subjects that bother and pursue us throughout our lives. I don't mean ruling passions that obsess one—as sex and money and power do—but unanswered, unshakable questions, such as religious faith or doubt, that haunt one. In my own case the question I can never resolve concerns equality; my attitude toward it oscillates constantly, like a trembling needle on a dial, and I've about decided that I'm never going to come to a still point on the subject, and be at rest with it. In its blessings and in its dangers, I think equality is the great, the basic American question.

² We are strengthened by equality, we are weakened by it; we celebrate it, we repudiate it. The question haunts Americans in particular because en-

graved early on our brainpans is the dubious assertion that "all men are created equal." If this means they are genetically equal, or born in similar circumstances or with similar prospects, then it's nonsense on the face of it. If, then, it means "equal in the sight of God," we are soon deep in the tortured theology of those Graham Greene thrillers where the miserable sinner, because he is bedeviled, seems more interesting to God than does the well-behaved faithful one; to even things up, you have to add in the notion of grace, to assure a heavenly welcome to those who seem lacking in all earthly merit. It is the earthly aspect of equality that fascinates me.

³ Equality, as in one man, one vote, is the essence of democracy; the notion that I'm as good as you are is at the heart of American informality. Yet equality also implies a leveling, a resistance to every individual's longing to stand out from the crowd, and thus wars with that other basic American trait, the pursuit of success and distinction. Equality is not a subject that can be seen whole; it shows itself clearly only in facets that catch the light at one moment. Perhaps these facets put together add up to a whole. I hope.

⁴ Start then with the fact that I am a child of equality, which has given me privileges I would never otherwise have known.

⁵ Alex Haley has surer roots than I have. On my mother's Irish side, I go back to a grandfather who emigrated from Ireland, helped lay tracks westward for the Northern Pacific Railroad, and settled where it came to an end in Tacoma, Washington. Back beyond that grandfather, Peter O'Reilly, I suspect my ancestors were never far from the bog, though my Irish relatives insisted we were lace-curtain. About my father's family I am even less clear: I never heard him mention his Welsh father or say what kind of work he did; my father was always skimpy on biographical detail unless it could be invoked in moralizing, to show that his childhood was harsher than ours. If it weren't for state universities with low tuitions, I wouldn't have gone to college; if it weren't for a $15-a-month student make-work New Deal job, I probably couldn't have stayed there.

⁶ So I begin in equality's debt. Growing up among the ordinary and hard-pressed, being one of them, I have a natural feeling for that large segment of Americans who seem so mysterious and threatening to others; I'm not tempted either to exaggerate their virtues or to ignore their merit. Later, in a fellowship at Harvard and in good jobs in New York City, I got to know people who had the advantages of family, position, and money I lacked, admired them for their ease and for their schooling, which was more literate and less utilitarian than mine. But I also discovered the walking wounded among the privileged—saw how advantage can sap the spirit of some, can create in others doubts that they can live up to the higher expectancies for them.

⁷ I learned the paradox that the disadvantaged have advantages. Today's real hard-luck kid may be surrounded by money, ignored by parents too centered on their own careers to pay him attention, living in a lonely maze of stepfathers, stepbrothers and sisters, and absent parents. Since my mother died

early I grew up orphaned, was farmed out to boarding houses, but at least I knew where I was at. There was no confusion about it.

[8] Beyond the reach of legislative remedy, more important than either race or income, the circumstances of family life and the character of one's parents really mark the inequality of all our beginnings.

[9] Sources of confusion: Most of us benefit some of the time from equality but gain more often from accepted inequality.

[10] Places where equality is (in principle at least) expected to reign: in being subject to the draft, or to jury duty. In bumper-to-bumper traffic jams. In lines, waiting "your turn"—at movies, bank windows, tollbooths, polling booths. In equal pay for equal work; most Americans get the "going scale" in their line of work, are governed by the union contract, the hourly wage, the in-grade pay level in the armed forces and civil service.

[11] Places where inequality prevails: wherever money permits one to jump the queue to win unequal treatment—first class vs. tourist; orchestra vs. balcony; expense-account restaurants, at the headwaiter's rewarded discretion.

[12] Wherever rank has its privileges—executive dining rooms, limos, private planes, gates that swing widely only for them.

[13] Wherever having got there first matters, particularly when it comes to owning land: this is the advantage of "old money" over new.

[14] Money is thus the approved American way of escaping the rigors of equality. "My money is as good as yours" has a democratic sound to it, but really means I have just as much right to pay for preferred treatment as you do. Money as "the great equalizer" works, except in a few enclaves of privilege— clubs, golf courses—which therefore seem doubly undemocratic, downright un-American.

[15] Inequality prevails too in taxes. Once everyone was supposed to pay an equal share of his earnings, then with the progressive income and inheritance taxes, the better off would be paying a greater share. In fact the rich pay proportionately less than the middle class . . .

[16] In lawbreaking, equal offenses are presumably equally punished, but the difference in the kind of lawyering one can afford is immense. A man may steal half a million dollars and not go to jail, while a street robber can get prison for stealing $50; the armed threat, not the sum, makes the difference. Crime in a white collar gets off easier.

[17] Other forms of inequality: health, bone structure and beauty, talent, temperament, humor, taste. "All other things being equal" . . . but they never are.

[18] The real pox of equality is envy, the notion that I'm as much entitled as he is, the smoldering resentment when someone else gets more, or gets away with more, than I do. Equality always feels threatened by diversity.

[19] The politics of revenge is the shabby side of egalitarianism; its better side is the politics of redress, which seek to even out life's inequities, to give

everyone an evener chance. This is like making the favorite carry additional weight in a horse race, but in the human race, not everyone starts from the same starting gate or at the same time. Helping the hindmost is an act of fairness; more than that, these days, it is an investment in public tranquillity.

[20] The classic American formula for modifying (without abolishing) inequality is the idea of "equality of opportunity," which has been defined as giving everyone a fair chance to leave the others behind. Its energizing spirit is incentive, but such competitiveness is now considered gauche, greedy, "overachieving" by those who (to use another vogue word) are "laid back." So we hear a proposition urged called "equality of results," a horse race in which everyone is to be equally rewarded no matter in what position he crosses the finish line. In the name of equality, torpor gets paid the wages of effort.

[21] Equality deserves better theory than that. Equality has a number of false friends, especially among academic apologists. Particularly noxious to me are the leveling views of Professor Herbert J. Gans, author of *More Equality*, who wants to eliminate "invidious status and other distinctions" between highbrow, middlebrow, and lowbrow levels of taste. "A culturally equal society would thus treat all ways of expressing oneself and acting as equal in value, status, and moral worth." Why? "Because they express the differing aesthetic standards of people in different socioeconomic and educational circumstances." This is condescension gone mad. It is possible to argue the creativity and quality of blues music, as it is of string quartets, but whose socioeconomic circumstances require giving the Melachrino Strings equal time?

[22] Equality is most in trouble when it drops its "e," and must deal with quality. Its usual method is to scorn its betters, and to complain of elites, a dirty word in democracy's dictionary. Elite sounds snobbish when used by those who belong, deplorable to those who don't. Yet elites are just another way, like money, of sorting ourselves out of the ruck. There are elites, of course, of achievement, of specialization, of status; but there are also elites of common interest—of knowledgeable basketball fans, of discerning music buffs—where people talk in shorthand and quick exchanges, comfortable together, consciously or unconsciously excluding those who can't keep up. Even the meanest street has its elite.

[23] The truth is that inequality has two strings to its bow, and equality but one. Equality is the world of fairness. Inequality at its worst is the world of privilege, unearned, uncaring, and often arrogant. But inequality is also the world of achievement, of excellence.

[24] A hankering for equality does not prevent one from knowing that many of one's fellow citizens can be petty and selfish, slobs, or bores. The onrush of guilty snobbery really begins when one has to admit that there are people who are the salt of the earth whom one would not want to spend the evening with. Sociability and sterling worth often move on quite different tracks.

[25] The urban songwriter who celebrates the simple values to be found only in small towns probably wouldn't live in one. The main difference between small-town wholesomeness and big-city wickedness is that one doesn't have to be as circumspect in a big city's anonymity. I prize the friends I knew back where I come from, and easily pick up again with them after not seeing them for long periods, but I also like the company I now live among, who share the big city's fast transfer of opinions and references, the big city's tastes, opportunities, experiences.

[26] Yet I realize that much of the rest of the country feels an animosity toward the metropolis—particularly toward the publicity capitals of New York and Los Angeles, where a foolish overvaluation of commercial success and celebrityhood is shown by the new arbiters of democratic taste, the talk shows and the people magazines. In this world of the relentlessly ambitious, the right to equality of attention in the name of fairness has no meaning where merit is such a random element. As if we all didn't know that a bump of talent doesn't necessarily enrich one's character, or that the itch to make a lot of money rarely enlarges one's heart. The world of the Beautiful People is a sideshow that thinks itself a center. But how eager the many are to read about the eccentric few, maybe to envy them for being overpaid and oversexed, then to say smugly, when these paragons fall, that they knew it would turn out that way. Whoever said, in the name of democracy, that everyone is nice?

ANALYTICAL READING

1. What does Griffith achieve in his discussion of two well-known quotations about equality in paragraph 2?

2. What is the point of the author's discussion of his life and family?

3. What do you think Griffith means by stating that "money is . . . the approved way of escaping the rigors of equality" (paragraph 14)? Does he believe this is good or bad?

4. Why does Griffith believe that the "politics of redress" is "an investment in public tranquillity" (paragraph 19)?

5. What does the word *elite* mean to you? How does Griffith use the word (paragraph 22)?

6. What is Griffith's point about New York and Los Angeles?

REFLECTING

Point: Summarize Griffith's views in one or two sentences. Try to incorporate several of his key ideas.

Organization: Is there any organizational pattern in the article? Does he imply there may be none?

Support: Point out several instances where Griffith uses comparison and contrast effectively. Is his horse race analogy in paragraph 19 helpful?

Synthesis: Isn't one person as good as another? Do you agree with Griffith's views about poor rich kids? What do you think of his placing such importance on "the circumstances of family life and the character of one's parents"? What equalities and inequalities did you observe in high school? Were they desirable or not? If you read Rubin's essay on competition (pages 238–42), relate his ideas to Griffith's. Which do you prefer?

Evaluation: How well does Griffith explain his views? Do you understand much more now about equality, particularly how in its "blessings and dangers" it is "the basic American question"? Are there weaknesses in Griffith's comparisons? His contrasts? Discuss.

FROM READING TO WRITING

1.   For your college newspaper, write an article about busing and equality.

2.   Do high school or college social organizations (fraternities and sororities) promote equality or inequality? Are they beneficial? Write about this subject in an article designed for a general audience.

3.   In his January 1981 address on the economy, President Reagan stated that "the taxing power . . . must not be used to . . . bring about social change." For an editorial in your college newspaper, agree or disagree with this statement, relating it to some of the ideas in Griffith's essay.

4.   Write an article for your college newspaper, commenting on the view of Professor Gans, who wants to eliminate the critical distinctions between "highbrow, middlebrow, and lowbrow levels of taste," such as the distinctions between classical and rock music.

HOLDEN AND HUCK: THE ODYSSEYS OF YOUTH

Charles Kaplan

BIOGRAPHICAL SKETCH

Charles Kaplan was born in Chicago in 1919. He received an undergraduate degree from the University of Chicago and M.A. and Ph.D. degrees in English from Northwestern University. He has taught at Roosevelt College and Los Angeles State College, and since 1959 he has been professor and chairman of the Department of English at California State University in Northridge. He has been awarded a Fulbright lectureship, has been co-author of a textbook, Technique of Composition, *and has written several other books, including* Literature in America: The Modern Age. *Kaplan has also written numerous articles on American literature and literary criticism.*

FROM *College English,* 18 (November 1956), 76–80. Copyright © 1956 by the National Council of Teachers of English. Reprinted by permission of the publisher and the author.

PRE-READING

1. How does the biographical sketch establish Kaplan as an authority?

2. Do both the title and the quotation from Thoreau relate to the thesis stated in the opening paragraph? From these, what do you expect the essay to deal with?

3. Does the final paragraph go beyond the scope of the first? Explain.

4. From the language used in the opening paragraph, what kind of audience do you think Kaplan is addressing?

¹ Henry Thoreau, himself an interior traveler of some note, says in *A Week on the Concord and Merrimac Rivers*: "The traveller must be born again on the road, and earn a passport from the elements, the principal powers that be for him." In Mark Twain's *Adventures of Huckleberry Finn* (1884) and in J.D. Salinger's *The Catcher in the Rye* (1951) we meet two young travelers—travelers in their native land and also in the geography of their souls. Their narratives are separated in time by almost seventy years, but the psychic connection between them eliminates mere temporal distance: Huck Finn and Holden Caulfield are true blood-brothers, speaking to us in terms that lift their wanderings from the level of the merely picaresque to that of a sensitive and insightful criticism of American life.

² Each work, to begin with, is a fine comic novel. Each is rich in incident, varied in characterization, and meaningful in its entirety. In each the story is narrated by the central figure, an adolescent whose remarkable language is both a reflection and a criticism of his education, his environment, and his times. Each is fundamentally a story of a quest—an adventure story in the age-old pattern of a young lad making his way in a not particularly friendly adult world. An outcast, to all intents without family and friends, the protagonist flees the restraints of the civilization which would make him its victim, and journeys through the world in search of what he thinks is freedom—but which we, his adult readers, recognize to be primarily understanding. Society regards him as a rogue, a ne'er-do-well whose career consists of one scrape after another; but the extent to which he is constantly embroiled with authority is exactly the index of his independence, his sometimes pathetic self-reliance, and his freedom of spirit. He is a total realist, with an acute and instinctive register of mind which enables him to penetrate sham and pretense—qualities which, the more he travels through the adult world, the more he sees as most frequently recurring. He has somehow acquired a code of ethics and a standard of value against which he measures mankind—including, mercilessly, himself. There are people and things—not many, however—that are (in Holden's term) "nice"; there are many more that are "phony." He does not understand the world, but he knows how one should behave in it. The comic irony that gives each novel its characteristic intellectual slant is provided by the judgments of these young realists on the false ideals and romanticized versions of life which they encounter on their travels.

³ The slangy, idiomatic, frequently vulgar language which Twain and Salinger put in the mouths of their heroes is remarkable for the clarity of the self-portraits that emerge, as well as for the effortless accuracy of the talk itself. F. R. Leavis describes Huck's colloquial language as a literary medium that is "Shakespearian in its range and subtlety." Likewise, Holden's twentieth-century prep-school vernacular, despite its automatic and somehow innocent obscenities and its hackneyed coinages, also manages to communicate ideas and feelings of a quite complex sort within its sharply delimited boundaries. The language, in each case, is personal, distinctive, and descriptive of character. Holden and Huck are moralists as well as realists: each has a deep concern with ethical valuation, and each responds fully to the experiences which life offers him. It is the tension between their apparently inadequate idiom and their instinctively full and humane ethics that both Twain and Salinger exploit for comic purposes.

⁴ "The traveler must be born again," said Thoreau; and Huck's voyage down the Mississippi is a series of constant rebirths, a search for identity. Beginning with the elaborately staged mock murder which sets him free from the clutches of Pap, Huck assumes a series of varied roles, playing each one like the brilliant improviser that he is. Twain counterpoints Huck's hoaxes against the villainous or merely mercenary pretenses of the Duke and the Dauphin; the boy's sometimes desperate shifts are necessary for his survival and to both his moral and physical progress. The series reaches a climax in the sequence at the Phelps farm, when Huck is forced to assume the identity of Tom Sawyer—when, for the first time, he cannot choose his own role.

⁵ This, it seems to me, is a significant variation, pointing to the world which begins to close in upon Huck toward the end of the novel. Not only is an identity forced upon him, but with the appearance of the real Tom Sawyer upon the scene, Huck surrenders the initiative in planning and, in effect, loses control of his own fate. This is the tragedy of Huckleberry Finn: that he has gone so far only to surrender at the end to the forces which have been seeking to capture him. For despite the apparent similarities, there is a vital difference between Huck and Tom: Tom behaves "by the book"; Tom relies on historical precedent; Tom operates within the conventions of the civilized world, accepting its values and standards, and merely play-acting at rebellion—Tom, in short, is no rebel at all, but a romanticizer of reality. Huck's term to describe Tom's method of doing things is that it has "style." Style it may have, but it lacks design. Huck's willingness to let Tom take over Jim's rescue indicates Twain's final acquiescence to the world which has been criticized throughout. True, Huck is going to light out again, he tells us in the last lines: "Aunt Sally she's going to adopt me and sivilize me, and I can't stand it. I been there before." But, despite the expression of sentiments pointing to another future escape—and the fact that the limiting article is not part of Twain's title—Huck, by the end of the novel, has been trapped. I should like to add my bit to the perennial debate concerning the artistic validity of the final sequence, and suggest that it is both ironical and true to life. Tom's playacting before Huck sets

off down the river—his ambuscade of the "A-rabs," for example—seems innocent and amusing; but the rescue of Jim seems, as I think it is meant to seem,
tedious and irrelevant. After all, something has happened to Huck—and to
us—between chapters 3 and 43.

⁶ Huck is trapped by a society whose shortcomings he sees, and he says,
"I can't stand it." Holden's terminology is "It depresses me" and "It kills me."
Ironically, he is revealed as telling us his narrative from an institution of some
kind—psychiatric, we are led to suspect—having also been trapped by the
people who want to "sivilize" him.

⁷ Holden's instinctive nonconformity asserts itself early in the novel. He
has been told by one of the masters at Pencey Prep, from which he is about to
be dismissed, that life is a game. "Some game," Holden comments. "If you get
on the side where all the hot-shots are, then it's a game, all right—I'll admit
that. But if you get on the *other* side, where there aren't any hot-shots, then
what's a game about it? Nothing. No game." At the age of seventeen he has
learned to suspect the glib philosophies of his elders, and to test the coin of
experience by determining whether it rings true or false for him, personally.

⁸ Like Huck, Holden is also a refugee. He flees the campus of Pencey Prep
before he is formally expelled, and returns to New York City to have three
days of freedom before rejoining his family. Pencey Prep is merely the most
recent in a series of unsatisfactory academic experiences for him. "One of the
biggest reasons I left Elkton Hills was because I was surrounded by phonies.
That's all. They were coming in the goddam window. I can't stand that stuff. It
drives me crazy. It makes me so depressed I go crazy."

⁹ Also like Huck, Holden assumes a series of guises during his lone wanderings. "I'm the most terrific liar you ever saw in your life. It's awful. If I'm on
the way to the store to buy a magazine, even, and somebody asks me where
I'm going, I'm liable to say I'm going to the opera. It's terrible." In a sequence
which reminds one forcibly of Huck Finn, Holden finds himself in conversation with the mother of one of his classmates, Ernie Morrow, whom he describes as "doubtless the biggest bastard that ever went to Pencey, in the whole
crumby history of the school." But Holden, adopting the name of "Rudolf
Schmidt" (the janitor), tells her what she wants to hear about her son, to her
wonder and delight. Holden's comment is: "Mothers are all slightly insane.
The thing is, though, I liked old Morrow's mother. She was all right." His
imagination rampant, Holden tells her a cock-and-bull story which includes an
impending brain operation and a trip to South America to visit his grandmother, but he stops just short of revealing himself completely. It is a wonder-
fully funny scene, showing Holden in several aspects: his instinctive evaluation
of the mother's "rightness" overcoming his profound distaste for her son, his
adolescent imagination in a frenzy of wild invention, and his own awareness of
the limits to which he can act his suddenly-adopted role of Rudolf Schmidt.

¹⁰ Huck's tortured decision not to "turn in" Jim is made on the basis of his
own feelings, which he automatically assumes to be sinful since they have so
often put him at odds with society. His personal moral code seems always to

run counter to his duty to society, a conflict which serves to confirm him in the belief that wickedness is in his line, "being brung up to it." In the crucial moral act of the novel, Huck must "decide, forever, betwixt two things, and I knowed it. I studied a minute, sort of holding my breath, and then says to myself, 'All right, then I'll *go* to hell.' " Huck's humanity overcomes the so-called duty to society. Holden, also, is "depressed" by the notion that he is somehow a misfit, that he does strange, irrational things, that he is fighting a constant war with society—but his awareness of his own weaknesses (his compulsive lying, for example) is the result of his searching honesty.

[11] The yardstick which Holden applies to the world is a simple one—too simple, perhaps, too rigorous, too uncompromising, for anyone but an adolescent (or, as the popular phrase has it, "a crazy mixed-up kid") to attempt to apply to a complex world: it is the test of truth. The world is full of phonies—so Holden dreams of running away and building his own cabin, where people would come and visit him. "I'd have this rule that nobody could do anything phony when they visited me. If anybody tried to do anything phony, they couldn't stay."

[12] Huck's world, realistically depicted as mid-America in the middle of the nineteenth century, is also the world where the established codes are penetrated as being either hypocritical or superficial; Huck finds peace and reassurance away from the haunts of man, out on the river. After the waste and folly of the Grangerford-Shepherdson sequence, for example, Huck retreats to the river:

> Sometimes we'd have that whole river all to ourselves for the longest time. Yonder was the banks and the islands, across the water; and maybe a spark—which was a candle in a cabin window; and sometimes on the water you could see a spark or two—on a raft or a scow, you know; and maybe you could hear a fiddle or a song coming over from one of them crafts. It's lovely to live on a raft.

But the idyll is interrupted shortly thereafter with "a couple of men tearing up the path as tight as they could foot it"—the Duke and the Dauphin imposing their unsavory world upon Huck's.

[13] Holden's world is post-war New York City, from the Metropolitan Museum to Greenwich Village, during Christmas week, where, in successive incidents, he encounters pompous hypocrisy, ignorance, indifference, moral corruption, sexual perversion, and—pervading all—"phoniness." Holden's older brother, a once promising writer, is now a Hollywood scenarist; the corruption of his talent is symptomatic to Holden of the general influence of the movies: "They can ruin you. I'm not kidding." They represent the world at its "phoniest" in their falsification of reality; in addition, they corrupt their audiences, converting them into people like the three pathetic girls from Seattle who spend all evening in a second-rate night club looking for movie stars, or like

the woman Holden observes at the Radio City Music Hall. She cries through the entire picture, and "the phonier it got, the more she cried . . . She had this little kid with her that was bored as hell and had to go to the bathroom, but she wouldn't take him. . . . She was about as kind-hearted as a goddam wolf."

[14] Holden's awareness of sham sensitizes him to its manifestations wherever it appears: in the pseudo-religious Christmas spectacle at Radio City ("I can't see anything religious or pretty, for God's sake, about a bunch of actors carrying crucifixes all over the stage"); in ministers with "Holy Joe" voices, in magazine fiction, with its "lean-jawed guys named David" and "phony girls named Linda or Marcia"; and in the performance of a gifted night-club pianist as well as that of the Lunts. His reactions to the performances of all three is a comment on the relationship between virtuosity and integrity: "If you do something *too* good, then, after a while, if you don't watch it, you start showing off. And then you're not as good any more." Both mock humility and casual bravura are dangerous to the integrity of the individual: Holden finds no "naturalness" in the finished and most artistic performers in his world. His world, he comes to feel, is full of obscenities, both figurative and actual; even a million years would be inadequate to erase all the obscenities scribbled on all the walls. His week-end in New York reminds him of the time an alumnus of Pencey visited the school and inspected the doors in the men's toilet to see if his initials were still carved there. While he searched for this memento of his past, he solemnly gave platitudinous advice to the boys. The glaring disparity between what even "good guys" say and what they do is enough to make Holden despair of finding anyone, except his sister Phoebe, with whom he can communicate honestly.

[15] A few things Holden encounters on his voyage through the metropolis make him "feel better." Like Huck, who has to retreat regularly to the river, to reestablish his contacts with his sources of value, Holden several times meets perfectly "natural" things which delight him: the kettle-drummer in the orchestra, who never looks bored, but who bangs his drums "so nice and sweet, with this nervous expression of his face"; a Dixieland song recorded by a Negro girl who doesn't make it sound "mushy" or "cute"; and the sight of a family coming out of church. But these incidents merely serve to reveal in sharper contrast the phoniness and the tinsel of the adult world which seeks to victimize Holden, and which, in the end, finally does. Like Huck, he finds himself at the mercy of the kindly enemy. The realist's sharp perceptions of the world about him are treated either as the uncivilized remarks of an ignorant waif or—supreme irony!—as lunacy.

[16] In addition to being comic masterpieces and superb portrayals of perplexed, sensitive adolescence, these two novels thus deal obliquely and poetically with a major theme in American life, past and present—the right of the noncomformist to assert his noncomformity, even to the point of being "handled with a chain." In them, 1884 and 1951 speak to us in the idiom and accent of two youthful travelers who have earned their passports to literary immortality.

ANALYTICAL READING

1. Explain the phrase "the level of the merely picaresque" (paragraph 1).

2. On what bases does Kaplan compare the two novels?

3. How does Kaplan integrate into his essay the quotation from Thoreau in the opening paragraph? What evidence does he offer from each book to illustrate the quote?

4. What points in the essay might be viewed as contrasts between the two books?

5. What points has Kaplan made throughout the essay that lead the reader to accept his contention that the books illustrate "the right of the noncomformist to assert his nonconformity" (paragraph 16)?

REFLECTING

Point: Using the information in the opening and closing paragraphs, write a one-sentence summary of Kaplan's thesis. What opinion does he express?

Organization: Make a brief outline of the paper. What comparison-and-contrast scheme does Kaplan follow?

Support: Indicate places where Kaplan uses quotations from the two novels as support. Discuss the variety of ways that he uses them. How do his comparison-and-contrast paragraphs support his thesis about the two books? Does his thesis demand a comparison-and-contrast approach? Explain.

Synthesis: If you have not read the books, did you find the information complete enough to enable you to identify with the two heroes? If so, at what points? If you have read one or both works, did you agree or disagree with any of Kaplan's points?

Evaluation: Do you think the writer handles the comparisons effectively? Are they easy to follow? Why or why not? What transitional devices do you find especially effective? Why? Has Kaplan supported his thesis adequately and written about the two books clearly, interestingly, and convincingly? Has he included any unnecessary material?

FROM READING TO WRITING

1. Write a critical paper comparing and contrasting some aspect of two works—novels, short stories, TV shows, movies—that have similar themes.

2. Write a critical paper comparing and contrasting two characters in a single work—novel, short story, TV show, movie—and how they relate to the themes in the work. Try to relate your discussion of the characters to real life, as Kaplan does.

Analysis
Analysis Using Example

DO AS I SAY, NOT AS I DO
Amitai Etzioni

BIOGRAPHICAL SKETCH

Amitai Etzioni was born in Cologne, Germany, in 1929. He received B.A. and M.A. degrees from Hebrew University and a Ph.D. from the University of California at Berkeley. He has been a professor of sociology and chairman of the Department of Sociology at Columbia University, and is currently the Director of the Center for Policy Research. Among his honors are a Guggenheim Fellowship and an appointment as a Fellow at the Center for Advanced Study for Behavioral Studies. In addition to serving on the editorial board of Science *magazine and writing numerous articles in professional journals, he is the author of twelve books, including* Modern Organizations, Studies in Social Change, The Active Society, *and* Genetic Fix.

PRE-READING

1. The title is a familiar maxim; what does it indicate to you about the subject matter of the essay?

2. Skim the first and last paragraphs. What do you think the subject and the writer's attitude toward it are?

3. From the biographical sketch, do you accept Etzioni as an authority?

[1] The hottest new item in post-Watergate curriculums is "moral education," an attempt by educators to instill moral values in youngsters by using newly designed teaching methods. With many believing that people in the United States do not live as moral and honest lives as they used to, according to Gallup, moral education is now favored by four out of every five Americans.

[2] But moral education means rather different things to different people—from teaching respect for the law as embodied in police officers and other authority figures, to instilling "good manners," to developing the capacity to form one's own standards and judgments. Though the goals of moral educa-

FROM *The New York Times Magazine,* 26 September 1976, pp. 44, 65–66. © 1976 by The New York Times Company. Reprinted by permission.

tion are at best contradictory, a significant number of the nation's public schools are nonetheless forging ahead.

3 Progressive educators are keenly aware that preaching ethics in the classroom is not likely to meet with much success. They also know that assigning "morals" readings in textbooks, the way children are taught, say, geography, is not likely to be anywhere near as productive for character building as such techniques are for developing factual understanding. In the search for an appropriate way to get moral value across, a variety of approaches are being tried.

4 In 1970, Jane Elliott, a teacher at Community Elementary school in Riceville, Iowa, wanted to teach her third-grade students the injustice of discrimination, but sensing that just talking about the arbitrariness and unfairness of race prejudice would be too academic to have much impact, her inspiration was to appeal directly to the children's capacity for emotional experience and empathetic insight by declaring a day of discrimination against the blue-eyed. She began by "explaining" the innate superiority of the "cleaner, more civilized, smarter" brown-eyed. When the children were, at first, disbelieving, she snapped sarcastically at a blue-eyed child, "Is that the way we've been taught to sit in class?" and then moved all the blue-eyed to the back of the room. To snickers from the brown-eyed, she then informed the blue-eyed that they would not be permitted to play on the big playground at recess and could only play at all if invited by a brown-eyed child. Throughout the day she was conspicuously more tolerant of mistakes made by brown-eyed children. The brown-eyed quickly started to enjoy lording it over the blue-eyed, who soon showed signs of growing insecurity and loss of confidence.

5 After reversing the roles for a day, Mrs. Elliott had every child write about how it felt to be discriminated against. Though to many adults her procedure may sound heavy-handed, as far as her students were concerned the experience "took." That it made a profound impression is apparent from such comments as "I felt dirty, left out, thought of quitting school." The children were not shy about saying how "rotten" it felt to be labeled inferior and how relieved they were to be equal again.

6 In the context of the current moral-education drive, what Jane Elliott did in 1970 is of particular interest because despite the successful results she was reported to have achieved, few schools have followed her lead.

7 One Monday morning, the students in a Pittsburgh junior high school started their civics class not with a rehash of government branches, the meaning of "checks and balances," or that pragmatic addition of recent years, how to fill out Form 1040A, but with a brief "moral dilemma": "Sharon and Jill were best friends. One day they went shopping together. Jill tried on a sweater and then, to Sharon's surprise, walked out of the store with the sweater under her coat. A moment later, the store's security officer stopped Sharon and demanded that she tell him the name of the girl who had walked out. He told the storeowner that he had seen the two girls together, and that he was sure that

the one who left had been shoplifting. The storeowner told Sharon that she could really get in trouble if she didn't give her friend's name."

[8] "Should Sharon tell?" the teacher asked. One student suggested that Sharon should deny knowing Jill. The teacher wanted to know if the student approved of lying for a friend. "Yah," was the answer. The teacher then inquired, "What is going to happen to all of us if everyone lies?" This elicited the following pupil observation: "If everyone goes around shoplifting, do you know what kind of life that would be? Everybody would just be walking around stealing everybody else's stuff." Another student interjected, "But everybody doesn't steal and everybody wouldn't, and, anyway, the storeowner probably has a large enough margin of profit to cover the few rip-offs." The first stuck to his guns: "But the store can't exist if everybody is stealing, there are so many people, and it is getting worse every day." A third student felt it was "like stealing from the rich and giving to the poor."

[9] What educators who favor this moral-dilemma approach stress is that, first of all, it elicits a discussion in which the teacher tolerates free expression of student viewpoints and, second, such give-and-take improves student awareness of moral issues, and leads to higher levels of moral reasoning.

[10] According to Harvard's Lawrence Kohlberg, most often cited by moral-dilemma advocates, children move from an amoral stage toward concern for the needs and feelings of others. It is useless, he argues, to try to get children at the most primitive stage of moral development—in the early years where they only do what is right to avoid punishment or to gain approval—to suddenly understand principles or modes of reasoning at the highest level. But it is possible, through proper classroom dialectics, to help children move toward a point where they wish to be ethical because they themselves think it's right.

[11] Just as in past years many whites who referred to adult black men as "boys" did not fully comprehend the offense they were giving, in numerous other situations many youngsters (and adults) simply do not perceive the moral issue at stake. Nearly 20 years ago, following the "$64,000 Question" quiz-show scandal, in which it was discovered that TV personnel had provided some contestants with the answers, Kurt and Gladys Lang asked a class of New York University students to rank various behaviors according to their relative unethicality. A year ago I used their questionnaire with Columbia University undergraduates and obtained similar results. One of the main findings of both surveys was that students tend to have a difficult time perceiving behavior as unethical if they can not identify individual victims. Thus, the Langs found, for example, that the students considered the behavior of a land speculator who made millions on a tip-off from city hall less unethical than that of a student who cheated on an exam—or of Charles Van Doren, the "cheating professor" of "$64,000 Question" fame.

[12] The students reasoned that a student who cheats gains an unfair competitive advantage over other students and that Van Doren had "let down" television viewers who believed in him, but they could not see that the land

speculator had harmed anyone. They had a hard time conceiving of the community—or business or government—as the victim of unethical conduct.

[13] By far the most prevalent method of classroom ethics teaching today is paper-and-pencil assignments. The main champion of this approach is Prof. Sidney B. Simon of the University of Massachusetts. One of the more than 1,000 schools using his "values-clarification kits" is the William W. Niles Junior High School in the Bronx. According to Claudia Macari, assistant principal for guidance, and Mildred W. Abramowitz, principal, who were responsible for introducing values clarification at William W. Niles, an example of the technique is as follows:

[14] Exercise one: "Write down 20 things you love to do." Pause. "Now that you have all made your lists, state *the five* things you love to do *best of all.* Check the things you love to do alone; X the things you love to do with other people; . . . things that cost less than $3 to do."

[15] Macari and Abramowitz explain that the purpose of having the students choose the five out of 20 things they like best is to make them aware of what it is they value. The whole idea of values clarification is *not* to instill or introduce any particular values, new or old, but to help students discover those they already have. Having to decide which 15 items to leave out, which five to include, leads the youngsters to an understanding of how values work, the choices inevitably involved.

[16] The items relating to gregariousness and money help the student gain insight into why he values what he does, and foster greater self-awareness.

[17] Values-clarification exercises differ from most other work-book assignments in one way: Any and all answers are considered "right" as long as one can give a reason for them. Asked whether a youngster might not, therefore, end up reaffirming "wrong" values, such as intolerance or thievery, the designers of the approach reply: "Our position is that we respect his right to decide upon that value."

[18] Some claim that it is precisely its amorality that makes the values-clarification package so popular in the public schools—it protects them from having to choose *whose* values to teach.

[19] Actually, despite the "rules" of such programs, when sensitive issues like abortion, women's rights and discrimination against minorities are discussed in the classroom, it is difficult for teachers to hide their feelings. Body language, tone of voice, allotment of more speaking time to children who have the desired point of view, will indicate to the student where his teacher stands.

[20] Whatever method of teaching morals is employed—there is not yet enough data available to support the superiority of any one technique—there are other ways schools communicate moral values.

[21] It has long been understood that children learn from their parents by emulation—as is acknowledged in the well-known saw: "Do as I say, not as I do!" The same notion is equally applicable to the ethics taught in school: The way teachers, administrators, coaches and other school officials interact with the children teaches ethical values by example. Mrs. Elsa Wasserman, a coun-

selor to the Cambridge, Mass., public schools, explains: "The governance structure of many schools teaches students that in school they have no significant control over their lives; that they must conform to arbitrary rules or be punished; and that they should go along with what the majority thinks and does even when they disagree." This is the "hidden curriculum."

22 Talking to students, one finds that the core of the hidden curriculum revolves around grades, athletics and student behavior. The attitudes and actions students observe on the part of school officials with regard to these are not often ones which convey the importance of standing up for ethical principles.

23 For example: In one Eastern Pennsylvania school, administrators became aware that some black pupils had formed gangs which collected 25 cents a day in "protection money" from younger, mainly white children. For a long time, these officials looked the other way. Why? Well, they said, they were afraid that active efforts to find out which children were in the extortion ring and to punish them would expose them to charges of "police tactics." The principal's main concern was that it was a "no-win" situation.

24 When some gang members were finally caught, he first suspended the extortionist pupils, then, when black parents protested, had them reinstated, then, when white parents were outraged, sent them to an experimental school, then, when the black parents charged "exile," had them returned. He felt no need to apologize for setting policy according to which ethnic group was protesting most. The main issue, as he saw it, was not what to do about extortion, or how his failure to do anything credible about it would affect the students, but how to negotiate a political tightrope.

25 In marked contrast to the idealism of a few years back that sought to replace grades with more meaningful evaluations, many of today's students believe their life's fate hangs on getting into the "right" college—which in turn depends on getting high grades. Thus, for quite a few students the notion that cheating on exams or term papers is a serious ethical issue is about as quaint as the medieval scholastic debate over how many angels can stand on the head of a pin.

26 Among the students with whom I have spoken, attitudes seem to be less cynical toward sports than toward grades. But each sport has its own "informal" rules of fair play. Basketball players, for instance, say they are trained to keep a keen eye on the referee and to push another player out of the way when the referee is not looking, although "really digging your elbow into the other guy" is considered going too far. Football seems to be the focus of the most intense pressures to win—and, therefore, the greatest temptations to win at any price.

27 Traditionally, one of the major justifications for lavishing large sums on school sports programs—especially competitive team-sports programs—has been that athletics are "character-building." And, indeed, they very likely are. The question that needs greater attention, however, is what kind of character are they building?

[28] The hidden-curriculum emphasis on high grades and winning in sports suggests that grades and sports are still considered important tools for instilling the American "success ethic" and that stimulating the drive for success is still a major mission of the American school. The success drive has ethics-undermining side-effects, however, if built into its creed is the attitude conveyed by the late football coach Vince Lombardi's oft-quoted motto: "Winning is not the most important thing, it's the only thing." Unbounded competition is incompatible with ethical codes because it puts self (or one's team) above the rules of the game.

[29] Of all the approaches to moral education, the one which focuses on reform of the hidden curriculum is likely to be both the most relevant and the most difficult to accomplish, because teachers and students are less aware of its moral implications than they are of the formal curriculum, and because its roots lie in the community. It is thus far from accidental that when Professor Kohlberg tried to apply his ideas about how best to foster higher levels of moral reasoning in the schools, he ended up having to set up an experimental, "alternate," school, in which 72 students selected from four high-school classes in the Cambridge High and Latin school, together with a volunteer staff, became a school-within-a-school run on principles of student participation. In Kohlberg's "just school," each student and each staff member has one vote and "no major decision or commitments are made without consulting the entire community."

[30] Most of America is probably far from ready for such a radically egalitarian approach in the public schools. But most schools may be ready for limited reforms to bring the hidden curriculum more in line with what is taught in ethics classes—awarding grades on the basis of merit rather than on conformity to the teacher's views or docility in the face of authority, emphasizing respect for the rules in sports rather than just playing to win.

[31] The objection may be raised that schools structured to produce more ethical youth would fail in their major mission of adequately preparing their students for later life, in which "success" often entails bending, if not violating, the rules. One could counter this criticism by maintaining that it is the schools' job to educate their students morally—over and above the prevalent societal standards. At the very least, then, the students will have some principles to compromise later on; and though their standards may become eroded, nonetheless they will not become as unethical as they would have had they started out with no scruples at all. True, most schools cannot proceed very far in promoting values not shared by the community at large. Before the schools can effectively provide moral education, the surrounding society must work to reform itself so that its members are less concerned with success and material achievements, and more concerned about quality of life and individual conduct.

ANALYTICAL READING

1. How do the first three paragraphs set up the basis for the classification in this article? What is it?

2.   List in one-sentence summaries the subclasses of "approaches to teaching moral values."

3.   What factors seem to be most important in making value judgments? Your answer should be an inference that you have drawn from reading the examples given in the article.

4.   Do you agree with the contention in paragraph 19? Can you cite some personal experience?

5.   In what ways are grades and sports compared and related?

6.   From reading the article, can you define the "hidden curriculum," giving its characteristics? Is it a positive or negative influence on students?

7.   How might emphasis on ethics interfere with students' success in the world?

8.   Does Etzioni think that the schools can do an effective job of teaching morality? Why or why not? How is his opinion on this revealed?

REFLECTING

Point: What else is achieved in the article besides listing methods of teaching moral values? How appropriate is the title for the essay?

Organization: Using the list you made in answer to question 2, work up an organizational scheme for the article, indicating the relationships involved.

Support: Do the examples act as support to the subclassification process? Explain. How are authorities used?

Synthesis: Have you had experience with any of the moral dilemmas dealt with in the article, such as shoplifting or cheating? Have you been encouraged in class to discuss controversial subjects that involve moral issues? Discuss. Are there nonreligious reasons for doing what is ethical? Compare Etzioni's views about sports with those expressed by Lipsyte in the selection from *SportsWorld* on pages 205–10.

Evaluation: What element of the essay did you find most effective? Why? Do you think the subject is an important one? Do you agree or disagree that schools should attempt to teach ethics? How much influence can teachers and principals have?

FROM READING TO WRITING

1.   Pick a topic about which people hold differing opinions, such as athletic scholarships, school discipline, open dorms. Write an analysis paper, not simply listing these opinions, but showing some relationship they share. Use examples as Etzioni does.

2.   Using examples, write an analysis of the different attitudes toward the grading system for your school newspaper.

BAD STUDY HABITS
Russell Baker

BIOGRAPHICAL SKETCH

Russell Baker, a graduate of Johns Hopkins University, was born in 1925 in Loudoun County, Virginia. After working as a reporter for the Baltimore Sun *and the* New York Times, *in 1962 he became the author of a nationally syndicated humorous column, "The Observer." He has been awarded honorary degrees by Princeton and several other universities. Among his six books are two novels and several collections of his essays, including* All Things Considered *and* Baker's Dozen. *In addition, he has contributed witty and satirical essays to numerous magazines, such as* Ladies' Home Journal, Sports Illustrated, Holiday, *and* McCall's.

PRE-READING

1. What information in the biographical sketch suggests the probable tone of the essay?

2. How is the tone revealed in the opening paragraph?

3. What does the final paragraph indicate about the general subject and Baker's attitude toward it?

¹ Had the Government simply refused to watch 58 women cook three meals a day for a week, no reasonable citizen would have complained, for the Government is terribly busy. But the Government did not refuse. This, after all, was a study, and if there is one thing the Government loves, it is a study.

² And so it assembled 58 women in a kitchen at the National Bureau of Standards and told them to start cooking. They cooked and they cooked. And while they cooked, the Government watched them on television cameras and through one-way mirrors.

³ They were not told why they were cooking, and so they did not know that their cooking habits were being scrutinized to determine the energy efficiency of the typical American cooker. The results are now in, and a more unexciting batch of results I have rarely seen.

⁴ For example, the women tended to cook on their stoves' right front burners, even when these were the biggest burners on the stove. What's more, many of the women left their oven doors open while they peeled potatoes.

⁵ The Government's conclusion is that Americans waste a lot of gas and electricity through bad cooking habits. This differs substantially from my own conclusion, which is that the Government wastes a lot of money and energy through bad study habits.

⁶ Any government half as efficient as ours wants its cooking citizenry to be would have nipped this study in the bud. It would have said, "Look here,

FROM *The New York Times Magazine,* 5 June 1977, p. 12. © 1977 by the New York Times Company. Reprinted by permission.

you're not only proposing to tie me up for a week watching 58 women who don't know why they're being watched, but you're also asking me to spend a lot of money on television cameras, one-way mirrors, psychologists, tabulators, report writers and similar gewgaws. And all you're going to learn is that people cook indiscriminately on the right front burner."

[7] "How can you be so sure?" the study director might have asked.

[8] To which a sagacious government would have replied, "Because most people are right-handed, and because Americans are a people who don't like to put things on the back burner."

[9] Our Government does not operate this way. Americans don't like to put things on the back burner, and the Government doesn't like to pass up the chance to conduct a study that will confirm what everyone has always known. A few years ago it conducted a study that discovered kissing transmits colds.

[10] As for the discovery that many people leave the oven door open while peeling potatoes, this is almost certainly wrong. The error in all probability results from elevating cookery to a laboratory enterprise.

[11] Every cook at some point in his or her development has left the oven door open while peeling potatoes. But only once. In a normal kitchen with its cramped space, an open oven door leads inexorably to cracked shinbone, perhaps broken leg and possibly severe burn. After the first encounter with an oven door in the typical American kitchen, the neophyte Escoffier rarely, if ever, leaves it open again dealing with the spuds.

[12] The women who did so in the Government's test probably had good reasons. Perhaps the Government's kitchens were as commodious as its purse and gave them a luxurious sense of spaciousness which allowed them to indulge a vice denied them in their homes. More likely, I suspect, since the women were kept in the dark about why they were cooking in this laboratory, some of the them tried to outguess the experimenters.

[13] If I were taken to the National Bureau of Standards and told to cook three meals daily for a week under close observation, and utterly without explanation, I might very well conclude that the Government was trying to discover whether I was wasting potatoes by peeling off too much potato with the skin. Under the intense strain of struggling to keep my potato peels paper thin, I might easily forget such normal kitchen habits as keeping the oven door closed.

[14] The Government doesn't pounce on this sensible explanation of why the oven doors were left open. Instead, it proposes to inflict yet another buzzer on the national nervous system. This buzzer would sound off with each opening of the oven and, of course, in the natural development of buzzers, acquire a mind of its own which would set it off whenever it became peevish, at all hours of the day and night, whether the oven is open or shut.

[15] We need only one more buzzer in America. This should go off in the Government's ear every time somebody proposes to study whether water is wet and whether fleas like dogs.

ANALYTICAL READING

1. What sentences in paragraphs 2, 3, and 5 indicate the author's attitude toward the Government study? Analyze how their structure achieves this effect.

2. Why is the word *government* not capitalized in the first sentence of paragraph 6? Can you rewrite this sentence to make it clearer?

3. Is the pun on *back burner* (paragraph 8) a logical or humorous statement in this context? What is the relationship between the statement about the back burner and the results of the study? What is the effect of this point and of Baker's imagined conversation between the Government and the study director?

4. Could you guess at the meaning of the allusion to *Escoffier* (paragraph 11), or did you look it up? How appropriate is the simile in paragraph 12? What specific words in the essay did you find particularly delightful and most effective in maintaining the tone?

5. How knowledgeable is Baker about cooking? On what evidence do you base your conclusion?

6. How does Baker render absurd a serious Government recommendation about adding a buzzer to stoves to save wasted energy?

REFLECTING

Point: Is the article mainly concerned with a particular study, most Government studies, Government waste of money, or all three? Answer this question by writing a summary statement of the essay.

Organization: Indicate how the essay is divided into its respective parts. Could the order of these parts have been changed without affecting the essay? Could any part have been omitted? How does the analogy in the last paragraph contribute to the author's organization?

Support: Does Baker offer sufficient examples to illustrate the nature of the Government study? Does he clearly explain his reasons for feeling that the study was unnecessary, the results inconclusive, and the recommendation impractical?

Synthesis: Do you agree with Baker about the study? What case can be made for it? Do you think that the 58 women watched under the conditions mentioned would have acted normally or would have been more careful than usual about leaving oven doors open and cooking on the most efficient burner? Is there any value in determining whether kissing transmits colds? Whether great amounts of saccharin produce cancer in laboratory rats?

Evaluation: How effective is Baker in analyzing the problem? Describe the voice he uses and indicate whether it contributes to or detracts from his essay. Is the essay written clearly, interestingly, and convincingly?

FROM READING TO WRITING

1. Write an essay about a high school study of homework, dating, driving, or some other student habits, showing how ridiculous the methodology, conclusions, or recommendations are.

2. If some campus rule, procedure, or proposal irritates you, write a letter to your college newspaper, emulating Baker's voice and tone.

3. Write a paper analyzing the changes you foresee in the use of drugs, restrictions on television, changes in family life, the nature of cars and transportation, the composition of the armed forces, the status of women, or some other subject. Consider changes resulting from both external and internal factors. Support your prediction by citing examples of recent changes.

Analysis
Analysis Using Statistics

INFLATION, EDUCATION, AND THE AFTER-SCHOOL JOB
David L. Manning

BIOGRAPHICAL SKETCH

Born in Manchester, New Hampshire in 1937, David L. Manning received an undergraduate degree at Boston College, a master's degree from Wesleyan University, and a master's degree and a doctorate from Boston University. A high school teacher for over twenty-two years, he is currently teaching social studies at Conard High School in West Hartford, Connecticut and is also a visiting professor at Fairfax University. His articles have appeared in the New York Times *and the* Wall Street Journal. *Recently, he was the writer of a Kettering committee report, "Transition of Youth to Adulthood: A Bridge Too Long."*

PRE-READING

1. Which word in the title provides the best clue to the specific subject of the article?

2. Which sentence in the first few paragraphs suggests the probable direction of the article?

3. Which sentence in the final paragraph seems to state the author's main concern?

[1] In complex and far-reaching ways, inflation is devastating the lives of far too many American high school students. It saps their buying power, skews their learning habits, and subverts their values.

[2] The most visible sign of inflation's impact on the life of the high school student is the part-time job. Working after school has become a pervasive part of youth culture. To a startling degree the part-time job has replaced the varsity team as the central focus in the lives of many high school students.

[3] The part-time job has long been part of the growing up process; what has changed dramatically, however, is the number of hours that high school

FROM The *Wall Street Journal*, March 11, 1980, p. 20. Reprinted by permission of The *Wall Street Journal*, © Dow Jones & Company, Inc., 1980. All rights reserved.

students work to cope with spiraling inflation. When the hours are totaled, part-time work often amounts to a full-time job.

⁴ Some insight into the dimensions of the problem is provided by a recent modest survey I made of the work-study habits of 148 juniors and seniors in six Connecticut high schools, essentially one classroom in each school. The schools represent a cross-section of Connecticut public high schools, including urban and suburban districts representing varying socio-economic levels. The students ranged in age from 15 to 19.

⁵ The survey results are revealing and cause for concern among parents, educators and employers. Seventy-seven percent of the students report that they work at part-time jobs. Slightly more than half are girls. Typically, the part-time job averages out to 20 hours each week. Incredibly, 11 students said that they worked 30 or more hours per week on a steady basis.

⁶ The survey indicates a strong inverse relationship between the number of hours that students work at part-time jobs and the number of hours that they spend on homework. As the number of hours on the part-time job increases, the time devoted to homework assignments decreases. Students who work after school report that they devote an average of only one hour per school night to their homework assignments. Equally alarming is the fact that three out of four of these students indicate that they have collegiate aspirations.

⁷ This growing disparity between labor for pay and study for a deferred benefit, gives rise to a condition in which students become increasingly deficient in the mastery of basic academic skills. Homework which is assigned to develop basic academic skills and concepts, if done at all, is done haphazardly or incompletely. This is hardly surprising. Only students with uncommon talents or with unusual pluck are willing and able to tackle several hours of demanding homework assignments following three to four hours of often tedious drudgery at a part-time job.

⁸ The end result is all too familiar. Increasing numbers of high school students fail to develop facility in writing, ease in linguistic form, and competence in mathematical processes. Teachers, in turn, are forced to direct their instructional efforts toward remediation in basic skill areas, and they are unable to sharpen and broaden basic skills to a point where students can begin to move beyond the basics.

⁹ As physical and mental fatigue creeps in from a steady diet of 12-hour stints of school and work, youthful effervescence gives way to languor. Yawns come earlier in the day and with greater frequency. Attention spans shorten. Youthful dispositions grow less pleasant. Tempers flare. Coping with one's teachers and peers becomes a formidable task. Frequent absence from school becomes a way to catch up on homework or to rest for the afternoon job.

¹⁰ Where does all the money go? Only 24% of the students I surveyed indicated that they were working to save money for a college education or for future needs; furthermore, only one student indicated that money from a part-time job was contributed to the family budget. Where is the rest of the money

spent? Most of it goes to gratify the sophisticated materialistic tastes of high school students—to buy gasoline for the numerous gas guzzlers that fill the parking lots of every high school, to buy tickets for an endless assortment of rock concerts and sporting events, to buy expensive jeans and exotic footwear, and to buy a veritable smorgasbord of fast foods.

[11] What is most troubling from this analysis is what it reveals about the needs and the values of high school students. The primary motive for part-time work appears to be indulgent self-interest. There is little evidence of a developing sense of responsibility for their own future needs, for the substantial financial sacrifices of parents, or for the instructional efforts of teachers.

[12] Many students find themselves locked in a troubling value dilemma: while 72% of the students who work after school admit that their schoolwork suffers as a result of the part-time job, most are unwilling to deviate from the lifestyles to which they have become accustomed. Instead, the tendency is to work longer hours to maintain them. As inflation continues to ratchet up the prices of the goods and services that students work for, their purchasing power stands still, locked into minimum and subminimum wage scales. All the while, powerful peer pressures conspire with the usual materialistic impulses to inspire them to purchase bigger and faster cars, more fashionable clothes and to finance ever more elaborate social gatherings.

[13] In no sense are we witnessing the rebirth of the Horatio Alger ethic; if anything, we are witnessing Algerism at its worst. Money in the pocket of a young person has immediate value; the value of a high school education, by contrast, cannot be measured in such utilitarian terms. When a part-time job dominates the life of a teen-ager, schooling suffers. A better balance is desperately needed.

ANALYTICAL READING

1. If Manning doesn't object to students taking part-time jobs, under what conditions might he approve?

2. How valid or representative does Manning's survey seem to you? Would you like any additional information about it?

3. Why does Manning feel homework is important? Do you agree with him? Why does he feel that students with jobs neglect their homework?

4. Describe the predominant sentence structure in paragraph 9. What is its effect? How are rhetorical questions used in paragraph 10?

5. What fault does Manning find with the way students spend the money earned from part-time jobs? What basic value judgment concern him?

6. What is the Horatio Alger ethic (paragraph 13)? Does Manning believe that the problems arising from part-time jobs will get worse in the future? Why or why not?

REFLECTING

Point: What sentence in the article best summarizes the author's main idea? Write a more complete summary in a sentence or two, making certain to include several of the causes and results.

Organization: Point out the main divisions of the article. What basic organizational pattern is followed?

Support: What evidence does Manning use to support his thesis? What assumption does he make about his readers' knowledge of students' academic skills? How does Manning establish that little time and effort devoted to homework result in poor academic performance?

Synthesis: Does the author exaggerate at any point? Does he overlook the benefits of part-time work? Do many students work because they find it more interesting, challenging, and fulfilling than their classes? If so, what is wrong with working? Why should Manning blame students for having the same values as their parents? And what difference does inflation make? If the inflationary rate were lower, would that have any effect on students' part-time work?

Evaluation: How clearly has Manning presented his ideas? Is he trying to persuade readers or make them aware of a current problem? How significant and well known is this problem? What additional evidence could Manning have used to make his point more convincingly about the impact of work on education?

FROM READING TO WRITING

1.   Manning's article appeared in the *Wall Street Journal*. Write a letter for publication in this newspaper, assuming that readers may not have read or recalled his article. Agree or disagree with it on the basis of the homework assigned to you in high school.

2.   For an essay contest sponsored by a group of local businessmen, write a paper about the value of working part-time while atending high school or college.

3.   People are generally concerned about the low student scores on national standardized tests. Write an article for a teachers' publication, suggesting reasons for these scores.

4.   For your college newspaper, agree or disagree with Manning's views about student values. If you wish, you may refer to his article.

Assessment of
Reading and Writing Skills:
Expository Writing

Step 1

Read the essay that follows with the aim of understanding and recalling the important ideas. When you finish, note how long it took you to read the selection. Then close your book and write a summary of the important information without referring again to the essay. Indicate also your impression of how the writer used form or structure to clarify meaning. You will be allowed 7 to 10 minutes to write; your instructor will establish the limit and tell you when the time is up.

NO MORE ISOLATION IN THE NUCLEAR FAMILY AND MONOTONOUS SUBURBS ... A RELAXING OF POLITICAL FRONTIERS

Margaret Mead

Changes in methods of child rearing are important not only because they contribute to changes in the character of the future citizens of the planet but because making changes in the way children are raised affects the character of those who raise them—parents, physicians, legislators. How children will be raised in the year 2000 can only be a more or less informed guess by someone who has specialized in the relationship of child rearing to other aspects of culture. But how we should raise our children is necessarily a program for a better future and a citizenry that can better deal with the great issues of the next century.

I hope that they will be raised in neighborhoods where they have warm relationships with many older people—grandparents or surrogate grandparents, teen-agers, currently unmarried adults, who have time to teach children special skills. I hope that such contacts will mean that children will no longer be confined to the isolated nuclear family in suburbs and housing developments, where all of the families are of the same class and ethnic group and have children of approximately the same age.

I hope that we will have redesigned our cities and suburbs so that there is a real outdoors for all little children's play, so that they can experience the unpredictability and endless fascination of growing things and be rescued from their current boredom with only-too-predictable toys and school tasks.

I hope that men and women will have come to design their married lives as parents who share, in many different styles, both the domestic tasks of homemaking and the tasks that contribute to the public life of the country, with all division of labor based on temperament and skill rather than on sex membership. Providing such an upbringing for children is the easiest and most efficient way to bring up children who will be persons first—individuals able to use their full potentialities—and members of one sex or the other second.

I hope that children can be raised with the recognition that since war can no longer protect any country, it is no longer appropriate to raise boys who will someday be asked to kill and die and girls who will concur in these activities. If boys are not raised to be soldiers, it will be easier to relax those political frontiers that are now powerless to protect us against the new enemies: nuclear death, overpopulation strangulation, ecological death of sea and air. We can relax the lines around the small family and around the state and raise children in continually widening circles of affection for family, community, country, and planet—children who will care enough for each circle to be willing to make any sacrifice for its well-being and who will not find life stale and meaningless, as they so often do now, but will find it exacting, exhilarating, and significant.

Step 2

Read the following essay as quickly as you can without sacrificing your comprehension of the material. You will have a maximum of 2 minutes, 45 seconds (200 words per minute) to glean as much information as you can. If you finish before time is called, note how long it took you to read the selection. Again, close your book and write a summary of the essay, including a statement about the organization. You will have 7 to 10 minutes for this task.

A CONCERTED EFFORT TO ELIMINATE ALL THE GIANT AND SUBTLE WAYS OF DETERMINING HUMAN FUTURES BY CASTE

Gloria Steinem

The year 2000. It has a hopeful, science-fiction ring, so perhaps we can predict that by then there will be an understanding of how caste functions in our child-rearing operations, that there will be a concerted effort to eliminate all the giant and subtle ways in which we determine human futures according to the isolated physical differences of race or sex.

That statement may sound simple or unnatural to many of us reading it now. Simple—to those of us who accept the fact that individual differences far outstrip the group differences based on race or sex. Unnatural—to those of us who assume that physical differences pervade and shape all human capabilities. But it seems to me that the problem of caste is the most profound and revolutionary of the crises we must face. Only by attacking the patriarchal and racist base of social systems of the past—tribal or industrial, capitalist or socialist—can we begin to undo the tension and violence and human waste that this small globe can no longer afford, and that the powerless, castemark majority of this world will no longer tolerate.

By the year 2000 we will, I hope, raise our children to believe in human potential, not God. Hopefully, the raising of children will become both an art and a science: a chosen and a loving way of life in both cases. Whether children are born into extended families or nuclear ones, into communal groups or to single parents, they will be wanted—a major difference from a past in which, whatever the sugar coating, we have been made to feel odd or unnatural if we did not choose to be biological parents. Children will be raised by and with men as much as women; with old people, as well as with biological or chosen parents; and with other children. For those children of single parents or nuclear families, the community must provide centers where their peers and a variety of adults complete the human spectrum. For those children born into communal groups or extended families, the community must provide space to be alone in and individual, one-to-one teaching. The point is to enlarge personal choice, to produce for each child the fullest possible range of human experience without negating or limiting the choices already made by the adults closest to her or to him.

It used to be said that this country was a child-centered one. Nothing could be further from the truth. Children have been our lowest priority, both in economic and emotional spending. They also have been looked upon as a caste, although a temporary one. And that caste has been exploited as labor by relatives as well as by business people. It has been used as a captive audience or a way of seeking social status. It has finally been reduced to the status of object—a possession of that caste known as adults.

By the year 2000 there should be no one way of raising children; there should be many ways—all of them recognizing that children have legal and social rights that may be quite separate and different from the rights or desires of the adults closest to them. At last we should be nurturing more individual talents than we suppress.

Step 3

Without looking back at the two essays, write a paragraph or two in which you evaluate them and explain how their ideas or issues are related. You may refer to your summaries, but not to the essays. Time: 10 minutes.

4 PERSUASIVE WRITING

Contrary to the popular understanding of the word *argument* as synonymous with *quarrel*, argument as a rhetorical form means persuasion, not pugnacity. In argument, writers express their opinion about a subject, but add verbal salesmanship. They attempt to "sell" an idea or solution to readers whose attitudes may be neutral, favorable, or unfavorable in various degrees. Writers cannot merely express and analyze their convictions and expect to persuade readers with contrary opinions to change their thinking. Instead, writers must supply convincing evidence and must consciously appeal to readers: to their sense of reason and fairness; to their ethical convictions; to their emotions; to their human sympathies; and sometimes to their individual self-interest. By employing one or a combination of these appeals, a writer is using informal argument. Formal argument, on the other hand, takes into consideration all possible objections or counterarguments that readers might voice. Writers choose formal argument because they can argue highly controversial topics more effectively if they anticipate and refute the many opposite viewpoints readers hold, as Senator Edward M. Kennedy does in his formal argument for gun control (pages 336–42). However, you need to realize that persuasive writing, no matter how masterful, will not always be effective: readers in agreement with your viewpoints need no persuasion; readers extremely hostile will not change their viewpoints. This reader response scale may help you determine when argument might be most effective.

TARGET AUDIENCE OF PERSUASION

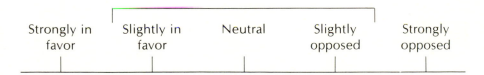

| Strongly in favor | Slightly in favor | Neutral | Slightly opposed | Strongly opposed |

As with expository writing, the kind of argument paper you write will depend largely on the subject, your purpose in arguing your case, and your readers' knowledge and attitudes toward it. If you want to argue against changing a situation, you might want to choose proposition argument—a paper that opens with a thesis stating a proposition (x *should* do _____) and then supports it with reasons and evidence. Proposition argument is also useful, if you want to change people's opinions about a well-publicized situation. But if you want to propose a new plan of action about which your audience has little knowledge, then you may wish to explain the problem before you present your arguments for an effective solution to it: problem-solution argument. Either type of organization can be handled as informal or formal argument.

KINDS OF PERSUASIVE WRITING

PROPOSITION ARGUMENT

Like exposition, proposition argument is usually organized in three sections—an opening that states the thesis proposition and provides some orientation to the problem, historical background, its effects on society or the ecology, and so on; a body that represents the supporting arguments; and a conclusion that in some way appeals to the reader for support of the writer's viewpoint. An effective organizational scheme might look like this:

OPENING

Thesis proposition
Orientation to the subject

BODY

Supporting argument I
Supporting argument II
Supporting argument III

CONCLUSION

Appeal to readers to adopt
action proposed

Formal Argument
would include
refutation of
counter arguments

Unlike expository papers, argument papers are designed to persuade readers to adopt a writer's personal convictions about a topic. Therefore, they should contain only those reasons and arguments that will lead readers to the conclusion stated in the thesis proposition. If argument papers fail to do this, then they do not persuade. Although facts are valuable as evidence, the main persuasive force in argument comes from the logical relationships that the writer establishes between the supporting arguments and the conclusion stated in the thesis. This relationship hinges on "therefore," as in James Fallows' article on the draft (pages 344–49):

Volunteer armies create divisive military class systems (argument); *therefore,* the U.S. should reinstate the draft (thesis proposition, conclusion).

If the writer organizes the argument so that the recommendation made in the thesis follows logically from the conditions and relationships set up throughout the paper, the argument will carry more persuasive force. Such organization forces both the writer and the reader into a special way of thinking known as "syllogistic reasoning"—one form that logical reasoning can take. The *therefore* relationship cited above is an example of syllogistic reasoning. At other times writers use *if. . .then* or *either. . .or* constructions, which impose conditions on the relationships: "If we continue to dump waste in our water supply, then irreparable pollution will result"; "*Either* we solve the nuclear waste problem *or* we must cease the production of nuclear plants." Because the logical form itself carries great persuasive power, people who are masters at persuasion learn to present sound reasons and hard evidence in the context of these forms, so that their arguments attain maximum persuasive effectiveness.

As a reader and a writer, however, you should be aware that because of its persuasiveness, syllogistic reasoning can be abused: arguments may seem reasonable and logical but actually be fallacious. For an entertaining look at some of these fallacies, read Max Shulman's "Love is a Fallacy," (pages 297–305).

You should also be aware that how you deal with the refutations or counterarguments of an argument can add to its persuasive force. Stating and negating an opponent's viewpoints not only counteracts them but establishes the writer as a careful, thorough, knowledgeable authority. It helps to establish the readers' confidence because it shows that the writer is well informed, having considered other possibilities before arriving at a conclusion. This formal aspect of persuasion, counter argument or refutation, may be a part of both proposition and problem–solution argument.

PROBLEM–SOLUTION ARGUMENT

As we indicated earlier, this kind of argument outlines the problem and then presents a solution. A lengthy discussion of the problem, common to this kind of argument paper, provides the writer with several advantages: it allows an opportunity to establish rapport with the readers; it prepares the ground for the arguments to convince the readers of the solution's benefits; and it delays the presentation of the writer's arguments until the readers have become more receptive to them. Sometimes, in problem–solution argument, the writer may not have a solution to suggest, but may instead offer possibilities for solutions or suggest a process by which a solution may be reached. This workable organizational scheme is often used by writers:

PROBLEM
Analysis of problem and
relevance to readers

SOLUTION
Explanation of solution; relation
of solution to problem;
superiority of proposed
solution over others

Formal Argument
would include
refutation of
counter arguments

TACTICS FOR READING ARGUMENT

PRE-READING

The special pre-reading skills for reading and understanding argumentative writing build on the suggestions made in earlier sections. In reading argument, as in reading exposition, you should search for the main idea before tackling the whole assignment. But in argument, you need to determine not only the subject but also the writer's recommendations about it, the stand the writer takes, and the purpose of the argument. It helps, also, to analyze your own feelings about the subject: do you agree or disagree with the writer's viewpoint? Before you read beyond the opening paragraph, try to list mentally the arguments you might present on the subject. Then as you read through the article, you can judge how well the writer deals with those points—either using them as support or refuting them as opposing views. But, if you are hostile to the writer's viewpoint, you may need to discipline yourself to read as objectively as possible so that you will give the writer's argument a fair hearing.

ANALYTICAL READING

An awareness of the organizational form of argument can greatly increase your persuasive skills. Ordinarily, arguments are organized around a proposition-thesis with a form like the following examples: "Seat belts *should not* be required by law"; "Young people *should* have the right to make their own religious choices"; "The U.S. *can* solve the automobile problem." As suggested earlier, the proposition may be stated early in the opening paragraphs, followed by supporting materials.

But when the writer's ideas are highly controversial, the supporting materials may be presented first and the proposition stated in the closing paragraphs. This order is also often evident in problem-solution arguments—the writer first outlines the problem, its causes and effects, and then states the solution as a proposition.

In addition to being aware of the organizational scheme as you read, you should also be alert to the rhetorical devices that writers use to support their arguments. Does the writer use comparison and contrast, comparing one situation with another, the present time with a previous era, one solution with another? Does the writer set up causal relationships, talking of effects and how they result from specific causes? Or perhaps the writer uses analogy, explaining a situation by finding logical relationships to a similar situation, as Wendell Berry (page 310) does in his analogy between the flesh of unclean animals and that of murder victims.

In reading persuasive writing, you should be especially alert to the writer's bias about the subject. Word choice is instrumental in establishing the writer's viewpoint and determining whether the argument is presented objectively and logically or emotionally. For instance, the language connotations of Ellen Goodman's "A Grateful Wife Has Second Thoughts' (pages 307–08) leave little doubt about her subjective attitude toward her topic.

Another caution to keep in mind as you read argument is to be aware of the hidden assumption—an unstated part of an argument. Make sure that you are aware of the underlying premise and decide whether you accept its truth and validity. As an example, the hidden assumption in the opening paragraph of Edward M. Kennedy's argument for gun control (pages 337–42) is that "people who possess firearms are more apt to commit murder." Before you can intelligently evaluate his arguments, you must decide whether you accept or reject that unstated premise.

REFLECTING

In argument, this stage of reading involves discerning not only the relationship of form to meaning but also the significance of form to the persuasive force of the argument. As you work your way through the POSSE approach, keep these questions and considerations in mind.

Point. Do you need to restate the proposition that you developed in the pre-reading stage? Where in the article is the writer's purpose best stated?

Organization. Is the proposition stated in the opening or the conclusion? How does the sequence of material serve the persuasive force of the argument? The writer's purpose? Does the thesis-proposition follow logically from the main arguments in the paper? From a "therefore" relationship?

Support. What devices does the writer use to develop and support the main points: example, citing of authority, cause-and-effect relationships, statistics, reasons, comparison and contrast, analogy? Does the choice of one of these work especially well in making the point clear and persuasive?

Synthesis. Do you agree or disagree with the writer's viewpoint and proposition? Does the writer deal adequately with your counter-arguments and with those of other viewpoints you may have encountered? Were you convinced by any of the arguments, or did the article reinforce your own attitudes toward the subject?

Evaluation. How effective do you find the argument to be? Are refutations tactfully and thoroughly handled? Is the tone offensive or persuasive? Does the writer effectively couple emotional or ethical appeal with logical argument? Does the author avoid fallacious argument? How valid do you find the writer's argumentative devices—syllogistic reasoning, analogy, causal relations, authoritative evidence? If a solution is proposed, is it practical, better than other solutions, and not likely to create more problems?

FROM READING TO WRITING

If you have developed an awareness of the form used for the articles you read, you can model your own organizational pattern after them. One word of caution, however. Remember that in writing an argument paper, you need to take into account the reading audience, the sensitive nature of the subject, and the purpose for writing. All of these influence your ordering of the paper—whether you state the proposition early, following it with your main ideas and support, or whether you wait until the conclusion to state the proposition because you feel the subject matter is so controversial that the supporting evidence should be presented first, helping to temper the effect of your proposition at the end. Even within the paper, the audience, subject, and purpose may influence your decisions about the order in which to present your supporting points. Thus, you see, you should avoid slavishly following any particular model, but should adapt it to your own writing situation.

Whether you plan to write an emotional or a logical argument, spend some time organizing your paper before you start. Argument works best when there is syllogistic reasoning involved in the organizational scheme; this adds persuasive force to your paper. To achieve that, you should see that your thesis serves as a conclusion of a syllogism and that your supporting arguments serve as premises that lead logically to the conclusion-thesis: "Point A is true; *therefore* thesis."

Also before writing, you should give some thought to the ways that you might treat the supporting evidence. Here are some suggestions for ways to handle your supporting ideas.

Comparison and contrast. There are two basic methods for organizing a comparison of several items. One is to deal with each item separately, discussing all the points to be made about it. The second is to handle each point showing how both items relate to it. These outlines may help to illustrate the two methods:

First Method	*Second Method*
Item A	Point 1
Point 1	Item A
Point 2	Item B
Item B	Point 2
Point 1	Item A
Point 2	Item B

Cause-and-effect analysis. As in reading, before you write you need to determine what are causes and what are effects. Traffic congestion, for instance, can be an effect; its causes might include rush-hour traffic, poorly coordinated traffic lights, lack of left-turn arrows, and so forth. But traffic congestion in another discussion might be a cause. In a paper arguing against constructing another shopping center in a particular district, traffic congestion might only be one of the causes resulting in the effect of an undesirable situation.

Again, you have at least two choices for arranging your material:

From Effect to Cause	*From Cause to Effect*
Effect	Cause A
↑	Cause B
Cause A	↓
Cause B	Effect

Other writing devices. Before writing, you should also determine whether you will find other devices useful for presenting evidence. These could include illustration or example, the citing of authority, or the use of statistical evidence. All these can effectively add weight and authority to your argument. Also, if you are planning a logical argument, give some thought to handling refutations of opposing views. Sometimes it is more effective to deal with all of them in the beginning; other times you may want to use them at places throughout the paper where they are related to a point you are making.

Another important consideration in writing argument is to avoid fallacious reasoning. After writing, you can often spot faulty reasoning by checking to see if you have been guilty of sweeping generalizations which you have skimpily supported, or whether you have stated a faulty conclusion—one based on too small a sample. Finally, test your points: see that they are logically supported by evidence.

Because most of us are stimulated by controversy, we find satisfaction in reading an argument, and even greater satisfaction in writing one. Persuasive writing gives us a chance not only to sharpen our views on a subject but also to exert an influence over other people—a chance to test the old adage that the pen is mightier than the sword.

Proposition Argument: Informal

THE NIGHTMARE OF LIFE WITHOUT FUEL
Isaac Asimov

BIOGRAPHICAL SKETCH

Isaac Asimov was born in Petrovichi, Russia, in 1912 and moved to the United States in 1923. Since receiving a Ph.D. from Columbia University, he has been an indefatigable writer, producing over 232 books. They range from science fiction to pure science, history, religion, literature, and geography. Among them are such classics as I Robot, the Foundation *trilogy, and Asimov's Guide to Science. His novel,* The Gods Themselves, *won several awards. Another work is* Murder at the ABA, *his first mystery novel in eighteen years. Asimov has also written innumerable articles and appeared on many television talk shows.*
permission.

PRE-READING

1. Combining your biographical knowledge of Asimov and his previous writings with the title, what do you speculate he might be attempting to deal with in this essay?

2. What does skimming the first paragraph add to your previous ideas about the essay?

3. Do the final short four paragraphs indicate a purpose to Asimov's view of the world of 1997?

¹ So it's 1997, and it's raining, and you'll have to walk to work again. The subways are crowded, and any given train breaks down one morning out of five. The buses are gone, and on a day like today the bicycles slosh and slide. Besides, you have only a mile and a half to go, and you have boots, raincoat and rain hat. And it's not a very cold rain, so why not?

² Lucky you have a job in demolition too. It's steady work. Slow and dirty, but steady. The fading structures of a decaying city are the great mineral mines and hardware shops of the nation. Break them down and re-use the parts. Coal is too difficult to dig up and transport to give us energy in the

amounts we need, nuclear fission is judged to be too dangerous, the technical breakthrough toward nuclear fusion that we hoped for never took place, and solar batteries are too expensive to maintain on the earth's surface in sufficient quantity.

³ Anyone older than ten can remember automobiles. They dwindled. At first the price of gasoline climbed—way up. Finally only the well-to-do drove, and that was too clear an indication that they were filthy rich, so any automobile that dared show itself on a city street was overturned and burned. Rationing was introduced to "equalize sacrifice," but every three months the ration was reduced. The cars just vanished and became part of the metal resource.

⁴ There are many advantages, if you want to look for them. Our 1997 newspapers continually point them out. The air is cleaner and there seem to be fewer colds. Against most predictions, the crime rate has dropped. With the police car too expensive (and too easy a target), policemen are back on their beats. More important, the streets are full. Legs are king in the cities of 1997, and people walk everywhere far into the night. Even the parks are full, and there is mutual protection in crowds.

⁵ If the weather isn't too cold, people sit out front. If it is hot, the open air is the only air conditioning they get. And at least the street lights still burn. Indoors, electricity is scarce, and few people can afford to keep lights burning after supper.

⁶ As for the winter—well, it is inconvenient to be cold, with most of what furnace fuel is allowed hoarded for the dawn; but sweaters are popular indoor wear and showers are not an everyday luxury. Lukewarm sponge baths will do, and if the air is not always very fragrant in the human vicinity, the automobile fumes are gone.

⁷ There is some consolation in the city that it is worse in the suburbs. The suburbs were born with the auto, lived with the auto, and are dying with the auto. One way out for the suburbanites is to form associations that assign turns to the procurement and distribution of food. Pushcarts creak from house to house along the posh suburban roads, and every bad snowstorm is a disaster. It isn't easy to hoard enough food to last till the roads are open. There is not much in the way of refrigeration except for the snowbanks, and then the dogs must be fought off.

⁸ What energy is left cannot be directed into personal comfort. The nation must survive until new energy sources are found, so it is the railroads and subways that are receiving major attention. The railroads must move the coal that is the immediate hope, and the subways can best move the people.

⁹ And then, of course, energy must be conserved for agriculture. The great car factories make trucks and farm machinery almost exclusively. We can huddle together when there is a lack of warmth, fan ourselves should there be no cooling breezes, sleep or make love at such times as there is a lack of light—but nothing will for long ameliorate a lack of food. The American population isn't going up much any more, but the food supply must be kept high even though the prices and difficulty of distribution force each American to eat

less. Food is needed for export so that we can pay for some trickle of oil and for other resources.

¹⁰ The rest of the world, of course, is not as lucky as we are. Some cynics say that it is the knowledge of this that helps keep America from despair. They're starving out there, because earth's population has continued to go up. The population on earth is 5.5 billion, and outside the United States and Europe, not more than one in five has enough to eat at any given time.

¹¹ All the statistics point to a rapidly declining rate of population increase, but that is coming about chiefly through a high infant mortality; the first and most helpless victims of starvation are babies, after their mothers have gone dry. A strong current of American opinion, as reflected in the newspapers (some of which still produce their daily eight pages of bad news), holds that it is just as well. It serves to reduce the population, doesn't it?

¹² Others point out that it's more than just starvation. There are those who manage to survive on barely enough to keep the body working, and that proves to be not enough for the brain. It is estimated that there are now nearly 2 billion people in the world who are alive but who are permanently brain-damaged by undernutrition, and the number is growing year by year. It has already occurred to some that it would be "realistic" to wipe them out quietly and rid the earth of an encumbering menace. The American newspapers of 1997 do not report that this is actually being done anywhere, but some travelers bring back horror tales.

¹³ At least the armies are gone—no one can afford to keep those expensive, energy-gobbling monstrosities. Some soldiers in uniform and with rifles are present in almost every still functioning nation, but only the United States and the Soviet Union can maintain a few tanks, planes and ships—which they dare not move for fear of biting into limited fuel reserves.

¹⁴ Energy continues to decline, and machines must be replaced by human muscle and beasts of burden. People are working longer hours and there is less leisure; but then, with electric lighting restricted, television for only three hours a night, movies three evenings a week, new books few and printed in small editions, what is there to do with leisure? Work, sleep and eating are the great trinity of 1997, and only the first two are guaranteed.

¹⁵ Where will it end? It must end in a return to the days before 1800, to the days before the fossil fuels powered a vast machine industry and technology. It must end in subsistence farming and in a world population reduced by starvation, disease and violence to less than a billion.

¹⁶ And what can we do to prevent all this now?

¹⁷ Now? Almost nothing.

¹⁸ If we had started 20 years ago, that might have been another matter. If we had only started 50 years ago, it would have been easy.

ANALYTICAL READING

1. According to Asimov, what has happened to the sources of energy? How plausible are his speculations about coal, nuclear fission, nuclear fusion, solar energy, and oil?

2. Is Asimov serious about the advantages of critical fuel shortages? Do you think he is suggesting some possible present reforms, or is he just portraying the future as he sees it?

3. How does Asimov move from a narrative beginning about a demolition worker to a world view of life in 1997?

4. What are the top priorities in this country in 1997? Explain.

5. What points is Asimov making about the population decline, undernutrition, and the armies? Are these ideas pertinent today?

6. How effective are the closing series of questions and the answers to them in the final three paragraphs?

7. Is Asimov's essay the development of a conclusion he reaches from current facts about the petroleum supply? Explain.

REFLECTING

Point: Why would you consider Asimov's essay to be an argument? What are some of the minor points he makes in his projection of future life with little fuel? How does the author's voice contribute to his purpose?

Organization: What are the main divisions in the essay? Do you find a logical organizational structure? Explain and suggest the advantage of this plan.

Support: How does Asimov use the narrative to support the major points in his argument? What logical evidence does he provide?

Synthesis: Do you think that Asimov has painted either too grim or too favorable a picture? How do your views of life in the future differ from his? Explain the different assumptions you may have about fuel and population. What specific ideas do you agree with? Which ones do you disagree with?

Evaluation: How plausible are Asimov's basic assumptions? Given these assumptions, does Asimov make an effective case for the nature of life in 1997? To what extent does his projection suggest the simple, healthy life that existed before the industrial age and that some people today are seeking in rural living? Overall, how effective is this scenario as an argument?

FROM READING TO WRITING

1. Using analogy or satire, write an informal proposition argument for readers familiar with Asimov's essay about the future types and uses of cars in view of the fuel problem.

2. The cost of medical and hospital care has increased rapidly during the past ten years. Write an argument against these huge increases by projecting a view of medical treatment in the future. Your audience consists of general readers.

3. Using Asimov's opening paragraph and the next three sentences, write a narrative of one day in this person's life. Use your ideas or Asimov's.

4. Strike out on your own by using Asimov's futuristic argumentative device to argue your case to a college audience for or against something that you favor or oppose.

FROM BANANA RIVER
Charles A. Lindbergh

BIOGRAPHICAL SKETCH

In May 1927 Charles A. Lindbergh (1902–1974) completed the first solo transatlantic flight, from New York to Paris, in 33½ hours. With this feat, he began the era of modern aviation. An international hero, "Lucky Lindy" lost some of his popularity during World War II by joining the isolationist America First Committee which opposed U.S. aid to Great Britain. When the United States entered the war, Lindbergh volunteered his services, trained fighter pilots in the Pacific, and participated in over fifty combat missions himself; he was eventually commissioned as a brigadier general in the U.S. Air Force Reserve. In his later years, he turned to ecology and environmentalism. He died of cancer in 1974 and by his request was buried on the Hawaiian island of Maui. The following selection appears in his recently published book, which consists of material from his unpublished 1,000-page memoir.

PRE-READING

1. Do you know anything about the author besides the information furnished in the biographical sketch? What general subject do you believe he would write about? Does the title give any indication of the subject?

2. What sentence in the first paragraph seems to suggest the particular subject?

3. What does the last paragraph suggest about Lindbergh's viewpoint toward the subject?

¹ Man feels he must conquer space. He works sometimes in the interests of pure science, sometimes for the practical needs of war. His reason may be convenient to his motive, but the spirit of adventure is beyond his power to control. Our earliest records tell of biting the apple and baiting the dragon, regardless of hardship or of danger, and from this inner drive, perhaps, progress and civilization developed. We moved from land to sea, to air, to space, era on era, our aspirations rising with our confidence and knowledge. Wheels and hulls and wings changed our present environment. Where will missiles fit in the human scale of values as they may be recorded ten centuries from now?

² I look at the faces around me: the civilians at instrument benches, the general at a window, the colonel and the captain with their check lists, the guards and workmen who have come inside for shelter, all intent on a missile and its mission—years of dreaming, designing, building brought to this moment, about to be tested by a firing. Their minds are concentrated on mechanical perfection. Who has time to think of what that rocket signifies in human values of the future? . . .

FROM Charles A. Lindbergh, *Banana River*, a part of *Autobiography of Values* (New York: Harcourt Brace Jovanovich, 1976), pp. 13–22. Copyright © 1976 by Harcourt Brace Jovanovich, Inc. and Anne Morrow Lindbergh. Reprinted by permission of the publisher.

[3] *"X minus two minutes?"* One feels the tenseness in the blockhouse although every man is trying to show an attitude of calm. A cigar tip accentuates the trembling of lips and a paper's flutter tattles on a hand.

[4] *"X minus sixty seconds!"* Words of command grow sharp, terse. Multiple recorders click in the background.

[5] *"X minus ten seconds! Nine! Eight! Seven! . . . Zero! Rocket away!"*

[6] A muffled roar, then flame, and great clouds of smoke burst outward from the tailpipe. The rocket thunders, rising slowly, as though uncertain of its strength, yet firm and erect with no sign of instability. It moves faster, leaps suddenly upward, streaks out of sight beyond the range of blockhouse windows. Steel doors are thrown open. Men shout, joke, laugh with success. The tension is broken, the responsibility has passed to other hands. The Control Center has taken over, and instruments will from now on tell the missile's story.

[7] I think of the long, sleek vehicle streaking out through space, far above our atmosphere's layer of interference. It is the prototype of man-made meteors that can be directed to atomize any spot on earth: Moscow, London, Tokyo, Rome, cities that can become a series of figures. Select your missile's destination, read the digits, set the dials. A cannon shell is sluggish, moving at a medieval pace, compared to this projectile in flight.

[8] Millions of lives, centuries of labor, can be wiped out by words of command spoken more than an ocean-width away! It is theoretical, so separate from the senses. Enclosed within a concrete blockhouse, your mind tells you the significance of what has taken place; but your flesh and bone do not feel it. There is no deafening scream, no hurricane of wind against the check, no sight of blood to assault the eye. You deal in contrivances, in ideas and imagination: a button pressed, a lever pulled, a city will disappear. I watched a cup of cold coffee tossed into a sink.

[9] A ballistic missile orbits dozens of miles outside our world: the dream of science and dread of man; the culmination of military power and ultimate in civilized destruction. I step through the open doorway and look up to a tranquil sky. How can a modern airman comprehend the devastation he causes? And how often that question has churned my mind before—at Wotje and Tarawa; at Jefman and Samate; at Rabaul and Kavieng. And yes, at Kavieng.

[10] Eyes of memory still see it clearly, the bombed city of Kavieng on New Ireland's northern coast. My vision shifts from Florida to South Pacific seas. Kavieng looked like an ant hill when I approached in my fighter-bomber on May 29, 1944. I was flying in a three-plane patrol from Major Joseph Foss's Marine Corsair Squadron VMF–115, Major Marion Carl and Lieutenant Rolfe F. Blanchard flanking me. My mind slips back easily through the stream of time, into that Corsair's cockpit. I feel the stick's vibration in my hand, and the pedals against my feet. My thumb has the power of TNT and my finger controls six machine guns.

[11] A few miles ahead, fifteen thousand feet below my altitude, a scorched-brown texture between blue of sea and green of jungle is our target—so min-

ute, so apparently trivial compared to the limitless expanse of land and water that rolls to the horizons. Careful scanning of the earth informs me that Kavieng, situated on the top of a peninsula, is sheltered from the sea by two islands and their reefs, and that the hulks of several sunken ships obstruct the harbor. Minute circles on the ground warn of enemy antiaircraft cannon. Group Intelligence officers told us to be wary of those gunners: "The 'Nips' have none better in the South Pacific."

[12] My exact target is an area of city in which Japanese troops are stationed. I want to kill some of those troops. In fact, I want to kill as many as possible. But when I tell myself I am going to kill, the idea somehow does not take hold inside me. I never have the feel of killing as I move the controls of my plane. Whenever I fly in my fighter-bomber, I seem to lose relationship to earth's community of men.

[13] Everything is quiet on the ground and in the sky. It is hard to realize that we can strike with deadly force across such a magnitude of space, that we have come to toss five-hundred-pound bombs at humans down below, and that at any moment black blooms in air around us will symbolize the hostility of our reception.

[14] An airman separates himself from the earth and its people when he follows a warplane's orbit. There are moments when the planet he is bound to seems as unrelated to his actions as does the moon, moments when he is completely isolated from the world's problems, its happiness and its sufferings, when the calculations of his mission appear as bloodless as the digits of astronomy. He guides his plane along independent courses through a space of air, watching dials, moving levers, caring no more about the lives he crushes than he would if the city below were an ant hill. How well I know the irresponsibility of the bomb's red button, and how often I have pressed it: in the Marshalls, over Noemfoor, in the Bismarks, above Kavieng. . . .

[15] The wings of Corsair 1 are rocking. We drop our dive brakes, purge our wing tanks, brighten gun sights. Corsair 1 peels off; it is Carl. Corsair 2 follows; it is Blanchard. I pull into a wingover, putting the sun behind my back, and nose steeply to the dive. I see the two Corsairs well below me, screaming toward the ground. My controls tighten, the altimeter needle touches ten thousand feet, air howls, wings tremble. At seven thousand feet I make a final adjustment to the trim tabs; six thousand feet, steady on the rudder; pipper beyond the target. Fifty-five hundred feet. NOW. My thumb presses, my arm pulls back. I kick right rudder toward the sea, reverse bank to throw off enemy ack-ack, reserve again, and look down to check my marksmanship.

[16] There was no sense of combat on that mission; it was like an exercise in aerial calisthenics. I saw no flashes on the ground to challenge my attack. I did not feel the bomb drop. One moment it was held firmly in its rack, completely under my control. Then my thumb moved ever so slightly against a small red button on the stick and death went hurtling earthward. I caught one glimpse of the bomb falling after I dropped my wing—cylindrical, inert, awkward, irre-

trievably launched on its mission; certain to destroy itself and the first object that it touched. In another second it was lost to sight. No power of man could countermand my action. If there was life where that bomb would hit, I had taken it; yet that life was still thinking, breathing when the bomb was still falling: there was still eternal seconds. Nothing had changed in my cockpit; nothing in my sky.

¹⁷ The little puff of smoke—the pebble-splash of debris—was centered in a row of buildings near the beach, an area where antiaircraft guns had been reported. What a slight scar it left! I could not even find it with my eyes after the smoke drifted away. So far as I could tell, Kavieng was no worse off for our visit. But in reality were there torn and writhing bodies in that pinprick I had made in the ground? Were they already out of sight behind me? Was a machine-gun nest wiped out? Had I eliminated a score of soldiers from the war? Was some child without a mother, a mother without a child? I felt no responsibility for what I had done. It was too far away, too disconnected.

¹⁸ How can an airman comprehend the devastation he causes? He must stand on the rubble of a destroyed city to sense the power of the bomb's red button. He must see flashing concussion waves tear across the ground, debris vomiting through air, and great columns of smoke billowing. He must take the hammer blows on his chest, the thunder against his ears, hear the cries of terror. When you look down at two human heads above a single body, at bones protruding from a mass of flesh a dozen feet away; when you stand at some cross street on a pile of brick and let your eyes travel its four directions over block after block of fire-blacked, shattered walls; when you watch clouds redden with the flames beneath them, and feel after a bombardment the white dust of death that settles over everthing—then your thumb's contact with the bomb button transmits significance.

¹⁹ Hiroshima lies flat and peaceful between plum-tinted mountain ranges and the island-studded beauty of Japan's Inland Sea. It is December 1947. I am in an Air Force transport plant, circling at three thousand feet. Two years have passed since the bomb was dropped. The aged mountains, the nestling city, the calm sea, all the crystal tranquility beneath me—it seems impossible that the people here witnessed the horror of that August day when an airplane soared overhead, barely specking the sky, yet leaving behind it excruciating pain and devastation. There is no sign to mark the gigantic mushroom cloud that once towered in the sky, no sign except, when I look more carefully, the shades on earth below.

²⁰ To see the terror of past war, an airman's eye must translate shadings. A city, like a human face, can show the pallor of death. A gray-ash saucer, a mile or so in width, marks the blasted, radiated, and heat-shriveled earth of Hiroshima. Surrounding it is a black halo of undamaged roots on the outskirts. The straw-colored stippling which glints now and then in sunlight, as we bank, is caused by the unpainted lumber of the newly built dwellings that have sprung up like fungi. Inside that gray saucer more than seventy thousand men,

women, and children were killed, and that many more were burned and mangled. Over one hundred and forty thousand casualties from a single bomb—from words of command—from the pressure of buttons.

[21] Since I flew over Hiroshima we have developed bombs of more than a thousand times the power. The kilotons and hours we used in our calculations at the end of World War II have been replaced by figures representing megatons and minutes. In planning for the possibility of an all-out nuclear conflict we discuss casualties running into tens of millions, huge uninhabitable areas caused by fallout. Will half or three-quarters of a continent's population be wiped out?

ANALYTICAL READING

1. What is the point of the scene in the Control Center? Which paragraph best conveys that point?

2. The first two paragraphs are linked by their references to missiles. In what other significant way are they related?

3. What is the connection between the account of the missile's launching and Lindbergh's own bombing run at Kavieng?

4. Analyze paragraph 8 closely. How does Lindbergh use comparison and contrast effectively to make his point? What is accomplished by the reference to the cold cup of coffee?

5. Discuss Lindbergh's thoughts about killing in paragraph 12. Does he want to kill or not? Is there a feeling that he must kill or be killed? What different effect might have been created by mention of Pearl Harbor and the many American deaths caused by Japanese soldiers?

6. How does he feel after the bombing run? What is the rhetorical effect in paragraph 17 of his concern for a child and its mother?

7. Note how Lindbergh describes his bombing experience, moving back and forth from vivid description to generalizations about the experience. Did you find this distracting? Why or why not? Is it appropriate in view of Lindbergh's purpose?

8. What emotions is Lindbergh appealing to in the description of his flight over Hiroshima?

9. What does Lindbergh mean at the beginning of paragraph 20 when he states that "an airman's eye must translate shadings"? Analyze the structure of that paragraph.

REFLECTING

Point: Is Lindbergh making a statement only to airmen and those involved in launching missiles, or is he appealing to a larger audience? Formulate his purpose in a sentence or two.

Organization: What are the main divisions in this essay? How are they linked? Would it have been more effective to have started with his bombing experience instead of the missile launching? Why or why not?

Support: What emotions does Lindbergh appeal to? Which of his examples best convey those emotions? How does he maintain interest? Discuss the tone and its appropriateness to the subject. Analyze the effect of the "ant hill" image in paragraph 10, point out where it is used again, and discuss any other images.

Synthesis: What significance does the essay have for you? What practical argument can be used against Lindbergh's discussion of future weapons? To what extent can Lindbergh's argument be extended into everyday life, to actions like shop-lifting, vandalizing a school building, or stealing a hubcap from an unknown person's car?

Evaluation: Does Lindbergh make his point clearly and convincingly? Does he leave you as troubled as he is, or can you remove yourself from his strong emotional appeal and look only at the practical side of war? Is his language forceful and thought-provoking? Select specific sentences that you felt were powerful and compelling. Do you think that you are likely to remember the essay? Why or why not?

FROM READING TO WRITING

1. On the basis of incidents in your school career, write an informal argument for a campus publication in favor of or against cheating on exams and out-of-class assignments.

2. Write a reply to Lindbergh's argument. Make your target audience a general one, and appeal to their emotions.

3. Referring to specific examples, write an argument for or against raising or lowering the present legal driving or drinking age in your state. Your audience is the state legislature.

THAT DISTINCTIVELY AMERICAN CHRISTMAS
Newspaper Editorial

PRE-READING

1. Does the title raise any suspicions about the author's treatment of the subject?

2. Can you point to any statement in the first paragraph that sheds light on the viewpoint of the editorial?

3. What does the last paragraph reveal about the tone of the writer? Is it serious or satirical? Does it demonstrate the use of irony (a figure of speech used in argumentation to discredit something by appearing to approve of it)?

FROM *Louisville Courier-Journal and Times*, 25 December 1973, p. A10. Copyright © 1973 by The Courier-Journal and Times, Louisville, Kentucky. Editorial reprinted with permission from the Opinion page.

¹ Christmas is being celebrated all over the world today, in the cathedral towns of Europe, in the squalid slums of Latin American metropolises, in the steaming jungles of Africa and on the overpopulated plains of India. But the diverse peoples of those distant lands, however worthy and devout they may be in other respects, do not understand the true meaning of Christmas, as we do. Our Christmas is a uniquely American product quite distinct in spirit and tone from lesser Christmases. In these uncertain times, when most of our institutions are suspect, it remains a source of national stability and pride.

² Let the flighty sophisticates of France and Belgium observe the winter solstice with their feasts and frivolity and midnight Masses. Let the Christian converts of Japan and Indonesia rejoice over the nativity of Our Lord. In our country, Christmas is, as it should be, a deadly serious business enterprise, a time for encouraging the combativeness of young men, and an ennobling ordeal. From the first appearance of plastic greenery in the department stores just before Halloween until the final hoarse cheer echoes across the Rose Bowl on New Year's Day, it is a splendid, glorious, incomparable festival that reflects the enduring strengths and values of our great land.

³ Christmas traditions have had their origins in many parts of the world. The ancient Romans first came up with the idea of a late December bash, which later merged with Christian ceremonies imported from the Mideast. The Teutonic tribes of central Europe added the evergreens, the wassailing and the yule log. Many of our favorite carols came from Britain and France. But Americans have made the greatest contributions, using their native ingenuity and technological skills to devise a Christmas celebration for the rest of the world to admire, envy and wonder at.

⁴ It was the business community of the United States, after all, that fully realized the potential of Christmas as a stimulus to commerce and trade. And it was the advertising industry of our native land that introduced parents to the pleasures of investing their annual savings in mountains of breakable toys for their deprived offspring, and that aroused the natural longings of infant children for battery-operated, three-speed blooper blappers.

⁵ The people who plan our Christmas seasons were the first in the world to recognize the harmonious relationship between hymns of peace and games of violence. Where else is it possible to combine family togetherness during the holidays with non-stop viewing of an immense number and variety of athletic contests?

⁶ Think of what our educational system has done to make Christmas pleasurable. The primary school teachers of America have singlehandedly made Christmas the mainstay of their curriculums for a full four weeks before the holiday, sending their pupils home with an endless succession of handcrafted Santa Clauses and snowmen, and helping to generate the frantic excitement and whining insolence that parents so value in their young.

⁷ And we can claim credit for so many other innovations that will eventually spread across the seas and bring cheer and good will to billions of people all over the world. In our suburbs, for instance, the decoration of homes and

yards has developed into a competitive sport, momentarily sidetracked by an energy shortage that frowns on conspicuous waste. The mass feeding of family and relatives has been elevated into a joyous opportunity for young wives to demonstrate their culinary skills. Where else is it possible to satisfy one's need to be charitable to the lonely and under-privileged simply by shedding tears over the sentimental slosh of television's Christmas specials? Moreover, Americans have wisely incorporated traditional pre-Lenten promiscuity into their Christmas celebrations, making it perfectly acceptable for a tipsy executive to lunge at his secretary while the wife is home making cookies.

[8] Nor should we overlook the role that our American Christmas has played in the advancement of psychiatry. The inevitable feelings of guilt, depression and unfulfilled expectations that follow Christmas often require extensive treatment, opening up an entire new industry for the medical profession. It is now rumored that a new disorder, tentatively known as the Reverse Scrooge Syndrome, has been identified. Its victims, normally kind, decent and generous people, are said to burst into uncontrollable rages when a small child looks up from his or her $7,000 electric train, which took an entire night to assemble, and says: "Is that all, daddy?"

[9] Christmas in our country is never static, never stays the same. Each year brings new delight and new excitement. This year, for instance, the women's liberationists have thoughtfully helped us to recognize that the careless selection of toys can cause our daughters to grow up to be as passive, vacuous and helpless as their mothers, and our sons to become as insensitive, militaristic and obnoxious as their fathers.

[10] Is there any way that Christmas in America can be made more rewarding? A few dissident pseudo-intellectuals, it is true, argue that the holiday season should be shorter and simpler and should have a narrower focus, with, perhaps, a greater religious orientation. Fie on them, we say. Washington may be awash with corruption, family life may be disintegrating and belief in God may be declining. But Christmas is a symbol of the rationality and essential virtuousness of our people and must remain pure and undefiled.

ANALYTICAL READING

1. What sentence in the second paragraph might you have underlined because of its importance?

2. According to the writer, what primarily caused the distinctive American celebration of Christmas?

3. What other groups have contributed to the American Christmas? Do you agree with the writer's selection of all these special groups?

4. What point is made about American psychiatry? If you had any doubt about whether the writer's intent was serious or not, what specific statements in paragraph 8 would clearly settle the question?

5. Explain the reference to the women's liberation movement in paragraph 9. Do you agree with this point or not?

REFLECTING

Point: What do you think the author's purpose is? Do you think his emotional appeal is more effective than a more logical, direct argument would have been? Explain.

Organization: Discuss the point of each paragraph. Then determine whether the writer has followed a particular plan. Could the sequence of certain paragraphs be changed without spoiling the effect?

Support: What assumption does the writer make? How does the writer appeal to readers to change the way Christmas is celebrated? Point to specific statements suggesting practices that should be changed. Also, point out phrases that are particularly delightful or effective.

Synthesis: How do you feel about the distinctive way that Americans celebrate Christmas? Do you agree with the author's ideas about the roles of business, advertising, the schools, home decorations, and feasts? Is this subject—or the approach to it—new? Where else has the subject been discussed? Are our celebrations of Christmas getting better or worse? Explain.

Evaluation: How convincing is the editorial? Does it gain most of its persuasiveness from the approach it takes? Is it more or less likely to affect people than a sermon on the subject? Are any points not pertinent? Could some additions be made? Compare this essay with Wendell Berry's on page 310.

FROM READING TO WRITING

1. Write an ironic argument for your college newspaper, using this indirect form of attack instead of the direct form. You might, for example, point out why women shouldn't be paid the same as men, why people should litter, why more violence should be presented on television, or some such subject. Have fun with your paper just as the author of this editorial did.

2. Write a proposal to your college newspaper for solving some current political or other problem. Your plan should be seriously presented but be utterly inhumane or preposterous, such as killing all convicted criminals or requiring all students with low grades to be sterilized.

LOVE IS A FALLACY
Max Shulman

BIOGRAPHICAL SKETCH

Max Shulman was born in St. Paul, Minnesota, in 1919, and graduated from the University of Minnesota. He has written fiction, nonfiction, plays, a television series, and film scripts. Among his eight novels are Barefoot Boy with Cheek *and* Rally

FROM *The Many Loves of Dobie Gillis* (Garden City, N.Y.: Doubleday and Company, 1953). Copyright © 1951 by Max Shulman, renewed 1979 by Max Schulman. Reprinted by permission of Harold Matson Co., Inc.

'Round the Flag, Boys. *The former was adapted to the stage and was a success on Broadway, as were two other plays,* The Tender Trap *and* How Now, Dow Jones. *Also popular was his television series,* The Many Loves of Dobie Gillis. *The best of Shulman's essays are collected in two anthologies,* Guided Tour of Campus Humor *and* Large Economy Size.

PRE-READING

1. What tone does the writer set in the opening paragraph? Does it give any hint of the subject?

2. From the title and the closing paragraphs, what do you think the subject of the paper is?

3. On the basis of the biographical sketch, how would you expect Shulman to handle any subject?

¹ Cool was I and logical. Keen, calculating, perspicacious, acute and astute—I was all of these. My brain was as powerful as a dynamo, as precise as a chemist's scales, as penetrating as a scalpel. And—think of it!—I was only eighteen.

² It is not often that one so young has such a giant intellect. Take, for example, Petey Burch, my roommate at the University of Minnesota. Same age, same background, but dumb as an ox. A nice enough fellow, you understand, but nothing upstairs. Emotional type. Unstable. Impressionable. Worst of all, a faddist. Fads, I submit, are the very negation of reason. To be swept up in every new craze that comes along, to surrender yourself to idiocy just because everybody else is doing it—this, to me, is the acme of mindlessness. Not, however, to Petey.

³ One afternoon I found Petey lying on his bed with an expression of such distress on his face that I immediately diagnosed appendicitis. "Don't move," I said. "Don't take a laxative. I'll get a doctor."

⁴ "Raccoon," he mumbled thickly.

⁵ "Raccoon?" I said, pausing in my flight.

⁶ "I want a raccoon coat," he wailed.

⁷ I perceived that his trouble was not physical, but mental. "Why do you want a raccoon coat?"

⁸ "I should have known it," he cried, pounding his temples. "I should have known they'd come back when the Charleston came back. Like a fool I spent all my money for textbooks, and now I can't get a raccoon coat."

⁹ "Can you mean," I said incredulously, "that people are actually wearing raccoon coats again?"

¹⁰ "All the Big Men on Campus are wearing them. Where've you been?"

¹¹ "In the library," I said, naming a place not frequented by Big Men on Campus.

¹² He leaped from the bed and paced the room. "I've got to have a raccoon coat," he said passionately. "I've got to!"

¹³ "Petey, why? Look at it rationally. Raccoon coats are unsanitary. They shed. They smell bad. They weigh too much. They're unsightly. They—"

¹⁴ "You don't understand," he interrupted impatiently. "It's the thing to do. Don't you want to be in the swim?"

¹⁵ "No," I said truthfully.

¹⁶ "Well, I do," he declared. "I'd give anything for a raccoon coat. Anything!"

¹⁷ My brain, that precision instrument, slipped into high gear. "Anything?" I asked, looking at him narrowly.

¹⁸ "Anything," he affirmed in ringing tones.

¹⁹ I stroked my chin thoughtfully. It so happened that I knew where to get my hands on a raccoon coat. My father had had one in his undergraduate days; it lay now in a trunk in the attic back home. It also happened that Petey had something I wanted. He didn't *have* it exactly, but at least he had first rights on it. I refer to his girl, Polly Espy.

²⁰ I had long coveted Polly Espy. Let me emphasize that my desire for this young woman was not emotional in nature. She was, to be sure, a girl who excited the emotions, but I was not one to let my heart rule my head. I wanted Polly for a shrewdly calculated, entirely cerebral reason.

²¹ I was a freshman in law school. In a few years I would be out in practice. I was well aware of the importance of the right kind of wife in furthering a lawyer's career. The successful lawyers I had observed were, almost without exception, married to beautiful, gracious, intelligent women. With one omission, Polly fitted these specifications perfectly.

²² Beautiful she was. She was not yet of pin–up proportions, but I felt sure that time would supply the lack. She already had the makings.

²³ Gracious she was. By gracious I mean full of graces. She had an erectness of carriage, an ease of bearing, a poise that clearly indicated the best of breeding. At table her manners were exquisite. I had seen her at the Kozy Kampus Korner eating the specialty of the house—a sandwich that contained scraps of pot roast, gravy, chopped nuts, and a dipper of sauerkraut—without even getting her fingers moist.

²⁴ Intelligent she was not. In fact, she veered in the opposite direction. But I believed that under my guidance she would smarten up. At any rate, it was worth a try. It is, after all, easier to make a beautiful dumb girl smart than to make an ugly smart girl beautiful.

²⁵ "Petey," I said, "are you in love with Polly Espy?"

²⁶ "I think she's a keen kid," he replied, "but I don't know if you'd call it love. Why?"

²⁷ "Do you," I asked, "have any kind of formal arrangement with her? I mean are you going steady or anything like that?"

²⁸ "No. We see each other quite a bit, but we both have other dates. Why?"

²⁹ "Is there," I asked, "any other man for whom she has a particular fondness?"

³⁰ "Not that I know of. Why?"

³¹ I nodded with satisfaction. "In other words, if you were out of the picture, the field would be open. Is that right?"

³² "I guess so. What are you getting at?"

³³ "Nothing, nothing," I said innocently, and took my suitcase out of the closet.

³⁴ "Where are you going?" asked Petey.

³⁵ "Home for the weekend." I threw a few things into the bag.

³⁶ "Listen," he said, clutching my arm eagerly, "while you're home, you couldn't get some money from your old man, could you, and lend it to me so I can buy a raccoon coat?"

³⁷ "I may do better than that," I said with a mysterious wink and closed my bag and left.

³⁸ "Look," I said to Petey when I got back Monday morning. I threw open the suitcase and revealed the huge, hairy, gamy object that my father had worn in his Stutz Bearcat in 1925.

³⁹ "Holy Toledo!" said Petey reverently. He plunged his hands into the raccoon coat and then his face. "Holy Toledo!" he repeated fifteen or twenty times.

⁴⁰ "Would you like it?" I asked.

⁴¹ "Oh yes!" he cried, clutching the greasy pelt to him. Then a canny look came into his eyes. "What do you want for it?"

⁴² "Your girl," I said, mincing no words.

⁴³ "Polly?" he said in a horrified whisper. "You want Polly?"

⁴⁴ "That's right."

⁴⁵ He flung the coat from him. "Never," he said stoutly.

⁴⁶ I shrugged. "Okay. If you don't want to be in the swim, I guess it's your business."

⁴⁷ I sat down in a chair and pretended to read a book, but out of the corner of my eye I kept watching Petey. He was a torn man. First he looked at the coat with the expression of a waif at a bakery window. Then he turned away and set his jaw resolutely. Then he looked back at the coat, with even more longing in his face. Then he turned away, but with not so much resolution this time. Back and forth his head swiveled, desire waxing, resolution waning. Finally he didn't turn away at all; he just stood and stared with mad lust at the coat.

⁴⁸ "It isn't as though I was in love with Polly," he said thickly. "Or going steady or anything like that."

⁴⁹ "That's right," I murmured.

⁵⁰ "What's Polly to me, or me to Polly?"

⁵¹ "Not a thing," said I.

⁵² "It's just been a casual kick—just a few laughs, that's all."

⁵³ "Try on the coat," said I.

⁵⁴ He complied. The coat bunched high over his ears and dropped all the way down to his shoe tops. He looked like a mound of dead raccoons. "Fits fine," he said happily.

[55] I rose from my chair. "Is it a deal?" I asked, extending my hand.

[56] He swallowed. "It's a deal," he said and shook my hand.

[57] I had my first date with Polly the following evening. This was in the nature of a survey; I wanted to find out just how much work I had to do to get her mind up to the standard I required. I took her first to dinner. "Gee, that was a delish dinner," she said as we left the restaurant. Then I took her to a movie. "Gee, that was a marvy movie," she said as we left the theater. And then I took her home. "Gee, I had a sensaysh time," she said as she bade me good night.

[58] I went back to my room with a heavy heart. I had gravely underestimated the size of my task. This girl's lack of information was terrifying. Nor would it be enough merely to supply her with information. First she had to be taught to *think*. This loomed as a project of no small dimensions, and at first I was tempted to give her back to Petey. But then I got to thinking about her abundant physical charms and about the way she entered a room and the way she handled a knife and fork, and I decided to make an effort.

[59] I went about it, as in all things, systematically. I gave her a course in logic. It happened that I, as a law student, was taking a course in logic myself, so I had all the facts at my finger tips. "Polly," I said to her when I picked her up on our next date, "tonight we are going over to the Knoll and talk."

[60] "Oo, terrif," she replied. One thing I will say for this girl: you would go far to find another so agreeable.

[61] We went to the Knoll, the campus trysting place, and we sat down under an old oak, and she looked at me expectantly. "What are we going to talk about?" she asked.

[62] "Logic."

[63] She thought this over for a minute and decided she liked it. "Magnif," she said.

[64] "Logic," I said, clearing my throat, "is the science of thinking. Before we can think correctly, we must first learn to recognize the common fallacies of logic. These we will take up tonight."

[65] "Wow–dow!" she cried, clapping her hands delightedly.

[66] I winced, but went bravely on. "First let us examine the fallacy called Dicto Simpliciter."

[67] "By all means," she urged, batting her lashes eagerly.

[68] "Dicto Simpliciter means an argument based on an unqualified generalization. For example: Exercise is good. Therefore everybody should exercise."

[69] "I agree," said Polly earnestly. "I mean exercise is wonderful. I mean it builds the body and everything."

[70] "Polly," I said gently, "the argument is a fallacy. *Exercise is good* is an unqualified generalization. For instance, if you have heart disease, exercise is bad, not good. Many people are ordered by their doctors *not* to exercise. You must *qualify* the generalization. You must say exercise is *usually* good, or exercise is good *for most people*. Otherwise you have committed a Dicto Simpliciter. Do you see?"

[71] "No," she confessed. "But this is marvy. Do more! Do more!"

[72] "It will be better if you stop tugging at my sleeve," I told her, and when she desisted, I continued. "Next we take up a fallacy called Hasty Generalization. Listen carefully: You can't speak French. I can't speak French. Petey Burch can't speak French. I must therefore conclude that nobody at the University of Minnesota can speak French."

[73] "Really?" said Polly, amazed. "*Nobody?*"

[74] I hid my exasperation. "Polly, it's a fallacy. The generalization is reached too hastily. There are too few instances to support such a conclusion."

[75] "Know any more fallacies?" she asked breathlessly. "This is more fun than dancing even."

[76] I fought off a wave of despair. I was getting nowhere with this girl, absolutely nowhere. Still, I am nothing if not persistent. I continued. "Next comes Post Hoc. Listen to this: Let's not take Bill on our picnic. Every time we take him out with us, it rains."

[77] "I know somebody just like that," she exclaimed. "A girl back home—Eula Becker, her name is. It never fails. Every single time we take her on a picnic—"

[78] "Polly," I said sharply, "it's a fallacy. Eula Becker doesn't *cause* the rain. She had no connection with the rain. You are guilty of Post Hoc if you blame Eula Becker."

[79] "I'll never do it again," she promised contritely. "Are you mad at me?"

[80] I sighed deeply. "No, Polly, I'm not mad."

[81] "Then tell me some more fallacies."

[82] "All right. Let's try Contradictory Premises."

[83] "Yes, let's," she chirped, blinking her eyes happily.

[84] I frowned, but plunged ahead. "Here's an example of Contradictory Premises: If God can do anything, can He make a stone so heavy that He won't be able to lift it?"

[85] "Of course," she replied promptly.

[86] "But if He can do anything, He can lift the stone," I pointed out.

[87] "Yeah," she said thoughtfully. "Well, then I guess He can't make the stone."

[88] "But He can do anything," I reminded her.

[89] She scratched her pretty, empty head. "I'm all confused," she admitted.

[90] "Of course you are. Because when the premises of an argument contradict each other, there can be no argument. If there is an irresistible force, there can be no immovable object. If there is an immovable object, there can be no irresistible force. Get it?"

[91] "Tell me some more of this keen stuff," she said eagerly.

[92] I consulted my watch. "I think we'd better call it a night. I'll take you home now, and you go over all the things you've learned. We'll have another session tomorrow night."

[93] I deposited her at the girls' dormitory, where she assured me that she had had a perfectly terrif evening, and I went glumly home to my room. Petey

lay snoring in his bed, the raccoon coat huddled like a great hairy beast at his feet. For a moment I considered waking him and telling him that he could have his girl back. It seemed clear that my project was doomed to failure. The girl simply had a logic–proof head.

[94] But then I reconsidered. I had wasted one evening; I might as well waste another. Who knew? Maybe somewhere in the extinct crater of her mind, a few embers still smoldered. Maybe somehow I could fan them into flame. Admittedly it was not a prospect fraught with hope, but I decided to give it one more try.

[95] Seated under the oak the next evening I said, "Our first fallacy tonight is called Ad Misericordiam."

[96] She quivered with delight.

[97] "Listen closely," I said. "A man applies for a job. When the boss asks him what his qualifications are, he replies that he has a wife and six children at home, the wife is a helpless cripple, the children have nothing to eat, no clothes to wear, no shoes on their feet, there are no beds in the house, no coal in the cellar, and winter is coming."

[98] A tear rolled down each of Polly's pink cheeks. "Oh, this is awful, awful," she sobbed.

[99] "Yes, it's awful," I agreed, "but it's no argument. The man never answered the boss's question about his qualifications. Instead he appealed to the boss's sympathy. He committed the fallacy of Ad Misericordiam. Do you understand?"

[100] "Have you got a handkerchief?" she blubbered.

[101] I handed her a handkerchief and tried to keep from screaming while she wiped her eyes. "Next," I said in a carefully controlled tone, "we will discuss False Analogy. Here is an example: Students should be allowed to look at their textbooks during examinations. After all, surgeons have X–rays to guide them during an operation, lawyers have briefs to guide them during a trial, carpenters have blueprints to guide them when they are building a house. Why, then, shouldn't students be allowed to look at their textbooks during an examination?"

[102] "There now," she said enthusiastically, "is the most marvy idea I've heard in years."

[103] "Polly," I said testily, "the argument is all wrong. Doctors, lawyers, and carpenters aren't taking a test to see how much they have learned, but students are. The situations are altogether different, and you can't make an analogy between them."

[104] "I still think it's a good idea," said Polly.

[105] "Nuts," I muttered. Doggedly I pressed on. "Next we'll try Hypothesis Contrary to Fact."

[106] "Sounds yummy," was Polly's reaction.

[107] "Listen: If Madame Curie had not happened to leave a photographic plate in a drawer with a chunk of pitchblende, the world today would not know about radium."

[108] "True, true," said Polly, nodding her head. "Did you see the movie? Oh, it just knocked me out. That Walter Pidgeon is so dreamy. I mean he fractures me."

[109] "If you can forget Mr. Pidgeon for a moment," I said coldly, "I would like to point out that the statement is a fallacy. Maybe Madame Curie would have discovered radium at some later date. Maybe somebody else would have discovered it. Maybe any number of things would have happened. You can't start with a hypothesis that is not true and then draw any supportable conclusions from it."

[110] "They ought to put Walter Pidgeon in more pictures," said Polly. "I hardly ever see him any more."

[111] One more chance, I decided. But just one more. There is a limit to what flesh and blood can bear. "The next fallacy is called Poisoning the Well."

[112] "How cute!" she gurgled.

[113] "Two men are having a debate. The first one gets up and says, 'My opponent is a notorious liar. You can't believe a word that he is going to say.' . . . Now, Polly, think. Think hard. What's wrong?"

[114] I watched her closely as she knit her creamy brow in concentration. Suddenly a glimmer of intelligence—the first I had seen—came into her eyes. "It's not fair," she said with indignation. "It's not a bit fair. What chance has the second man got if the first man calls him a liar before he even begins talking?"

[115] "Right!" I cried exultantly. "One hundred percent right. It's not fair. The first man has *poisoned the well* before anybody could drink from it. He has hamstrung his opponent before he could even start. . . . Polly, I'm proud of you."

[116] "Pshaw," she murmured, blushing with pleasure.

[117] "You see, my dear, these things aren't so hard. All you have to do is concentrate. Think—examine—evaluate. Come now, let's review everything we have learned."

[118] "Fire away," she said with an airy wave of her hand.

[119] Heartened by the knowledge that Polly was not altogether a cretin, I began a long, patient review of all I had told her. Over and over and over again I cited instances, pointed out flaws, kept hammering away without letup. It was like digging a tunnel. At first everything was work, sweat, and darkness. I had no idea when I would reach the light, or even *if* I would. But I persisted. I pounded and clawed and scraped, and finally I was rewarded. I saw a chink of light. And then the chink got bigger and the sun came pouring in and all was bright.

[120] Five grueling nights this took, but it was worth it. I had made a logician out of Polly; I had taught her to think. My job was done. She was worthy of me at last. She was a fit wife for me, a proper hostess for my many mansions, a suitable mother for my well-heeled children.

[121] It must not be thought that I was without love for this girl. Quite the contrary. Just as Pygmalion loved the perfect woman he had fashioned, so I

loved mine. I determined to acquaint her with my feelings at our very next meeting. The time had come to change our relationship from academic to romantic.

122 "Polly," I said when next we sat beneath our oak, "tonight we will not discuss fallacies."

123 "Aw, gee," she said, disappointed.

124 "My dear," I said, favoring her with a smile, "we have now spent five evenings together. We have gotten along splendidly. It is clear that we are well matched."

125 "Hasty Generalization," said Polly brightly.

126 "I beg your pardon," said I.

127 "Hasty Generalization," she repeated. "How can you say that we are well matched on the basis of only five dates?"

128 I chuckled with amusement. The dear child had learned her lessons well. "My dear," I said, patting her hand in a tolerant manner, "five dates is plenty. After all, you don't have to eat a whole cake to know that it's good."

129 "False Analogy," said Polly promptly. "I'm not a cake. I'm a girl."

130 I chuckled with somewhat less amusement. The dear child had learned her lessons perhaps too well. I decided to change tactics. Obviously the best approach was a simple, strong, direct declaration of love. I paused for a moment while my massive brain chose the proper words. Then I began:

131 "Polly, I love you. You are the whole world to me, and the moon and the stars and the constellations of outer space. Please, my darling, say that you will go steady with me, for if you will not, life will be meaningless. I will languish. I will refuse my meals. I will wander the face of the earth, a shambling, hollow–eyed hulk."

132 There, I thought, folding my arms, that ought to do it.

133 "Ad Misericordiam," said Polly.

134 I ground my teeth. I was not Pygmalion; I was Frankenstein, and my monster had me by the throat. Frantically I fought back the tide of panic surging through me. At all costs I had to keep cool.

135 "Well, Polly," I said, forcing a smile, "you certainly have learned your fallacies."

136 "You're darn right," she said with a vigorous nod.

137 "And who taught them to you, Polly?"

138 "You did."

139 "That's right. So you do owe me something, don't you, my dear? If I hadn't come along you never would have learned about fallacies."

140 "Hypothesis Contrary to Fact," she said instantly.

141 I dashed perspiration from my brow. "Polly," I croaked, "you mustn't take all these things so literally. I mean this is just classroom stuff. You know that the things you learn in school don't have anything to do with life."

142 "Dicto Simpliciter," she said, wagging her finger at me playfully.

143 That did it. I leaped to my feet, bellowing like a bull. "Will you or will you not go steady with me?"

[144] "I will not," she replied.

[145] "Why not?" I demanded.

[146] "Because this afternoon I promised Petey Burch that I would go steady with him."

[147] I reeled back, overcome with the infamy of it. After he promised, after he made a deal, after he shook my hand! "The rat!" I shrieked, kicking up great chunks of turf. "You can't go with him, Polly. He's a liar. He's a cheat. He's a rat."

[148] "Poisoning the Well," said Polly, "and stop shouting. I think shouting must be a fallacy too."

[149] With an immense effort of will, I modulated my voice. "All right," I said. "You're a logician. Let's look at this thing logically. How could you choose Petey Burch over me? Look at me—a brilliant student, a tremendous intellectual, a man with an assured future. Look at Petey—a knothead, a jitter-bug, a guy who'll never know where his next meal is coming from. Can you give me one logical reason why you should go steady with Petey Burch?"

[150] "I certainly can," declared Polly. "He's got a raccoon coat."

ANALYTICAL READING

1. How does Shulman establish the rationality of the narrator—his concern with logic and reason?

2. What logical fallacies does Shulman present? How does he make them interesting? Define each briefly and cite the paragraphs in which they are mentioned. (Your instructor may want to substitute other names for them.)

3. How much character development is in the article? How does this contribute to Shulman's argument?

4. How does Shulman use irony to develop humor in relation to the fur coat, to Polly Espy and logic, and to the narrator's logic?

5. Do you think the article reveals the weakness of logic or of human nature? Discuss.

6. How do the events of the story change the reader's attitudes toward the narrator portrayed in the opening paragraphs?

REFLECTING

Point: If Shulman had a stated thesis proposition, what would it be?

Organization: What advantage is gained by the narrative, chronological order? Is there another organizational scheme buried within the narrative—problem-so-lution argument? Try to outline the article in two ways.

Support: How are the fallacies themselves used to support Shulman's contention about logic and human behavior? What part does language play, especially metaphor and slang?

Synthesis: Can you think of other situations in which humans seem unable to act logically and rationally? Could the thesis of Shulman's article be applied to any of the subjects discussed in this section of the book—for example, religion, gun control, testing, abortion? Explain.

Evaluation: How effective do you think the essay is? Does Shulman succeed in making a dull subject interesting? Is Shulman himself guilty of a fallacy—stereotyping? Discuss.

FROM READING TO WRITING

1. Using the proposition "People cannot live by logic alone," write a paper for a college newspaper that illustrates how human behavior reflects logical fallacies. For example, you might write a narrative about someone you know who believes in superstitions, or someone who is blind to the fallacious reasoning in advertising. Try to establish a satirical tone.

2. Write an argument paper to your local newspaper exposing and condemning the use of one of the article's logical fallacies in the advertising of a particular product.

3. Write an argument for your college newspaper in favor of or against some current fad.

A GRATEFUL WIFE HAS SECOND THOUGHTS

Ellen Goodman

BIOGRAPHICAL SKETCH

Born in Newton, Massachusetts in 1941, Ellen Goodman graduated summa cum laude from Radcliffe College. She was a reporter for Newsweek, *a feature writer for the Detroit* Free Press *and a columnist for the Boston* Globe *before becoming a syndicated columnist for the Washington* Post *in 1976. She has received a Nieman Fellowship and several awards for her newspaper columns, appears occasionally on the CBS radio program* Spectrum, *and the NBC* Today *show, and is the author of* Close to Home *and* Turning Points.

PRE-READING

1. What does "to have second thoughts" mean to you? Does the phrase signal a possible bias of the writer's?

2. From the biographical information given above and the information in the opening two paragraphs, who do you think is the "grateful wife"?

3. Is the thesis in the opening or the closing paragraph? What is it?

FROM Louisville *Courier-Journal*, December 11, 1979. pp. 31.© 1979, The Boston Globe Newspaper Company/Washington Post Writers Group. Reprinted with permission.

[1] I know a woman who is a grateful wife. She has been one for years. In fact, her gratitude has been as deep and constant as her affection. And together they have traveled a long, complicated road.

[2] In the beginning, this young wife was grateful to find herself married to a man who let her work. That was in 1964, when even her college professor said without a hint of irony that the young wife was "lucky to be married to a man who let her work." People talked like that then.

[3] Later, the wife looked around her at the men her classmates and friends had married and was grateful that her husband wasn't threatened, hurt, neglected, insulted—the multiple choice of the mid-60's—by her job.

[4] He was proud. And her cup overran with gratitude. That was the way it was.

[5] In the late '60s when other, younger women were having consciousness-raising groups, she was having babies and more gratitude.

[6] You see, she discovered that she had a Helpful Husband. Nothing in her experience had led her to expect this. Her mother was not married to one; her sister was not married to one; her brother was not one.

[7] But at 4 o'clock in the morning, when the baby cried and she was exhausted, sometimes she would nudge her husband awake (wondering only vaguely how he could sleep) and ask him to feed the boy. He would say sure. And she would say thank you.

[8] The Grateful Wife and the Helpful Husband danced this same pas de deux for a decade. When the children were small and she was sick, he would take charge. When it was their turn to car-pool and she had to be at work early, he would drive. If she was coming home late, he would make dinner.

[9] All you have to do is ask, he would say with a smile.

[10] And so she asked. The woman who had minded her P's and Q's as a child minded her pleases and thank yous as a wife. Would you please put the baby on the potty? Would you please stop at the store tonight for milk? Would you please pick up Joel at soccer practice? Thank you. Thank you. Thank you.

[11] It is hard to know when gratitude first began to grate on my friend. Or when she began saying please and thank you dutifully rather than genuinely.

[12] But it probably began when she was tired one day or night. In any case, during the car-time between one job and the other, when she would run lists through her head, she began feeling less thankful for her moonlighting job as household manager.

[13] She began to realize that all the items of their shared life were stored in her exclusive computer. She began to realize that her queue was so full of minutia that she had no room for anything else.

[14] The Grateful Wife began to wonder why she should say thank you when a father took care of his children and why she should say please when a husband took care of his house.

[15] She began to realize that being grateful meant being responsible. Being grateful meant assuming that you were in charge of children and laundry and running out of toilet paper. Being grateful meant having to ask. And ask. And ask.

[16] Her husband was not an oppressive or even thoughtless man. He was helpful. But helpful doesn't have to remember vacuum–cleaner bags. And helpful doesn't keep track of early dismissal days.

[17] Helpful doesn't keep a Christmas–present list in his mind. Helpful doesn't have to know who wears what size and colors. Helpful is reminded; helpful is asked. Anything you ask. Please and thank you.

[18] The wife feels, she says, vaguely frightened to find herself angry at saying please and thank you. She wonders if she is, indeed, an ingrate. But her wondering doesn't change how she feels or what she wants.

[19] The wife would like to take just half the details that clog her mind like grit in a pore, and hand them over to another manager. The wife would like someone who would be grateful when she volunteered to take *his* turn at the market, or *his* week at the laundry.

[20] The truth is that after all those years when she danced her part perfectly, she wants something else. She doesn't want a helpful husband. She wants one who will share. For that, she would be truly grateful.

ANALYTICAL READING

1.   What role playing does Goodman describe in the essay?

2.   How would you characterize the tone of the essay?

3.   To what audience do you think Goodman is directing her case? What kind of reader do you think would be persuaded by her arguments?

4.   What does she mean by these phrases: "danced this same pas de deux," "minded her Ps and Qs"(paragraphs 8 and 10)? How do these phrases contribute to her argument?

5.   What does Goodman mean in paragraph 15 when she says "being grateful meant being responsible"?

6.   In paragraph 10, what is the effect of placing the *Thank you's* at the end? (Try ordering them immediately after each question.) In what other places does the author use a similar device?

REFLECTING

Point: What point of view is Goodman "selling"? Is it stated or implied? Explain. State her proposition in one sentence.

Organization: What persuasive advantage does the chronological organization give her? Outline her organizational scheme, showing her main points.

Support: How does Goodman use definition to support her argument? How does she add persuasive force through repetition? Point out how she uses details and figurative language effectively.

Synthesis: How do the stereotype roles the author describes correspond to some you have observed or experienced? Have you ever learned to resent a role forced on you by a long–lasting relationship?

Evaluation: How effective was Goodman's argument? Did she elicit a sympathetic response? Why or why not? What advantage was there in using third person? in employing satire? What are some of the counterarguments that she chose to ignore?

FROM READING TO WRITING

1. Calling upon personal experiences in which you followed some role model, write an informal proposition argument for your classmates, using Goodman's title format: "A _____ Has Second Thoughts." Suggestions might include "a dutiful son/daughter; an honor student; a high-school jock; big brother/sister; a good girl/boy. You may wish to treat the paper satirically as Goodman did.

2. Think of other relationships that have involved social stereotypes and that have changed since your parents were young: parent-child, man-woman, teacher-student, black-white, for example. Using Goodman's approach, write a paper directed to a specific audience in which you argue that the change needs further revision.

3. Write a paper arguing the helpful husband's case. Make your target audience a cross-section group of college-age students.

A FEW WORDS FOR CANNIBALISM
Wendell Berry

BIOGRAPHICAL SKETCH

A Kentucky poet, novelist, and essayist, Wendell Berry received his B.A. and M.A. degrees from the University of Kentucky, where he later taught creative writing. His many works include the novels A Place on Earth *and* The Memory of Old Jack; *books of poetry (*The Broken Ground, The Country of Marriage, Clearings) *and several essay collections (*A Continuous Harmony, The Long-Legged House). *A farmer and a dedicated proponent of conservation, he is an active participant in organizations committed to the preservation of the earth and its environment. Besides contributing to publications such as* The Whole Earth Catalog *and* Organic Gardening, *he has written two books that outline his philosophy about mankind's relationships to nature and to the soil:* An Unforeseen Wilderness *and* The Unsettling of America.

PRE-READING

1. What is the effect of the title? What writing purpose does the word *for* suggest?

2. In the opening paragraph, are you aware that Berry is being ironic? How?

3. Explain the relationship between the last sentence of the essay and the title.

¹ I must admit at the outset that my purpose here somewhat astounds me. For I remember the days of my youth when I contributed numberless nickels and dimes toward the conversion of cannibals. In my fantasies of those days, in fact, I used to tremble for fear that the Lord would call *me* into the "mission field," where I would be eaten by the beneficiaries of my goodness. (The shepherd eaten by his sheep! Perhaps it is in the metaphor that most of the horror lies.) That it might be at least equally unpleasant to be killed before being eaten didn't occur to me for several years. I seem to have gone on the assumption that I would somehow be present at the feast.

² Later, when I became a man, I re-examined the practice in the light of all I had learned, and to my surprise was able to find nothing much wrong with it. Indeed it seemed to me that the cannibals probably stood at the apex of civilization, rather than at its foot as I had assumed previously. I asked myself why we, who scarcely blink at the wholesale burning alive of families, should yet quail and sicken at the thought of eating those we have not only killed but cooked. Such fastidiousness, it seemed to me, was far more curious and eccentric than cooking missionaries, especially when I considered that the missionaries were usually killed beforehand.

³ These thoughts, I assure you, turned my head around so vigorously as to threaten the integrity of my neck. But as I hope to be an honest man, I was not long a defender of cannibalism before I became its advocate. Even supposing it to be a sin, cannibalism hardly makes a visible stain upon murder. It may, rather, be thought to mitigate somewhat the sin of murder by the virtue of frugality, for after all a dead man is meat, and meat is either to be eaten or wasted.

⁴ I would propose for a start—believing that reform should be accomplished by gentle phases—that as a curtailment to murder we should have a law requiring every murderer to eat whomever he has killed. It is not that a murderer would *necessarily* hesitate to eat his victim, but that a law *requiring* that the victim be eaten would tend to cause the prospective murderer to reflect a moment beforehand on the palatability of the prospective victim. And who knows but what in that moment conscience might be able to catch up and prevent the murder from happening? For my own part I am sure that I would hesitate to kill and eat certain of my enemies once I took time to consider that they have spent their lives sweating cool oily sweats in little offices, eating frozen pre-cooked dinners and sleeping with detestable women. The flesh of such people, I am sure, is spongy and foul to the taste. With such a law I foresee that our killing of one another—at present our major industry, not to say our way of life—might come to be governed by a sort of bag limit. In short, mankind might once again aspire to the decency of wild animals, which rarely kill more than they can eat. With patience and luck, we might even reach a new Golden Age when we would hope to emulate *most* animals, which do not kill their own kind at all.

ANALYTICAL READING

1. What change in attitude is described in the first two paragraphs? What persuasive advantages does this description provide?

2. What analogies does Berry use in presenting his arguments?

3. How does he propose that cannibalism could become a deterrent to murder?

4. From the biographical sketch, you see that Berry believes in conservation and respects nature. How are these attitudes reflected in his essay?

REFLECTING

Point: What is Berry really advocating in the essay? State it as a thesis proposition.

Organization: The essay is a proposition argument (see page 278–79). Construct an outline of the main arguments showing a *therefore* relationship between them and the thesis.

Support: How do the analogies that you discussed in question 2 (Analytical Reading) help to support the ideas in the essay?

Synthesis: This essay is closely related to a famous argument by Jonathan Swift—"A Modest Proposal." If you have read it, explain how the two are similar. Berry's essay was written during the Vietnam conflict when U.S. forces were using napalm on villages. How is this reflected in the essay?

Evaluation: Did you find the essay effective? Did Berry provide enough signals that the essay was satirical? Explain. Do you think shock can contribute to the art of persuasion? Can you illustrate situations that have been remedied because of some shocking accident or incident?

FROM READING TO WRITING

1. Advocate a shocking suggestion for a serious social situation as Berry does in this essay. Choose an audience that would be a natural target for such an argument.

2. Write a letter to Wendell Berry refuting his proposition that cannibalism could inhibit murder. You may wish to offer some other plan.

3. Propose a novel approach to some school or community problem, such as cheating, vandalism, littering, or parking in handicapped zones. You may be serious or humorous in this article for your college paper.

Proposition Argument: Formal

WHAT'S RIGHT WITH SIGHT–AND–SOUND JOURNALISM

Eric Sevareid

BIOGRAPHICAL SKETCH

Eric Arnold Sevareid was born in the small town of Velva, North Dakota, in 1912. He graduated from the University of Minnesota and worked as a reporter for several newspapers before embarking on a career as a radio and television commentator, originally abroad and then as a regular editorialist for CBS. The recipient of Peabody Awards for distinguished reporting in 1949, 1964, and 1968, Sevareid was generally acknowledged to be the dean of American broadcasters before his retirement in 1977. He is the author of five books and is a frequent contributor to magazines.

PRE-READING

1. What does the title say about the subject and the direction of the article?

2. How does the biographical sketch establish the writer as an authority?

3. What ideas does the opening paragraph suggest the article will deal with?

4. Although the ending is personal, what logical point can you infer from it?

[1] A kind of adversary relationship between print journalism and electronic journalism exists and has existed for many years. As someone who has toiled in both vineyards, I am troubled by much of the criticism I read. Innumerable newspaper critics seem to insist that broadcast journalism be like *their* journalism and measured by their standards. It cannot be. The two are more complementary than competitive, but they *are* different.

[2] The journalism of sight and sound is the only truly new form of journalism to come along. It is a *mass* medium, a universal medium, as the American public-education system is the world's first effort to teach everyone, so far as that is possible. It has serious built-in limitations as well as advantages, compared with print. Broadcast news operates in linear time, newspapers in lateral space. This means that a newspaper or magazine reader can be his own editor

FROM *Saturday Review*, 2 October 1976, pp. 18–21. Copyright © 1976 by the Saturday Review Corporation.

in a vital sense. He can glance over it and decide what to read, what to pass by. The TV viewer is a restless prisoner, obliged to sit through what does not interest him to get to what may interest him. While it is being shown, a bus accident at Fourth and Main has as much impact, seems as important, as an outbreak of a big war. We can do little about this, little about the viewer's unconscious resentments.

[3] Everybody watches television to some degree, including most of those who pretend they don't. Felix Frankfurter was right; he said there is no highbrow in any lowbrow, but there is a fair amount of lowbrow in every highbrow. Television is a combination mostly of lowbrow and middlebrow, but there is more highbrow offered than highbrows will admit or even seek to know about. They will make plans, go to trouble and expense, when they buy a book or reserve a seat in the theater. They will not study the week's offerings of music or drama or serious documentation in the radio- and TV-program pages of their newspaper and then schedule themselves to be present. They want to come home, eat dinner, twist the dial, and find something agreeable ready, accommodating to *their* schedule.

[4] For TV, the demand–supply equation is monstrously distorted. After a few years' experience with it in Louisville, Mark Ethridge said that television is a voracious monster that consumes Shakespeare, talent, and money at a voracious rate. As a station manager once said to a critic, "Hell, there isn't even enough mediocrity to go around."

[5] TV programming consumes eighteen to twenty-four hours a day, 365 days of the year. No other medium of information or entertainment ever tried anything like that. How many good new plays appear in the theaters of this country each year? How many fine new motion pictures? Add it all together and perhaps you could fill twenty evenings out of the 365. As for music, including the finest music, it is there for a twist of the dial on any radio set in any big city of the land. It was radio, in fact, that created the audiences for music, good and bad, as nothing ever had before it.

[6] Every new development in mass communications has been opposed by intellectuals of a certain stripe. I am sure that Gutenberg was denounced by the elite of his time—his device would spread dangerous ideas among the God-fearing, obedient masses. The typewriter was denounced by intellectuals of the more elfin variety—its clacking would drive away the muses. The first motion pictures were denounced—they would destroy the legitimate theater. Then the sound motion picture was denounced—it would destroy the true art of the film, which was pantomime.

[7] To such critics, of course, television is destroying everything.

[8] It is destroying conversation, they tell us. Nonsense. Non-conversing families were always that way. TV has, in fact, stimulated billions of conversations that otherwise would not have occurred.

[9] It is destroying the habit of reading, they say. This is nonsense. Book sales in this country during the lifetime of general television have greatly increased and well beyond the increase in the population. At the end of a pro-

gram with Hugo Black, we announced that if viewers wanted one of those little red copies of the Constitution such as he had held in his hand, they had only to write to us. We received about 150,000 requests—mostly, I suspect, from people who didn't know the Constitution was actually down on paper, who thought it was written in the skies or on a bronze tablet somewhere. After my first TV conversation with Eric Hoffer, his books sold out in nearly every bookstore in America—the next day.

[10] TV is debasing the use of the English language, they tell us. My friend Alistair Cooke, for one. Nonsense. Until radio and then TV, tens of millions of people living in sharecropper cabins, in small villages on the plains and in the mountains, in the great city slums, had never heard good English diction in their lives. If anything, this medium has improved the general level of diction.

[11] The print–electronic adversary relationship is a one-way street. Print scrutinizes, analyzes, criticizes us every day; we do not return the favor. We have tried now and then, particularly in radio days with "CBS Views the Press," but not enough. On a network basis it's almost impossible because we have no real national newspapers—papers read everywhere—to criticize for the benefit of the national audience. Our greatest failure is in not criticizing ourselves, at least through the mechanism of viewers' rebuttals. Here and there, now and then, we have done it. It should have been a regular part of TV from the beginning. The Achilles heel of TV is that people can't talk back to that little box. If they had been able to, over the years, perhaps the gas of resentment could have escaped from the boiler in a normal way; it took Agnew with his hatchet to explode it, some years ago. The obstacle has not been policy; it has been the practical problem of programming inflexibilities—we don't have the fifteen-minute program anymore, for example. If we could extend the evening news programs to an hour, as we have wished to do for years, we could do many things, including a rebuttal period from viewers. It is not the supposedly huckster-minded monopolistic networks that prevent this; it is the local affiliates. It was tough enough to get the half-hour news; apparently it's impossible to get an hour version.

[12] I have seen innumerable sociological and psychological studies of TV programming and its effects. I have never seen a study of the quality—and the effect—of professional TV criticism in the printed press.

[13] TV critics in the papers tell us, day in and day out, what is wrong with us. Let me return the favor by suggesting that they stop trying to be Renaissance men. They function as critics of everything on the screen—drama, soap operas, science programs, musical shows, sociological documentaries, our political coverage—the works. Let the papers assign their science writers to our science programs, their political writers to our political coverage, their drama critics to the TV dramas.

[14] Let me suggest also that they add a second measurement to their critiques. It is proper that they judge works of fiction—dramas, for example—entirely on the basis of what they see on the little screen because in that area the producers, writers, and performers have total control of the material. If the

result is wrong, *they* are wrong. News and documentaries are something else—especially live events, like a political convention. Here we do not have total control of the material or anything like it. On these occasions, it seems to me, the newspaper critic must also be a reporter; he must, if he can, go behind the scenes and find out why we do certain things and do not do other things; there is usually a reason. In the early days such critics as John Crosby and Marya Mannes would do that. A few—Unger on the *Christian Science Monitor*, for example—still do that, but very few.

¹⁵ Let me suggest to their publishers that a little less hypocrisy would become them. Don't publish lofty editorials and critiques berating the culturally low common denominator of TV entertainment programming and then feature on the cover of your weekly TV supplements, most weeks of the year, the latest TV rock star or gang-buster character. Or be honest enough to admit that you do this, that you play to mass tastes for the same reason the networks do—because it is profitable. Don't lecture the networks for the excess of violence—and it *is* excessive—on the screen and then publish huge ads for the most violent motion pictures in town, ads for the most pornographic films and plays, as broadcasting does not.

¹⁶ Now, at this point the reader must be thinking, what's this fellow beefing about? He's had an unusually long ride on the crest of the wave; he's highly paid. He's generally accepted as an honest practitioner of his trade. All true. I have indeed been far more blessed than cursed in my own lifework.

¹⁷ But I am saying what I am saying here—I am finally violating Ed Murrow's old precept that one never, but never, replies to critics—because it has seemed to me that someone must. Because the criticism exchange between print and broadcasting is a one-way street. Because a mythology is being slowly, steadily, set in concrete.

¹⁸ Why this intense preoccupation of the print press with the broadcast press and its personae? Three reasons at least: broadcasting, inescapably, is the most personal form of journalism ever, so there is a premium on personalities. The networks are the only true national news organs we have. And, third, competition between them and between local stations is intense, as real as it used to be between newspapers.

¹⁹ So the searchlight of scrutiny penetrates to our innards. Today we can scarcely make a normal organizational move without considering the press reaction. Networks, and even some stations, cannot reassign a reporter or anchorman, suspend anyone, discharge anyone, without a severe monitoring in the newspapers. Papers, magazines, wire services, don't have to live with that and would very much resent it if they did.

²⁰ We live with myths, some going far back but now revived. The myth that William L. Shirer was fired by Ed Murrow and fired because he was politically too liberal. He wasn't fired at all; but even so good a historian as Barbara Tuchman fell for that one. The myth that Ed Murrow was forced out of CBS. At that point in his great career, President Kennedy's offer to Ed to join the government, at cabinet level, was probably the best thing that could have

happened to him. The myth that Fred Friendly resigned over an issue of high principle involving some public-service air time. There are other such myths, and a new generation of writers are perpetuating them in their books, which are read and believed by a new generation of students and practitioners of journalism.

[21] We have had the experience of people leaving, freely or under pressure, then playing their case in the papers to a fare-thee-well; they are believed because of that preconceived image of the networks in the minds of the writers. What does a big corporation do? Slug it out with the complainant, point by point, in the papers? Can it speak out at all when the real issue is the personal character and behavior of the complainant, which has been the truth in a few other cases? It can't. So it takes another beating in the press.

[22] There is the myth that the CBS News Division—I am talking about CBS of course, because it is the place I know and because it is the network most written about these days—has been somehow shoved out to the periphery of the parent corporation, becoming more and more isolated. What has happened is that it has achieved, and been allowed, more and more autonomy because it is fundamentally different from any other corporate branch. Therefore it is more and more independent.

[23] There is the myth that the corporation is gradually de-emphasizing news and public affairs. In the last sixteen years since CBS News became a separate division, its budget has increased 600 percent, its personnel more than 100 percent. It does *not* make money for the company; it is a loss leader, year after year. I would guess it spends more money to cover the news than any other news organization in the world today. This is done because network news servicing has become a public trust and need.

[24] There is the myth that since the pioneering, groundbreaking TV programs of Murrow and Friendly, CBS News has been less daring, done fewer programs of a hard-hitting kind. The Murrow programs are immortal in this business because they were the *first*. Since then we have dealt, forthrightly, with every conceivable controversial issue one can think of—drugs, homosexuality, government corruption, business corruption, TV commercials, gun control, pesticides, tax frauds, military waste, abortion, the secrets of the Vietnam War—everything. What shortage has occurred has been on the side of the materials, not on the side of our willingness to tackle them.

[25] In case I had missed something myself, I have recently inquired of other CBS News veterans if they can recall a single case of a proposed news story or a documentary that was killed by executives of the parent organization. Not one comes to anyone's mind. Some programs have been anathema to the top executive level, but they were not stopped. Some have caused severe heartburn at that level when they went on the air. Never has there been a case of people at that level saying to the News Division, "Don't ever do anything like that again."

[26] For thirteen years I have done commentary—personal opinion inescapably involved—most nights of the week on the evening news. In that time exactly three scripts of mine were killed because of their substance by CBS

News executives. Each one by a different executive, and none of them ever did it again. Three—out of more than 2,000 scripts. How many newspaper editorialists or columnists, how many magazine writers, have had their copy so respected by their editors?

[27] There is the perennial myth that sponsors influence, positively or negatively, what we put on the air. They play no role whatever. No public-affairs program has ever been canceled because of sponsor objection. Years ago, they played indirect roles. When I started doing a six P.M. radio program, nearly thirty years ago, Ed Murrow, then a vice-president, felt it necessary to take me to lunch with executives of the Metropolitan Insurance Company, the sponsors. About fourteen years ago, when I was doing the Sunday-night TV news, a representative of the advertising agency handling the commercials would appear in the studio, though he never tried to change anything. Today one never sees a sponsor or an agency man, on the premises or off.

[28] There is the myth, which seems to be one of the flawed premises of so successful a reporter as David Halberstam, that increased corporate profitability has meant a diminished emphasis on news and public affairs. The reverse, of course, is the truth.

[29] There is the new myth, creeping into print as writers rewrite one another, that an ogre sits at the remote top of CBS Incorporated, discouraging idealistic talents down the line, keeping the news people nervous, if not cowardly. His name is William S. Paley,[1] and the thesis seems to be that the tremendous growth of CBS News in size and effectiveness, its unmatched record of innovation and boldness in dealing with public issues, its repeated wars with the most powerful figures of government and business, have all taken place over these forty years or more in spite of this man's reluctance or downright opposition. The reverse is much closer to the truth. *Only* with a man of his stripe could all this have been done. Think what it is to sit up there all those years, whipped by gales of pressures from every public cause group, politicians, Presidents, newspapers, congressional committees, the FCC, affiliates, stockholders, and employees, individually and organized. To sit up there under unrelenting pressures of an intensity, a massiveness, rarely endured by any print publisher and still keep the apparatus free and independent and steady on its long course. After all, in this country networking might at its inception have become an appendage and apparatus of government; it might have gone completely Hollywood. It did neither. It grimly held to every freedom the law allows, and it fights for more. This has not been accomplished by weak or frightened men at the top.

[30] I am no appointed spokesman for William Paley. We are not intimates. I owe him nothing; I have earned my keep. I have not got rich. I have had my differences with him, once or twice acutely. I have been a thorn in his side a number of times. But we had our differences out, and never once was his treatment of me less than candid and honorable. He is now in the evening of his career; I am now pretty much the graybeard of CBS News. I must soon go

---

[1] William Paley was the vice-president of CBS during Sevareid's last years as a news analyst.

gently into that good night of retirement. But I shan't go so gently that I shall not say what I think of the mythologists who now surround us, what I think of these ignorant assaults on Paley. It would be cowardly of me not to say that many of these critics are simply wrong—wrong in their attitude, wrong in their premises, repeatedly wrong in their facts.

[31] We are not the worst people in the land, we who work as journalists. Our product in print or on the air is a lot better, more educated, and more responsible than it was when I began, some forty-five years ago, as a cub reporter. This has been the best generation of all in which to have lived as a journalist in this country. We are no longer starvelings, and we sit above the salt. We have affected our times.

[32] It has been a particular stroke of fortune to have been a journalist in Washington these years. There has not been a center of world news to compare with this capital city since ancient Rome. We have done the job better, I think, than our predecessors, and our successors will do it better than we. I see remarkable young talents all around.

[33] That's the way it should be. I will watch them come on, maybe with a little envy, but with few regrets for the past. For myself, I wouldn't have spent my working life much differently had I been able to.

ANALYTICAL READING

1. What distinctions does Sevareid make between print journalism and electronic journalism? Why does he make these distinctions?

2. What charges do the critics of television make? How does Sevareid refute these charges? Do you agree with him? Is his evidence sufficient?

3. What does Sevareid mean in stating that "the Achilles heel of TV is that people can't talk back to that little box" (paragraph 11)? Do you know of any recent solutions to this problem?

4. In what ways does Sevareid criticize the TV critics and their publishers? Do you think that he is justified in pointing out their hypocrisy?

5. Why do you suppose that Ed Murrow, one of the first great radio and television journalists, felt that critics should be ignored? For what three reasons has Sevareid violated this precept?

6. What are some of the myths about television journalists or CBS that Sevareid refutes? Do you accept his evidence? Why or why not?

7. In what ways do you think Sevareid is right in saying that journalists affect the times (paragraph 31)? Refer to specific events.

8. Note that in the closing paragraphs, Sevareid links print and electronic journalists. How does this support a concept stated in the opening paragraph? What is the effect of this association at the end of his argument?

REFLECTING

Point: What audience is Sevareid addressing? How does that influence his purpose? What is his specific purpose besides defending television journalism? Formulate in a sentence or two the main points in his argument.

Organization: How does paragraph 16 link two sections of the article? What are these sections? What is Severeid's main strategy throughout the article in defending television journalism?

Support: Sevareid uses the first person throughout. Why is this particularly effective here? Is his tone angry, annoyed, even-tempered, or what? How effective is the repetitious use of the word *nonsense* in paragraphs 8, 9, and 10 twice as a one-word sentence? What do you think of the repetitious use of myths in the topic sentences of many of the paragraphs from 20 to 29? Where and how is comparison and contrast used effectively? What justification is there for the single sentence in paragraph 7?

Synthesis: What is your general criticism about television news? Has Sevareid made you aware of factors that you had not considered previously? If so, what are they? Do you think that television has interfered with your family conversations, reduced your reading time, or affected your use of the English language? If so, how?

Evaluation: Does Sevareid portray television journalism too favorably? Has he overlooked any significant criticism of either television programming or news reporting? Are his refutations of criticisms and myths convincing? Does his argument gain from his own reputation as a respected TV journalist?

FROM READING TO WRITING

1. For a general audience, write a paper entitled "What's Right with _____," using some of Sevareid's strategies.

2. Write an article for TV Guide attacking, defending, or modifying some of the points mentioned by Sevareid, such as the importance of studying TV schedules instead of watching indiscriminately; the need to allow viewer response; or the criticism of newspapers for their hypocritical appeal to low tastes.

STANDARDIZED TESTS: THEY REFLECT THE REAL WORLD

Robert L. Ebel

BIOGRAPHICAL SKETCH

Robert Louis Ebel was born in Waterloo, Iowa, in 1910. He received a B.A. from Northern Iowa University and an M.A. and Ph.D. from Iowa University. After teaching and serving as a school superintendent in Michigan, he was vice-president of the Educational Testing Service for six years before joining the faculty at Michigan State University, where he is now a professor of educational psychology. He has also served as a consultant for various school systems and educational associations in this

FROM *The New York Times*, 1 May 1977, Sec. 12, pp. 1 ff. © 1977 by The New York Times Company. Reprinted by permission.

country and others. Ebel's writing includes several books and numerous scholarly articles, mainly about testing and its reliability and social consequences.

PRE-READING

1. What does the title imply to you after a reading of the first paragraph?

2. What does the final paragraph reveal about the subject?

[1] Are standardized tests headed for extinction? To judge from news reports, magazine articles and some popular books the answer might seem to be yes. A variety of charges have been laid against them, and there is substance to some. But the effects are neither so overpowering nor so harmful as the critics imply. On balance the case for standardized tests is persuasive.

[2] A common accusation is that some pupils have, and others lack, a special talent for taking tests and that tests end up measuring this ability rather than academic achievements. Only on a carelessly or ineptly constructed test, though, can a pupil inflate his score by special test savvy. Most widely used standardized tests have been constructed carefully by experts. Unfamiliarity with the item types or response modes employed in a standardized test can indeed handicap a naïve examinee. But that kind of naïveté can be removed quite easily by careful instructions and practice exercises.

[3] Bear in mind that the test score reports only the level of knowledge the pupil possesses, not how frequently or how effectively he makes use of it. It reports what the pupil can do, not what he typically does. What a pupil does, and how well he does it, depends not on his knowledge alone. It depends also on his energy, ambition, determination, adroitness, likableness and luck, among other things. A pupil's knowledge as measured by a standardized or any other test is one ingredient—but only one—of his potential success in life.

[4] The simplicity with which answers to multiple-choice questions can be recorded on an answer sheet, and the objectivity and speed with which correct answers can be detected and counted by modern scoring machines, offends some devotees of the other common type of examination, the written essay. They confuse the simplicity of the process of recording an answer with the complexity of the process of figuring it out. Some of them charge that multiple-choice questions test only rote learning, or superficial factual information. That is clearly not true. Consider this question:

The sides of a quadrilateral having two consecutive right angles are consecutive whole numbers. The shortest side is one of the two parallel sides. What is the area of the quadrilateral in square units? (a) 11 (b) 18 (c) 25 (d) 36 (e) Not given

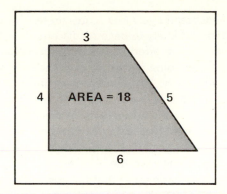

[5] Multiple-choice questions can be trivial or irrelevant. They need not be.

[6] Critics of tests and testing sometimes provide examples of questions that seem to be ridiculously trivial or impossibly ambiguous. In some cases their criticisms are justified. Bad questions have been written and published. But few of these come from professionally constructed standardized tests of achievement. In other cases the criticism is not justified. The objection is based on a possible but unlikely interpretation different from the clearly intended sense of the question. One who sets out to discover how a question might conceivably be misconstrued is likely to find some way to misconstrue it. Language, after all, is not a flawless means for the precise communication of thought.

[7] Another charge is that standardized testing harms children. It is said that the tests threaten and upset pupils, that if a pupil gets a low score he will be seriously damaged and that standardized testing is incompatible with educational procedures designed to support the child.

[8] There is, no doubt, anecdotal evidence to support some of these claims. However, common sense suggests that the majority of pupils are not harmed by testing, and as far as I know there is no substantial survey data that would contradict common sense on this matter. The teachers I talk with seem much more often to be concerned with pupils who don't care enough how well or how poorly they do on such tests, than with the relatively rare instances of pupils who care too much.

[9] It is normal and biologically helpful to be somewhat anxious when facing any real test, regardless of one's age. But it is also a necessary part of growing up to learn to cope with the tests that life inevitably brings. Of the many challenges to a child's peace of mind, caused by such things as angry parents, playground bullies, bad dogs and shots from the doctor, standardized tests must surely be among the least fearsome. Unwise parental pressure can in some cases elevate anxiety to harmful levels. But usually the child who breaks down in tears at the prospect of a test has problems of security, adjustment and maturity that testing did not create and that cannot be solved by eliminating tests.

[10] A pupil who consistently gets low scores on tests of what that pupil has tried hard to learn is indeed likely to become discouraged. If this does happen, the school cannot claim to be offering a good educational program, and the teacher cannot claim to be doing a good job of teaching. Most low scores on tests, however, go to pupils who, for one reason or another, have not tried very hard to learn. In the opinion of the teachers of such pupils, it is the trying rather than the testing that is most in need of correction.

[11] It is sometimes charged that tests distort school curriculums by causing schools to teach to the tests and by thus hampering curricular innovation.

[12] A school that is teaching what the tests test will surely teach many other things besides. Even in the basic areas that the test does sample, there will be time and cause to venture into areas of learning not covered by the standardized tests. Standardized tests can dominate local curriculums only to the extent that school administrators and school teachers allow them to.

[13] There are, of course, some programs of open education that are satisfied merely with maximum pupil freedom, trusting nature alone to do what others employ the art and science of teaching to help nature do. To say that standardized tests of achievement are inappropriate for such programs may imply more criticism of the programs than of the tests.

[14] Standardized tests are also charged with encouraging harmful comparisons of one pupil with another. Let a pupil measure his achievements against his potential, or against his own past performance, say the critics, not against his classmates.

[15] I believe they are wrong. What they should criticize is unwise reactions to comparison, not comparison itself. For those who are interested in excellent education find it difficult to believe that comparisons of educational achievement are irrelevant or unnecessary. No proud parent believes it. No capable teacher believes it. It simply is not true.

[16] The only basis for judging a human performance excellent, acceptable, or inferior is in comparison with other human performances. The only basis for setting reasonably attainable objectives for pupil learning is knowledge of what similar pupils have been able to learn. Of course it is good for a pupil to compare his present performance with his own past performance. But that is no substitute for comparing his present performance with the present performances of his classmates. Surely it is cold comfort to a pupil when his arithmetic teacher says, "For you, five out of ten is quite good."

[17] Only in some eyes have tests lost favor. Quite clearly they are not headed for extinction. They are much too useful to the competent, concerned educator. They are much too essential to the pursuit of excellence in education.

ANALYTICAL READING

1. Does Ebel effectively refute the accusation that some students have special skills for taking standardized tests?

2. What importance does he place on such tests?

3. What is the purpose of Ebel's example of a multiple-choice question? How typical is this example?

4. How satisfactorily does Ebel refute the contention that standardized tests are damaging to low-scoring children? Explain.

5. Explain and discuss Ebel's statement at the end of paragraph 12 to the effect that teachers and administrators determine the extent to which standardized tests dictate curriculums.

6. Does Ebel point out the positive value of standardized tests? If so, where? Can you formulate a syllogism of this point? If so, do you agree with the basic assumption?

REFLECTING

Point: What is the purpose of the article? How is it accomplished? In one or two sentences, state the main points of the argument.

Organization: Where does the proposition appear? Why do you think Ebel chose this form? In a paragraph-by-paragraph analysis, explain his strategy as reflected in the article.

Support: What is the role of voice and tone in the article? What evidence does Ebel use to refute most of the claims made by opponents of standardized tests?

Synthesis: How do you feel about standardized tests? Do such tests seem fair? Do you know students who have been harmed by them? Do you think that essay tests are preferable to multiple-choice tests? Do the tests seem to rate you and your friends as your teachers do? Do you agree with Ebel's final statement that standardized tests "are much too essential to the pursuit of excellence in education"?

Evaluation: How effective are the examples or reasons? How thoroughly has Ebel refuted counter-arguments? How convincing is he? Explain.

FROM READING TO WRITING

See the suggestions after the essay by Taylor and Lazarus (page 327).

STANDARDIZED TESTS: THEY DON'T MEASURE LEARNING

Edwin P. Taylor and Mitchell B. Lazarus

BIOGRAPHICAL SKETCH

Edwin P. Taylor was born in Oberlin, Ohio. He graduated from Oberlin College and earned M.A. and Ph.D. degrees in physics from Harvard. After teaching at Wesleyan University for about twelve years, he became a senior research scientist of the Education Research Center at the Massachusetts Institute of Technology. He has published numerous articles in scholarly journals, mainly about subjects related to mechanics, special relativity and quantum physics, and computer-assisted learning.

Mitchell B. Lazarus was born in Montreal in 1942, received a B. Eng. degree from McGill University and an S.M. in electrical engineering, and a Ph.D. in psychology from Massachusetts Institute of Technology. In addition to teaching at MIT, Lazarus taught at George Mason College and Northern Virginia Community College before becoming associated first with MIT's Education Research Center and then with the Education Development Center at Newton, Massachusetts, where he is currently a senior staff associate. His articles about the teaching of mathematics, testing, and educational television have appeared in educational journals.

PRE-READING

1. This essay is also concerned with standardized testing. What is the purpose of the title?

2. How do the opening and closing paragraphs add to your knowledge of the argument?

¹ The controversy over achievement testing starts from a simple fact: Achievement tests reward test-taking skills as much as they reward achievement. Different children who know a subject equally well can still receive very different scores on a multiple-choice achievement test.

² Some children work fast, not taking time to think deeply: they may make quick conventional guesses on some questions, be tidy and accurate in shading boxes on answer sheets and have suburban, middle-class backgrounds—useful for quickly grasping the words and pictures on most tests. These children get credit, perhaps, for what they know about the subject matter.

³ Other children may work slowly, think through too many possibilities, be too insecure to guess fast or be sloppy with the answer sheet. Children come from a variety of cultural and linguistic backgrounds. Thus many children's test scores will probably not reflect their grasp of the subject, even if they know the subject well.

⁴ And nearly every achievement test is a reading test first, before it is a test of anything else.

⁵ Neatness, accuracy, speed and good reading are useful skills, worth encouraging in children. But as long as test scores depend so much on skills that supposedly are not being tested, the results are bound to be inaccurate.

⁶ All questions on standardized achievement tests are multiple choice. The child must (1) read the question and (2) think of the answer—but not write it down! Instead, he or she must (3) try to find this answer among those given; (4) and when it is not there, pick one that is; (5) keep track of its number or letter, and (6) shade in the correct little box on the answer sheet. Only two of these six steps concern the subject being tested. The other four help the computer grade the test.

⁷ Multiple-choice questions distort the purposes of education. Picking one answer among four is very different from thinking a question through to an

answer of one's own, and far less useful in life. Recognition of vocabulary and isolated facts makes the best kind of multiple-choice questions, so these dominate the tests, rather than questions that test the use of knowledge. Because schools want their children to perform well, they are often tempted to teach the limited sorts of knowledge most useful on the tests.

[8] Questions are often badly worded, confusing, or downright wrong. For many questions, the thoughtful or imaginative student can see several acceptable answers among those given.

[9] There is an easy defense against the charge of poor question quality: make the questions better. But after many decades of testing, the proportion of defective questions seems about the same—enough so that missing the defective ones can change a first-rate performance into a mediocre score. For at least two reasons—test secrecy and use of multiple-choice questions—the proportion of defective questions is unlikely to go down in the future.

[10] Aside from the content of the tests, there is the fact that some children are intimidated by the testing procedures—vastly different from ordinary classroom activity—and perform poorly.

[11] "Keep quiet. Sit with an empty row of desks between you and your neighbor. Listen hard to the instructions. Don't mind the teacher stalking up and down between the rows during the test. Remember how much your future depends on your score—but don't be nervous. Imagine what your folks will say if you land in a low percentile. If you tighten up under pressure, you are in real trouble. Hurry. Stay calm. Hurry. Stay calm."

[12] There are many stories of children breaking down during a test or being physically ill the night before. But life is full of trials and fears; why should we protect children? Because they are children; because we want to find out, for example, how well they are learning rather than how well they stand stress, and because those children already hobbled by insecurity, past failure or discrimination will be the most vulnerable in a vicious cycle.

[13] Once the tests are administered and scored, the purpose to which the results are put—comparing children using numbers—is of no use.

[14] Every person is complicated, everyone has unique skills and difficulties. But each test score reduces the pattern of a child's strengths and weaknesses to a single number. Why? To compare the child with others around the country. Why? To tell if the schools are doing their job. But the single numbers and averages carry no hints about how to improve either the schools or individual children.

[15] Healthy competition encourages excellence. But competition in standardized tests encourages intellectual narrowness and triviality.

[16] Society does need to measure people's achievement and school performance, and could do so in much better ways. Imagine school tests set up like the test for a driver's license, each test matched to the skills under test and each child doing "well enough" or not, with a chance for those who did not to try again later. In judging a school, attention would focus on the fractions of its children who passed various tests at various ages.

[17] Your children's future depends in part on tests you are not allowed to

see. There is growing expert opinion that this violates your rights and those of your children. It also puts the test publishers beyond public criticism—and that's one reason the tests remain so bad.

[18] The publishers say that the tests must be secret so children cannot prepare for them. But if the tests were good, preparing for them would be a fine idea. Everyone knows the range of questions that will be on the driver's license tests, and by practicing and preparing for them, it is possible to become a better driver. Children could become better thinkers in much the same way if they were given good, open tests.

[19] In the past we developed an unjustified faith in numbers, and then in computers. Objectivity and statistical analysis became major virtues; automatic data analysis often replaced thoughtful evaluation. Now we are learning that numbers can misrepresent children and can lead to wrong decisions about their lives. There can be no true objectivity in a heterogeneous society, and all data analysis is subject to the GIGO principle: garbage in, garbage out.

[20] The task is to find out how well children are learning. The present standardized multiple-choice achievement tests are doing it badly, sometimes destructively. There are better ways to find out, without compressing children into uniform molds that misrepresent their accomplishments.

ANALYTICAL READING

1. What is the meaning of the reference to "middle-class backgrounds" in paragraph 2?

2. Why do Taylor and Lazarus contend that "many children's test scores will probably not reflect their grasp of the subject" (paragraph 3)?

3. Explain what Taylor and Lazarus mean by their claim that multiple-choice questions fail to "test the use of knowledge" (paragraph 7)?

4. To what extent do you think that the authors would find essay tests more acceptable than multiple-choice tests?

5. Do you think paragraph 11 provides a representative or exaggerated example of the testing procedure? Support your answer with references to your own experience.

6. If the purpose of school is to prepare children for life, why do Taylor and Lazarus feel that they should be protected from stress and tension?

7. Do Taylor and Lazarus state that it is important to evaluate students and their schools? How do they propose that it be done, if not by standardized tests?

REFLECTING

Point: What are the main ideas in this proposition argument against standardized tests?

Organization: What are the main divisions of the essay? Can you find an organizational pattern in the first section?

Support: What group of readers is the article addressed to? Do you think they would agree with the point that test questions are poorly worded? What is the purpose of the analogy between achievement tests and driver's license tests? How appropriate is this analogy?

Synthesis: What role has reading ability played in the standardized tests you have taken? Do you feel that some or many children are intimidated by such tests? Would the fact that the average score of one high school's students on ACT or SAT tests was higher than another school's average indicate that the former was better than the latter? Is there any way to prepare for the tests? Don't such tests provide the simplest and easiest way to evaluate student learning?

Evaluation: Which points have the authors argued most convincingly? Least convincingly? Explain. How clear and practical are their solutions? How effective are their examples? Why would their audience probably agree or disagree with them?

FROM READING TO WRITING

1. For readers familiar with the two essays on testing, write a proposition argument stating which viewpoint on achievement tests is better and why.

2. Pretend you are the dean of admissions in a college or university with more students applying than you can accept. Write an argument explaining and defending your procedure for choosing students.

3. Argue for or against standardized testing in an article intended for your college newspaper.

4. Write a letter to high school seniors, trying to persuade them to sign up for the special study course offered by your company to help them raise their ACT or SAT scores.

5. Write a letter to your former high school principal, suggesting some change in the use or application of standardized tests.

6. Write an argument for a PTA audience discussing measures other than standardized test scores that might be used in evaluating schools.

7. In paragraph 10 of his essay (page 322), Ebel contends that only students who do not try very hard to learn receive low scores on standardized tests. Write an argument for your school newspaper agreeing or disagreeing with or modifying this view.

GIVE THE PEOPLE A VISION
Rev. Jesse L. Jackson

BIOGRAPHICAL SKETCH

Jesse Louis Jackson was born in Greenville, North Carolina, in 1941. He earned a B.A. in sociology from the Agricultural and Technical College in North Carolina and did postgraduate work at the Chicago Theological Seminary, from which he later received an honorary degree. A Baptist preacher and close friend of Martin Luther King, Jr., he was active in the civil rights movement for many years, particularly as one of the leaders of Operation Breadbasket, a Chicago organization devoted to increasing jobs for black people. Jackson, as head of the Chicago-based Operation PUSH (People United to Save Humanity), has launched a national crusade to improve black schools and students.

PRE-READING

1. While the title is interesting and inviting, it does not indicate the direction of the article. But when you add the title to the information in the first paragraph, what do you know about Jackson's subject and purpose?

2. Does the last paragraph specifically indicate Jackson's "vision"? If so, what is it?

¹ It is time, I believe, to reexamine the causes of the social and economic plight in which black Americans—and particularly the poor blacks of the Northern cities—still find themselves, despite the legal advances of the 60's. Since so many past analyses of this problem have failed to bring about satisfactory improvement, I think it is time to suggest some new approaches, based largely on new values. It is my view that such a fresh start offers the best hope not only of lifting up the black people but of saving America's cities.

² I also believe that it is fruitful to think of these problems within a larger context—the relationship between the United States and the third world. For the white racist attitudes that are part of the problem at home have also been an often unconscious element in the policy failures of the white political leadership via-à-vis the emerging nations, most recently in Africa. And the natural pride of American blacks in the achievement of black leaders abroad is a factor in their own struggle.

³ As a starting point, let us take a noteworthy statistic: There are now 130 black mayors in the United States. We blacks have populated the cities; we must now learn to run them. The need is urgent. The ethical collapse, the heroin epidemic, the large numbers of our people who are out of work and on welfare, and the disruptive violence in our schools all indicate that the cities may be destroying us.

⁴ The thrust of my argument is that black Americans must begin to accept

FROM *The New York Times Magazine*, 18 April 1976, pp. 13, 71–73. © 1976 by The New York Times Company. Reprinted by permission.

a larger share of responsibility for their lives. For too many years we have been crying that racism and oppression have kept us down. That is true, and racism and oppression have to be fought on every front. But to fight any battle takes soldiers who are strong, healthy, spirited, committed, well-trained, and confident. This is particularly true when the enemy is as tough and elusive as American racism. I don't believe that we will produce strong soldiers by moaning about what the enemy has done to us.

⁵ It is time, I think, for us to stand up, admit to our failures and weaknesses and begin to strengthen ourselves. Here are some of the things I am talking about:

⁶ There is a definite welfare mentality in many black communities that derives perhaps from slavery but that must now be overcome.

⁷ We have beome politically apathetic. Only 7 million out of 14 million eligible black voters are registered to vote. Yet politics is one key to self-development. In terms of votes, we have more potential strength than labor or any other single bloc. We have responsibility to use it to the full.

⁸ We too often condemn blacks who succeed and excel, calling them Toms and the like, when the ideal ought to be for all of us to succeed and excel.

⁹ We are allowing a minuscule minority of criminals in our midst to create disorder, ruin our schools and sap the energy we need to rebuild our neighborhoods and our cities.

¹⁰ Many leaders who are black, and many white liberals, will object to my discussing these things in public. But the decadence in black communities—killings, destruction of our own businesses, violence in the schools—is already in the headlines; the only question is what we should do about it. Others will object that to demand that we must meet the challenge of self-government is to put too much pressure on the victims of ancient wrongs. Yet in spite of these objections, in spite of yesterday's agony, liberation struggles are built on sweat and pain rather than tears and complaints.

¹¹ In facing up to the new reality of black concentration in the Northern cities, the flight of whites to the suburbs, and the decay of the inner cities—particularly their black communities—in many parts of the country, many black and white leaders demand Federal aid as the only solution. More Federal aid is certainly needed, but money alone, or in combination with minor reforms, will not significantly change the welfare system, reduce crime, build enough new houses, improve education, restore stable families or eliminate drug abuse. A multitude of Federal antipoverty and urban-renewal programs should have proved that by now. But if more Federal money will not solve the problem, what will?

¹² I believe we should look to the third world for an answer. The message from there is clear: Through the proper use of money and a positive attitude, we can stimulate self-development and give the people a vision. It has been fascinating for me to observe what has happened in South Vietnam in the past year. The new Saigon leaders have spent little time talking about the Ameri-

cans who carpet-bombed and defoliated their country. Instead, they have concentrated on rebuilding, putting people to work, inculcating new values and
attitudes. They did it with military authority and a liberated attitude. We black
Americans can rebuild our communities with moral authority. We need a
blueprint, such as an urban Marshall Plan, but at its base there must be moral
authority and sound ethical conduct.

[13] This is not unrealistic. It was the moral authority of the civil-rights
movement, not the Federal marshals—who stood back initially and let whites
have their way with the demonstrators—that changed the face of the South. It
was a disciplined struggle—and such a struggle can be waged again, to good
purpose, in the cities of the North.

[14] We need to tell our young people in those cities: "All right, we'll get all
the state and Federal money that we can; but first and foremost, we need to put
your hands and your bodies and your minds to work building our communities." What we must do for our young people is challenge them to put hope in
their brains rather than dope in their veins. What difference does it make if the
doors swing wide open if our young people are too dizzy to walk through
them?

[15] I often wonder what would happen if Coleman Young, the Mayor of
Detroit, who has inherited a city of much moral and economic decay, were to
go into one of Detroit's stadiums and had 50,000 or 60,000 people in there—
just as Jomo Kenyatta has done, and Castro, and President Samora Machel of
Mozambique—and delivered a resounding State of Detroit message.

[16] "All right, people" he could say, "Detroit needs 200 doctors in the next
10 to 15 years, and here is what we will do to make certain that it happens.
And we will need 200 lawyers and 400 electricians and 250 nurses, and here is
what we will do to make sure it happens. I cannot pass a law about these
things, but I am appealing to you parents and you children to cooperate. Parents, you must keep your children at home every night from 7 to 9 to study,
and get them into bed by 10. Every morning the city will provide physical-
training directors in city parks. We will close off one block in every neighborhood for half an hour every morning for exercise—we want you out there
getting your bodies healthy for this struggle for independence."

[17] I have been visiting major cities across the country, preparing for a
crusade next fall that will stimulate people along these lines. Everywhere I go,
from Washington to Los Angeles, I meet young people in schools that the
politicians have given up on. I frequently find myself addressing 3,000 or 4,000
young people in a rundown assembly hall. Each time I suggest a program of
self-development, they respond with overwhelming enthusiasm. Black teen-
agers—some of the roughest, most street-wise dudes you will ever meet—
respond to that appeal.

[18] There is another parallel with the third world that is very much to the
point. The emerging countries have had to proceed by stages—from a situation
in which they were outright colonies, and their white rulers simply grabbed up
the countries' natural resources; to a state of neocolonialism, in which the

people attained nominal independence but the former colonizers remained in de facto control of the resources, which they continued to exploit primarily for their own benefit; to a situation of real independence in which the people take over control of their resources and work out mutually beneficial production arrangements with the former colonizers.

[19] We black Americans feel we have been exploited, too, although the natural resources we had to offer were not minerals in the ground or produce in the field but the human resources of brain and brawn. And we feel we are at a stage at which we can emulate the third-world countries by moving from "neocolonialism," as it were, to real "independence." The lessons, of course, must be applied to situations that often are vastly different from those facing the leaders of the economically underdeveloped countries of Africa, Asia and Latin America, but the principle of self-reliance in place of dependency is the same.

[20] Let me give a practical example. In the 60's, many black leaders, myself included, were picketing in front of Sears and A. & P. and other supermarkets in the black neighborhoods, demanding more and better jobs for blacks and more equitable financial arrangements with the community. And we succeeded. Some of these stores began to appoint black managers, put products of black companies on their shelves, hire black contractors for building new stores, and place their accounts in black-controlled banks. But today we find ourselves in Chicago, East Orange, N.J., and elsewhere, lying down at Sears' back doors begging the man not to fire us all and close down.

[21] We want those white-owned branches, with the services and jobs they provide, to stay, but if they want to go, we should not be left with nothing to take their place. The point is that if we had pulled together in the intervening decade, if we had not lost so many good minds to the jails and the drug culture, if we had taken the pooling of our money more seriously, we would today have the ready capital and trained managers and communal organization to buy out those white-controlled stores that want to close down, direct all black business to them, and make them economically successful. But that takes discipline and purpose and dedicated leadership at many levels, and that is where I think the experience of the third-world countries can be of help to us.

[22] It is bad to be in the worst slums in the country; it is even worse if those slums are internalized, become part of you. Hence the therapeutic effect of the Black Power symbolism of the 60's. But some black students became so caught up in the symbolism of black nationalism and black liberation that they forgot about such basic skills as reading, writing and thinking.

[23] God knows that I recognize the need for black self-pride. But that monument must be built on a solid foundation; we must not, as Dr. Martin Luther King, Jr. used to say, confuse symbolism with substance. When I stand in front of an audience of 3,000 black high-school or college students and we chant back and forth, "I am somebody, I am somebody," I can feel them tell me: "I need to be told I am somebody, I need to know I am somebody." But shouting "I am somebody" is only the first small step toward independence.

24 In the last 10 to 12 years, many of us missed the chance to grow intellectually and chased Superfly instead. Many of us spent more time on lottery and luck than looking for a job. Many of us did not use the opportunities we had. But it is time to cut that now. That backward trend goes against our own best traditions. Africa's great leaders, from Nkrumah to Machel, have all been learned men.

25 Preoccupation with symbolism has also made it hard for many of us to dintinguish service from servility.

26 As I travel around the country, I often eat in restaurants run by the Nation of Islam. One reason is that the waiters are the most courteous and prompt you will find anywhere. They enjoy serving black people: you will never find a Muslim waiter with an "attitude." Unfortunately, the same is not true of all blacks. I know of black contractors who have gone out of business because their black workers were not prompt or had negative attitudes. I know young black workers who talk with pride about going to work any hour they feel like it, taking a day off when they feel like it, wearing Apple Caps on the job, playing loud portable radios on the assembly line. They're rebelling against the system, they say: they're exhibiting their independence. (There are many white workers, it should be added, who do the same.) What they're really exhibiting is ignorance of a tradition of work in the black community that is one of our proudest legacies.

27 Slavery is over now, but you can't free a man who still has a slave mentality, just as you can't enslave a man who has a free spirit. We don't need to carry chips on our shoulders, fearing we are being treated in a servile manner. This does not mean we cannot be angry and loud and ornery on occasion, as all mortals have a way of being, but we should always try to use the power that derives from true courtesy.

28 The process of "internalizing" conditions that should instead be banished has another tragic effect.

29 According to black historian Lerone Bennett Jr., the first black people arrived in America in 1619. That means that black people have been in this land for 357 years. For 244 of those years we were slaves; for 113 years we have been technically free; but real freedom has only just come since the turn of the 20th century. Although welfare was set up mainly to aid poor whites, and two-thirds of the recipients today are white, our history of slavery and oppression, and the decades of forced dependency, do seem to have carried over into what I call the welfare mentality. There are black families that have not had an opportunity to be independent of a white-controlled system of one kind or another for as many generations back as they can account for. It is time for that syndrome to end. We cannot afford it any longer.

30 My own approach to the welfare situation is mixed. We need all the reforms the progressives argue for—guaranteed minimum income; an end to the humiliating spying and investigating by case workers; passage of the Humphrey-Hawkins full-employment bill now before Congress; an end to the

"make a dollar, take a dollar" regulations that penalize people on welfare who get part-time jobs; incentives to encourage people on welfare to go to school and improve themselves. On the other hand, as the job market expands, we must inspire people to get off that debilitating welfare system and say to them: "We need you to help us rebuild our communities." Then we must supply the tools for the urban poor to work with. We need jobs, for self-esteem, self-confidence and character—not just money.

[31] The greatest potential for self-development is to be found in the public schools in our cities. That is also where there is now the greatest potential for explosions. Predominantly black schools in most urban areas with high concentrations of black people—New York, Washington, Detroit, Chicago, Los Angeles, St. Louis, Boston—are largely out of control. Violence against students and teachers, perpetrated by students, is steadily and dangerously increasing. Drug abuse is an accepted fact of life; pushers operate freely in many schools, and police patrol the corridors. Discipline has broken down. In a number of New York schools, teachers complain that the places are run not by the principals but by the gangs. We need to change this because it is morally right, because it is necessary for our development, and because no one else is going to do it for us.

[32] The principals are not alone: Parents, teachers, superintendents, school boards have all failed to impose discipline and create a proper atmostphere for learning. And if our young people are not learning today, we will not have the doctors, engineers, lawyers, mechanics, nurses, clerks and accountants that we will need to manage the cities.

[33] A few years ago there was sizable movement for community control of the public schools. But the community-control movement never did seriously address the problem of control of the students by their parents. Many black students turned the movement into a cynical rebellion against any authority—black or white, sympathetic or unsympathetic, healthy or destructive. A people seeking independence cannot tolerate that.

[34] A related problem is the misconception, perpetrated on many parents, that a parent with little formal education is in a position to dictate on pedagogical matters to teachers and educators. Parents have something more fundamental to offer: motivation, love, care, discipline—and sometimes chastisement. Children cannot be allowed to play the game of "teach me if you can catch me." Children must be taught that they have a responsibility to learn as well as a right to an education. Busing is absolutely necessary, but without a will to learn, busing is irrelevant.

[35] With all that in mind, PUSH (People United to Save Humanity), the organization that I direct from Chicago, has begun a national program, "PUSH for Excellence," to address urban problems, beginning with the public schools. The models for this project are in Washington, Los Angeles and Chicago, but we have already found great interest in the approach in other cities.

[36] We have begun in Washington by stimulating high-school students to

organize a city-wide Council Against Drugs, Racism and Violence and for Discipline. A student conference will be held by this council in the spring. We have had large numbers of students turn out for planning meetings, and we have aroused substantial mass support at high-school assemblies. Parallel and sometimes coordinated meetings have been held with teachers, athletic coaches, superintendents and school boards. Mayor Walter Washington has shown great interest—as have Mayors Maynard Jackson of Atlanta, Coleman Young of Detroit, Richard Hatcher of Gary, Ind., and Thomas Bradley of Los Angeles for similar initiatives in their cities.

[37] Our program is simple. We want to get black men from the neighborhoods to replace the police in patrolling the school corridors and the street corners where the dope pushers operate. We want all parents to reserve the evening hours of 7 to 9 for their children's homework. We want student leaders and athletes to help identify and solve discipline problems before they get out of control. We want the black-oriented media to find ways to publicly reward achievers. We want the black disc jockeys, who reach more black kids than the school principals, to inform and inspire as well as entertain.

[38] A crucial element in our program is the black church. The church is the most stable influence in the black communities. It is the only place where all segments of the community come together, once a week. An estimated 11 to 13 million men, women and children are members of black churches. Historically, the black church has been involved in or behind every black movement of any significance. I have been involved with high schools in Washington, Chicago and Los Angeles that are working with churches, and if there is anything the experience has shown me, it is that black ministers still carry moral authority with our people, except for a hard-core few, and most people want moral authority.

[39] America is in the midst of a crisis, both in regard to its cities and in regard to its position in the world. Black Americans, inheritors of the role of the restless and disenfranchised minorities of the past who helped make America strong, have a historic opportunity to show that the cities can be saved. We can do so by stimulating change in the schools and the communities we control.

[40] Also by virtue of our special empathy for the colored peoples of the third world, and particularly Africa, black Americans can contribute to the foreign-policy debate by exposing the racism at the root of some of our Government's worst domestic and foreign blunders. It would be tragic if our nation lost its potential for true greatness by letting racist legacies deflect it from its proper course.

[41] Vital though this second task may be, it must, for the moment, take second place. The first and immediate task for American blacks is to rise up from the decadence in which we too often find ourselves in the cities, and to do so by the force of our will, our intellect, our energy and our faith in ourselves. It is a historic opportunity we cannot afford to miss.

ANALYTICAL READING

1. What problems concern Jackson? Have political changes occurred in the United States or elsewhere that allow for the possibility of new solutions to these problems?

2. Why are the old solutions inadequate? Have they failed completely?

3. What four specific failures does Jackson point out early in his essay? Which one do you think concerns him most?

4. What objections to his argument does Jackson note, and how does he refute them?

5. Why is Jackson confident about relying on moral authority and sound ethical conduct? Does he base his appeal on morality or group self-interest?

6. Why does Jackson look to the Third World as an example? Do these African countries face some of the problems of American blacks? What solutions does he find that might be adopted by American blacks?

7. What did Dr. Martin Luther King, Jr., mean by the statement that blacks should not "confuse symbolism with substance" (paragraph 23)? Does Jackson believe that black symbolism is of some importance? Why or why not? Does it present any problems? Explain.

8. How does he use cause and effect to discuss "slave mentality"?

9. Whom does Jackson blame for the problems in the schools? What solutions does he propose?

10. If, as Jackson states, the church in black communities is such a stabilizing force, why have the churches been so ineffective in helping to improve the circumstances of their members?

REFLECTING

Point: Jackson's article originally appeared in the *New York Times Magazine*. What audience is he addressing? Would he write differently for a general public periodical than for a black magazine, such as *Ebony?* What is his thesis and what do you suppose is his purpose?

Organization: After the first two introductory paragraphs, Jackson starts his argument with a statistic. Is this effective? Why or why not? How does he handle the four failures he mentions near the beginning of the essay? What is the persuasive advantage of (1) downplaying the currently favored solution to black problems—more federal money—early in the essay and (2) saving his specific proposals for near the end? Discuss the overall organization of the article.

Support: What examples does Jackson use? How pertinent and effective are they? What evidence is offered to show that his plan is practical? What part does his analogy to the Third World play in supporting his arguments?

Synthesis: To what extent is Jackson's argument applicable to whites? Why is it important to whites? From your personal experience in urban or other schools, do you agree with his assessment of many black students? How do you feel about discipline in the schools? Do you agree with his ideas about the role of parents in the schools?

Evaluation: Are you convinced that an educational problem exists? Do you accept Jackson's contention that present solutions are inadequate? Does he offer evidence that his solution is practical enough to appeal to teenagers, or do you believe it is too idealistic? Does Jackson write clearly and convincingly?

FROM READING TO WRITING

1. Write a letter to your high school principal arguing that the schools themselves, rather than black students, are at fault for learning failures. Use examples to support your contentions.

2. For a talk to a church group, write a proposition argument about the influence of the church today, either in the black or white community, or with black or white young people.

3. For a PTA presentation, write a proposition argument about the influence parents have on their children, either blaming them for failing to discipline and provide a model for their offspring or relieving them of the major blame for the faults of their children.

4. Write a letter to your mayor favoring, modifying, or repudiating Jackson's PUSH program.

THE NEED FOR GUN CONTROL LEGISLATION
Edward M. Kennedy

BIOGRAPHICAL SKETCH

Edward M. Kennedy, born in 1932, is the youngest son of Joseph P. and Rose Kennedy and the brother of the late President John Kennedy and Senator Robert Kennedy. He holds a B.A. from Harvard University (1954) and a law degree from the University of Virginia. Since 1962, he has been a Democratic Senator from Massachusetts, holding the position of majority whip from 1969 to 1971, and chairing the powerful Judiciary Committee until the Republican victory of 1980 forced him to relinquish the post. In 1980, he conducted an unsuccessful campaign for the presidential nomination.

PRE-READING

1. What do the title and the first paragraph indicate about the subject of the article and Kennedy's stand on it?

FROM *Current History*, July/August 1976, pp. 26, 27, 28, 31. Reprinted by permission of the publisher.

2. What do the last two paragraphs state about possible general solutions to the problem indicated in the title and opening paragraph?

¹ The case for effective firearms legislation can be logically and clearly explained on the basis of the daily tragedies reported in our nation's newspapers. Over 25,000 Americans die each year because of shooting accidents, suicides and murders caused by guns, primarily because too many Americans possess firearms. When guns are available, they have proved to be a far too easily accessible tool for the destruction of human life. Because of the senseless deaths and injuries caused by guns I strongly support the public demand for legislation to provide a uniform, nationwide system to control the abuse and misuse of firearms. A brief review of the conditions involving firearms in this country makes it clear that the proliferation of firearms, particularly handguns, must be halted.

² My interest in the need for effective firearms legislation goes back at least to 1963. I have introduced firearms bills in the Senate on several occasions. I offered gun control amendments to pending legislation on the Senate floor. Since I have been in the Senate, I have heard much of the testimony presented by nearly 200 witnesses, during more than 40 days of hearings on gun control. The issues never change. The arguments never vary. The statistics never recede. In 1963, handgun murders totaled 4,200. Eleven years later, in 1974, handguns were used to murder 11,000 Americans. The tragic toll of handgun suicides and accidental handgun deaths pushes the annual figures well beyond reasonable limits for a society that claims to respect life and personal security.

³ Gun manufacturers produce more guns each year, and American gun deaths increase right along with the output of firearms. Advocates for stronger controls are understandably alarmed by production figures showing that the annual output of handguns increased from 568,000 in 1968 to over 2.5 million in 1974.

⁴ Many experts insist that a gun, and particularly a handgun, is such a viciously lethal weapon that no citizen deserves to wield the awesome power of a gun. Our complex society requires a rethinking of the proper role of firearms in modern America. Our forefathers used firearms as an integral part of their struggle for survival. But today firearms are not appropriate for daily life in the United States.

⁵ The arguments used to oppose gun controls are old and hackneyed. The same lament has been used in one of the following forms time and time again:

First.   Gun controls cannot limit the supply of guns enough to reduce violence.
Second.   The Constitution protects the citizen's right to bear arms.
Third.   There is no need to ban guns because guns are not killers; people do the killing.
Fourth.   Criminals will always find a way to obtain guns. Thus, controls will only disarm those who obey the law.

Fifth.   Registration and licensing procedures are so cumbersome and inconvenient that they would create unfair burdens for legitimate gun owners.

[6] Opponents of effective gun controls believe that these objections are valid. But a thorough examination of each of these claims reveals that not one of them is well founded.

[7] First, can laws limit the supply of guns enough to reduce violent crime?

[8] Of course, such laws, properly enforced, can reduce the availability of handguns. In 1968, when importers anticipated the enactment of a new gun law, about 1.2 million handguns were rushed into the American market. In 1969, pistol and revolver imports fell to less than 350,000 and have not risen substantially above that total since then.

[9] Today, nearly three million new handguns enter the American market every year because handgun parts are still legally imported and because American manufacturers are still authorized to produce them. The legislation I have introduced would not only reduce the number of handguns assembled from imported parts, but it would also drastically curtail the output of domestically manufactured handguns.

[10] In June, 1934, President Franklin D. Roosevelt signed the National Firearms Act, which outlawed civilian ownership of machine guns. Perhaps this is the law that best illustrates the way in which legislation can effectively restrain the availability of firearms. Since enactment of that measure over 40 years ago, machine guns have been virtually eliminated in the United States. Obviously, a machine gun has no legitimately useful place in a civilized society. Easily concealed pistols and revolvers are also out of place in today's highly urbanized and complex society.

[11] Opponents of handgun control insist that it is impossible to prevent a criminal from obtaining a handgun. But if a criminal has to steal a gun before he can use a gun, he will use a gun much less frequently.

[12] An effectively enforced ban on the output of these deadly devices is the most direct way to reduce the deaths and injuries caused by guns.

[13] Second, it is claimed that the second amendment to the constitution protects the citizen's right to bear arms. Anyone who believes that "the right to bear arms" is guaranteed in the constitution has conveniently ignored the language of the second amendment, which provides that:

A well regulated militia being necessary to the security of a free state, the right of the people to keep and bear arms shall not be infringed.

[14] The United States Supreme Court has repeatedly said that this amendment has nothing to do with the right to personal ownership of guns but only with the right of a state to establish a militia.

[15] In perspective, the purpose of the second amendment emerges clearly. Debates in the first and second Congresses were naturally affected by the re-

cently won independence of the new government. And in Massachusetts it was bitterly recalled that the British Crown had quartered its troops but forbade the organization of a colonial militia. Congressional debates of early Congresses support the view that the second amendment was designed to protect and preserve the state militias. No mention was made of any individual's "right" to possess, carry, or use arms, and there is no indication of any concern with the need to do so. The new government was far more interested in maintaining state militias to defend the hard-won liberty. That fledgling government feared the establishment of a federal standing army as a threat to the basic authority of the several states.

[16] Indeed, in December, 1791, when the Bill of Rights was ratified, all but one of the 14 states of the Union adopted a constitution or a declaration of rights under which their people were governed.

[17] Rhode Island still operated under its charter of 1663, which authorized the colony to organize a militia. But there was no mention of any "right" to bear arms.

[18] Eight states—Delaware, New Jersey, Connecticut, Georgia, South Carolina, Maryland, New Hampshire, and New York—operated under constitutions that made no mention of any "right" to bear arms, although each authorized a state militia.

[19] Three states—Massachusetts, North Carolina, and Virginia—expressly recognized the right of the people to bear arms for the defense of the state.

[20] Two states—Pennsylvania and Vermont—included language in their constitutions which acknowledged that:

> The people have a right to bear arms for the defense of themselves and the State.

[21] However, that sentence was included in a paragraph that was concerned with the prohibition against a standing army and the guarantee of civilian control of the militia. Considering the history of the right to bear arms, reason defines the phrase "defense of themselves" as referring only to collective defense. That phrase did not include individual defense.

[22] It appears, therefore, that both the states and the Congress were preoccupied with the distrust of standing armies and the importance of preserving state militias. It was in this context that the second amendment was written and it is in this context that it has been interpreted by the courts.

[23] Third, a common refrain against firearm controls is that "guns do not kill, people do." This argument contends that people who use guns to commit crimes should be dealt with severely but that efforts to control weapons are not necessary. Yet, a glance at the statistics and common sense tell us that it is when guns are in hand that two-thirds of the people who kill other people do so; it was when guns were in hand that over 250,000 robberies were committed in 1973; it was when guns were in hand that one-fourth of the nation's 400,000 aggravated assaults were committed in 1973.

[24] Murder is usually committed in a moment of rage. Guns are quick and

easy to use. They are also deadly accurate, and they are all too often readily accessible. It is estimated that there are over 35 million handguns in private ownership in this country. Each year, 2.5 million new handguns are introduced into the marketplace for civilian use. Because handguns are available people use them.

[25] An attacker makes a deliberate choice of a gun over a knife. But because the fatality rate of knife wounds is about one–fifth that of gun wounds, it may be concluded that using a knife instead of a gun might cause 90 percent fewer deaths.

[26] Fourth, others argue that because criminals have guns, gun control will simply disarm law–abiding citizens. Lawless citizens, according to that argument, will not feel obliged to abide by gun restrictions.

[27] Perhaps there is truth in this argument. And for this reason, I am convinced that gun restrictions can be effective in limiting the wholesale misuse of firearms. Strict gun restrictions will aid in disarming anyone who fails to register his weapons or to obtain a license for ownership. Indeed, the enforcement of licensing and registration laws will isolate precisely those citizens who flaunt the law, because such legislation makes it a crime merely to possess an unregistered firearm. The commission of a crime with such a weapon compounds the wrong of any criminal action.

[28] Fifth. It may be that the greatest number who protest gun controls do so because the administrative requirements for registration are cumbersome and inconvenient. Since 1969, Congress has attempted several times to remove the 1968 gun control law's record–keeping requirements with regard to sales of .22 caliber ammunition.

[29] I have repeatedly objected to any move that would eliminate the requirement that sales of such ammunition must be recorded. Between 6 billion and 7 billion rounds of ammunition are produced in this country each year. At least 85 percent of those bullets are .22 caliber. Records maintained to control the sale of ammunition may be useful in restricting access to those gun owners who intend to use their weapons for legitimate purposes.

[30] I believe that any measure that will substantially reduce the misuse of firearms will at the same time enhance whatever pleasures may be derived from the so–called recreational pursuits of gun ownership.

[31] Among the nations of the world, the United States stands in the bloodiest pool of deaths by gunfire. Americans are not only ranked No. 1, but No. 2 lags so far behind that a tally of gun deaths in all civilized nations probably would not equal the excessive fusillade Americans train on their fellow citizens.

[32] In 1973, the total gun murder rate in the United States was 6.2 per 100,000 population. Thus, even the United States handgun murder rate was 62 times the rate in Scotland, the Netherlands, and Great Britain and Japan, 31 times the rate in Denmark, France, Sweden, and Switzerland, and 20 times the rate in New Zealand, Germany and Italy. (See Table 1.)

Table I: Total Number of Homicides and Rate per 100,000 Population

Country (year is the latest for which figures are available)	Total Homicide		Gun Homicide	
	Number	Rate	Number	Rate
United States, 1973	19,510	7.5	11,249	6.2
Australia, 1970	190	1.5	71	.6
Denmark, 1971	48	1.0	12	.2
England and Wales, 1972	384	.8	41	.1
France, 1970	373	.7	124	.2
German Federal Republic, 1971	802	1.3	203	.3
Ireland, 1971	21	.7	—	—
Italy, 1970	442	.8	239	.4
Japan, 1971	1,380	1.3	20	.0
Netherlands, 1972	72	.5	13	.1
New Zealand, 1971	25	.9	8	.3
Scotland, 1972	73	1.4	3	.1
Sweden, 1971	76	.9	19	.2
Switzerland, 1972	57	.9	12	.2

Source: International Statistical Classification of Diseases, Injuries and Causes of Death (Geneva: World Health Organization, 1971, 1972, 1973, 1974).

[33] Among civilized societies that have acted to control guns the United States is a glaring exception. In Italy, West Germany, France, Britain, and the Soviet Union, "the right to bear arms" is a strictly regulated privilege. In Japan, private gun ownership is all but prohibited. Five European countries totally prohibit the private possession of handguns. A 1968 State Department survey of 102 of its diplomatic posts revealed that 29 European countries require either a license to carry a firearm or registration of the ownership or sale of each privately owned firearm, or both.

[34] Legislation to control the violence caused by firearms is essential in a national campaign to reduce handgun deaths. At the same time, public education and ongoing research in the relationship between firearms and violence is also important.

[35] The gun mystique fascinates and excites the imagination. Films, novels and dramatic presentations that depict gun violence are enjoyed and readily understood by all members of our society. The role of the handgun in American society has been distorted. A complete reform of the role of the handgun is needed. It is clearly not a weapon of entertainment, and only rarely is it used for sporting purposes. Many Americans insist that a handgun provides comfort and security in a menacing environment where assailants threaten the weak, the helpless, and the lonely. Yet the proliferation of handguns seems to involve a vicious cycle that sees more and more people buying guns to protect themselves from more and more people who have guns.

[36] I am convinced that this national evil of handgun roulette must be interrupted before the two–gun family becomes as common as the two–car family.

[37] In April, 1976, the House of Representatives' Subcommittee on Crime

reported a bill to begin to establish controls on the use of handguns. If this measure is enacted, it will establish the foundation for a full system of controls that can stem the unbridled flow of firearms violence.

[38] From other sources, it has also been recommended that handgun production quotas must be imposed upon the nation's firearms producers. Because the American people have repeatedly expressed the demand for an end to firearms violence, I look forward to the enactment of effective and enforceable controls on the use of firearms.

Sources

Bakal, Carl. *The Right to Bear Arms*. New York: McGraw–Hill, 1966.

Newton, George D. and Franklin Zimring. *Firearms and Violence in American Life—Staff Report to the National Committee on the Causes and Prevention of Violence*. Washington, D.C.: U.S. Government Printing Office, 1968.

Senate Subcommittee on Juvenile Delinquency. "Hearing on the Saturday Night Special." Washington, D.C.: U.S. Government Printing Office, 1971.

Sherrill, Robert. *Saturday Night Special*. New York: Charterhouse Books, 1973.

ANALYTICAL READING

1. What is the effect of Kennedy's mention in paragraph 2 of his personal involvement in gun control legislation?

2. Is the machine gun analogy in paragraph 10 valid? Why or why not?

3. Are the conclusions Kennedy bases on the figures in Table 1 acceptable? How would you reply to the counter argument that the United States has a much greater population than all the other countries cited, so it inevitably has more handgun murders?

4. How does Kennedy refute the argument that the Constitution guarantees "the right to bear arms"?

5. Consider the following analogy: cars do not kill, people do; thus we do not need safer cars and highways, but better education for drivers. Similarly, guns do not kill, people do; hence we need better education for people. Do you agree? Why or why not?

6. How does Kennedy reply to the slogan, "When guns are outlawed, only outlaws will have guns"?

7. Does Kennedy respond directly, indirectly, or not at all to the argument that gun controls would be "cumbersome and inconvenient"? Explain.

8. Why does Kennedy refer to restrictive policies in other countries? Aren't Americans different by tradition, upbringing, and environment?

9. What does Kennedy find wrong with the fact that more and more people are buying guns to protect themselves from criminals? Do you agree or disagree? Discuss.

10. Is there a "gun mystique" in the United States (paragraph 35)? What does this phrase mean, and how do you feel about this theory?

REFLECTING

Point: Write a statement about the purpose of Kennedy's article, but do not try to incorporate each of the five arguments he refutes. Instead, summarize them in some way and show what the article contains besides these refutations. What single sentence states the thesis proposition?

Organization: What is the function of the first four paragraphs? What other major divisions do you find in the article? Explain the general purpose of each and discuss the effectiveness of this organization. Discuss the short paragraphs, pointing out where some could have been combined and indicating why Kennedy perhaps did not combine them.

Support: What does Table 1 contribute to the argument? Does Kennedy let the facts speak for themselves, or does he discuss the information given in the table? Do you think that Kennedy's argument would have been aided by a direct reference to the assassination of his two brothers? Why do you suppose he did not refer to them? Describe the voice and tone used. What is the effect of the concession Kennedy makes at the beginning of paragraph 27? Are the references to "handgun roulette" and "the two-gun family" (paragraph 36) in keeping with the style of the article? Are they effective or not?

Synthesis: Do you or your family or friends have any firearms or handguns? What are your feelings about the article? Does your church take a position on handguns? Should it? Do you feel comfortable or more secure with a gun in the house? Explain. Polls show that more than 70 percent of Americans favor a registration and licensing law similar to the ones for automobiles. Why do you think that little has been done to comply with the wishes of the majority of Americans?

Evaluation: How thorough is Kennedy in treating his subject? Has he failed to consider all the objections, and has he adequately refuted the ones he does mention? Has he conveyed a sense of the seriousness of the problem? Does the need for a solution appear to be urgent? Do his proposed solutions seem to be practical? Would they raise other serious problems? Has he presented his argument clearly, logically, and effectively? Why or why not?

FROM READING TO WRITING

1. Since this article was published, singer John Lennon has been killed, President Ronald Reagan and Pope John Paul were seriously wounded in assassination attempts. Taking these events into account, write a letter to your minister or rabbi, pointing out that he or she should speak out in favor of or against gun control. Be sure to include counterarguments.

2. Write a reply to Kennedy's argument, opposing gun control. Use logical argument to refute Kennedy's arguments.

3. As of December 8, 1976, handgun sales were prohibited in San Francisco. Write a letter to your community newspaper, urging that your city council and state

legislature either enact or reject a similar law. You may wish to do some research on how effective the law has been in deterring handgun crimes. Use Kennedy's documentation techniques to incorporate the research into your argument.

THE DRAFT: WHY THE COUNTRY NEEDS IT

James Fallows

BIOGRAPHICAL SKETCH

James Fallows, who was born in Phildelphia in 1949, graduated with a BA degree from Harvard, where he was elected to Phi Beta Kappa and won a coveted award for outstanding undergraduate writing. Later, he attended Oxford University as a Rhodes scholar, receiving a diploma in economic development. After writing for the Washington Monthly *and the* Texas Monthly, *he became Washington editor of the* Atlantic Monthly. *A former speech writer for President Carter, he has written* The Water Lords, *coauthored* Who Runs Congress?, *and recently received acclaim for his* National Defense.

PRE-READING

1. Can the title be restated as a proposition? What side do you expect the writer to take?

2. How does the writer use the letter and the opening paragraph to establish his point of view?

> I am more than angry. I did not give birth to my one and only son to have him snatched away from me 18 years later. My child has been loved and cared for and taught right from wrong and *will not* be fed into any egomaniac's war machine.
>
> Our 18– to 25–year–olds have not brought this world to its present sorry state. Men over the age of 35, down through the centuries, have brought us here, and we women have been in silent accord.
>
> Well, this is one woman, one mother, who says *no.* I did not go through the magnificent agony of childbirth to have that glorious young life snuffed out.
>
> Until the presidents, premiers, supreme rulers, politburos, senators and congressmen of the world are ready to physically, as opposed to verbally, lead the world into combat, they can bloody well forget my child.

Unite mothers! Don't throw your sons and daughters away. Sometime, somewhere, women have just got to say *no*.

No. No. No. No. No. Never my child.

—Louise M. Saylor

(Letter published in the Washington *Post*, January 28, 1980.)

¹ Nor my child, Mrs. Saylor. Nor either of my mother's sons when, ten years ago, both were classified 1–A. But *whose*, then? As our statesmen talk again of resisting aggression and demonstrating our will—as there is talk, that is, of sending someone's sons (or daughters) to bear arms overseas—the only fair and decent answer to that question lies in a return to the draft.

² I am speaking here not of the health of the military but of the character of the society the military defers to. The circumstances in which that society will choose to go to war, the way its wars will be fought, and its success in absorbing the consequent suffering depends on its answer to the question Whose sons will go?

³ History rarely offers itself in lessons clear enough to be deciphered at a time when their message still applies. But of all the hackneyed "lessons" of Vietnam one still applies with no reservations: that we wound ourselves gravely if we flinch from honest answers about who will serve. During the five or six years of the heaviest draft calls for Vietnam, there was the starkest class division in American military service since the days of purchased draft deferments in the Civil War. Good intentions lay at the root of many of these inequities. The college–student deferment, the various "hardship" exemptions, Robert McNamara's plan to give "disadvantaged" youngsters a chance to better themselves in the military, even General Hershey's intelligence test to determine who could remain in school—all were designed to allot American talent in the most productive way. The intent was to distinguish those who could best serve the nation with their minds from those who should offer their stout hearts and strong backs. The effect was to place the poor and the black in the trenches (and later in the coffins and the rehabilitation wards), and their "betters" in colleges or elsewhere far from the sounds of war. I speak as one who took full advantage of the college–student deferment and later exploited the loopholes in the physical qualification standards that, for college students armed with a doctor's letter and advice from the campus draft counseling center, could so easily be parlayed into the "unfit for service" designation known as 1–Y. Ask anyone who went to college in those days how many of his classmates saw combat in Vietnam. Of my 1200 classmates at Harvard, I know of only two, one of them a veteran who joined the class late. See how this compares with the Memorial Roll from a public high school in a big city or a West Virginia hill town.

⁴ For all the talk about conflict between "young" and "old" that the war caused, the lasting breach was among the young. To those who opposed the

war, the ones who served were, first, animals and killers; then "suckers" who were trapped by the system, deserving pity but no respect; and finally invisible men. Their courage, discipline, and sacrifice counted for less than their collective taint for being associated with a losing war. Most veterans knew the honor they had earned, even as they knew better than anyone else the horror of the war. They came to resent being made to suppress those feelings by students who chose not to join them and who, having escaped the war without pain, now prefer to put the whole episode in the past. Perhaps no one traversed that era without pain, but pain of the psychic variety left arms, legs, life intact and did not impede progress in one's career. For people of my generation—I speak in the narrow sense of males between the ages of twenty-eight and thirty-six or thirty-seven—this wound will never fully heal. If you doubt that, sit two thirty-two-year-olds down together, one who served in Vietnam and one who did not, and ask them to talk about those years.

⁵ At least there was theoretical consistency between what the students of those days recommended for others and what they did themselves. Their point was that no one should go to war, starting with them.

⁶ I hear little of that tone in the reaction to President Carter's muted call for resumption of draft registration. Within a week of his request in the State of the Union address, I spent time at two small colleges. At both, the sequence of questions was the same. Why is our defense so weak? When will we show the Russians our strength? *Isn't it terrible about the draft?*

⁷ Senator Kennedy, who so often decried the unfairness of the draft during Vietnam, won cheers from his college audience for his opposition to draft registration, in the same speech in which he suggested beefing up our military presence in the Persian Gulf. Kennedy did go on to argue that we should not shed blood for oil, which is more than most anti-draft groups have done to date. It would have been reassuring to hear the students say that they oppose registration *because* they oppose a military showdown in the Persian Gulf. Instead many simply say, We don't want to go. I sense that they—perhaps all of us—have come to take for granted a truth so painful that few could bear to face it during Vietnam: that there will be another class of people to do the dirty work. After seven years of the volunteer Army, we have grown accustomed to having suckers on hand.

⁸ That the volunteer Army is another class can hardly be denied. The Vietnam draft was unfair racially, economically, educationally. By every one of those measures, the volunteer Army is less representative still. Libertarians argue that military service should be a matter of choice, but the plain fact is that service in the volunteer force is too frequently dictated by economics. Army enlisted ranks E1 through E4—the privates and corporals, the cannon fodder, the ones who will fight and die—are 36 percent black now. By the Army's own projections, they will be 42 percent black in three years. When other "minorities" are taken into account, we will have, for the first time, an army whose fighting members are mainly "non-majority," or, more bluntly, a black and brown army defending a mainly white nation. The military has been

an avenue of opportunity for many young blacks. They may well be first–class fighting men. They do not represent the nation.

[9] Such a selective bearing of the burden has destructive spiritual effects in a nation based on the democratic creed. But its practical implications can be quite as grave. The effect of a fair, representative draft is to hold the public hostage to the consequences of its decisions, much as children's presence in the public schools focuses parents' attention on the quality of the schools. If citizens are willing to countenance a decision that means that *someone's* child may die, they may contemplate more deeply if there is the possibility that the child will be theirs. Indeed, I would like to extend this principle even further. Young men of nineteen are rightly suspicious of the congressmen and columnists who urge them to the fore. I wish there were a practical way to resurrect the provisions of the amended Selective Service Act of 1940, which raised the draft age to forty–four. Such a gesture might symbolize the desire to offset the historic injustice of the Vietnam draft, as well as suggest the possibility that, when a bellicose columnist recommends dispatching American forces to Pakistan, he might also realize that he could end up as a gunner in a tank.

[10] Perhaps the absence of a World War II–scale peril makes such a proposal unrealistic; still, the columnist or congressman should have to contemplate the possibility that his son would be there, in trench or tank. Under the volunteer Army that possibility will not arise, and the lack of such a prospect can affect behavior deeply. Recall how, during Vietnam, protest grew more broad–based and respectable when the graduate school deferment was eliminated in 1968. For many families in positions of influence, the war was no longer a question of someone else's son. How much earlier would the war have ended had college students been vulnerable from the start?

[11] Those newly concerned families were no better and no worse than other people at other times; they were responding to a normal human instinct, of the sort our political system is designed to channel toward constructive ends. It was an instinct that Richard Nixon and Henry Kissinger understood very well, as they deliberately shifted the burden of the war off draftees and finally off Americans, to free their hands to pursue their chosen course. Recall how fast protest ebbed with the coming of the volunteer Army and "Vietnamization" in the early 1970's. For this reason, the likes of Nixon and Kissinger might regard a return to the draft as a step in the wrong direction, for it would sap the resolve necessary for a strong foreign policy and introduce the weakening element of domestic dissent. At times leaders must take actions that seem heartless and unfair, and that an informed public would probably not approve. Winston Churchill let Coventry be bombed, because to sound the air–raid sirens and save its citizens would have tipped off the Germans that Britain had broken their code. But in the long run, a nation cannot sustain a policy whose consequences the public is not willing to bear. If it decides not to pay the price to defend itself, it will be defenseless. That is the risk of democracy.

[12] What kind of draft? More than anything else, a *fair* one, with as few holes as possible to wriggle through. "Fairness" does not mean that everyone

need serve. This year 4.3 million people will turn eighteen, 2.2 million women and 2.1 million men. For the last few years, the military has been taking 400,000 people annually into the volunteer Army—or, in raw figures, only one in ten of the total available pool. Using today's mental and physical standards, the military knocks off 30 percent of the manpower pool as unqualified, and it excludes women from combat positions. When these calculations are combined with the diminishing number of young men—only 1.6 million men will turn eighteen in 1993—the military projects that it will need to attract one of every three "qualified and available men" by the end of the 1980's.

[13] Read another way, this means that a draft need affect *no more* than one in three—and probably far fewer. To make the draft seem—and be—fair, the pool of potential draftees should be as large as possible, even if only a few will eventually be picked. Those who are "disabled" in the common meaning of that term—the blind, paraplegics—should be excluded, but not the asthmatics and trick-back cases who are perfectly capable of performing non-combat military jobs. The military's physical requirements now assume that nearly all men must theoretically be fit for combat, even though only 14 percent of all male soldiers hold combat jobs. The proportion of draftees destined for combat would probably be higher, since those are the positions now most understrength; if actual fighting should begin it would be higher still. But combat will never represent the preponderance of military positions, and its requirements should not blindly dictate who is eligible for the draft. Instead, everyone without serious handicap should be eligible for selection by lottery—men and women, students and non-students. Once the lottery had determined *who* would serve, assignments based on physical classifications could determine where and how.

[15] The question of women's service is the most emotionally troubling aspect of this generally emotional issue, but the progress of domestic politics over the last ten years suggests that the answer is clear. If any sexual distinctions that would deny a woman her place as a construction worker or a telephone pole climber have been forbidden by legislators and courts, what possible distinction can spare women the obligation to perform similar functions in military construction units or the Signal Corps? If women are drafted, they have an ironclad case for passage of the Equal Rights Amendment. If they are not, their claim for equal treatment elsewhere becomes less compelling. At the same time, it is troubling to think of women in combat, or of mothers being drafted, and a sensible draft law would have to recognize such exceptions.

[16] There should be no educational deferments except for students still in high school, and possibly in two other cases. One would be for college students who enroll in ROTC; like their counterparts in the service academies, they would be exchanging four years of protected education for a longer tour of duty as an officer after graduation. The other exception might be for doctors, possessors of a skill the military needs but cannot sensibly produce on its own. If potential doctors wanted to be spared all eligibility for the draft, they could enter a program like the Navy's V–12 during World War II, in which they

could take a speeded–up college course and receive a publicly subsidized medical education, after which they would owe several years' service as military doctors. Except in the most far–fetched situations, "hardship" cases should be taken care of by compensation rather than by exemption. If these are permitted, they become an invitation to abuse: who can forget George Hamilton pleading hardship as his mother's sole supporting son? Instead, the government should offset hardship with support payments to the needy dependents.

[17] One resists the idea of lottery, because it adds to the system the very element of caprice and unfairness it is so important to remove. But since only a fraction of those eligible to serve are actually required, there seems no other equitable way to distribute the burden. With a well–established lottery, every male and female might know at age eighteen whether he or she was near the top of the list and very likely to be called, or near the bottom and almost certainly protected. How far the draft calls went down the list would depend on how many people volunteered and how many more were needed.

[18] None of these concerns and prescriptions would matter if the volunteer Army were what it so often seemed in the last few years—a stand–in, a symbol, designed to keep the machinery running and the troops in place, not to be sent into action for any cause less urgent than absolute survival. But now we hear from every quarter that the next decade will be a time of testing, that our will and our strategy and our manpower will be on the line. The nature of this challenge, and the style of our response, are what we should be thinking and talking about now. Our discussions will never be honest, nor our decisions just, as long as we count on "suckers" to do the job.

ANALYTICAL READING

1. What reasons does Fallows give for the "lasting breach" (paragraph 4) among those who were young during the Vietnam war?

2. Why does he refer to the volunteers in the army as "suckers" (paragraph 4)? What do you think his argumentative purpose is in the use of the term?

3. What shortcomings does he list for the volunteer army system?

4. Fallows often uses *if . . . then* sentences. Examine a few to see if they involve syllogistic arguments.

5. What is his definition of a "fair draft"?

6. How does he think the draft should be applied? What persuasive advantage is gained from his long discussion?

7. How does the closing paragraph enhance his argument?

REFLECTING

Point: What sentence best states Fallows' proposition? Where in the article does it appear?

Organization: List his main arguments. What counterproposals does he refute?

Support: How does Fallows use historical events to support his proposition? Does he appeal to the public interest? To the reader's sense of decency and fairness?

Synthesis: Do recent movies about the Vietnam conflict help to verify his points about the societal problems that the inequitable deferments have caused? What about the reaction of the Vietnam veterans to the welcome of the Iranian hostages? How do you feel about women being drafted?

Evaluation: Is the writer's argument convincing? If so, what devices did he use that made it so? Do you think his argument that a draft would act as a deterrent to war is a valid one? Why or why not?

FROM READING TO WRITING

1. For readers of *The Atlantic,* write a paper that argues for one of the possibilities Fallows rejects: volunteer army, educational deferments, draft by lottery. In your paper, refute possible counterarguments or counterproposals.

2. Fallows' argument that drafting older people would serve as a war deterrent could be treated satirically. For your college newspaper, write a piece using the format in the Berry article (page 310). You might wish to include the material in the fourth paragraph of the quoted letter at the beginning of Fallows' essay.

3. Fallows could have used the problem-solution organization suggested on page 279 in his argument. Using his material and points, construct an organizational scheme for such a paper and write it as a letter to student activists who oppose the draft.

Problem–Solution Argument: Informal

IRRATIONAL BEHAVIOR OR EVANGELICAL ZEAL?

Michael Mewshaw

BIOGRAPHICAL SKETCH

Michael Mewshaw was born in Washington, D.C., in 1943 and holds a B.A. from the University of Maryland and a Ph.D. from the University of Virginia. Besides his four novels—Man in Motion (1970), Walking Slow (1972), The Toll (1972), and Earthly Bread (1976)—he has published many articles and reviews. Earthly Bread is about a young Catholic priest who helps to "deprogram" a "Jesus freak"; Mewshaw's research for this novel stimulated his interest in such "deprogramming."

PRE-READING

1. What do the title and the biographical sketch prepare you for?

2. When the first paragraph provides inadequate clues about an article, as this one does, then you should read on until you gain more insight into the subject. How far do you have to read before you feel reasonably confident that you know the subject of this essay?

3. The title poses an either-or question. From skimming the last paragraph, how do you suppose the author would answer the question?

[1] As the radio ads have announced—to the accompaniment of spooky music, shrieks, and the burble of green pea soup—*The Exorcist* is back. But one wonders whether it ever went away. Judging by the recent spate of books and movies dealing with demonic possession, it seems to have spawned clones and provided a self-replenishing resource for publishing and film companies.

[2] This phenomenon, odd as it is, would deserve no more than a footnote in a pop-culture thesis if it weren't for the fact that grotesque parodies of

FROM *The Chronicle of Higher Education*, 18 October 1976, p. 32. Copyright © 1976 by Editorial Projects for Education, Inc. Reprinted by permission of the author and *The Chronicle of Higher Education*.

exorcism are performed whenever pentecostal Christians, Moon people, and Hare Krishna chanters are kidnapped, confined for days with little food and sleep, and badgered into recanting their beliefs.

3 Euphemistically called "deprogramming," the process amounts to little more than a methodical and sometimes violent attempt to exorcise not Satan, but unpopular, misunderstood, or inarticulate notions about God.

4 During the last four years as I researched, wrote, and published a novel concerning this subject, I ran into very few people—except for direct participants—who had much substantive knowledge about deprogramming. Although most victims of these systematized efforts at brainwashing are college or graduate students, or members of the free-floating communities that congregate around universities, my academic colleagues were either oblivious to the situation or else felt that evangelical Christianity wasn't intellectually respectable and therefore its *dévotés* deserved whatever they got. At the start, I myself was ill-informed, and, though a practicing Catholic, I scarcely qualified as a pentecostal or charismatic believer. Yet driven by curiosity and convinced of the basic decency of the "born-again" Christians in my classes, I decided to take a closer look at the problem.

5 What I learned surprised and dismayed me. Much as I might disagree with the theology of certain evangelical groups, they struck me as no more deluded or neurotic than others on campus. Yet from parents I repeatedly heard the same justification of deprogrammings. They claimed their children were misguided, distressingly inclined to give away money, incapable of making mature decisions, maybe even demented. In cases where the "children" turned out to be college graduates in their 20's and 30's and sometimes mothers and fathers themselves, the charges grew more dramatic. The "kids," I was told, had been abducted, hypnotized, or—shades of Patty Hearst—forced into joining a cult which then held them captive against their will.

6 Just recently a distraught mother confronted me and tearfully asked what I would do if my own son had joined a religious group and would no longer communicate with me. Wouldn't I consider kidnapping him and trying to talk sense to him? It was only after I had sympathized with her that she revealed that her son was 26, a Phi Beta Kappa graduate of Notre Dame, and a former student at the Sorbonne. I suggested that since he sounded like a gifted, responsible boy she should perhaps try to understand and accept his decision. Our conversation was then broken off by hysterical sobs and her accusation that I didn't know what I was talking about.

7 The woman may have been right; I may be wrong. But I must say I never encountered any of the irrational, robot-like zealots I heard about, and, to my knowledge, none of the sensational allegations against unorthodox religious groups has ever stood up in court.

8 Gradually I've come to believe the problem may be semantic as much as anything else. For example, what parents call propaganda and coercion the religious groups invariably call evangelical zeal. After all, don't Catholics and Protestants also send out missionaries? What the parents see as irrational behavior the groups say is ritualized devotion. Don't most religions encourage

ideas and rites that strike outsiders as bizarre, if not insane? What the parents interpret as extortion or embezzlement the groups view as voluntary charity. Don't all organized churches accept—and in some instances demand—contributions?

⁹ Yet, while parents have failed to prove their charges, they have managed to convince a crucial segment of the media and the public that their children are in danger. Thus young people continue to be captured, imprisoned, and physically and emotionally abused because of their beliefs. Civil libertarians have shown no great eagerness to get involved, and some local police forces have admitted that they actually encouraged and assisted deprogrammers. There have been a few cuts and bruises, broken bones, and chipped teeth. Fortunately no one has been killed or maimed so far, but substantial damage has been done to our constitutional guarantees of religious freedom.

¹⁰ All of this prompts questions about America's commitment to the First Amendment and to human rights in general. While the country retains its capacity for selective indignation, it often appears to relinquish one old liberty for each new one it wins. For instance, recent court rulings have affirmed the right of adolescent girls, regardless of age, to undergo abortions without parental approval. Yet both by their decisions and by their refusal to hear certain cases, the courts have suggested that the same young girl who has gained complete control over her body might have to accept familial interference with her soul. And this interference won't necessarily end when she reaches 21. Even marriage offers no sanctuary, for many people have paid to have their spouses kidnapped and deprogrammed.

¹¹ Frequently I have been asked questions by students and young people who have been harassed because of their theology, their dress, and their behavior. Why have "born-again" Christians been singled out? Why aren't dope dealers or pornographers kidnapped and deprogrammed? How would the public respond if a Protestant pulled his son out of a seminary and kept him incommunicado until he gave up his vocation? What would the Vatican do if a Catholic dragged his daughter from a convent? How would the Black Muslims react if their congregation was picked off one by one? Would Jews consider it just if Reform members grabbed Orthodox believers and put them through a crude form of behavior modification?

¹² These questions, I think, deserve careful consideration—and honest answers. As a country committed to the separation of church and state and to freedom of worship, we may not always approve of what others believe or the way they express their beliefs, but we have no moral or legal right to intervene except in the most extreme circumstances. It would be a shame . . . if America was not mature and wise enough to insist upon that religious liberty that was one of its founding principles and is still one of its greatest claims to international respect.

ANALYTICAL READING

1. What was Mewshaw's attitude before he began research for his novel, and how did other professors feel about deprogramming?

2. Why do you suppose parents are so upset about their children joining evangelical religious groups?

3. What does the author mean when he says that "the problem may be semantic" (paragraph 8)?

4. According to the author, how do many people feel about deprogramming? Do you agree with his appraisal?

5. What is so ironic about the rights that courts have granted and denied to young people?

6. Does Mewshaw believe in the absolute right of religious freedom, or does he suggest that some restriction might be placed upon it? If so, what kind of restriction might be imposed and why?

REFLECTING

Point: What is the main idea in Mewshaw's essay? Where do you find it best expressed? What do you suppose was his purpose in writing the essay?

Organization: In what part of the essay does the author discuss the problem? What solution does he suggest? Write an outline of his problem–solution organization.

Support: Does Mewshaw load his argument by associating exorcism with deprogramming, or is this a sound analogy? Does the author's voice reveal him to be a fair, reasonable, and sympathetic person? Why or why not? Do you feel that the abortion and deprogramming analogy in paragraph 10 adds valid support? What about the analogies implied in the rhetorical questions in paragraph 11? Does Mewshaw deal with the rights of parents or of spouses?

Synthesis: What do you know personally of this problem? Should young people over twenty-one have the right to join any religious cult? Since in many states young people can drive at sixteen, vote at eighteen, and buy liquor at twenty-one, might it not be wise to give them unlimited religious freedom, which may call for greater emotional and intellectual maturity, at twenty-five?

Evaluation: Does Mewshaw appear to have treated the problem fairly, fully, and logically? Could it be argued that his research experiences were not typical? How convincing would he be to parents? What audience do you think he is writing to? How convincing do you think he would be with this audience? Why?

FROM READING TO WRITING

1. Write a letter to the editor of a local newspaper, arguing for the freedom of young people to make their own religious choices.

2. Write for or against a California plan (struck down by a higher court) that allowed parents to have custody for a thirty-day period of their children, who were followers of the Reverend Sun Myung Moon. (It might interest you to know that of five, who ranged in age from twenty-one to twenty-five, three chose to return to their parents, two returned to Moon's Unification Church.)

3. In a letter to *Newsweek,* Carol Mays, Director of Christian Education in Blacksburg, Va., commented that it is fortunate Mary did not have Jesus deprogrammed for leaving a promising career as a carpenter and following his conscience. Write a reply letter to *Newsweek,* arguing for or against Ms. Mays' statement.

STRIKE OUT LITTLE LEAGUE
Robin Roberts

BIOGRAPHICAL SKETCH

Robin Roberts was born in 1926 in Springfield, Illinois. He graduated from Michigan State, where he excelled in baseball and basketball. Although he pitched for several major league teams, he is best known for his many years with the Philadelphia Phillies, who were then mainly a second division club. Despite that fact, he was a twenty-game winner for five consecutive years (1950–1955). Elected to the Hall of Fame in 1976, he was called "one of the greatest pitchers in National League history." Now living in Philadelphia, he is active in coaching young players and working with school boards.

PRE-READING

1. From the title, what do you think the author's views are about Little League?

2. What word in the opening paragraph particularly expresses his attitude?

3. To what extent does paragraph 15 seem to summarize the article?

[1] In 1939, Little League baseball was organized by Bert and George Bebble and Carl Stotz of Williamsport, Pa. What they had in mind in organizing this kids' baseball program, I'll never know. But I'm sure they never visualized the monster it would grow into.

[2] At least 25,000 teams, in about 5,000 leagues, compete for a chance to go to the Little League World Series in Williamsport each summer. These leagues are in more than fifteen countries, although recently the Little League organization has voted to restrict the competition to teams in the United States. If you judge the success of a program by the number of participants, it would appear that Little League has been a tremendous success. More than 600,000 boys from 8 to 12 are involved. But I say Little League is wrong—and I'll try to explain why.

[3] If I told you and your family that I want you to help me with a project from the middle of May until the end of July, one that would totally disrupt your dinner schedule and pay nothing, you would probably tell me to get lost.

That's what Little League does. Mothers or fathers or both spend four or five nights a week taking children to Little League, watching the game, coming home around 8 or 8:30 and sitting down to a late dinner.

⁴ These games are played at this hour because the adults are running the programs and this is the only time they have available. These same adults are in most cases unqualified as instructors and do not have the emotional stability to work with children of this age. The dedication and sincerity of these instructors cannot be questioned, but the purpose of this dedication should be. Youngsters eligible for Little League are of the age when their concentration lasts, at most, for five seconds—and without sustained concentration organized athletic programs are a farce.

⁵ Most instructors will never understand this. As a result there is a lot of pressure on these young people to do something that is unnatural for their age—so there will always be hollering and tremendous disappointment for most of these players. For acting their age, they are made to feel incompetent. This is a basic fault of Little League.

⁶ If you watch a Little League game, in most cases the pitchers are the most mature. They throw harder, and if they throw strikes very few batters can hit the ball. Consequently, it makes good baseball sense for most hitters to take the pitch. Don't swing. Hope for a walk. That could be a player's instruction for four years. The fun is in hitting the ball; the coach says don't swing. That may be sound baseball, but it does nothing to help a young player develop his hitting. What would seem like a basic training ground for baseball often turns out to be a program of negative thoughts that only retards a young player.

⁷ I believe more good young athletes are turned off by the pressure of organized Little League than are helped. Little Leagues have no value as a training ground for baseball fundamentals. The instruction at that age, under the pressure of an organized league program, creates more doubt and eliminates the naturalness that is most important.

⁸ If I'm going to criticize such a popular program as Little League, I'd better have some thoughts on what changes I would like to see.

⁹ First of all, I wouldn't start any programs until the school year is over. Any young student has enough of a schedule during the school year to keep busy.

¹⁰ These programs should be played in the afternoon—with a softball. Kids have a natural fear of a baseball; it hurts when it hits you. A softball is bigger, easier to see and easier to hit. You get to run the bases more and there isn't as much danger of injury if one gets hit with the ball. Boys and girls could play together. Different teams would be chosen every day. The instructors would be young adults home from college, or high-school graduates. The instructor could be the pitcher and the umpire at the same time. These programs could be run on public playgrounds or in schoolyards.

¹¹ I guarantee that their dinner would be at the same time every night. The fathers could come home after work and relax; most of all, the kids would have

a good time playing ball in a program in which hitting the ball and running the bases are the big things.

[12] When you start talking about young people playing baseball at 13 to 15, you may have something. Organize them a little, but be careful; they are still young. But from 16 and on, work them really hard. Discipline them, organize the leagues, strive to win championships, travel all over. Give this age all the time and attention you can.

[13] I believe Little League has done just the opposite. We've worked hard with the 8- to 12-year-olds. We overorganize them, put them under pressure they can't handle and make playing baseball seem important. When our young people reach 16 they would appreciate the attention and help from the parents, and that's when our present programs almost stop.

[14] The whole idea of Little League baseball is wrong. There are alternatives available for more sensible programs. With the same dedication that has made the Little League such a major part of many of our lives, I'm sure we'll find the answer.

[15] I still don't know what those three gentlemen in Williamsport had in mind when they organized Little League baseball. I'm sure they didn't want parents arguing with their children about kids' games. I'm sure they didn't want to have family meals disrupted for three months every year. I'm sure they didn't want young athletes hurting their arms pitching under pressure at such a young age. I'm sure they didn't want young boys who don't have much athletic ability made to feel that something is wrong with them because they can't play baseball. I'm sure they didn't want a group of coaches drafting the players each year for different teams. I'm sure they didn't want unqualified men working with the young players. I'm sure they didn't realize how normal it is for an 8-year-old boy to be scared of a thrown or batted baseball.

[16] For the life of me, I can't figure out what they had in mind.

ANALYTICAL READING

1. What fault does Roberts find with Little League instructors? Why might he refer to them as *instructors* instead of *coaches*? Does he praise them in any way? If so, what effect does this have on readers?

2. What reason does Roberts offer for saying that Little League baseball is not helpful in teaching baseball fundamentals?

3. In what ways would Roberts' proposed changes remedy the faults he finds in Little League?

4. What appears to be his main reason for suggesting the changes?

5. In paragraph 15, does Roberts add any new charges?

6. What does he achieve in that paragraph by mentioning again the Williamsport organizers of Little League?

REFLECTING

Point: Which sentence best indicates what Roberts proposes to do in his article?

Organization: Show how the essay is divided into two main parts. Discuss the function of the last four paragraphs. Should Roberts have mentioned some of the advantages of Little League? Why or why not? Should he have considered other solutions? Why or why not?

Support: What purpose does the historical and statistical information in the first two paragraphs serve? To what extent does Roberts support specific points with evidence? To what extent does he rely on the fact that most 1976 readers of *Newsweek* would have remembered him as a great pitcher?

Synthesis: How do your Little League experiences or those of your friends compare with the ones Roberts describes? Are his criticisms valid today? To what extent are coaches at fault? Parents? What do you think of his solution? Is it practical? Do you have other solutions? Is the growing popularity of slow pitch baseball related to problems mentioned by Roberts?

Evaluation: How convincing does Roberts appear to his audience? Does he seem to be fair, sincere, reasonable, and honest in his criticism? Does his argument gain force from the fact that he was a well-known baseball player? Should he have indicated how he was so knowledgeable about Little League or provided more evidence to support his contentions?

FROM READING TO WRITING

1. Write a response to Roberts for publication in *Newsweek*, arguing for or against his views.

2. Write an article for *Little League Coach* (an imaginary publication, we believe) in which you try to convince readers to make some changes in Little League, such as requiring that all children get a chance to play, allowing the coaches to pitch, or banning parents from the games.

3. Write an article for eight- to twelve-year olds, urging them not to participate in Little League.

4. Write an article for the *PTA Journal*, trying to persuade parents to take a more constructive approach to Little League.

5. Write an article for general readers trying to persuade them that some activity or organization involving young children creates problems and should be changed. You might want to argue, for example, that the Boy Scouts and Girl Scouts should be merged into one organization for all scouts. Rely on your knowledge and experience for evidence.

LET THE CONVICTED PERSON DECIDE
Marvin L. Coan

BIOGRAPHICAL SKETCH

Born in Louisville, Kentucky, in 1948, Marvin L. Coan graduated with a B.A. from the University of Indiana and a law degree from the University of Kentucky. While a law student, he became interested in the death penalty, publishing an article about it in the Kentucky Law Review. *After serving with the Justice Department in Washington, where he received a special commendation award from the Attorney General, he returned to Louisville to practice law. Several of his other articles have appeared in the* Louisville Courier-Journal.

PRE-READING

1. From the title, what do you think is the general subject of the article?

2. How does Coan restrict the subject in the second paragraph and suggest the problem to be discussed?

¹ The time has come when American society should begin to resolve some of the seemingly insoluble ethical and legal problems that divert our attention from achieving loftier goals such as attaining energy independence and raising the standard of living for all citizens.

² Since the 1979 execution of Gary Gilmore in Utah ended the 12-year moratorium on carrying out the death penalty, every case involving the possible execution of an individual has become circus-like.

³ Each imposition of the death penalty—a highly charged emotional issue—causes attorneys to race between state and federal courthouses seeking a stay of execution. Meanwhile, the family of the victim curses the delays inherent in such legal maneuvering. Furthermore, members of the condemned person's family are often left with open anguish over whether and when their loved one is going to be put to death.

⁴ The psychological dilemma imposed upon all the actors in this drama—from judge to jury to the respective families and the condemned person—is severely in need of being resolved. The process has become even more complicated since in many instances the condemned person is either unaware of or indifferent to the issue of whether or not the appeal process is worthwhile and may even be totally opposed to further legal action to save him from execution.

⁵ My proposed solution to the death penalty dilemma would involve amending Kentucky laws (and hopefully pertinent federal statutes) so that all crimes now punishable by death would be changed to carry a punishment of life imprisonment without privilege of parole.

FROM the Louisville (KY) *Courier-Journal*, August 1, 1980, sec. A, p. 9. Reprinted by permission of the author.

⁶ In this respect, society would be adequately protected from those individuals who deserve such severe punishment and there still would be a great deterrent to others who might be inclined to perform heinous acts. Our only sacrifice as a society would be the elimination of any possible "benefit" to be derived from retribution for the sake of revenge alone.

⁷ The next and perhaps most revolutionary step in this proposed solution to the death–penalty dilemma would entail a decision made solely by the condemned person facing life imprisonment without privilege of parole. That person, *as opposed to society*, would be permitted to elect self–imposition of death as a sentence alternative with government authorities simply serving to see that death occurred in the most humane way available to medical science.

⁸ For instance, if the administration of a deadly drug could cause instant death, it would be made available at a specified time, with witnesses chosen by the prisoner available to observe the self–administration of the drug by the condemned person.

⁹ Society's moral and ethical dilemma will be greatly eased, if not totally eliminated, since the condemned person would make the ultimate freedom–of–choice decision—a life of imprisonment without parole or death self–administered in the most humane fashion known.

¹⁰ This proposed solution is not at all unrealistic or farfetched, since so many individuals sentenced to death throughout the nation since the Gilmore execution have openly expressed the preference for death when balanced against the option of life imprisonment without parole.

¹¹ The only pre–condition that would need to be satisfied when allowing self–imposed death would entail a determination of competency. This, however, would be largely resolved when the question of competency to stand trial for the crime is made by the trial court. Only in rare instances would it be necessary to have a second "competency hearing" upon election of self–imposed death by the person—for example, when a pattern of abnormal behavior presented itself after completion of the trial proceedings.

¹² My proposal could effectively eliminate the moralistic debate by pro– and anti–capital punishment factions. Society will have fulfilled its duty to protect the citizenry through life imprisonment without parole while doing away with the unenviable task placed upon judges, juries and state officials who have in the past been required to recommend, impose and carry out the death penalty.

¹³ Even those who base their opposition to the death penalty on the Constitution's Eighth Amendment "cruel–and–unusual–punishment" clause should respect this proposal, since it bestows absolute freedom of choice in death–penalty cases solely upon the convicted person. Since state and/or federal officials would participate in the actual imposition of death *only* by making the means of carrying out the penalty available to the convicted person, their roles would no longer be subject to endless controversy.

¹⁴ Seemingly insoluble issues such as the death penalty, abortion and ending discrimination but causing reverse discrimination in the process, must be solved practically and more expeditiously than has been the case in the last

several decades. As a nation of multitudinous special–interest groups, we must begin to realize that resolution of such problems cannot be accomplished until there is a relaxation of absolutist principles by opposing factions. Only in this manner can a workable consensus be achieved.

¹⁵ Until the various factions on both sides of moral and ethical problems of contemporary American society realize that there will never be a true winner or true loser emergent from the fray, real progress in advancing the living standards of all Americans will remain an elusive goal.

ANALYTICAL READING

1. What does Coan find wrong with the present system of imposing the death penalty? What does he mean by calling it a "psychological dilemma" (paragraph 4)?

2. To what extent does Coan think that life imprisonment without parole maintains the three objectives achieved by the death penalty?

3. What objection does Coan hope to negate by suggesting that the death sentence be administered humanely?

4. Explain Coan's probable purpose in establishing a second competency hearing.

5. In paragraph 14, what does Coan mean by "a relaxation of absolutist principles." Apply this meaning to the problem he examines.

REFLECTING

Point: Write a sentence expressing Coan's thesis.

Organization: Explain the problem–solution organization of the article. How does Coan indicate that his solution should satisfy readers who favor or oppose the death penalty? Explain the function of the introduction and conclusion.

Support: How does Coan make readers aware of the problem? Should he have mentioned the electric chair or the firing squad? How does he show that his solution would be practical and should be acceptable?

Synthesis: Do you favor the death penalty or not? How do you feel about Coan's solution? Do you think it is morally right to allow a convicted person to choose death? Wouldn't this be a form of legal suicide (see Matthews, pages 363–67 on suicide)? What should happen if a convicted person chose life imprisonment but decided years later to die?

Evaluation: Will Coan's description of the problem convince most readers that something should be done about the present system of treating condemned persons? Does his solution seem generally practical, effective, and acceptable? Has he omitted any significant ideas about the subject? Should he have developed any points more clearly or completely?

FROM READING TO WRITING

1. Write a letter to your senator or congressman, arguing for Coan's proposal and urging that any federal laws prohibiting it be changed. Structure your letter as an informal problem–solution argument.

2. Write a letter to the *Courier-Journal* in response to Coan's article, arguing against his proposal.

3. Assume that the wife and two young children of a popular professor on your campus have been brutally murdered. Write a letter to your campus newspaper, arguing for or against the death penalty for the crime.

Problem–Solution Argument: Formal

VOLUNTARY EUTHANASIA: THE ETHICAL ASPECT

W. R. Matthews

BIOGRAPHICAL SKETCH

Reverend Walter Robert Matthews (1881-1973) was born in London, England, where he attended King's College, receiving the degrees of doctor of divinity and doctor of literature. After serving at the college as a lecturer and professor of philosophy, he became dean of Exeter Cathedral for three years and then was appointed dean of St. Paul's Cathedral in London, where he remained from 1934 to 1967 and in an emeritus role until his death in 1973. Among his numerous honors and degrees was the Order of the British Empire, the Freedom Cross of King Haakon VIII (Norway), and an S. T. D. from Columbia University. He wrote or edited over forty books, including Following Christ, God in Christian Experience, The Moral Issues of War, The British Philosopher as Writer, *and* The Search for Perfection. *In addition, he was the author of numerous booklets, papers, broadcast addresses, and journal articles.*

PRE-READING

1. From a reading of the first paragraph, which side of the issue do you think the author favors? Why?

2. What do you learn about the author's beliefs from the second and the last paragraphs?

¹ The proposal to legalize, under stringent conditions, voluntary euthanasia, has called forth much criticism from Christians. We ought not to be surprised at this, because the sacredness of human life and personality is a fundamental tenet of the Christian faith. Some of its earliest battles against paganism

FROM *Death: Current Perspectives*, ed. Edwin S. Schneidman (Palo Alto, Calif.: Mayfield Publishing Co., n.d.) Originally published in *Euthanasia and the Right to Death*, ed. A. B. Downing (N.Y.: Nash Publishing Co., 1970), pp. 25–29.

were fought against customs which presupposed that human lives could rightly be disposed of according to the convenience or pleasure of the State, or of some other human institution, such as the family. From the first the Church stood against the exposure of unwanted babies and against gladiatorial shows, in which human lives were sacrificed for the amusement of the populace. The racial theories and practices of the Nazis remind us that this emphasis on the sacredness of human personality is needed today, and I should like to make it quite clear that I have no sympathy whatever with any design either to breed or to destroy human beings for some purpose of the State. I hold firmly the doctrine of the sacredness of human personality.

2 When a Christian first hears of the proposal to legalize voluntary euthanasia he naturally thinks that it is a dangerous one, because it may weaken, or even seem to contradict, the principle of the sacredness of human personality. That was my own primary reaction and, therefore, I wish to treat opponents of voluntary euthanasia with respect and to recognize that they have a case. I have come, however, to believe that they are mistaken, and I will try to state briefly the reasons which have caused me to change my mind.

3 It seems plain to me that the principle of the sacredness of human personality cannot be stretched to cover the case of those whom the proposed legislation has in mind. We have to present to ourselves the condition of a man who is incurably ill and destined to a period of agonized suffering, relieved only by the administration of narcotic drugs. The situation here, in many instances, is that a disintegration of the personality occurs. Nothing could be more distressing than to observe the gradual degeneration of a fine and firm character into something which we hardly recognize as our friend, as the result of physical causes and of the means adopted to assuage intolerable pain. It is contended that the endurance of suffering may be a means of grace and no Christian would deny this, but I would urge that, in the case of a man whose existence is a continuous drugged dream, this cannot be alleged.

4 Though we must readily agree that endurance of suffering in the right spirit may be a means of grace for the deepening of the spiritual life, we are bound to hold that, in itself, suffering is evil. If it were not so, how could it be a duty to relieve it as far as we are able? We should all revolt against a person who complacently regarded the suffering of someone else as "a blessing in disguise" and refused to do anything about it on those grounds. It seems to be an incontrovertible proposition that, when we are confronted with suffering which is wholly destructive in its consequences and, so far as we can see, could have no beneficial result, there is a prima facie duty to bring it to an end.

5 We sometimes hear it said that voluntary euthanasia is an attempt to interfere with the providential order of the world and to cut short the allocated span of life. It seems to be assumed by those who argue in this way that God has assigned to each one a definite number of days—"the term of his natural life"—and that to take any measure to reduce this number must in all circumstances be wrong. But we must observe that this argument would cut both ways and would equally condemn any attempt to lengthen the term. All medi-

cal treatment, which after all is an interference with the natural processes, would on this assumption be wrong, and many of us who are alive now because doctors have saved our lives have in effect no right to continue to exist in this world. Surely this view of the providential order is not the true one. Worked out to its logical conclusion it would lead to intolerable absurdities and even to the doctrine that every human effort to lengthen life or improve its condition is to be reprobated as contrary to the will of God.

⁶ No one is really prepared to act on this assumption. I suggest that a truer view of the providential order would be as follows: The Creator has given man reason, freedom, and conscience and has left him with the possibility of ordering his own life within limits. He is to do the best he can with the material presented to him, and that means that it is the will of God that we should use our reason and conscience and our power to choose when we are faced with evils that have a remedy. My view of Providence then leads me to suppose that we are required by our belief in God to give the most earnest consideration to the proposal to legalize voluntary euthanasia. We are not at liberty to dismiss it on some preconceived prejudice.

⁷ The less reflective critics of voluntary euthanasia allege that it would be legalized murder, or suicide, or both. But surely before we fling these ugly words about we should be careful to inquire what we mean by them.

⁸ Legally, since the Suicide Act of 1961* (passed without any opposition), it is no longer a criminal offence for any person to commit suicide or to attempt to do so, although it remains an offence, punishable by heavy penalties, to assist a suicide. Morally the act of the suicide may be wrong because he takes his own life solely on his own judgment. It may be that he does so in a mood of despair or remorse and thus evades the responsibility of doing what he can to repair the wrong or improve the situation. He may fling away his life when there is still the possibility of service and when there are still duties to be done. The proposals for voluntary euthanasia . . . have nothing in common with this kind of suicide. The choice of the individual concerned—a person faced with hopeless and useless suffering—is submitted to the objective judgment of doctors, and his decision can only be carried out with their assistance.

⁹ Murder consists in the taking of the life of another person with deliberate intention, "with malice aforethought." Very few people are prepared to take the command "Thou shalt not kill" as universally applicable and admitting no exceptions. If we did so, we should all have to be vegetarians. But supposing the command to apply only to human life, we can all imagine circumstances in which it would be a duty to kill. For example, if an innocent person is being murderously assaulted and there is no other way of defending him, we ought to try to kill the assailant. The suggestion that voluntary euthanasia—under the conditions considered by the contributors to this volume—is murder, seems to me absurd. The life which is abbreviated is one which the patient ardently wishes to resign; there is no malice in the hearts of those who

*Rev. Matthews is referring to the 1961 Act passed in England.—ED.

co–operate, but rather love and compassion; the community is not deprived of any valuable service. None of the conditions which constitute the sin of murder are present in voluntary euthanasia as envisaged in this volume.

[10] Something must be said in reply to those who deprecate the raising of these questions and would prefer to leave things as they are. "Why not leave it to the doctor?" they cry, imagining—I do not know with what justification— that doctors often take measures to shorten the suffering of the hopelessly ill.

[11] This attitude appears to me to be really immoral, because it is an excuse for shuffling off responsibility. By what right do we place this terrible burden on the individual doctor? We have to remember that, as the law stands at present, if he does not do all he can to preserve the tortured life up to the last possible gasp, he renders himself liable to grave penalties—even perhaps to the charge of murder. Is this a position in which one's conscience can be easy? The answer must be, no. There is no honorable way of dealing with the question except by making up our minds whether or not voluntary euthanasia under proper safeguards is ethically justifiable and, if we decide that it is, embodying that conclusion in the law. Moreover, if the legitimacy of properly safeguarded euthanasia at the request of a patient is accepted, every sufferer *in extremis* and in severe pain has a right to be able to choose it. It is unjust that he should have to depend upon the views of the individual doctor who happens to attend him.

[12] I have met the argument that we can never be certain that any illness is incurable; that "while there is life there is hope." It is of course true that we hear of remarkable recoveries which confound the prognosis of the physician. I do not disregard the potentialities of "spiritual healing," nor would I exclude even the possibility of miracle, but I do not see how anyone who has had any experience of visiting the sick can question the proposition that there are cases where nothing but a miracle could restore the patient or stave off his dissolution within a brief period, and where nothing but useless agony can be anticipated. We cannot regulate our conduct at all unless we assume that it must be guided by the knowledge that we have. We take for granted that known causes will be followed by known effects in the overwhelming majority of cases. Any other assumption would strike at the roots of sanity.

[13] The advance of medical science has changed the conditions of human life. It is true that the ultimate principles of Christian morals do not change. The root of all Christian morality is the injunction to love God and our neighbor; as St. Paul says, "love is the fulfilling of the law." But though the fundamental principles do not change, their application may differ as the needs of the time require. Rules which were once valid and useful may become obsolete and even an obstacle to the true "fulfilling of the law." We must beware lest, in holding fast to "the letter," we betray "the spirit." In my belief it is the vocation of the Christian to be alert to see where the law of love points to "new duties."

[14] The great master principle of love and its child, compassion, should impel us to support measures which would make voluntary euthanasia lawful

and which, as stated by the Euthanasia Society, "would permit an adult person of sound mind, whose life is ending with much suffering, to choose between an easy death and a hard one, and to obtain medical aid in implementing that choice."

ANALYTICAL READING

1. What is the effect of the first two paragraphs on the readers that Reverend Matthews appears to be writing for?

2. What are Matthews' views on suffering? Why does he explain them?

3. In discussing what he refers to as "the providential order of the world," (paragraph 5) does Reverend Matthews distinguish between shortening (or taking) life and lengthening it? Should he?

4. How does the author distinguish ethically between suicide and voluntary euthanasia? Why does he approve of the latter and not the former?

5. How does Reverend Matthews distinguish ethically between murder and voluntary euthanasia?

6. What does he find wrong with our present informal policy of allowing doctors to decide what to do about the suffering of terminally ill patients? Aren't doctors best qualified to decide?

7. Doesn't Reverend Matthews believe that doctors may be wrong, miracles may occur, or new cures found? If so, how can he believe in voluntary euthanasia?

8. If voluntary euthanasia is morally right, how would Matthews account for the fact that it was not approved in the past?

REFLECTING

Point: In a few sentences, write a summary of the reasons why Matthews feels that the arguments against voluntary euthanasia are not convincing.

Organization: In this article, Matthews assumes that readers are familiar with the problem and the details of proposed solution. What then is he trying to do? How does he go about it? Do you perceive any reason for the order in which he presents his ideas?

Support: To what extent does Matthews use examples, facts, personal experiences, or reasons to support his solution? Where does he rely on comparison-and-contrast or cause-and-effect reasoning?

Synthesis: Do you agree with Matthews? If not, at what point do you find his solution weak? Do his arguments apply only to Christians? Why or why not? What experiences have you had or heard about involving the suffering of a terminally ill person? How do you feel about leaving the decision to doctors? Should family members be involved?

Evaluation: Do you think Matthews has written an argument that might convince many of his readers? Why or why not? Explain why his introduction and conclusion are effective or not.

FROM READING TO WRITING

1. For your college paper, write an ethical argument for or against voluntary euthanasia. Assume that readers are not familiar with the proposed plan to legalize it and Matthews' article.

2. For the same readers, write an argument on whether capital punishment is ethically right or not.

3. For a regional meeting of a church or temple organization, write a paper advocating that a person should or should not have the right to commit suicide.

4. For a woman's periodical such as *Redbook*, write an article arguing for or against the abortion of a fetus whose chromosomes indicate that it would have severe mental retardation and physical impairment after birth.

ORDER IN THE CLASSROOM
Neil Postman

BIOGRAPHICAL SKETCH

Neil Postman, who was born in 1931 in New York City, received a B.S. degree from SUNY at Fredonia, and M.A. and Ph.D. degrees with a major in linguistics from Columbia University. A university professor, presently a professor of communication arts and sciences at New York University, he has also taught in elementary and secondary schools. The best known of his several books is the coauthored Teaching as a Subversive Activity *(1967). A new book,* The Disappearance of Childhood, *which is scheduled to be published in 1982, and this article more accurately reflect his current views about education.*

PRE-READING

1. How helpful is the title in suggesting the subject?

2. Explain how the final paragraph contributes to an understanding of Postman's thesis.

¹ William O'Connor, who is unknown to me in a personal way, was once a member of the Boston School Committee, in which capacity he made the following remark: "We have no inferior education in our schools. What we have been getting is an inferior type of student."

² The remark is easy to ridicule, and I have had some fun with it in the past. But there are a couple of senses in which it is perfectly sound.

³ In the first place, a classroom is a technique for the achievement of certain kinds of learning. It is a workable technique provided that both the

FROM *Teaching As a Conserving Activity* by Neil Postman. Copyright © 1979 by Neil Postman. Originally appeared in *Atlantic Monthly*. Reprinted by permission of Delacorte Press.

teacher and the student have the skill and, particularly, the attitudes that are fundamental to it. Among these, from the student's point of view, are tolerance for delayed gratification, a certain measure of respect for and fear of authority, and a willingness to accommodate one's individual desires to the interests of group cohesion and purpose. These attitudes cannot be taught easily in school because they are a necessary component of the teaching situation itself. The problem is not unlike trying to find out how to spell a word by looking it up in the dictionary. If you do not know how a word is spelled, it is hard to look it up. In the same way, little can be taught in school unless these attitudes are present. And if they are not, to teach them is difficult.

[4] Obviously, such attitudes must be learned during the years before a child starts school; that is, in the home. This is the real meaning of the phrase "preschool education." If a child is not made ready at home for the classroom experience, he or she usually cannot benefit from any normal school program. Just as important, the school is defenseless against such a child, who, typically, is a source of disorder in a situation that requires order. I raise this issue because education reform is impossible without order in the classroom. Without the attitudes that lead to order, the classroom is an entirely impotent technique. Therefore, one possible translation of Mr. O'Connor's remark is, "We have a useful technique for educating youth but too many of them have not been provided at home with the attitudes necessary for the technique to work."

[5] In still another way Mr. O'Connor's remark makes plain sense. The electronic media, with their emphasis on visual imagery, immediacy, non–linearity, and fragmentation, do not give support to the attitudes that are fundamental to the classroom; that is, Mr. O'Connor's remark can be translated as, "We would not have an inferior education if it were the nineteenth century. Our problem is that we have been getting students who are products of the twentieth century." But there is nothing nonsensical about this, either. The nineteenth century had much to recommend it, and we certainly may be permitted to allow it to exert an influence on the twentieth. The classroom is a nineteenth–century invention, and we ought to prize what it has to offer. It is one of the few social organizations left to us in which sequence, social order, hierarchy, continuity, and deferred pleasure are important.

[6] The problem of disorder in the classroom is created largely by two factors: a dissolving family structure, out of which come youngsters who are "unfit" for the presuppositions of a classroom; and a radically altered information environment, which undermines the foundations of school. The question, then, is, What should be done about the increasing tendency toward disorder in the classroom?

[7] Liberal reformers, such as Kenneth Keniston, have answers, of a sort. Keniston argues that economic reforms should be made so that the integrity and authority of the family can be restored. He believes that poverty is the main cause of family dissolution, and that by improving the economic situation of families, we may kindle a sense of order and aspiration in the lives of

children. Some of the reforms he suggests in his book *All Our Children* seem practical, although they are long–range and offer no immediate response to the problem of present disorder. Some Utopians, such as Ivan Illich, have offered other solutions; for example, dissolving the schools altogether, or so completely restructuring the school environment that its traditional assumptions are rendered irrelevant. To paraphrase Karl Kraus's epigram about psychoanalysis, these proposals are the Utopian disease of which they consider themselves the cure.

[8] One of the best answers comes from Dr. Howard Hurwitz, who is neither a liberal reformer nor a Utopian. It is a good solution, I believe, because it tries to respond to the needs not only of children who are unprepared for school because of parental failure but of children of all backgrounds who are being made strangers to the assumptions of school by the biases of the electronic media.

[9] During the eleven years Dr. Hurwitz was principal at Long Island City High School, the average number of suspensions each year was three, while in many New York City high schools the average runs close to one hundred. Also, during his tenure, not one instance of an assault on a teacher was reported, and daily student attendance averaged better than 90 percent, which in the context of the New York City school scene represents a riot of devotion.

[10] Although I consider some of Dr. Hurwitz's curriculum ideas uninspired and even wrong–headed, he understands a few things of overriding importance that many educators of more expansive imagination do not. The first is that educators must devote at least as much attention to the immediate consequences of disorder as to its abstract causes. Whatever the causes of disorder and alienation, the consequences are severe and, if not curbed, result in making the school impotent. At the risk of becoming a symbol of reaction, Hurwitz ran "a tight ship." He holds to the belief, for example, that a child's right to an education is terminated at the point where the child interferes with the right of other children to have one.

[11] Dr. Hurwitz also understands that disorder expands proportionately to the tolerance for it, and that children of all kinds of home backgrounds can learn, in varying degrees, to function in situations where disorder is not tolerated at all. He does not believe that it is inevitably or only the children of the poor who are disorderly. In spite of what the "revisionist" education historians may say, poor people still regard school as an avenue of social and economic advancement for their children, and do not object in the least to its being an orderly and structured experience.

[12] All this adds up to the common sense view that the school ought not to accommodate itself to disorder, or to the biases of other communication systems. The children of the poor are likely to continue to be with us. Some parents will fail to assume competent responsibility for the preschool education of their children. The media will increase the intensity of their fragmenting influence. Educators must live with these facts. But Dr. Hurwitz believes that as a technique for learning, the classroom can work if students are ori-

ented toward its assumptions, not the other way around. William O'Connor, wherever he is, would probably agree. And so do I. The school is not an extension of the street, the movie theater, a rock concert, or a playground. And it is certainly not an extension of the psychiatric clinic. It is a special environment that requires the enforcement of certain traditional rules of controlled group interaction. The school may be the only remaining public situation in which such rules have any meaning, and it would be a grave mistake to change those rules because some children find them hard or cannot function within them. Children who cannot ought to be removed from the environment in the interests of those who can.

¹³ Wholesale suspensions, however, are a symptom of disorder, not a cure for it. And what makes Hurwitz's school noteworthy is the small number of suspensions that have been necessary. This is not the result of his having "good" students or "bad" students. It is the result of his having created an unambiguous, rigorous, and serious attitude—a nineteenth-century attitude, if you will—toward what constitutes acceptable school behavior. In other words, Dr. Hurwitz's school turns out to be a place where children of all backgrounds—fit and unfit—can function, or can learn to function, and where the biases of our information environment are emphatically opposed.

¹⁴ At this point I should like to leave the particulars of Dr. Hurwitz's solution and, retaining their spirit, indicate some particulars of my own.

¹⁵ Let us start, for instance, with the idea of a dress code. A dress code signifies that school is a special place in which special kinds of behavior are required. The way one dresses is an indication of an attitude toward a situation. And the way one is *expected* to dress indicates what that attitude ought to be. You would not wear dungarees and a T-shirt that says "Feel Me" when attending a church wedding. That would be considered an outrage against the tone and meaning of the situation. The school has every right and reason, I believe, to expect the same sort of consideration.

¹⁶ Those who are inclined to think this is a superficial point are probably forgetting that symbols not only reflect our feelings but to some extent create them. One's kneeling in church, for example, reflects a sense of reverence but also engenders reverence. If we want school to *feel* like a special place, we can find no better way to begin than by requiring students to dress in a manner befitting the seriousness of the enterprise and the institution. I should include teachers in this requirement. I know of one high school in which the principal has put forward a dress code of sorts for teachers. (He has not, apparently, had the courage to propose one for the students.) For males the requirement is merely a jacket and tie. One of his teachers bitterly complained to me that such a regulation infringed upon his civil rights. And yet, this teacher will accept without complaint the same regulation when it is enforced by an elegant restaurant. His complaint and his acquiescence tell a great deal about how he values schools and how he values restaurants.

¹⁷ I do not have in mind, for students, uniforms of the type sometimes

worn in parochial schools. I am referring here to some reasonable standard of dress which would mark school as a place of dignity and seriousness. And I might add that I do not believe for one moment the argument that poor people would be unable to clothe their children properly if such a code were in force. Furthermore, I do not believe that poor people have advanced that argument. It is an argument that middle–class education critics have made on behalf of the poor.

[18] Another argument advanced in behalf of the poor and oppressed is the students' right to their own language. I have never heard this argument come from parents whose children are not competent to use Standard English. It is an argument, once again, put forward by "liberal" education critics whose children *are* competent in Standard English but who in some curious way wish to express their solidarity with and charity for those who are less capable. It is a case of pure condescension, and I do not think teachers should be taken in by it. Like the mode of dress, the mode of language in school ought to be relatively formal and exemplary, and therefore markedly different from the custom in less rigorous places. It is particularly important that teachers should avoid trying to win their students' affection by adopting the language of youth. Such teachers frequently win only the contempt of their students, who sense that the language of teachers and the language of students ought to be different; that is to say, the world of adults is different from the world of children.

[19] In this connection, it is worth saying that the modern conception of childhood is a product of the sixteenth century, as Philippe Aries has documented in his *The Centuries of Childhood*. Prior to that century, children as young as six and seven were treated in all important respects as if they were adults. Their language, their dress, their legal status, their responsibilities, their labor, were much the same as those of adults. The concept of childhood as an identifiable stage in human growth began to develop in the sixteenth century and has continued into our own times. However, with the emergence of electronic media of communication, a reversal of this trend seems to be taking place. In a culture in which the distribution of information is almost wholly undifferentiated, age categories begin to disappear. Television, in itself, may bring an end to childhood. In truth, there is no such thing as "children's programming," at least not for children over the age of eight or nine. Everyone sees and hears the same things. We have already reached a point where crimes of youth are indistinguishable from those of adults, and we may soon reach a point where the punishments will be the same.

[20] I raise this point because the school is one of our few remaining institutions based on firm distinctions between childhood and adulthood, and on the assumption that adults have something of value to teach the young. That is why teachers must avoid emulating in dress and speech the style of the young. It is also why the school ought to be a place for what we might call "manners education": the adults in school ought to be concerned with teaching youth a standard of civilized interaction.

[21] Again, those who are inclined to regard this as superficial may be un-

derestimating the power of media such as television and radio to teach how one is to conduct oneself in public. In a general sense, the media "unprepare" the young for behavior in groups. A young man who goes through the day with a radio affixed to his ear is learning to be indifferent to any shared sound. A young woman who can turn off a television program that does not suit her needs at the moment is learning impatience with any stimulus that is not responsive to her interests.

[22] But school is not a radio station or a television program. It is a social situation requiring the subordination of one's own impulses and interests to those of the group. In a word, manners. As a rule, elementary school teachers will exert considerable effort in teaching manners. I believe they refer to this effort as "socializing the child." But it is astonishing how precipitously this effort is diminished at higher levels. It is certainly neglected in the high schools, and where it is not, there is usually an excessive concern for "bad habits," such as smoking, drinking, and in some nineteenth–century schools, swearing. But, as William James noted, our virtues are as habitual as our vices. Where is the attention given to the "Good morning" habit, to the "I beg your pardon" habit, to the "Please forgive the interruption" habit?

[23] The most civilized high school class I have ever seen was one in which students and teacher said "Good morning" to each other and in which the students stood up when they had something to say. The teacher, moreover, thanked each student for any contribution made to the class, did not sit with his feet on the desk, and did not interrupt a student unless he had asked permission to do so. The students, in turn, did not interrupt each other, or chew gum, or read comic books when they were bored. To avoid being a burden to others when one is bored is the essence of civilized behavior.

[24] Of this teacher, I might also say that he made no attempt to entertain his students or model his classroom along the lines of a TV program. He was concerned not only to teach his students manners but to teach them how to attend in a classroom, which is partly a matter of manners but also necessary to their intellectual development. One of the more serious difficulties teachers now face in the classroom results from the fact that their students suffer media–shortened attention spans and have become accustomed, also through intense media exposure, to novelty, variety, and entertainment. Some teachers have made desperate attempts to keep their students "tuned in" by fashioning their classes along the lines of *Sesame Street* or the *Tonight* show. They tell jokes. They change the pace. They show films, play records, and avoid *anything* that would take more than eight minutes. Although their motivation is understandable, this is what their students least need. However difficult it may be, the teacher must try to achieve student attention and even enthusiasm through the attraction of ideas, not razzmatazz. Those who think I am speaking here in favor of "dull" classes may themselves, through media exposure, have lost an understanding of the potential for excitement contained in an idea. The media (one prays) are not so powerful that they can obliterate in the young, particularly in the adolescent, what William James referred to as a "theoretic instinct":

a need to know reasons, causes, abstract conceptions. Such an "instinct" can be seen in its earliest stages in what he calls the "sporadic metaphysical inquiries of children as to who made God, and why they have five fingers. . . ."

[25] I trust that the reader is not misled by what I have been saying. As I see it, nothing in any of the above leads to the conclusion that I favor a classroom that is authoritarian or coldhearted, or dominated by a teacher insensitive to students and how they learn. I merely want to affirm the importance of the classroom as a special place, aloof from the biases of the media; a place in which the uses of the intellect are given prominence in a setting of elevated language, civilized manners, and respect for social symbols.

ANALYTICAL READING

1. In what respect does Postman agree with William O'Connor about schools getting an inferior type of student?

2. Does Postman consider other solutions to the problem of classroom disorder? If so, what are they, and what are his responses to them?

3. How does Postman account for Dr. Hurwitz's success in dealing with classroom disorder?

4. Why does Postman believe that proper dress and language are important?

5. Explain how the modern concept of childhood is related to Postman's view of order in the classroom.

6. What faults does he find with the electronic media?

7. What does he view as the basic causes of classroom disorder? Does he offer solutions for these causes? Explain. Why does he feel that his solutions will be effective?

REFLECTING

Point: Write a sentence stating Postman's thesis. Try to include not only his solution but his specified causes.

Organization: What does Postman gain by quoting from William O'Connor in the introduction? To what extent does Postman assume that readers are familiar with the problem of classroom disorder and its causes? What is the advantage of his mentioning other solutions before his own? Of his discussing Dr. Hurwitz's approach before his own solutions?

Support: Does Postman use statistics effectively? Explain. Do you accept the analogy that compares a male teacher's attitude about dressing for an elegant restaurant with his attitude about dressing for class? Why or why not? Does Postman suggest in any way that he himself is an authority on the subject?

Synthesis: From your own experience, do you agree with Postman that disorderly children come mainly from troubled families? Did your high school principal run a tight ship? If so, how effective was this policy? If not, would your school have been improved by authoritarian teachers and administrators? What do you think of a dress code? Of teachers who speak like students? Do you wish you had been a member of the highly "civilized" class that Postman visited? Why or why not? To what extent did teachers use "razzmatazz" in your classes?

Evaluation: Who is Postman's audience? Should he have described the problem for his readers at greater length? Anticipated more opposition to his ideas? Explained why his ideas would be practical and effective? Suggested how they could be implemented?

FROM READING TO WRITING

1. Write a letter to Postman disputing any idea in his article.

2. Write a letter to your high school principal trying to persuade that person to institute a change suggested by Postman.

3. Write an article for *TV Guide* designed to persuade network officials, television producers, and sponsors to improve programs for children.

4. Write an article for a teacher's publication proposing a solution for some school problem.

5. Write an article for *Parent's Magazine*, trying to persuade readers to prepare their children for going to school.

THE AGE OF INDIFFERENCE
Philip G. Zimbardo

BIOGRAPHICAL SKETCH

Born in New York in 1933, Philip G. Zimbardo graduated with a degree in psychology from Brooklyn College, and received the M.S. and Ph.D degrees from Yale. He has taught there, at New York, Barnard, and Columbia Universities and the University of Hawaii. Since 1968 he has been a professor at Stanford University. Among his eight books and many articles are Psychology and Life *(10th edition) and* Shyness: What It Is and What to Do About It. *Due soon for publication are* The Stanford Prison Experiment *and* The Rational Basis of Madness. *Among Zimbardo's many interests are social psychology, social influence, violence, madness, hypnosis, and the improvement of the quality of life.*

PRE-READING

1. How do the first two paragraphs restrict the meaning of "indifference" in the title?

2. What general solution to the problem of the hacker mentality does Zimbardo mention in the last paragraph?

Reprinted FROM *Psychology Today Magazine*, August 1980, pp. 71–76. Copyright © Ziff-Davis Publishing Company.

¹ In some schools where computers are used as tutors, children have reported developing a closer, friendlier relationship with their ever–reliable machine than with Ms. Dove and her sundry personal idiosyncrasies. As these kiddies mature, some of them are likely to become "hackers," members of a new subculture of grown–up electronic whiz kids obsessed by interacting with computers. Hackers spend long hours at night or early in the morning, when "downtime" is shorter, playing with their programs and sending messages via electronic bulletin boards to hacker associates seated at terminals a few feet away. Fascination with the computer becomes an addiction, and as with most addictions, the "substance" that gets abused is human relationships.

² Not just in schools but in society as a whole, the hacker mentality is upon us, with or without the computer as a rationalization for putting other people at the bottom of our priority stack. There are forces at work in society increasing both the sense and the reality of our separateness from one another. It is as if we were suffering from a mysterious kind of "legionnaire's disease" of which the chief symptoms are isolation and a loss of naturalness in our relations with other people.

³ I used to believe that this separateness was the exclusive problem of the timid, introverted shys. For the past eight years I have been studying the personal and social dynamics of shyness, and I know that 40 percent of Americans quietly claim to be of that disposition. I also know that a surprising 25 percent of these sufferers became shy *after* leaving the universal self–concern and awkwardness of adolescence. I am aware, too, that self–help books for the shy are selling well; that shyness clinics are springing up; that social psychologists who used to be interested only in social affiliation are writing textbooks including chapters on loneliness, based on research and scientific meetings devoted to this fascinating phenomenon.

⁴ But shyness alone does not account for all of the isolation that marks contemporary society. My research team has surveyed, interviewed, observed, experimented upon, and done therapy with a vast number of shy people (reported in part in *Shyness: What It Is, What To Do About It*). While we were documenting their conversational awkwardness, passivity, reluctance to initiate social contact, and general social phobia, a curious discovery emerged—about a comparison group of nonshys. They do not show the same motivated avoidance and inhibition syndrome characteristic of their shy peers; theirs is an apparently unmotivated indifference. Unlike the shys, many of whom still *want* to connect, to have friends, date, marry, share intimate feelings, the nonshys often seem not to mind being isolated. Their conversations are rather banal and minimal, usually humorless, without signs of spontaneity, personal involvement, or joy in sharing ideas and feelings with friends. One gets the impression of watching a generation of clones of Mr. Spock from "Star Trek." Human speech is there, intelligence is evident, but the executive command programming does not include feeling or affection.

⁵ This fall, the class of 1984 will take its place in colleges and high schools, and it will be time to find out whether or not George Orwell's Big

Brother prophecy of mind control comes true. By the time these students have graduated, I believe, the message they will have learned will prove to be not Orwellian but Garboesque: "Big Person is *not* watching you. He doesn't have time to care about you anymore. She'd rather be alone."

⁶ Don't get me wrong; I'm an optimist. I have always believed that people can control their destinies by work, self–discipline, humor, love of life, concern for other people, and a sensitivity to the tactics of manipulation by the authorities. But tonight is different from all previous nights in America, and tomorrow will be even worse. As the father of three children, it is with sadness that I make such an assertion, and with the hope it will be shown to be a false alarm.

⁷ I believe that the basic quality of our social lives is being diluted, distorted, and demeaned by a host of profound structural changes in society. Because these new forces are systemic and not just transient developmental stages, they won't simply be outgrown but are likely to become permanent fixtures in our daily existence. The consequences are serious. I know of no more potent killer than isolation. There is no more destructive influence on physical and mental health than the isolation of you from me and of us from them. It has been shown to be a central agent in the etiology of depression, paranoia, schizophrenia, rape, suicide, mass murder, and a wide variety of disease states.

⁸ There is no dearth of research, anecdotes, and observations demonstrating the pervasiveness of the disorder I am talking about. A recently published report by Ralph Larkin, a sociologist, on the crises facing surburban youth underscores some aspects of this new malaise of the spirit. The children of American affluence are depicted as passively accepting a way of life that they view as empty and meaningless. The syndrome includes a constricted expression of emotions, a low threshold of boredom, and an apparent absence of joy in anything that is not immediately consumable; hence the significance of music, drugs, alcohol, sex, and status–symbol possessions.

⁹ According to a high school guidance counselor, the current generation of students differs in at least one way from the young people of their parents' day: "Kids hate school much more now than they did then. I mean the word *hate* and underline it." But this hatred is among the few strong emotions they allow themselves to feel about anything.

¹⁰ Where do we witness displays of strong emotion anymore, except at sports events and rock concerts? And even when we witness them, how many of us will acknowledge as much or dare to share the emotion? On my way to visit my sister because she is dying of cancer, I explain the reason for my absence to student assistants.

¹¹ "Have a nice trip!" chortles one. "See you when you get back," says another. And that is all they say. They haven't learned to extend comfort to another in distress. Too heavy.

¹² Another anecdote, different but just as telling: "I hate myself for having this daydream, but I can't help enjoying it every time it pops into my head," confides Denny, a sophomore in my introductory psychology class of 680 stu-

dents. "Everyone else fails the final exam, all hundreds upon hundreds of them, the nerds, the jocks, the freaks, and I get an A. Mine is the only A, floating high and dry in a sea of failure. Then somebody, everybody, would have to notice me, because I'd be special."

[13] Assuming that the narcissism of shyness was fueling this fantasy, I launched into my counseling spiel of "shyness–can–be–overcome–if–you–work–at–it–and . . ." "Hold on, don't get me wrong," he objected. "I'm out–going, an extravert. I used to make friends easily, but it seems as if there's no value to that anymore. No one has time to go beyond the superficial level of 'How's it going?' 'Have a nice day!' 'See you around,' and stupid stuff like that. There must be something wrong with *me*, because I just can't seem to connect in any meaningful way to the people I live with. We are all working so hard to make it that maybe we don't have any energy left over for making it with each other."

[14] The student health service at the university reassured this young man that his problem was a common psychiatric symptom of alienation and loneliness. In fact, it ranks near the top of the list of symptoms students present to this and similar clinics at other colleges when they seek professional help for their "attachment deficiencies."

[15] Signs of alienation show up long before college. Visit the Serramonte Mall in San Francisco, the Smithtown Mall in Long Island, Florida's Broward County Mall, the Glendale Shopping Mall in Arizona. What you witness when school is out are mass minglings of kids too young to drive wandering about in the artificial air of a totally enclosed space amid artificial flowers, canned music, junk–food dispensers, and plastic twittering canaries. In smaller clusters are the elderly, keeping warm in winter and cool in summer, but never talking with the youngsters, except when the generations become adversaries over a particular piece of Astroturf.

[16] When the shopping–center kids get a little older, they escape the anxieties attendant on formal social dating (one–next–to–one) by dating in clusters. "We're all going for a pizza, wanna come along?" The tone seems to add, "No big deal if you say yes, no loss if you don't come."

[17] Plenty of young adults who do date as couples find it less than satisfying. A handsome, successful television director tells me he has problems with women after the fifth date. He is concerned, wants help. For the first five innings, he has exciting, preprogrammed scripts for entertaining his dates. He strikes out when he runs out of scenarios and has to "be himself." Like many of his peers, he has never learned to be intimate, to relate closely to one other person, to make disclosures about his past, about his fears, frustrations, and future plans; in short, to reveal the private self behind the public façade. Disclosure presupposes trust, which in turn is nourished by sharing and gives substance and meaning to intimate contacts. But whom can you really trust these days?

[18] If you yourself have switched from being a team player in life to going it alone more often, if you seek out your friends less often than you used to, it

may be good for you, but it is a loss for the rest of us. Maybe you switched because we "weren't saying anything anyway," or because we "no longer turned you on," or because you had come to expect more of us while giving less of yourself. Or maybe, as a woman told me in Atlanta, "There's times peoples just be tired of peoples." Or then again, the message might be the one that the mother of one of my shy freshmen passed along to him: "Do you realize how boring you are?" Better not to play the game at all than to be seen as boring by the other players?

[19] Yet another sign of how alienated people are: not one of a dozen students in my wife's college seminar on sex roles could realistically imagine making a long-term commitment to one partner. "It would be nice if it happened, but it's not very realistic to expect it," a student said.

[20] What about short–term commitments simply to pass the time of day with people occupying common space with you? Our world is becoming like an elevator: "No talking, smiling, or eye contact allowed without written consent of the management." Next time you shop in a supermarket, do a study, make a word count of the conversations between shoppers in line or with the checkout person. Then try to use your data to prove that your subjects are not mute or deaf.

[21] Our brave new world is one in which the basic social unit is the large, impersonal institution. In such institutions, authority is concentrated in the hands of a few remote power brokers. Decision making begins with concerns for cost–effectiveness, profitability margins, and efficient management of behavior, and ends with rules that must be followed—or else. If the rules are followed, everything runs smoothly, and the mark of impersonality is stamped on each product, each of us. Institutions can't do their thing unless they can count on the predictability and compliance of those they "serve." Thus there can be no spontaneity, impulsivity, strong emotion, dissent, opposition, time to think anything over, no time to be "just people." Today's young people are being forged into cogs in the corporate structure. And they are the ones who will eventually control our world.

[22] Cult leaders and their management teams know all this. There they come, at least 2,000 strong, offering simple solutions to complex problems, love–bombing affection-starved youngsters. Cults attract a following not necessarily through political, religious, or economic ideology, but through offering the illusion of friendship, of noncontingent love. You exist, you are one of us, you get your fair share of our love and respect. (Wasn't that the message families once communicated?)

[23] If there is a Devil, it is not through sin that he opposes God. The Devil's strategy for our times is to trivialize human existence in a number of ways: by isolating us from one another while creating the delusion that the reasons are time pressures, work demands, or anxieties created by economic uncertainty; by fostering narcissism and the fierce competition to be No. 1; by showing us the personal gains to be enjoyed from harboring prejudices and the losses from not moving out whenever the current situation is uncomfortable. Fostering in

us the illusion of self–reliance, that sly Devil makes us mock the need for social responsibility and lets us forget how to go about being our brother's keeper—even if we were to want to.

[24] Surely one cause of the growing sense of disengagement in our society is the rise in middle–class affluence since the 1950s, which has allowed an enormous number of people to buy space, privacy, and exclusive–use permits and services. The move to suburbia is a move away from too many people too close. The well–tended front lawn is the modern moat that keeps the barbarians at bay. Every occupant in a separate bedroom with private toilet, personal television, telephone, and hi–fi reduces hassles and conflicts. No need to share.

[25] In the quest for upward mobility, moreover, the middle class sends its children away to prestigious colleges, moves to wherever its jobs demand, and does more and more of its business on the road. The consequence is a generation of children who have been uprooted time after time until, as one said to me, "I don't want to bother making friends. It's not worth the effort, because we'll be gone soon and it hurts more to leave good friends than casual acquaintances." The same is true of parents, who may find it even more difficult to make new friends in strange places. And as more of us take our paper–work jobs home or our jobs take us away from home, there is less time for family and neighborhood contacts.

[26] Geographical mobility also strains the bonds of extended families. With relatives thousands of miles apart, ritual gatherings become rarer, and relatives become curious aliens to our children. The zero population growth movement has as one of its unintended consequences children with few siblings or cousins and eventually with few aunts or uncles. The paucity of relatives, coupled with the fact of delayed childbearing and the high divorce rate, mean there will be fewer of us with a sense of primal ties to many kin and of roots that run deep into one place, our "home."

[27] By 1990, about one–third of all young people under 18 will have parents who have divorced at least once. Almost 60 percent of divorced couples have one or more children now under 18 years old. The number of children involved in divorce has risen from half a million in 1960 to 1.1 million now. Divorced mothers of children under 18 are increasingly likely to be in the labor force, which takes them away from home for long periods. I think a lasting legacy for the children of divorce is a deeply felt loss of trust in authorities (like parents, who have let them down) and in institutions (such as marriage, whose for–better–or–worse slogan won't sell even in Peoria).

[28] Finally, youthful cynicism has been fed by watching, on the evening news, or in some cases, "up close and personal," almost everyone going out on strike for better bucks—teachers, police, fire departments—all, apparently, in it for the money, not love of a profession. Widespread cynicism about institutions seems to be evident across the board. How to trust anything, given the moral disgrace of Watergate, the vision of criminals being media–hyped to

promote their best selling exposés, and the weakening of national pride after Korea, Vietnam, OPEC control of economy, and the Bay of Pigs rerun in the desert of Iran?

²⁹ As corny and unsophisticated as it sounds, the only escape from hacker-dom is to think of people as our most cherished resource. We need to work hard at reestablishing family rituals, such as family meals without TV and with meaningful conversation. Parents and teachers should show more concern for the social–emotional development of children and put less emphasis on intellectual competition. We must oppose systems and procedures that deny our uniqueness while spreading depersonalization and anonymity in the guise of efficiency.

³⁰ Social–support networks provide emotional sustenance, informative feedback, and validation of self–worth. They have been shown to buffer the adverse impact of change on physical and mental health, and it is important to create enough of them for everyone to have a chance to become a valued part of a life–support system.

³¹ Maybe the economic downturn the nation is facing is a blessing in disguise. Parents will not be able to afford divorce as readily and may eventually discover that they have something of value in common—as many of our parents did. More children may return home after college, and communal living and expanding, elastic family structures may become necessities. Sharing instead of hoarding, and caring instead of flaunting, may even become fashionable.

³² While waiting for all that to happen, it is well to reevaluate the survival strategies that many of the poor—immigrants, blacks, and other minorities—have used to advantage in the past when their money was soft and times were hard. Without a false sense of personal invulnerability, and with an accurate appraisal of the power of the "system" to overwhelm all in its path, they maintained their dignity by reaffirming family values and by tightening the bonds of friendship. Survival demands collective action; "alone" is for gravestones in hacker cemeteries.

ANALYTICAL READING

1. What is gained by Zimbardo's reference to his research? By his reference to himself as an optimist?

2. In paragraph 7, he states that "the basic quality of our social lives is being diluted, distorted, and demeaned by a host of profound structural changes in society." Does he identify them? If so, what are they?

3. Explain the meaning and the rhetorical effect of Zimbardo's statement that if the Devil exists, he does not oppose God through sin (paragraph 23).

4. Does Zimbardo use a consistent voice throughout the article? Is it that of a lecturing social scientist or a chatty father of three children?

5. Point out several examples of his effective use of parallelism in sentences.

REFLECTING

Point: Is Zimbardo mainly concerned with identifying a problem, proposing a solution, or both? Explain.

Organization: Analyze Zimbardo's introduction, showing how it attracts readers' interest and then moves to a statement of the thesis. What is the general pattern of organization in the discussion of the problem? Point out how Zimbardo arranges and links together examples of the hacker mentality.

Support: What kinds of evidence does Zimbardo use to show that the problem is widespread? How representative and reliable is this evidence? Does his reference to cults help his argument? How?

Synthesis: Do Larkin's findings about suburban youth (paragraph 8) apply to your high school classmates? Do young people *hate* school? Are strong emotions confined only to sports and rock concerts? Does dating consist mainly of formal one-to-one relationships or informal group gatherings? Do you feel that your friends could make a long-term commitment to a marriage partner? Are young people generally cynical about institutions and people? Do you think the hacker mentality is widespread? Do you agree with Zimbardo's stated causes of this mentality? What do you think of his solutions?

Evaluation: Is Zimbardo writing for the general reader or a well-educated reader? Is he writing mainly about all Americans or only affluent ones? Does he write convincingly to his readers about the existence of the problem? Does he persuade them that the problem is widespread and serious? How effective and practical are his conclusions? Does he anticipate and counter any objections to his solutions? Have you gained any important insight as a result of reading the article?

FROM READING TO WRITING

1. Write a reply to Zimbardo's article, arguing that most young people enjoy school and that they express their emotions in ways other than at sports and rock concerts.

2. Write an article for your college newspaper, arguing that your college is a large impersonal institution and stating ways to change it.

3. Based on Zimbardo's article, write an article for *Parent's Magazine*, explaining the appeal of cults and suggesting ways for parents to build strong family relationships.

4. Write an article for general readers, trying to persuade them that young people are cynical and proposing ways to combat this destructive attitude.

Assessment of Reading and Writing Skills: Persuasive Writing

Step 1

Read the essay that follows with the aim of understanding and recalling the important ideas. When you finish, note how long it took you to read the selection. Then close your book and write a summary of the important information without referring again to the essay. Include a discussion of the persuasive techniques the writer uses. You will be allowed 7 to 10 minutes to write; your instructor will establish the limit and tell you when the time is up.

NO RETREAT ON ABORTION
John D. Rockefeller III

It is ironic that in this Bicentennial year there is a strong effort across the nation to turn the clock back on an important social issue. Ever since the Supreme Court legalized abortion in January 1973, anti–abortion forces have been organizing to overturn the decision. They have injected the issue into the campaigns of 1976, including the appearance of a Presidential candidate who ran on the single issue of opposition to abortion.

There have been efforts within the Congress to initiate a constitutional amendment prohibiting abortion. There is litigation being pressed in state courts and appeals to the Supreme Court. Last November the National Conference of Catholic Bishops issued a "Pastoral Plan for Pro–Life Activities" calling for a wide–ranging anti–abortion effort in every Congressional district, including working to defeat any congressman who supports the Supreme Court decision.

Those who oppose abortion have won the battle of the slogans by adopting "Right to Life" as theirs. And, by concentrating on the single issue of the fetus, they have found abortion an easy issue to sensationalize. Thus, they have tended to win the publicity battle, too.

In contrast, those who support legalized abortion—and opinion polls demonstrate them to be a majority—have been comparatively quiet. After all, they won their case in the Supreme Court decision. Legalized abortion is the law of the land. It is also in the mainstream of world opinion. The number of countries where abortion has been broadly legalized has increased steadily, today covering 60 percent of the world population.

In this situation, there is a natural tendency to relax, to assume that the matter is settled and that the anti–abortion clamor will eventually die down. But it is conceivable that the United States could become the first democratic nation to turn the clock back by yielding to the pressure and reversing the Supreme Court decision. In my judgment, that would be a tragic mistake.

The least that those who support legalized abortion should do is try to clarify the issue and put it in perspective. The most powerful arguments about abortion are in the field of religious and moral principles—and this is where the opposing views clash head–on. Abortion is against the moral principles defended by the Roman Catholic Church, and some non–Catholics share this viewpoint. But abortion is *not* against the principles of most other religious groups. Those opposed to abortion seek to ban it for everyone in society. Their position is thus coercive in that it would restrict the religious freedom of others and their right to make a free moral choice. In contrast, the legalized abortion viewpoint is non–coercive. No one would think of forcing anyone to undergo an abortion or forcing doctors to perform the procedure when it violates their consciences. Where abortion is legal, everyone is free to live by her or his religious and moral principles.

There are also strong social reasons why abortion should remain legalized. In a woman's decision to have an abortion, there are three key considerations—the fetus, the woman herself, and the future of the unwanted child. Abortion opponents make an emotional appeal based on the first consideration alone. But there is steadily growing understanding and acceptance of a woman's fundamental right to control what happens to her body and to her future. In the privacy of her own mind, and with whatever counseling she seeks, she has the right to make her decision, and no one is better qualified. If she is denied that right, the result may well be an unwanted child, with all the attendant possibilities of abuse and neglect.

Finally, as a practical matter, legalization of abortion is a much more sound and humane social policy than prohibition. Banning abortions does not eliminate them; it never has and it never will. It merely forces women to go the dangerous route of illegal or self–induced abortions. Even worse, it makes abortion a "rich–poor" issue. At a high price, a well–to–do woman can always find a safe abortion. But, unable to pay the price, the poor woman all too often finds herself in incompetent hands.

Experience in three Catholic countries of Latin America that I visited provides dramatic evidence of a high incidence of abortion even when it is against the law. Estimates are that there is one abortion for every two live births in Colombia, and that more than half a million illegal abortions are performed every year in Mexico. In Chile, hospital admissions caused by illegal abortions gone wrong exceed 50,000 per year.

In contrast, the access to safe procedures in the United States has resulted in a drastic decline in deaths associated with abortion. In the period 1969–74, such deaths have fallen by two–thirds. Statistics also strongly suggest that about 70 percent of the legal abortions that have been performed would still have occurred had abortion been against the law. The only difference is that they would have been dangerous operations instead of safe ones.

When you combine the religious, moral and social issues raised above with the fact that women need and will seek abortions even if they are illegal, the case for legalized abortion is overwhelming. We dare not turn the clock back to the time when the religious strictures of one group were mandatory for everyone—not in a democracy.

We must uphold freedom of choice. Moreover, we must work to make free choice a reality by extending safe abortion services throughout the United States. Only one–fourth of the non–Catholic general hospitals and one–fifth of the public hospitals in the country now provide such services. It is still extremely difficult to have a legal and safe abortion if you are young or poor or live in a smaller city or rural area.

On a broader front, we must continue the effort to make contraceptive methods better, safer and more readily available to everyone. Freedom of choice is crucial, but the decision to have an abortion is always a serious matter. It is a choice one would wish to avoid. The best way to do that is to avoid unwanted pregnancy in the first place.

Step 2

Read the following essay as quickly as you can without sacrificing your comprehension of the material. You will have a maximum of 5 minutes, 36 seconds (200 words per minute) to glean as much information as you can. If you finish before time is called, note how long it took you to read the selection. Again, close your book and write a summary of the article, including a statement about the persuasive tactics used by the writer. You will have 7 to 10 minutes for this task.

DISCRETIONARY KILLING
George F. Will

It is neither surprising nor regrettable that the abortion epidemic alarms many thoughtful people. Last year there were a million legal abortions in the U.S. and 50 million worldwide. The killing of fetuses on this sale is a revolution against the judgment of generations. And this revolution in favor of discretionary killing has not run its course.

FROM *Newsweek*, 20 September 1976, p. 96. Copyright 1976 by Newsweek, Inc. All rights reserved. Reprinted by permission.

That life begins at conception is not disputable. The dispute concerns when, if ever, abortion is a *victimless* act. A nine–week–old fetus has a brain, organs, palm creases, fingerprints. But when, if ever, does a fetus acquire another human attribute, the right to life?

The Supreme Court has decreed that *at no point* are fetuses "persons in the whole sense." The constitutional status of fetuses is different in the third trimester of pregnancy. States constitutionally can, but need not, prohibit the killing of fetuses after "viability" (24 to 28 weeks), which the Court says is when a fetus can lead a "meaningful" life outside the womb. (The Court has not revealed its criterion of "meaningfulness.") But states cannot ban the killing of a viable fetus when that is necessary to protect a woman's health from harm, which can be construed broadly to include "distress." The essence of the Court's position is that the "right to privacy" means a mother (interestingly, that is how the Court refers to a woman carrying a fetus) may deny a fetus life in order that she may lead the life she prefers.

Most abortions kill fetuses that were accidentally conceived. Abortion also is used by couples who want a child, but not the one gestating. Chromosome studies of fetal cells taken from amniotic fluid enable prenatal diagnosis of genetic defects and diseases that produce physical and mental handicaps. Some couples, especially those who already have handicapped children, use such diagnosis to screen pregnancies.

New diagnostic techniques should give pause to persons who would use a constitutional amendment to codify their blanket opposition to abortion. About fourteen weeks after conception expectant parents can know with virtual certainty that their child, if born, will die by age 4 of Tay–Sachs disease, having become deaf, blind and paralyzed. Other comparably dreadful afflictions can be detected near the end of the first trimester or early in the second. When such suffering is the alternative to abortion, abortion is not obviously the greater evil.

Unfortunately, morals often follow technologies, and new diagnostic and manipulative skills will stimulate some diseased dreams. Geneticist Bentley Glass, in a presidential address to the American Association for the Advancement of Science, looked forward to the day when government may require what science makes possible: "No parents will in that future time have a right to burden society with a malformed or a mentally incompetent child."

At a 1972 conference some eminent scientists argued that infants with Down's syndrome (Mongolism) are a social burden and should be killed, when possible, by "negative euthanasia," the denial of aid needed for survival. It was the morally deformed condemning the genetically defective. Who will they condemn next? Old people, although easier to abandon, can be more inconvenient than unwanted children. Scientific advances against degenerative diseases will enable old people to (as will be said) "exist" longer. The argument for the discretionary killing of these burdensome folks will be that "mere" existence, not "meaningful" life, would be ended by euthanasia.

The day is coming when an infertile woman will be able to have a laboratory–grown embryo implanted in her uterus. Then there will be the "surplus embryo problem." Dr. Donald Gould, a British science writer, wonders: "What happens to the embryos which are discarded at the end of the day—washed down the sink?" Dr. Leon R. Kass, a University of Chicago biologist, wonders: "Who decides what are the grounds for discard? What if there is another recipient available who wishes to have the otherwise unwanted embryo? Whose embryos are they? The woman's? The couple's? The geneticist's? The obstetrician's? The Ford Foundation's? . . . Shall we say that discarding laboratory–grown embryos is a matter solely between a doctor and his plumber?"

But for now the issue is abortion, and it is being trivialized by cant about "a woman's right to control her body." Dr. Kass notes that "the fetus simply is not a mere part of a woman's body. One need only consider whether a woman can ethically take thalidomide while pregnant to see that this is so." Dr. Kass is especially impatient with the argument that a fetus with a heartbeat and brain activity "is indistinguishable from a tumor in the uterus, a wart on the nose, or a hamburger in the stomach." But that argument is necessary to justify discretionary killing of fetuses on the current scale, and some of the experiments that some scientists want to perform on live fetuses.

Abortion advocates have speech quirks that may betray qualms. Homeowners kill crabgrass. Abortionists kill fetuses. Homeowners do not speak of "terminating" crabgrass. But Planned Parenthood of New York City, which evidently regards abortion as just another form of birth control, has published an abortion guide that uses the word "kill" only twice, once to say what some women did to themselves before legalized abortion, and once to describe what some contraceptives do to sperm. But when referring to the killing of fetuses, the book, like abortion advocates generally, uses only euphemisms, like "termination of potential life."

Abortion advocates become interestingly indignant when opponents display photographs of the well–formed feet and hands of a nine–week–old fetus. People avoid correct words and object to accurate photographs because they are uneasy about saying and seeing what abortion is. It is *not* the "termination" of a hamburger in the stomach.

And the casual manipulation of life is not harmless. As Dr. Kass says: "We have paid some high prices for the technological conquest of nature, but none so high as the intellectual and spiritual costs of seeing nature as mere material for our manipulation, exploitation and transformation. With the powers for biological engineering now gathering, there will be splendid new opportunities for a similar degradation of our view of man. Indeed, we are already witnessing the erosion of our idea of man as something splendid or divine, as a creature with freedom and dignity. And clearly, if we come to see ourselves as meat, then meat we shall become."

Politics has paved the way for this degradation. Meat we already have become, at Ypres and Verdun, Dresden and Hiroshima, Auschwitz and the Gulag. Is it a coincidence that this century, which is distinguished for science and war and totalitarianism, also is the dawn of the abortion age?

Step 3

Without looking back at the two essays, write a paragraph or two evaluating them and explaining how the arguments are related. You may refer to your summaries, but not to the essays. Time: 10 minutes.

INDEX OF AUTHORS AND TITLES

A 1
B 2
C 3
D 4
E 5
F 6
G 7
H 8
I 9
J 0